Plato's Political Philosophy

Plato's Political Philosophy

Mark Blitz

The Johns Hopkins University Press
Baltimore

The author would like to thank the Earhart Foundation and the Henry Salvatori Center of Claremont McKenna College for supporting this work.

Printed in the United States of America on acid-free paper
9 8 7 6 5 4 3 2 1

The Johns Hopkins University Press
2715 North Charles Street
Baltimore, Maryland 21218-4363
www.press.jhu.edu

Library of Congress Cataloging-in-Publication Data

Blitz, Mark.
    Plato's political philosophy / Mark Blitz.
        p.   cm.
    Includes bibliographical references and index.
    ISBN-13: 978-0-8018-9764-1 (hardcover : alk. paper)
    ISBN-10: 0-8018-9764-5 (hardcover : alk. paper)
    ISBN-13: 978-0-8018-9765-8 (pbk. : alk. paper)
    ISBN-10: 0-8018-9765-3 (pbk. : alk. paper)
    1. Plato—Political and social views.   I. Title.
    JC71.P62B55 2010
    320.092—dc22   2010006886

A catalog record for this book is available from the British Library.

Special discounts are available for bulk purchases of this book. For more information, please contact Special Sales at 410-516-6936 or specialsales@press.jhu.edu.

The Johns Hopkins University Press uses environmentally friendly book materials, including recycled text paper that is composed of at least 30 percent post-consumer waste, whenever possible. All of our book papers are acid-free, and our jackets and covers are printed on paper with recycled content.

To Ellen, Evan, and Grant

Contents

Plato's Political Philosophy

Introduction

This book concerns Plato's political philosophy. Political philosophy is about forms of government and the common good. As Plato makes clear, political philosophy also concerns pleasure, virtue, nobility, goodness, justice, wealth, persuasion, divinity, and the arts. Politics serves human happiness generally, and, therefore, political philosophy studies human happiness generally. Its topic is both the best way to govern and the best way to live.

The philosophical life is among the matters whose contribution to happiness we must judge. Political philosophy, thus, also tries to clarify the purpose of philosophic activity. In fact, the worth of philosophy is Plato's guiding theme.

That it is proper for political philosophy to consider such topics as nobility, divinity, and justice is more obvious in some instances than others. One reason to study Plato is because he is the first to discern the lineaments of the subject and therefore articulates it with special freshness and urgency. As an intelligent man observing a scene largely undistorted by other views, much that he describes is likely to be true. Were this not so, why would one study him? I therefore treat Plato as living, not dead, and from a scientific, not historical, point of view. That Plato has been studied for so long is useful, for through him we come close to the source of thought. This advantage, however, does not mean that what he sees is never false, or wholly true.

Plato's aged intelligence offers an added benefit. A chief obstacle to philosophy today is that it seems unimportant, a plaything of academic specialists, or an annoying appendage to serious work. In Plato, however, we see philosophy before it is overcome by our natural sciences or becomes a minor servant to the practical world. We can observe its true scope, depth, and intention, and retrieve its proper task here and now.

II

One might doubt the seriousness, possibility, and need for philosophy for still other reasons. Plato provides a useful antidote to such doubts. Some confuse philosophy with airy thoughts about airy matters (philosophy united with astrology and the occult on bookstore shelves) or airy thoughts about trivial matters (my "philosophy" of gardening or real estate sales.) Plato shows us the cause of such confusions and provides a defense against them. He also shows the shortcomings of claims that philosophy is impossible because all "truth" is relative to individual opinion and perception. That truth is not relative, however, does not mean that it is unbendingly "absolute."[1]

Philosophy also differs from faith.[2] It is meant to be the rigorous, thoughtful examination of important things. It leaves nothing untouched by rational reflection. Faith, by contrast, always threatens to elevate the mysterious, uncanny, and awesomely powerful above the rational and to forget that nothing irrational can speak truly to what is divine in man.[3] Plato's political philosophy deals with or, indeed, first addresses this perennially urgent division, both through its own rational example and in its subjects. Faith finds its most powerful home in laws we believe gods have commanded, and in public ritual. But Plato shines the light of his rational reflection on government's integral connection to piety and priests. The Platonic enlightenment is the first great enlightenment.

III

The nature of the political and ethical topics that Plato discusses makes easy distinctions between beginners and scholars difficult to draw. It does not take someone "advanced" to think about pleasure. Plato's dialogues, indeed, are mostly conducted with friends, students, and amateurs, although not often with stupid ones.

I intend my book for all who wish to think together with Plato about the topics that most concern him. His thought can move far enough from its origin in evident questions, however, that it involves issues that look academic and controversies that today interest scholars alone. In fact, these issues are crucial for understanding the grip and range of the distinctions, desires, and uncertainties that orient and motivate all human beings from the start of our awareness. I therefore hope to make clear to beginners the importance of these more refined, complicated, or abstract thoughts, and to offer reflections about them that benefit the more advanced. I also hope to remind us all how Plato's most abstract thought is rooted in ordinary political and moral questions and to uncover his practical answers to them.

General books about Plato's political philosophy are not in fashion.[4] In recent years, however, there have been many fine translations of individual dialogues and commentaries on them. I draw on these liberally. One advantage of my generalizing approach is to bring together Plato's separate conversations. What are the connections among his several discussions of courage? How do they modify his several discussions of moderation? One disadvantage of my approach could be to lose the drama of distinct conversations. I hope to recapture this drama by summarizing and commenting on several dialogues in the course of the book.

IV

Plato's dialogues are dialogues, so we wonder how to read them. Our interest is in what he says about justice, happiness, virtue, and the like, so we obviously must attend to the arguments that Socrates (Plato's usual chief interlocutor) and other characters make. Does this mean, however, that the give and take among discussants is mere window dressing, or is it integral to the substance? If it is integral to the substance, in what ways is this so? Are Socrates' many obvious contradictions merely bad arguments, for example, or are they intentional? Does a structure underlie the occasionally abrupt transitions among topics, or are matters as formless as they sometimes seem?

A dialogue enables us to see an argument's being addressed to someone in order to teach or persuade him. It does not occur in the vacuum of a treatise or book such as the one you hold in your hand. Our first thought, therefore, is that Socrates' goal with a particular interlocutor directs each argument that he makes. Because his interlocutors are enmeshed in particular political and religious practices, moreover, and begin from certain opinions, he must often adjust or distort what he says. Socrates is famous for the irony that enables him to address different audiences with the same words, for without this irony he might not succeed or be allowed to continue.[5] Nonetheless, Socrates' goal with an interlocutor need not require that each argument be distorted, because the truth may do the job. Socrates makes many arguments and statements that ought to win assent from anyone competent.

To understand Socrates' intention, therefore, we need to grasp the character, wishes, opinions, and prospects of the people with whom he converses. We also need to attend to the flow of the conversation, to moments of anger, befuddlement, and silence, to changes from one interlocutor to another, and to Socrates' comments when he is narrating a dialogue. These show us the effect an argument is having on the person to whom it is addressed.

If dialogues are meant to persuade, to what are they persuading? If they mean to educate, what do they teach? Socrates' ethical goals range from pointing out a practical danger to himself or others to elevating his interlocutors toward something virtuous and just. His intellectual teaching ranges from loosening sclerotic opinions that restrict thought to opening someone's understanding of his experiences to their fuller unity and cause. Moral and intellectual persuasion differ, but they work together.

The persuasive aspects of a dialogue modify its subject by adjusting what and when we hear about it. They also clarify the subject by teaching something that the formal argument may not. Plato's dialogue on courage, for example, the *Laches,* is oriented to its interlocutors and, especially, to its title character. We do not see what courage is simply and purely. The *Laches* puts courage in a wide context by showing its different effects in different situations, indicating the strange relation between our experiences and what we say about them, and revealing courage's connections to other subjects. Some of courage's full power is revealed in ways that the formal discussion of the subject does not bring obviously to light.

This rhetorical directing of the argument occurs in several ways. Socrates uses without comment terms that are significant for the dialogue's subject to characterize the conversation in which he is engaged. He makes important points while encouraging or chastising his interlocutors and himself. He describes generally a procedure that he follows but does not analyze it. He chooses examples whose salience is not obvious. He refers to scenes in epics or tragedies that point to wider comparisons than the ones he makes explicitly. Plato sometimes replaces Socrates with other chief interlocutors, has Socrates or another character narrate a dialogue rather than present it directly, or entitles a dialogue by subject, not character, for reasons he does not state.

The examples, indications, omissions, characterizations, oaths, replies, opening scenes, and persuasive flow modify what is argued explicitly, and expand our understanding. We can say provisionally that Plato discusses a dialogue's subject in terms of a theme that he expresses through its title. The *Republic* examines justice in terms of the (best) form of government; the *Laches* examines courage in terms of Laches' leading characteristics and opinion. The theme is only one place where the subject shows its power, so it is narrower than the subject. But the theme is broader than the subject, in another sense, because it involves more. Plato clarifies matters by showing this twofold limit. Laches improperly treats part of courage as all of it, for example, but he also experiences it in terms of ridicule, war, and the arts, that is, in terms of matters broader than courage. By examining Laches' and Nicias' views, Socrates lets us glimpse both the whole of courage and its interconnections.[6] A dialogue seeks to isolate a subject as it acts in a cosmos oriented to its title figure or action.[7]

We progress in understanding Plato if, in addition to these points, we keep in mind three questions. What elements of a subject does a dialogue uncover even if it is inconclusive? (What is left unchallenged even when contradictory opinions are presented?) What is the central distortion Socrates uses to confuse an interlocutor? (What does he overstate or ignore?) How does the philosophic life itself exemplify or modify the subject discussed?[8]

V

My goal is to bring to the fore Plato's basic articulation of the realm of political philosophy. I especially wish to recapture the novelty, necessity, and uncertainties of the political-philosophical world as Plato first sees it. That man's "good" is the "soul's" "virtue," that virtue is "noble" or beautiful, and that the goal of "politics" is "justice" or the "common" good are truths at once surprising and inevitable.

I divide the bulk of my study into three parts: politics and virtue, politics and philosophy, and politics and knowledge. I concentrate on certain dialogues in each section and also discuss subjects generally.[9] I conclude each part by exploring one of Plato's three political dialogues. In these ways I hope to move along Plato's spiraling paths while not losing his thought in a maze of uncertainty or stepping through a false exit.[10]

Part One
Politics and Virtue

CHAPTER 1

The World of the Dialogues

The world of Plato's dialogues is largely familiar to us. We encounter ambitious young men, political discussion, and war; talk of physicians, trainers, cooks, captains, mathematicians, painters, and poets; exhortations to virtue, piety, love, and education. Whatever the odd details that distinguish Plato's time from ours, characters usually talk about and do what we talk about and do, with occasionally astounding openness and freedom.

This familiar atmosphere separates the pulse and nerve of the dialogues from what we read about and see in the life of remote tribes, or even from the world of the Old Testament, and helps to account for their attraction or charm. Plato's world is old but not especially old-fashioned and surely not primitive; on the whole, it consists of familiar activities conducted in familiar ways. The dialogues enable us to see a world ripe for enlightenment—indeed, already to some degree enlightened; they also enable us to see the darkness from which Platonic enlightenment arises, from the point of view of the attempt at enlightenment itself.

One way to begin to comprehend this world is to understand the opinions, practices, desires, feelings, and terms of praise and blame on which Plato's characters implicitly rely. Political philosophy is nothing but examining the actions, shortcomings, and contradictions in these phenomena, and seeking the farther shores from which we can better view and reconcile them. Were there nothing to observe or no conflicts to adjudicate there would be no possibility or at least no need for philosophy. Before we examine Plato's teaching about virtue and politics, therefore, we should study this world of implicit understanding. The familiar should not remain too familiar.

The world of the dialogues is in some ways strange, although the oddity is dulled because we expect it. We come across characters such as rhapsodes, whose activities require footnoted explanation.[1] Lawyers and journalists are strangely absent, women are not prominent, and slavery exists; we hear apparently serious conversation about gods and not only God, and our machines and appliances have disappeared.

Some of these peculiarities are softened by the dialogues' ample talk of love, rulers and ruled, and piety. Moreover, sophists, rhetoricians, and philosophers, and the dialogues' intimate atmosphere of gossip and acquaintance, may well replace our law schools, media networks, and research institutes. The activities of sophists, rhetoricians, diviners, and rhapsodes nonetheless remain elusive. To understand the world from which enlightenment arises, therefore, we must explore the dialogues' understanding of such anomalies.[2] The odd, also, should not seem too familiar or remain unexamined.[3]

I begin to examine the dialogues' world by exploring what Socrates' interlocutors want from him. Why do they seek him out? Why do they listen to him whether or not they seek him out? I point out five reasons: fathers' worries about their sons' education; the ambitions of young men; concerns of love and seduction; punishment or chastisement; and friendship, respect, or the pleasure of his company. The overall atmosphere of most dialogues combines the serious with the urbane.

Fathers and Sons

The natural starting point for discussion with Socrates, and for human concern, is parents' worries about their children. Three dialogues begin or almost begin with fathers' concerns about their sons' education.[4] Many others consider whether fathers can educate sons or wards and what it means that they cannot.[5] These concerns make evident that authoritative direction for bringing up sons no longer clearly exists. The practical question, or the need for advice, does not arise where customs are transmitted without tension.[6] One worries then about whether one is living up to a divine code but not about whether, or even how, to do so. The fathers' questions in Plato's discussions, however, are radical.

I

In the *Laches,* two men, Lysimachus and Melesias, with distinguished fathers but undistinguished themselves, seek advice from two leading Athenians about whether a new kind of military training is worthwhile. Nicias, the more prominent, says yes; Laches, the other, says no. Socrates, with whom the sons but not the fathers are familiar, and who is known by Nicias and Laches, is present. Called to offer his counsel, he turns matters toward the proper object of advice. With a view toward what end are they considering whether this military art is worthwhile? The purpose, they decide, is to enhance or secure courage, which they then proceed to discuss inconclusively, never directly returning to the art itself.

The central perplexity to which the fathers' question leads—what is education or advice about or for—is not mysteriously alien, philosophic, or scientific in our sense. We ask and examine it commonsensically. It is not pursued on a remote plane where, say, we look at Freudian or brain psychology, survey statistically derived samples, examine the ontology of questioning, or study the Greek meaning of advice. In his own way Plato deals with or moves toward such possibilities, but not immediately.

Although we see how important it is to clarify the true subject of advice once Socrates points this out, it is hard to discern the importance of this question by oneself. The subject is often more obscure than Socrates suggests initially. Military prowess may aid safety, security, victory, or freedom as much or more than it promotes courage. Individual display (which this art encourages) may not be best for the army as a whole. The strength or beauty that training enhances could seem an end in itself or useful for obtaining love or wealth. It is easy to see that one takes medicine to restore health, but unless health is the highest or only good, doing everything to preserve it is not always the best course.[7] Courage, after all, is inseparable from risk. In general, not only ends but also their connections to other goods are surprisingly ambiguous.[8]

These ambiguities are among the issues Socrates brings out in his discussions, and they befuddle the old and young men with whom he talks. Indeed, Socrates often chooses to heighten or intensify paradox and confusion rather than to diminish or assuage it. Nonetheless, it is clear that the true point of advice about an art is indeed to secure an end (courage, victory, or healthy eyes) and not merely to learn good techniques.

Fathers' concerns about how to improve or propitiate their sons lead them to another difficulty, the paradox of advising. How can we know whether an expert gives good advice when we lack his expertise? Crito, in the *Euthydemus*, places himself in Socrates' hands for his own and his sons' learning, while doubting the entire activity he associates with Socrates. How, indeed, could the nonmilitary Lysimachus and Melesias judge anyone's advice about whether fighting in armor is good in war or whether Stesilaus is the best artisan from whom to learn to fight that way?

The fathers are not entirely ignorant. They have some opinion about what they want (political distinction for their sons), where to look for it (military officers), and whom to ask about it (not slaves or ordinary artisans, although, occasionally, diviners). We can deal practically with the paradox of advice. If the experts all agree and have visible successes, why should we doubt them?[9] If one expert exists whom the others hold in highest repute, surely he is the one to consult. Although we can evade the paradox practically, however, we can never wholly eliminate it. It becomes visible when the experts contradict each other. Even if they agree, they all could be wrong, as even the best ancient physicians so often were. The advisee's perplexity, especially in the face of unfamiliar or amorphous goals, seems unavoidable.

A third concern of fathers is the advisors' honesty, frankness, and consent. To need a counselor does not ensure that he wishes to help or will offer help honestly. Why, after all, would someone aid a father in need? If he is not family, the expert needs to be persuaded.[10] The obvious means of persuasion is pay. One can suitably teach skills such as music or letters for pay. Is it proper to take money from a friend, however, or even from an acquaintance, merely to give him advice about which arts to pursue and which artisans to consult? Finders' fees are one of the practices by which the vulgarity of Hollywood or New York stands out from the liberality of Athens. Would a moral man take a fee to teach morality, assuming that he knows what virtue is and can teach it?

Payment is the obvious way to persuade, but it is insufficient to guarantee that a job will be done honestly or well. If money secures counsel, the artisan may work not for you but for the highest bidder; if money is the only incentive, he assuredly will do so. The highest bidder may occupy all of the better teachers' time, moreover, or be your enemy. In the *Hipparchus*, Socrates and his nameless interlocutor discuss dishonest pilots and physicians whose love of gain intentionally produces death. Honesty must supplement payment, so that deals are consummated and good results attempted. We normally expect, but sometimes doubt, such honesty: trust but verify. When a father seeks for his son so nebulous a product as courage, wisdom, or philosophy, moreover, the possibility of dishonesty is more vital and pressing than when he purchases his produce in the market. The fact that it is so easy to cheat when one sells goods such as wisdom or education in virtue is one reason the sophists who retailed such goods were disreputable. Hippocrates in the *Protagoras* seeks to learn from Protagoras but blushes at the suggestion that he wishes to become a sophist himself.

Pay is only one incentive for advisors. Lysimachus and Melesias believe that Laches and Nicias will advise them because they too have sons. Common need moves them to pay attention; their experience in war enables Laches and Nicias to pay intelligent attention. Just as their experience does not prevent them from giving contradictory advice, however, so too is need insufficient to direct them fully to Melesias and Lysimachus' concerns. Laches and Nicias cannot help sparring with each other. They seek victory in argument, and it is not obvious that their combat serves the need of Lysimachus and Melesias or their sons.[11]

Fathers and sons dimly see the shortcomings of payment and common need as incentives for advisors. Socrates' friend Crito expects Socrates to share his concern for his son Critobulus. Once he realizes that Socrates is the son of his good friend Sophroniscus, Lysimachus is pleased to learn that Socrates comes from his neighborhood. He hastens to explain why he has ignored Socrates and did not recognize him. Acquaintance promotes but does not guarantee loyalty and care.

Seeking advice is difficult because the advisee neither knows nor can trust sufficiently.[12]

II

Why are fathers ignorant of so much that they wish their sons to learn? Neither Socrates nor Theages doubts that the father is sufficient to teach farming, nor do men doubt that artisans can transmit what they know to their offspring. Why, however, do courage, wisdom, or virtue generally prove to be such obscure goals and so difficult to clarify? One reason is that clients who seek counsel about such matters are not always frank when they seek advice. Lysimachus tells Nicias and Laches (and Socrates, who overhears them) that he is speaking to them frankly, that is, that not everyone in his situation speaks frankly or (perhaps) should. Theages' father does not declare his son's tyrannical intention and seeks Socrates' sympathy or understanding once it comes out. Those who in the *Apology* call Socrates a corrupter of the young do not know precisely what they mean, or of what this corruption consists. Yet, they proceed.

The case of Lysimachus is especially significant. He frankly blames his renowned father for neglecting him while he was attending to the city's business. Aristeides the Just did not care sufficiently for his own.[13] This neglect meant that Lysimachus became an unimportant figure; he does not wish this outcome for his son. His frankness consists in condemning his father and the city and its demands, for he claims his father's failing is typical of those in power. Yet, if it is typical, how has Nicias been able to attend to his son's education? Why are some, say, Pericles, apparently able to rise without special help from their fathers or guardians while others, say, Alcibiades, rise with it? Why do others, such as Alcibiades' brother Cleinias and Pericles' sons, not rise at all?[14] Lysimachus covers his own weakness by speaking openly about his father's faults, and he then covers his father's faults by blaming the city, or its heads.

Frankness (or modesty) about need is implicated in the advice one receives and its ability to succeed. Lysimachus' frankness allows him to explain his need, but it conditions his companions' estimation of him. Theages and his father's original coyness forces Socrates to clarify Theages' goal by testing him. Just as a physician cannot treat certain illnesses unless the patient reveals their shameful origin, so, too, we cannot fully hide weakness of soul if we are to overcome it. We sometimes cannot seek knowledge without revealing our laziness, corruption, pretentiousness, or misplaced pride. We may therefore not seek it at all. Socrates asks Charmides early in the *Charmides* whether Critias' report that he is moderate is true. Charmides blushes, because answering either "yes" or "no" would demonstrate immodesty. A certain frankness or shamelessness (and sometimes a certain dissembling) is required for one to improve and for others to help. Fathers' need for advice shows us much about the ordinary milieu of modesty and frankness within which conversations take place, and which directs and limits them. The tension between "philosophy" (knowledge) and "politics" (morality) is at play from the beginning of each dialogue.[15]

The paradox of advice makes evident how ignorance is a bar to its own relief because one cannot fully grasp the advice one receives. Yet, that the true subject of advice is often not what it seems but, rather, the end one should have in mind, affords a step away from paradox, because we usually more easily grasp the goal (say, health) than the means (say, medicine). Or, so it seems because Socrates is then able to show that goals such as courage are perplexing, and to question whether anyone can teach them. We cannot be certain, furthermore, that possibly unjust, untrustworthy, or even friendly counselors will do all that they believe is best for us. Our own dissembling, moreover, makes it difficult to seek honest advice. Truth is elusive in practical affairs, and ignorance difficult to confront.[16]

Political Ambition

A second reason Socrates is approached is political ambition. We cannot separate this motive completely from the first, of course, but Socrates characteristically conducts conversations with the ambitious young when they are alone, and no longer in their fathers' immediate care. In the *Protagoras*, Hippocrates hopes to study with Protagoras in order to further his wish for political prominence; he expects Socrates to make the introductions and awakens him for that purpose. In the *Menexenus*, Socrates displays an appropriate funeral oration to an ambitious young friend. In the *Alcibiades I,* Socrates teases from Alcibiades an acknowledgement of the breadth of his ambition, his wish to rule the world.

Socrates' young interlocutors do not often boldly state and admit their ambition. Their relative reticence suggests that voicing extreme ambition is questionable, either because they should show prudence before others or because they are hesitant to face up to their desires. Few characters in the dialogues are as frank as Theages, and he converses with Socrates in private. Political ambition, when proclaimed, is often vague or limited.

The usual reticence about ambition does not keep Socrates from noticing it, however. Sometimes he pretends to be shocked; other times, as with Alcibiades, he visibly, if subtly, fans the flames. Socrates' care for the ambitious is noteworthy because it shows that he is not concerned only with those already slated for restful academic chairs in analytical philosophy. Even when he does talk with such a type—his look-alike Theatetus is the obvious example—he worries about his passion, not only his reason. Socrates wants to converse with young men such as Glaucon (in the *Republic*), Critias, and Charmides who are marked for politics or rule. Sooner or later they wish to spend time with him.

With Alcibiades, indeed, Socrates suggests that he alone can help him to speak well before the assembly.

Why does Socrates sometimes appear as a useful friend to the ambitious young? One reason is to calm or redirect them. Socrates presents himself in the *Apology,* where he is on trial for his life, as annoyingly moralistic, someone who hectors and pesters people to be just.[17] Such hectoring, however, has little counterpart in Plato's portrait of Socrates' conversations. He does not pester anyone to be moral. Rather, he offers arguments that silence but do not always convince interlocutors who have ignoble (and sometimes commonsensical) views, or he moderates them while claiming that more talk is needed.[18] Perhaps, indeed, Socrates deals with the ambitious primarily because he learns more about human affairs from talking to the gifted than to the average. The breadth of ambition belongs to the natural gifts that Socrates believes necessary for philosophy. So, he seems always to be on the scene when someone prominent is in town, and he attends to the ambitious even though he steers clear of ordinary politics.

How does Socrates deal with his young political friends? He drives them to questions similar to those that inform his discussions with fathers and sons. About what, say, does Alcibiades seek to address Athens' assembly? Experts deal with each issue, Socrates argues—physicians with public health, builders with public works. What, then, is Alcibiades' subject? Socrates brings out the perplexing vagueness of politics' comprehensive goal or standpoint. Indeed, Alcibiades can barely state this goal, and when Socrates helps him state it—virtue or justice—Alcibiades hardly knows what justice is. Hippocrates seeks skill in speaking, but about what is mysterious. Gorgias, Polus, and Callicles defend Gorgias' rhetoric, but its aim is unclear. Callicles does not even grasp the nature of the purpose—pleasure—to which he ostensibly subordinates politics. Socrates brings out our uncertainty about the goal of ruling, even when we believe we seek it only for pleasure and wealth. How should we use our wealth once it is attained? Who would be satisfied with a life of nothing but the joy of scratching itches?[19]

Not only politics' end but also the content of the art or science that reaches the end is hazy. What does a rhetorician know if some other artisan—say, a physician or shoemaker—always speaks more reasonably about any specific measure? What remains for the political scientist to know if someone else always knows more whenever we face a particular task? A rhapsode such as Ion declaims Homer's *Iliad* and *Odyssey;* these poems form the ambitions of many

young men. He defends Homer's comprehensive knowledge and his own peer-
less knowledge of Homer. Is he not, then, forced to claim that his knowledge
of these masterful chronicles of battle means that he knows more about war
than any general? Yet, is not such a claim by someone who has never been
elected general absurd?

Socrates inspires his interlocutors to see that virtue, not tyranny or mere
pleasure, is the proper goal of their political ambitions. He inspires them to
consider what this virtue is. At the same time, he questions whether virtue is
teachable, that is, whether it is knowledge in the same way that an art or science is knowledge, or whether it is knowledge at all. Neither Meno nor Critias
ever learns conclusively what virtue is, although Socrates discusses it amply
with them. Cleinias, for whom all in the *Euthydemus* have great hopes, receives
from Socrates encouragement to learn political science, only to have this encouragement fade in the mists of confusion about the virtue at which political
science aims and the relation of the science to the goal. Socrates both elevates
and confuses his ambitious young interlocutors, and he sets the stage for the
still more elevated and perplexing path of philosophic inquiry. Indeed, Socrates
occasionally uses ambition to move beyond political to philosophic virtue.
This approach is most evident in the *Republic*.

Political ambition is central in the dialogues, a key element of the co-philosophic world. Socrates can maneuver the ambitious to perplexity about their
goals. What actually are virtue and happiness, and what is their seat in the
body and soul? What is the status of the skills that enable one to rule, skills
more obscure than a carpenter's or shoemaker's? What remains for political
men to know once particular arts exist? If we exercise virtue only to acquire
and maintain rule, for what end do we exercise rule?[20] As with fathers and
sons, when Socrates deals with the ambitious young, our uncertain knowledge
of human ends, and the perplexing connection between knowledge and its
noble use, arise as fundamental topics.

Love

Socrates is also approached for counsel about love. Phaedrus (in the *Phaedrus*)
and Hippothales (in the *Lysis*) solicit Socrates' counsel about seduction. Love,
as well as ambition and educational advice, belongs to the dialogues' co-philosophical world and indicates questions that open to the philosophic way of
life.

Socrates sometimes suggests that he is an expert on love and only love. He claims to be a midwife, as is his mother Phaenerete, skilled in helping others to deliver (their thoughts), and a matchmaker, and to himself be in love with all the young and beautiful.[21] These claims may be true, but they are not the whole truth about him. Socrates also says he is related to Daedelus through his father, the stone-worker Sophroniscus, and that he is accompanied by a demon who restrains his actions.[22] As others see him, moreover, he is a sometimes arrogant, word-splitting, opponent-numbing, logic chopper.[23] And, he is not above true or pretended anger or annoyance.[24] Plato may subtly connect some or all of these skills and characteristics to Socrates' erotic art, but they are not identical to it.

Socrates' love discussions observe the conventions of place and time. As he tells Phaedrus, he is satisfied to believe conventional myths and to not spend time explaining them rationally; he is concerned, rather, with self-examination. Although Socrates observes the conventions, however, his goal is not conventional seduction or helping others to seduce. Rather, he seeks to understand. In the *Phaedrus* he questions how they can discuss successful love rhetoric before knowing what love is; in the *Lysis* he studies friendship by asking who experiences it, and for what. Were, say, Hippothales genuinely to imitate Socrates' discussion with Lysis (Hippothales' beloved), he might break Lysis' composure, as Socrates does, but his goal would be transformed through this imitation.

The conventions about love also bring out the dialogues' urbanity. Phaedrus and Socrates make fun of each other, as does Ctessipus of his lovesick friend Hippothales. The *Symposium* displays the remarkable talent of several Athenian aristocrats and the timeless brilliance of Socrates and Aristophanes. Related to this urbanity is many dialogues' transgressive air. Socrates shows the young Lysis limits to the parental or familial love he takes for granted. The *Protagoras* and *Symposium* have about them an atmosphere of decadence and luxury, the *Protagoras* occurring at the home of the notorious Callias, and the *Symposium* racked by the drunken entrance of Alcibiades. Socrates in the *Phaedrus* invents a beautiful story about love, gods, and men that belies his self-asserted conventionalism. In the *Protagoras* (where Phaedrus and Alcibiades are present) Hippias praises those gathered for their attachment to nature and freedom from convention. The dialogues' sophisticated transgressions do not go unnoticed, however, and they contain challenges and threats, especially to Socrates. Attacks for apparent corruption and charges of insolence also enliven the dramas.[25]

So, Socrates' involvement with lovers displays some of the needs (here, the desire to seduce) that political philosophy transforms, the urbanity with which most of his conversations are conducted, the conventions or threats that, however playfully, display some of his discussions' limits, and the priority for Socrates of questions about what things are and the goals they serve.

Socrates uses several methods to encourage men to listen to him. We see these clearly in his own seducing, which shows us how he treats those who are reluctant and recalcitrant at the start. He then uses similar procedures to advance discussion in less unyielding conversations.

A good example is his care for Alcibiades as we see it in *Alcibiades I* and as Alcibiades recounts it in the *Symposium*. Socrates makes himself look remarkable; he appears unconcerned with sex, rule, wealth, and other ordinary cares, and impervious to the elements and to ordinary fears.[26] He seems generally to worry merely about virtue and to love only learning, discussion, and wisdom. He presents himself as a god, remarkable in his persistence (say, in pursuing Alcibiades when others have fled), in his ability to trace his ancestry back to Apollo (through Daedelus), in his having a unique "demonic" warning voice, in his ability to divine or foretell the future, and in his being aware of the soul's possibilities before and after the present life.[27] Moreover, he seems to be endlessly inventive, attractive not only as strangely superhuman but also as wonderfully playful and resourceful.[28] Socrates is not above wheedling or cajoling as lovers do, but it is especially his attentive concern for, say Glaucon and Adeimantus in the *Republic,* Theatetus in the *Theatetus,* Phaedrus in the *Phaedrus,* and Simmias and Cebes in the *Phaedo* that displays his seductive focus. He can discern their hopes and character and connect these to their experience. Beyond this, his own neediness or desire is somehow graceful or noble, showing itself in love for the beautiful and in eager love of conversation.[29] Socrates is able to attend to others by calling attention to himself.

Socrates is not fraudulent. He (and Plato's Strangers) do seek wisdom and virtue. But his presence is complex. If wisdom is elusive, virtue difficult and impossible to teach purely, pious dogma forever present, insolence and injustice permanently threatening, and vulgarity often attractive, Socrates could hardly allow himself to appear to others precisely as he appears to himself. He requires and masters practices of love; in seduction, indeed, we permit or encourage actions and statements that we otherwise condemn.[30]

The everyday environment of love, the familiar yet unpredictable eruption of the extraordinary into the usual, is more than a starting point for Socrates' conversations. It is also one of Plato's chief subjects. Love is mysterious in its power and potency. How does it affect, move, and direct us: how does it achieve what it achieves? Examining love may also lead us to ask what we should truly seek, and whether some knowledge exists to find and encompass it. The sometimes inchoate wishes to learn, rule, and seduce suggest the deeper or higher attractions, confusions, and capabilities that stimulate our ordinary hopes.

Compulsion

Still another reason Socrates talks is legal or political compulsion. The obvious examples are the dialogues that surround his trial and conviction, the *Euthyphro, Apology, Crito,* and *Phaedo.* Socrates must have these conversations because he is on trial, in jail, or answering an indictment, and, therefore, unable to stay silent easily. In the *Republic,* Socrates is compelled by greater numbers to discuss justice; in the *Cleitophon* he tries to discover why Cleitophon attacks his reputation as a teacher of justice. The dialogues that feature compulsion do not involve force alone, as is shown by the path from the setting of the *Cleitophon,* in which Socrates initiates the conversation but then only listens, to the quasi-compulsory setting and remarkably open conversation of the *Republic,* to the almost compulsory setting and topic (piety) of the *Euthyphro,* to the literal compulsion of the setting and order of speech in the *Apology,* to the compulsory setting in jail and discussion of obedience and death in the *Crito* and *Phaedo.* Rather, others try to show Socrates something about justice and law, and he, in turn, teaches them.

What most obviously underlies such works is the link between law and piety.[31] Some details of Athens' rituals and practices are specific to it and places like it, and, of course, we are not polytheists. This difference between Plato's time and ours may lead us to believe that Plato considers piety unreflectively or that the connection in his work between law and piety is local or accidental.

It is wrong to dismiss these matters so easily. Socrates is not unquestioning about piety: this is the very issue of the *Euthyphro.* Indeed, the link between gods and poets rarely is far from Plato's sight.[32] The status of gods is not indisputable. The *Republic* begins with religious novelty and goes on to legislate about dogma unconventionally. The government that Plato's Eleatic Stranger outlines in the *Statesman,* and the *Republic*'s rule of philosophers, do not center on gods and priests. Plato's presentation of the connection between law and piety, thus, does not stem from historical blindness but from this link's being central to everyday experience, and a starting point on the path to natural, or free, understanding.

What issues emerge from the conversations caused by legal and political compulsion? One is the problem we see in advising: What truly is under discussion? Speakers take for granted what they fail to understand. With compulsion and righteousness, indeed, interlocutors' assuredness is greater than in dialogues of education (where they believe there is something they do not know). Compulsory dialogues' action is directly or self-consciously motivated by their certainty. Euthyphro is sure that his actions are pious; Socrates' accusers act as if they know he deserves to be indicted; Crito is certain Socrates should try to escape from prison. The issue of the being, goodness, and truth of the opinions and aims that motivate these compulsory discussions is a central conundrum of everyday action. Socrates tries to bring out perplexity or ignorance where certainty reigns.

The gap between speaking and acting correctly is especially salient in these conversations. In the *Crito*, Socrates tries to convince Crito that he owes so much to the law that he should not disobey it to help Socrates escape. Crito does as he is told, but the split between what everyone says Crito should do (help his friend to escape) and what the law demands remains nonetheless. In the *Apology* Socrates claims he would disobey a law forbidding him to philosophize, that is, that there are limits to proper obedience. In the *Republic* the question of the connection between political rule and philosophic questioning proves to be justice's heart. The atmosphere of pious law that infuses some dialogues reminds us of the ordinary pervasiveness of this phenomenon; the inherent limits to legal piety that Plato brings out remind us of the natural ground of philosophy and our own liberalism.

Pleasure

Socrates' interlocutors sometimes wish to speak with him for the pleasure of his company and conversation. The delight of friendship and friendly leisure, of seeing, talking, and being with, is a central element of the dialogues' world. The *Symposium* is one example, the *Republic* another. In the *Symposium* Socrates is one of several guests at a banquet where he talks about love. Neither he nor his host, the poet Agathon, knew in advance that love would be discussed. In the *Republic* his interlocutors encourage him to stay and talk, with (mock) force and persuasion. Their goal seems to be to enjoy his company. In the *Phaedo*, friends gather to be with and converse with him on his final day. As his wife Xanthippe wails, this will be the last time Socrates will talk with them. In the *Charmides,* he rushes to his usual gymnastic haunts after returning from battle to discover who among the young is reputed to be beautiful and what is new in philosophy. He is hailed by his fellows and pressed for information. Socrates and Crito are friends, apart from Crito's concern with his son.

Why is Socrates such a desirable companion? His acquaintances sense that being with him will improve them, even when they have no special request in mind. We see this with Nicias in the *Laches,* Aristeides in the *Theages,* and with his companions in the *Phaedo.* Another reason is love of learning or, more accurately, love of listening. Socrates claims not to be able to deliver long, beautiful speeches; the dialogues belie this modesty, and his interlocutors do not take him at face value.[33] They also recognize that he prefers questions and answers, and grasp something of his irony; some primarily enjoy the fireworks when he is around.[34]

These phenomena suggest the link between friendship and conversation. Socrates indicates the ground of this link when, in the *Apology,* he claims that it is "a very great good for a human being" "to make speeches every day about virtue."[35] The openness of some to friendship in speech, combined with the wish of some to be better (i.e., their lack of complete self-satisfaction), provides an opportunity for philosophy. It also produces the danger of sophistic talk that looks similar to Socrates' activity, and the distortion through unjust political ambition of the wish to improve.

Sophists

This brings us to the next feature of Socrates' everyday world, the presence of sophists. Plato presents five conversations with them (*Protagoras, Gorgias, Greater Hippias, Lesser Hippias,* and *Euthydemus*), one about them (*Sophist*), one heavily influenced by them (*Meno*), and others in which they and their teachings appear. Hippocrates wakes Socrates because he wishes to meet the sophist Protagoras. Meno (in the *Meno*) and Protarchus (in the *Philebus*) refer to Gorgias and his teachings. Socrates' companions expect that he has heard of Hippias. Socrates himself asks Theodorus in the *Sophist* to compare the sophist, statesman, and philosopher.[36]

The sophists are among those whose knowledge the ambitious young and their fathers seek. They seem to be educators or useful adjuncts to politicians.

After all, they are named for wisdom. Some of what people want from Socrates is what they want from sophists; they think he is an especially smart or odd one.[37] Socrates' concern is to differentiate himself from sophists but also to understand better through them what is imitative, fraudulent, rhetorical, and showy. Beauty, pleasure, virtue, and error are his chief subjects when he talks with them.

That sophists belong to the co-philosophic world of everyday Athens makes clear that it is not mutely or piously prephilosophic. Rather, political philosophy emerges in a civilized and sophisticated environment. Socrates, the Strangers, and other characters refer to Parmenides, Heraclitus, and Anaxagoras, and the teachings of the sophists are connected to them. Many characters justify and explain themselves in terms they have learned from sophists and philosophers. Political philosophy is born in a world that already is interpreted, not one altogether immediate, if such a human world can in fact exist. The interpretation not only is composed of piety and ritual but also is "wise." In Socrates' Athens, the cave of ordinary opinion has already been invaded by intellectuals.

The sophists distinguish between nature and convention.[38] They are thus formed by the split that makes possible philosophy's orientation to truth and permanence as opposed to fleeting distortions. This similarity causes difficulties for Socrates, who cannot help but look like them. It also means that a kinship exists between Socrates and the sophists that he does not share with those unaware of nature.[39] Because the sophists are aware of a split between the natural and conventional, they also see some of the limits of religion and politics. The home of convention is the political world, and the political world is inseparable from piety, reverence, and attachment to one's own. Sophists, who travel from city to city, are able to see how variable and, therefore, questionable conventions are.

Sophists' understanding of the natural is oriented to individual tyranny or, at least, to pleasure, not to nature unblinkingly observed.[40] The city, for them, is conventional; what is natural is the individual good, for which political affairs are a means. Natural rule is rule of whoever is strong, courageous, and clever enough to do what he wishes, which is to satisfy himself endlessly, arrogantly, and at will. What is natural is tyranny, individual pleasure, gain, power, and excess, and the courage and intelligence to achieve them.

Because sophists do not think justice can be natural, they do not try to elevate the city to what is naturally right. They on the whole live within the law, manipulating it or teaching others how to do so. The city is to be used. For all their naturalism and occasional bizarreness, the leading sophists are in some ways oddly ordinary.[41] They accept the dominance of the Athenian many or the Spartan few, teaching mostly aristocratic young men how to prevail in Athens and its sister cities. They seem not to question the apparent contradiction between their teachings about powerful individuals and the strength of Spartan tradition or the combined force of the citizenry of Athenian democracy.

Sophists are also characterized by the importance they ascribe to speech, to teaching and practicing rhetoric, to beautiful public displays, to sowing confusion with tendentious distinctions and similarities that make everything seem identical. The link between their naturalism and their elevation of speech is most visible in the rhetoric of law courts and assemblies. How else but through rhetoric could the selfish and supposedly powerful individual prevail over the more obvious strength of convention and force? The sophists teach how to defend oneself against charges, true or false. They show how to advise assemblies persuasively. They display how to convince others to do one's bidding. They do not teach just defense, service to the common good, or virtuous persuasion but claim that their education can also be used in these noble ways. They believe that the pleasure of powerful men is the natural guide.

The importance sophists give to speech is another way they and Socrates look alike.[42] Socrates must protect the source of their similarity and, therefore, protect them, but he also must make clear the differences and, therefore, protect himself and philosophy. Socrates and the sophists are both alike and unalike.

Socrates differs from the sophists about the substance of nature and the power of speech. The paradox that what seems completely conventional (the city's laws) could be oriented to a natural standard is central to his political thinking. He seeks to know whether natural justice exists; he does not think it a chimera. He explores common, not just individual, goods. In fact, he explores the possibility of common entities generally: what virtues have in common is central to his conversation with Protagoras; the marvel that two is in neither of the ones that comprise it is the denouement of his dialogue with Hippias.

If justice might be natural and common goods exist, we must change our understanding of individuals and their good. Socrates uncovers the soul, not a topic to which sophists or earlier thinkers gave serious rational reflection. The individual soul, its link to the body, and its orientation through thinking to common truths all suggest that sensual pleasure is not the only natural good. Socrates explores the rationality, limits, and variations of pleasure much more fully in the *Protagoras, Philebus, Republic,* and *Gorgias* than do Protagoras, Gorgias, or their students themselves.

Pleasure's amenability to reason, and the desirability of thought, indicate limits to sophistic hedonism. Sensual pleasure cannot be fully pleasurable if its amounts are miscalculated or if it is impure. No one believes seriously that the dumb, brute, instantaneous pleasure of a bedbug, or scratching the bedbug-caused itch, is the only human good. What is missing in this sophistic view is the complexity of thought and, therefore, of pleasure's (and our other powers') subtle relation to it. Sophists misconstrue the soul.

They especially misunderstand reason. They are men of speech, as we said, so they look like Socrates, but he explores reason as such and the life devoted to it. He chooses speech for its own sake, true speech, correct reason, philosophy. For Socrates, knowledge is the end, but for sophists speech—true or, more likely, false—is only the means. Their rhetoric intends to achieve wealth, pleasure, power, or gain. Speaking or thinking truly is not the point. Yet, such speech looks like Socratic search and persuasion. How could someone inexperienced—how could even some who are experienced—tell the difference? Sophists ignore not just the being of naturally common goods but the worth of understanding them.

Because sophists do not properly understand speech, they also do not come to grips with the pressing evidence of its limits. These limits are visible in the Spartan tradition that does not take sophists seriously, in contempt for sophists among those who profess attachment to old Athenian ways, and in the power of the many, who cannot be tamed successfully at every moment.[43] Sophists flatter the powerful without facing up to what the need to flatter implies. Socrates, on the other hand, sees the limits of speech clearly because his end is to comprehend. He grasps the importance of force, the irrationality of belief, and the limits to understanding. Sophists tend not just to proclaim but to believe that they are wise; the nature of the wonders and perplexities we humans face generates in Socrates much greater caution.

Socrates must deal with experiences described and views expressed by sophists and by those who talk in their terms. He must contend with those who think him a sophist for hire. He finds it necessary to defend natural justice (and much virtue) from the sophistic view that they are teachable only because they are conventional. He finds it especially imperative to defend the philosophical quest by differentiating dialectic from sophistic disputation, and differentiating education from mere rhetoric.

Given that sophists see something of nature and the importance of speech, they and, of course, their more truly philosophic forefathers are in a sense Socrates' allies.[44] Indeed, not all sophists are identical. Some such as Prodicus engage in activities from which one can learn, some such as Euthydemus and Dionysodorous uncover in their madcap discussions more serious distinctions and connections than meet the eye, and some such as Gorgias make visible the power of speech, in however perverted a fashion.

Because sophistry distorts the natural independence and generality of philosophic inquiry, we can clarify certain matters by attending to it. Just as Socrates' conversations motivated by love, ambition, fatherly hopes, and law teach him something about the causes and limits of our aspirations and perplexities, so too does the pervasiveness of sophistry teach him something significant. Socrates listens in the *Sophist* as a Stranger from Elea discusses with Socrates' look-alike Theatetus the central question that sophistry implicitly poses: the truth of falsity, or the being of what is not.

The Arts

Socrates conducts most arguments by referring to the arts—humble ones, such as shoemaking, and exalted ones, such as statesmanship. They are his constant examples.[45] His references to them rarely befuddle interlocutors immediately, but he can use them to reach perplexing results. Much about Socrates' methods and goals, the ordinary aspirations and questions from which philosophy begins, and the dissatisfactions that press it forward, become evident if we attend to Plato's use of the arts and sciences. The prevalence of the arts is another element of the Socratic world.

I

The arts exemplify knowledge as opposed to ignorance. They help us see the standard that Socrates has in mind when he criticizes presumed knowledge and opinion. Men are physicians, pilots, weavers, or carpenters because they know something, and their knowledge is not produced by divine inspiration, lucky guesses, or even wide experience.[46] Rather, artisans can produce their product more or less on demand and tell us how they effect their result. They can educate others of their type, moreover, and point out their own teachers. Plato largely replaces the grandiloquent or mystical talk we hear in so many works from far away countries and times; where it still exists in his dialogues, it is always supplemented by the cold bath of artistic competence.[47] Socrates' clarity about the importance of the arts, moreover, is the most visible evidence that his wish to know advances the simple and plain (and in this way the democratic) at the expense of the priestly or conventionally aristocratic. In fact, Socrates' continued reference to shoemakers is part of what makes him appear so unusual to the aristocratic young men with whom he spends his time.[48]

The arts are a chief way that knowledge raises its claim in ordinary affairs. When Socrates is teaching Alcibiades that he knows nothing about politics, the childish arts are useful examples of what it is to know something that not everyone knows or can teach equally well. Although the arts exemplify knowledge, however, Socrates rarely says just why this is so. He usually takes for granted that interlocutors know the difference between someone who teaches them letters, the cithara, or gymnastics, and someone who cannot. The external signs of artistic knowledge are teachers, students, and products: these visible facts, rather than a theory of knowledge, mark them.[49]

In the *Gorgias* Plato indicates what makes an art an art, differentiating the sham art of rhetoric from true arts. Arts, Socrates announces, are pursuits we do not carry out by guessing, experience, or routine. Rather, an artist can give a *logos*, a reasoned account, of the things he administers. The artist knows the nature of what he cares for and the cause of what he does. The shoemaker, for example, can tell us why and when he does what he does, given the nature of leather, feet, and their use.

This description and, therefore, artistic knowledge, is more ambiguous than it seems. Is the leading cause that the artist has in mind the shoes' use, the leather's properties, the foot's shape, or his own effort? Does the account he gives chiefly go through the steps of production, or does it primarily outline the shape of the finished product? Socrates says in the *Gorgias* that an artisan looks to his work and places each thing into a fitting, harmonized arrangement. The work to which he looks is less the making than the thing to be made.

Ambiguities about fit and form lead to questions to which we will turn in due course. They should not detract, however, from what distinguishes an art from other pursuits: the artisan can give a step by step account of how he brings about a product whose arrangement he can clearly describe. One could even attempt to abstract from use, moreover, and isolate more directly what shows the scientific factor in (some) arts. In the *Philebus,* Socrates treats the truest arts as those that most involve numbers and arithmetic. From this viewpoint, the carpenter who precisely measures lines and shapes is more an artisan than the musician who to some degree always guesses the note. Arts embody precise knowledge and enumerable steps—the more precise, the more artistic. This view, however, is not Plato's only word, for it ignores the too much and too little of an ordered fit that is guided by the purpose of the art's product, a measure that distinguishes the productive arts, such as weaving, from precise if purposeless counting.[50]

II

The combination of clarity and confusion about an art's purpose is another element that characterizes Socrates' discussion of arts. He indicates the perplexity here without obliterating our usual grasp of the arts as scientific.

Socrates often treats an art and its product as self-sufficient. Health is the end of medicine, beauty and strength the goal of gymnastics, a house the object of the carpenter, safe passage the directive of the pilot, and victory the purpose of the general. One can also see, however, that this picture is easy to complicate, and Plato often complicates it: the products of some (or all) arts are subordinate to others. In the *Theages,* Socrates lists a variety of artisans or activities who serve the carpenter: borers, planers, and the like. In the *Statesman,* the Eleatic Stranger discusses the master-builder to whom the carpenter is himself subordinate.[51] The Stranger also develops the distinction between weavers and the carders, fullers, spinners, and twisters below them. In these cases, Plato's purpose is to suggest the hierarchy or rule in the arts to which we can liken the rule of political science. Political science is so hazy, however, that Plato sometimes treats it as identical to household management or, even, despotism.[52]

One also sees that arts' products are subordinate to users who may not be artisans. Is it the physician, general, assembly, or individual who properly decides when health must be risked? Is it the blacksmith or owner who decides how we should use a horse (and, therefore, his shoes)? Does the weaver, general, or ruler choose whether the army's coats are to be winter or summer weight or how elaborate a cloak's decoration should be? Plato uses these ambiguities to suggest the complexities involved in politics' goals, the intricate connection among use, benefit, and beauty, and the limits of artistic knowledge. These ambiguities enable Socrates to treat an art either as sufficient or as incomplete, depending on the imperative of his argument at any point.

It is also clear that some arts have more than one end or use. Gymnastics trains for beauty and strength; they are not identical goals. Medicine restores health generally or the health of, say, the eye or the ear; these therapies may differ and compete for resources. Does the shepherd (or his master) have in mind lamb chops or wool coats? These ambiguities allow us to see the short-comings of some of Socrates' arguments and analogies, and they allow him to make convincing claims in different circumstances. He takes Charmides on a quick journey from speaking of treating a headache to treating it well only by treating the whole body, and thence to treating the whole body well only by treating the soul and, thus, needing to understand the soul's health or excel-lence, namely, moderation. In other places, however, the difference between eye and ear or body and soul is a large difference indeed.[53]

Rivalry among the arts is also obvious, once Socrates or the Eleatic Stranger points it out. Different arts deal with the same good, end, or task; they com-pete about or treat the same bodies or material. In the *Statesman,* we see that different artisans believe themselves to be the preeminent caretakers of human beings, although we all agree that a shepherd is at once cook, physician, and matchmaker for his sheep. In other places, cooks are subordinate to train-ers—or is it to physicians? Is the diviner or the general master of the army? Is the priest or judge master of the law?[54] These rivalries cannot all be avoided by rationally subordinating one art to another because the goods and arts that deal with them are not all naturally ordered. (Is the farmer always superior to the house builder, for example; are both always superior to the shoemaker?) The natural superiority of gymnastically perfecting the body to medically re-storing its health may, nonetheless, sometimes permit the priority of the phy-sician over the trainer—when, say, resources must urgently be diverted to secure health. Socrates can make different and even opposing cases convinc-ingly because the ambiguous relation of artisans, arts, and goods enables so many statements to be visibly true, but not the whole truth.

Connected to these issues are Plato's inquiries about which arts are truly arts, and which not. This is central in discussing sophistry. In several dialogues, Socrates treats cooking as an art.[55] In the *Gorgias,* however, cooking is a sham art because it involves guessing about and experience of what pleases, not precise knowledge of what medically corrects. We may wonder, however, whether it is the unscientific method or the goal of pleasure that is the true issue, for Socrates plays in the *Protagoras* with a calculus of pleasure and never simply separates it from the human good. Some pleasures are nobler than others.

Exactly what makes a so-called art bogus is thus less clear than it seems. When Socrates examines the rhapsode Ion, the thrust of his conversation is that Ion has no art because he cannot explain how he does what he does—

why, for example, he is able to talk about Homer but not Hesiod and what the subjects are about which he supposedly knows something. Socrates, as we said, pushes Ion into making the preposterous claim that he should be general. Yet, for all Ion's self-proclaimed inspiration, he also keeps an eye on his audience to see what works and what does not. His actions are not random, although they perhaps rely on guessing and experience. When Socrates discusses learning to play the cithara, he usually treats the teachers as artisans. In the *Gorgias,* however, he does not, because the goal is pleasure. In the *Philebus,* the cithar-er's art is less artistic than arts that measure more precisely.

Divining (or soothsaying) is an art whose artistic status is also ambiguous.[56] It (and rhetoric) is visibly but imprecisely related to rhapsody. The diviner predicts the future. Does his prediction arise from art or from a fit? Socrates does not claim that it is nonsensical. Rather, he sometimes commonsensically treats divining as an art because people think diviners know something; at other times he groups it casually with fake arts; at still other times he subtly suggests that a general or statesman should control it. Genuine arts apparently have true, properly ordered goals that they serve in the knowing, precise, re-producible way we outlined earlier.

The ambiguity of the arts can also extend to their novelty. In the *Sophist* and *Statesman,* the Stranger discovers arts that have no names, and he divides activities into parts that are controlled by arts we usually do not recognize. In the *Statesman,* for example, the Stranger discerns arts that deal with all coverings and protections, and in the *Sophist* he attaches a separate art to each different implement or motion we use in fishing. In the *Statesman,* he discerns a separate artisan for each process into which he divides weaving and further decides that each belongs either to syncritics or diacritics. Henry Ford's thousand-fold division of assembly line tasks takes a back seat to Plato's diacritical inventiveness. In general, then, the arts are so well understood in Plato's world that he can appeal to them as activities and types of knowledge, but he can also employ the uncertainty of their scope and relations to invent, differentiate, or debunk them. They help to guide, inspire, and exemplify his inquiry into knowledge of the common good.[57]

Knowledge

Plato's interlocutors implicitly understand what counts as knowledge. Such comprehension is what allows artisans to stand forth as exemplary; in turn, the arts help to make our ordinary understanding more exact. This everyday grasp of knowledge helps to constitute the dialogues' world, and Plato brings it to bear on his inquiries. Socrates uses it to clarify his goals and defeat others' arguments. Its elements are measures or marks of the discussions' successes and inadequacies. One of Plato's political-philosophical paths is to develop the nature of this understanding.

I discuss three of these criteria: clarity or plainness; precision, accuracy, or exactness; and sufficiency or adequacy.[58] I also look briefly at Socrates' use of ordinary logical arguments, especially contradiction, and touch on his view of perplexity and stability.

These criteria of ordinary understanding are connected to what makes arts arts. One obvious connection is Socrates' frequent suggestions that interlocutors are not speaking precisely, exactly, or accurately.[59] To be precise is to do or leave nothing extraneous or superfluous—no extra material for the tailor or shoemaker, no wasted or useless steps for the weaver. It is to do the thing and only the thing. An obvious example is mathematics, calculation, or geometry. A precise understanding hits its object just so, as a hammer strikes a nail or an arrow a target. (Perhaps Socrates has this fit partly in mind when he calls an argument just.) Socrates nowhere discusses precision exhaustively or precisely, but Plato addresses it explicitly in the *Statesman*.

For something to be understood precisely, it must stand out independently and be visible. Socrates (and his interlocutors) also often suggest that someone should be (or complain that they are not) speaking or seeing clearly (*delos*) or plainly (*saphes*).[60] To see or speak clearly is to not see or speak obscurely and confusedly. It is to see things in sharp outline, as one sees a shape plainly or hears a sound that rings true. It is to grasp what one seeks apart from the occlusions that cover or block access to it. It is also to see it as it stands out from what surrounds it.

Clarity and plainness suggest perception, knowing not as calculating, deducing, speaking, and arguing, but as seeing or hearing more or less directly. Plato discusses perception in several places, notably the *Theatetus*. He also explores perception in his subtle, variegated, discussions of images. He sometimes treats material things as images of a permanent, unblemished instance or form. A simple replica such as a tiny statue, however, differs from a depiction that must keep in mind distortions of distance and perspective. An instance of something, moreover, may not be an image at all, but a full version of the thing itself, as one dollar bill fully exemplifies each. The great complexity of images makes the question of clarity, plainness, or obviousness much more confused than it might otherwise seem. Nonetheless, Socrates and his interlocutors seek and decry the absence of clarity and plainness in the ordinary sense of seeing what visibly stands out, unshrouded and unblemished.

Clarity and plainness are also connected to sufficiency or adequacy.[61] Socrates seeks to see or know things sufficiently. While precision involves something's presentation (or being grasped) with no excess or extraneous attachments, sufficiency involves leaving nothing out. To see sufficiently is to see enough of a thing to know it as what it is; "enough" ranges from adequate to the full range of wholes, parts, genera, species, and classes to which the thing is connected. This full range is full sufficiency. When Socrates and his interlocutors examine something, they try to see enough of it so that nothing relevant is left out, try to see it precisely so that nothing extraneous belongs to it, and try to see it clearly, so that nothing blocks the way to it. They seek the truth (i.e., the clear, unblemished, truth), the whole truth (i.e., the sufficient or adequate truth) and nothing but the truth (i.e., the precise or exact truth.)

Many of Socrates' arguments are intentionally false or incomplete. He teaches by confusing as much as by assuring. The ways through which he confuses are allied to (often by reversing) precision, clarity, and sufficiency. He sometimes takes an ordinary view of a topic, say, virtue, and drops this view in and out of the conversation, so that what is achieved in more precise discussion once more becomes confused.[62] He often leaves concepts bunched together the way we do ordinarily and uses this impression of unity to occlude the issue at hand: he characteristically acts as if, say, virtue's being noble and/or good means that it is completely or nothing but noble and/or good.[63] He often obscures the fit of one concept into a larger class and the range of classes within which the concept is included.[64] In general, he sows confusion through arguments that address their subjects imprecisely and insufficiently.

Socrates' purpose in doing this is to bring out the relations among things while not letting these relations ossify into technical categories, and to grasp the living existence of what I have just called concepts—their presence in things as images and forms, and their full being as objects of knowledge. To grasp such matters is what it means to understand.

Almost everyone in the dialogues concedes that contradictory arguments are bad and that if we contradict ourselves about something we do not know it.[65] Interlocutors' common view that contradictions are to be eschewed is a condition for entrée into Socrates' conversations. What is contradictory is less a harmful characteristic of speech, however, than an impossible characteristic of things. Because something cannot be itself and its opposite in the same respect, at the same time, and so on, a contradictory speech cannot capture it correctly. The oddness of factual contradictions, in turn, the apparent existence of contrary versions of the same thing (say, the colors black and white) and the occasional existence of two opposites of one thing (say, foolishness and licentiousness as counters to moderation) allow Socrates to bewilder interlocutors.[66] The peculiarities involved in something's being both like other things and different from them are an endless source of confusion, amusement, and impetus to exploration, and a basis for understanding.[67]

Socrates sometimes searches for the "stability" at the ground of things so that statements will not contradict.[68] If this stability is at root immaterial, the locus of contradiction may be in "logic," that is, in what is speakable, although not necessarily in speaking. Yet, we find contradiction, unclarity, imprecision, and insufficiency not only in what we try to know but also in what we desire, fear, experience, and enjoy. The gap between speech, passions, and their objects is not transparent. Knowledge in Plato is never far from the excellence that organizes affairs. The place of the mind in virtue is one expression of the central political-philosophical theme.

CHAPTER 2

Virtue

If there is one point that orients the world of Socrates and his interlocutors it is that virtue is the proper goal of paternal advice, ambition, and punishment. So, examining Plato's understanding of virtue is our inquiry's next natural step. This understanding proves to be subtle and complex, and Plato develops it in many dialogues. I concentrate here on seven, the *Theages, Euthyphro, Laches, Charmides, Gorgias, Meno,* and *Protagoras.* Each of the first five addresses one of the basic virtues that Plato analyzes: wisdom, piety, courage, moderation, and justice.[1] The last two examine virtue generally. I also consider virtue in subsequent chapters.

Plato sees virtue in several dimensions, which he explores as he unveils it. Viewing virtue in the light of these dimensions, and they in its, exemplifies his dialectical understanding. This understanding uncovers contradictions and complexities, so Socrates does not reach crisp conclusions. When he apparently does reach such a conclusion, it means little until explored further. When, say, he looks for the "same" courage in everything courageous, he does not seek a pale abstraction: the similarity of all courageous things is not necessarily a bare identity. Courage, moreover, causes the courageous. It perfects, completes, forms, and attracts action and thought. It is noble or beautiful. Nobility and similar matters, however, are themselves controversial and must be explored dialectically. Hence, Plato's investigations are continuing spirals that elevate and expand their starting points and, consequently, root them more deeply.

To make this point in another way, Plato does not seek narrow definitions but examines phenomena. In the *Republic,* for example, the search for justice uncovers the variety and different degrees of justice's presence in communities and individuals. This range is likely contained in justice's definition there (justice is each doing it's own, or what nature fits it for), but this is not obvious. In any event, to understand what the definition means requires showing it at work in opinions, political orders, and activities of the soul. It requires, at a minimum, considering the *Republic* as a whole. Virtue occurs in several places, and we can understand it only as we observe it within these different limits.

The dimensions that complicate Plato's discussion of virtue are chiefly of three sorts. One looks to the question: virtue of what? Where is the virtue at work? Is courage primarily in soldiers as a class, so we mean by courage excellence in the city or its laws? Is it primarily in individuals, so we mean by courage our combined actions of body and soul, political or not? Is it primarily in our souls, so we mean the steadfast form of our dispositions and passions, not just our actions?

If a virtue such as courage belongs in all these places, moreover, can it be one? If a virtue is not one, however, what accounts for the likenesses among its appearances? If piety is not unified, for example, how can we explain the evident similarity in obedient public ritual, humble individual prayer, fastidiously reticent desire, and meticulously studious reason? Each of these homes of virtue contains its own complexities, moreover, whose unity is also difficult to grasp. There are many forms of government, not just one political order. The meaning of the spiritedness and desire that the soul's courage and moderation form is complex. The connections among philosophical reason, thoughtful prudence, and sound or unsound opinion are murky. Yet, forms of government, passionate desires, and users of reason are manifestly alike among themselves, although they differ from each other.

The second dimension involves the goods and ostensible harms that virtues deal with and distribute. To examine courage is to examine fear. To say what justice is is to say what goods are to be distributed and what makes them good. To consider moderation and excess is to consider pleasure. To explore wisdom is to explore understanding and knowledge. Socrates' interlocutors could hardly say what a virtue is without having in mind the goods that the virtue properly bypasses, possesses, or limits. What they see, however, is ordinarily only a dim reflection of the fully convoluted presence of the good in question. Socrates, for example, takes the immediacy of pleasure and brings out its complex nature. Yet, although the discussions of virtue cannot escape subtleties about goods, we can make our analyses accurate only if we attend to what evidently separates one good (say, pleasure) from another (say, wisdom.)

Plato's discussion of virtue also characteristically involves the question of entire ways of life. This sometimes obvious and sometimes hidden theme combines the other two dimensions. The virtues, their homes, and their objects come together in the political and philosophical ways of life, and their varieties and imposters. Plato explores how philosophic virtue is compatible with a gentleman's political virtue, or how it extends and radicalizes political virtue on its own terms. He also considers what philosophic virtue requires from the community. We will see how the *Theages* lays bare everyday conditions for Socratic wisdom, how the *Euthyphro* shows Socrates' compatibility with ordinary piety and courage, how the *Gorgias* and *Republic* radicalize conventional wisdom and justice, and how the *Gorgias* and *Protagoras* display Socrates' concern with sophistic look-alikes.

Plato also examines the virtue that we manifest in philosophical examination as such, the attempted perfection of reason and measure in their own domain. Here, too, he considers reflections, or imposters. In other instances, he looks directly at virtue in politics or economics, with the question of philosophy and philosophers in the background. The *Laws* is the most extensive example of this approach. The relative ability of different ways of life to enliven virtue is central in understanding and ranking them.

Wisdom

I begin with the *Theages* because wisdom is philosophy's goal. Although the *Theages* is subtitled "on wisdom," however, Socrates does not mention virtue, the soul, or philosophy in it.[2] Its true topic is the conditions and requirements for Socrates' activity, and his likeness to fathers, sophists, gentlemen, rulers, and gods. The issue is the connection of Socratic "wisdom" to other ways of life, not the theoretical elements of knowing.[3]

I

The first conditions for Socrates' activity are leisure and privacy. The dialogue begins when Theages' father, Demodocus, asks Socrates whether he has leisure to talk with him privately and, if not, to make time "for my sake." Demodocus is ashamed to say directly what Theages desires (tyranny), and he has been putting his son off. Socrates assures Theages that their conversation now has a witness (himself). Witnesses, we may say, at once increase dissembling because we keep up appearances and decrease it because it is hard to lie tomorrow about what we say publicly today.[4] Socrates politely accedes to Demodocus' request. We see that he needs a good reputation as well as leisure. He cannot seem to be a corrupter.[5]

Demodocus wants Socrates' counsel about Theages' desire "to become wise" and about placing him with a sophist.[6] Socrates suggests that they must agree on what they are counseling about. What wisdom do they seek, and is this the wisdom Theages desires? Indeed, Socrates' searches radicalize such questions but never break free of them. In his inquiries, the subject becomes ever more general and precise, and our desire to explore it is increasingly clarified. Socrates seeks to elevate "agreements" and "witnesses" that constitute or depend on opinion and sight to what is truly common and public, that is, to what the mind as such sees and hears.

II

Socrates begins to question Theages. What wisdom does he desire? Not a pilot's or charioteer's, for although they rule, it is over ships and horses. Rather, he desires wisdom in ruling human beings. Which ones? Not a farmer's art of ruling reapers and harvesters, or a carpenter's of how to rule sawyers, borers, planers, and turners. He desires knowledge of how to rule all the public artisans and private men and women.

The purpose of (some) of the arts Socrates uses as examples is unclear. Is the pilot's goal victory, safety, or wealth? Is the charioteer's art used for his benefit or his team's? Is the musician's purpose pleasure, beauty, or reverence? Such ambiguities come to a head in the rule over all. What is this rule's purpose? Socratic "wisdom" is concerned with what political rule exemplifies: the end, good, or purpose of the whole. But it adjusts or replaces the ruler's breadth by seeking to know all; its object is the unity of what we can articulate and understand. Socrates presents images of this whole here by listing the artisans or actions subordinate to farmers and carpenters. Each subordinate contributes to what the carpenter produces or the farmer grows, but none has his own end.[7] When we rule farmers or carpenters politically, however, we direct independent men, not mere subordinates. Socrates seeks especially to understand the duality of combination and independence.

III

Socrates now pushes Theages to name the knowledge he desires, and he lists several illegitimate rulers over all people in the city. Theages agrees to call them tyrants "on account of their identical rule," the same as two diviners are diviners, and he affirms his desire to tyrannize. If, as Euripides says, tyrants are wise by keeping company with the wise, in whose company might Theages become a wise tyrant? And, in what are they wise? Theages again says that he (and, he supposes, all men) would pray to "rule over all the citizens," although he would "probably rather become a god." He then claims, however, that he does not desire to rule by violence as tyrants do but over the willing, as do those such as Themistocles who are clever (as Socrates says) in political things.[8]

We see here further elements of Socratic wisdom. Theages treats the tyrant as if he is almost a god, and he and Socrates compare him to a diviner, who knows what gods will do. Socratic inquiry is a different type of godlike understanding; it transforms the desire or prayer of the would-be tyrant. Socrates also replaces the poets, for he serves here as Euripides' spokesman. What Socrates seeks that is divine in scope and permanence is what he calls here "sufficient knowledge that results from inquiry."

IV

Socrates and Theages agree that to become wise in horsemanship Theages should go to horses' owners and users. Similarly, to become wise about politics, should he not spend time with those who are clever about political things? Theages demurs, for political men's sons are no "better than the sons of shoemakers."[9] What, then, would Theages do, Socrates asks, if his own son desired to become a good painter but were unwilling to study with painters? Theages swears that he does not know. He therefore should not wonder at and blame his father, Socrates tells him. They will place Theages at no cost with an Athenian gentleman who deals with political things. Is not Socrates one of these gentlemen, Theages asks? It "will suffice and [he] will seek no one else" if Socrates is willing to keep company with him.

Plato displays here some of Socrates' methods, and his ordinary, conventional, helpfulness. He lets Theages see, through supposition, his possible sameness to his father. He clarifies politics by likening it to other activities. He mentions painting first among the arts. Socrates' inquiries involve supposing, likening, and imitating. One way Socrates retains his reputation with Athenian gentlemen is by seeming to be one (he does not take pay) and helping them (as he does here). Socrates' conversations may at first separate sons from fathers by expanding the sons' view of what is properly human or their "own," but he can then reconcile them by showing our limits.[10]

V

Socrates cannot deny that he is a gentleman, so he first tries to turn Theages back to his father, who has held many offices. Theages, however, "looks down on" the political men.[11] Perhaps, then, they can seek Prodicus, Gorgias, Polus, and others who claim to be able to educate the young. Socrates says that he himself knows none of the "blessed and noble subjects of knowledge" but, rather, "I always say . . . that I happen to know so to speak nothing except a certain small subject of knowledge, the erotic [things]." Theages tells Demodocus that Socrates is playing. He knows worthless boys who, after spending time with Socrates, appeared better than those to whom they had been inferior.

V A

Socrates' claim to know nothing of the noble subjects of knowledge is pregnant, not empty. Knowing nothing is having a knowledge of differences—that this is not that. Socrates, after all, differentiates political men here from pilots, charioteers, chorus masters, trainers, physicians, farmers, carpenters, horsemen, and javelin throwers. He also sees their similarities. How far knowledge of difference and similarity can go is one measure of the sufficiency of wisdom as the completed goal of inquiry.[12]

Socrates also claims to know erotic things. This knowledge is connected to knowing nothing, because knowledge of love, desire, wish, and prayer is knowledge of lacking and seeking. It is also, therefore, knowledge of what could satisfy: Socrates quickly saw that Theages desired what he himself only vaguely understood to be tyranny. Socrates knows the erotic because he is concerned with education. This concern fits with his playfulness, which is designed to elevate, not diminish.

Socrates has moderated the object of Theages' desire from tyranny, to rule over the willing, to being a gentleman, to being or merely appearing better than other youths. This apparent reduction in aspiration is poised to become the philosophic elevation of aspiration in which one becomes better than oneself. For this to occur, however, Theages would need to display a greater scope and intensity of eros, fuller intelligence, and more spiritedness than he has. Socrates earlier had to prod him to answer more eagerly. His father is wracked by fear. Theages attends to diviners.[13] Socrates thus does not mention philosophy. The self-improvement to which he orients Theages involves ordinary citizenship and ill-defined achievement.[14]

VI

Theages claims that if Socrates wished he could make Theages like those who are now better than others. It escapes your notice, Socrates tells him, that a demon from god follows Socrates and signals him and friends who consult him not to act. There are witnesses to this. Theages, for example, "will hear from many," "the things I said about the destruction of the (Sicilian) expedition."[15]

If the sign opposes, one cannot spend time with Socrates and benefit. Those "whose intercourse the power of the demonic thing contributes to" are the ones Theages has noticed. They make immediate, rapid, progress. Some retain the benefit "in a firm and lasting way." Many others, such as Aristeides, make wonderful progress while with Socrates but are no different from others once they go away.[16] If Socrates' and Theages' intercourse is "dear to the god," Theages "will make very great and rapid progress, but if not, not."[17]

Theages suggests a trial. If the demon permits, "that will be best." If it opposes, they will deliberate about whether to keep company or try to persuade it "with prayers, sacrifices, and in whatever way the diviners prescribe." The dialogue ends when Socrates agrees with Demodocus to stop opposing Theages: "if it seems that's the way it has to be done, then that's the way we'll do."[18]

VI A

This section suggests that Socrates requires intimacy, not just privacy. Socrates' peculiar eroticism radiates its own presence and magnetism, and (through the demon) manifests an allied principle of repulsion. Because privacy and intimacy endanger rulers, Socrates must secure his public reputation.[19] He thus displays his sound politics by claiming to have foreseen difficulty in Sicily.[20] Above all, he protects his reputation with his story of his demon. So far from being a sophist who takes all paying customers, demon-guided

Socrates eschews possible associates. Theages takes the demon to be a god amenable to prayers and sacrifices. Among the conditions for Socrates' success (or for his survival despite the risks he takes) is to appear as a god, a divine, or, at least, unaccountable presence, who draws something like love from Aristeides, Alcibiades, and others.[21]

Piety

I turn next to piety because discussing it shows how the orthodox understanding in which most people live can be moderated and elevated naturally. I explore it by examining the *Euthyphro*, where Socrates discusses piety directly. Plato displays philosophy's radical impiety by having Socrates question the essence of piety itself, as no pious man would, by reminding us of Socrates' indictment for introducing new gods, and by displaying piety's extremism. At the same time, he shows us how Socrates tries to support convention, moderate extremism, and associate philosophy with precise attention to what is worth revering.

I

The link between piety and justice is especially strong, both generally and in the *Euthyphro*. Euthyphro is bringing a suit against what he is certain is an unjust act that will pollute him if it goes unpunished. This link may strike us as odd, because toleration makes religion for us primarily private.[22] A moment's reflection on the past or on today's Islam, however, shows that the same law can be both divine and civic. When law is unquestionable because divine, philosophical exploration and human freedom gain footing only with great difficulty.[23] Socrates, therefore, must find safe ways to relax the identity of political and divine authority. The unique openness of everyday life in Athens is especially useful in this endeavor.[24]

Euthyphro begins by asking Socrates what is new. Why is he at the King's Porch, not the Lyceum? (Would strict piety allow anything new?)[25] Socrates tells him that he has been indicted. Meletus accuses him of corrupting the young; yet, how could one as young as Meletus know what corruption is? He is correct to care for the young, however, as farmers do; if he clears out corrupters of youths he will cause great goods. We may say that we know the proper human beginning—care for the young—more evidently than we know the proper end or outcome. We saw this in Demodocus' love. Plants are natural growths whose end we do know, but farmers cannot succeed without good luck, for which they hope and pray.[26]

Euthyphro thinks that Meletus will do the city evil by doing Socrates injustice. According to Socrates, Meletus asserts that Socrates makes new gods and does not believe in the ancient ones. (As with plants, corrupting human beings starts at the beginning, which includes denigrating the old gods.) Euthyphro takes "new gods" to refer to Socrates' demon. Euthyphro's own predictions about divine things are ridiculed as if he is mad. Socrates claims, however, that he is not merely ridiculed; Athenians' spiritedness is aroused against those they believe teach them wisdom. (Socrates' difficulty is not merely that he produces new gods but other Socratics.)

Socrates then asks about Euthyphro's suit, which Euthyphro could be defending or prosecuting. (Euthyphro shares more of Athens' prosecutorial indignation than does Socrates.) Euthyphro is prosecuting his father for murder; Socrates is surprised and swears his only oath. He suggests that only someone advanced in wisdom (as Euthyphro agrees he is) could believe (as opposed to the many) that this way is correct. Euthyphro is prosecuting his father on behalf of one of their laborers who in drunken anger had killed a servant. The father had left the laborer bound and exposed, and he died before the father could hear from the exegete of the gods what to do. For Euthyphro, what matters is whether the killing was just (as he is certain it was not), not whether the killer belongs to one's family. Associating with the unjust pollutes one.

Euthyphro does not dispute his family's view that the father is not a murderer.[27] He does dispute their view that prosecuting a father is impious, "they knowing badly, Socrates . . . how the divine is disposed concerning the pious and the impious."[28] Euthyphro's piety breaks the bond of family that pieties such as honoring parents and the incest prohibition were originally meant to protect. For him, what is central is his own righteousness. He subordinates political justice and family to himself.

Socrates asks if Euthyphro supposes his knowledge of divine and pious things to be so precise that he does not fear his act might be impious. Euthyphro claims that without precise knowledge he would not benefit or differ from the many. Socrates is thus able to suggest subtly to us that we cannot separate piety from knowledge of it.[29]

II

Socrates then questions Euthyphro about piety.[30] He asks what sort of things the pious are and suggests through a question what he means. Isn't the pious the same in itself in every action, and opposite to the impious, which is similar to itself and has one idea in accordance with impiety? At 6D he adds that the idea or *eidos* of piety is that by which pious things are pious, and at 6E that it can be gazed at as a pattern, allowing one to declare what it is like as pious. At 11A, he suggests that to say what the pious is is to give its being, not how it affects and is affected. We see no fuller description in any other dialogue of the characteristics of ideas, which Socrates sometimes presents as the objects of his understanding. An idea is the same in every action, is similar to itself, is one, has strict opposites, causes things to be what they are, can be seen as a pattern that things are like, is something's being, and answers the question, What is . . . ? The singularity of an idea such as piety thus hides a multiplicity of ways that ideas are. Ideas are simple, yet difficult to understand.[31]

Euthyphro agrees "entirely" with Socrates' statement. (Is an idea a unity as an entirety, as a whole, or in some other way?) What the pious is is what he is doing now, with regard to injustice. The law is disposed not to give way to impious things, even when it is parents who are impious. The proof is that Zeus, whom humans believe to be best and most just, bound his father for unjustly swallowing his sons, and Zeus' father Kronos castrated his own father "because of other such things." We see that Euthyphro, despite Socrates' help, makes a mistake similar to that of interlocutors in other dialogues. He does not say what piety is but gives what he believes are instances of it. Moreover, he identifies Zeus' actions with justice and goodness, identifies justice with law, and presents our laws as imitating, not (merely) obeying, the gods. An idea (piety) implicitly becomes for him a law or a set of laws that fully and without exception embodies the gods' example.

III

Socrates reminds Euthyphro of the "what is" question. Euthyphro now "beautifully" gives a single statement: What is beloved by (dear to) the gods is pious; what is not beloved by them (indeed, what they hate) is impious. We do not become angry when we differ about numbers, greater and less, or heavier and lighter, Socrates then suggests, because we can easily calculate, measure, or weigh. Rather, we are angry enemies about the just (and unjust), noble, and good; we cannot decide about them sufficiently.[32] The gods' quarrels must be about these: they love what they believe is noble, good, and just, but the gods differ about them. So (given Euthyphro's statement) the same things are both pious and impious (i.e., they have not found piety's idea.) Euthyphro agrees readily to all but the last step.

III A

Socrates' conclusion is clear. It is not evident, however, that his rubric captures anger that is caused by attachment to our own things. Perhaps the gods too seek to protect and defend their own, rather than differing (only) about the noble, good, and just.[33] This attachment could cause anger even if they believe the same things to be noble or, indeed, because of this. For, they (and we) might compete for equally valued but scarce rule, wealth, and worshipful admiration. Euthyphro, for example, seems to be guided not primarily by a difference from others about justice, but by his purity, his difference qua Euthyphro. His piety, and piety generally, exacerbates the tendency to equate the just with one's own.

Because the gods differ, we can say of no thing with confidence that it is pious.[34] By seeking piety as an idea, however, as something open to all, non-competitively, Socrates allows it to be rationalized and, thus, to soften it as a source of anger and difference.

IV

Euthyphro now claims that the gods do not dispute that whoever acts unjustly should pay the penalty. Socrates then asks Euthyphro to show him that all gods believe his action against his father is correct. Socrates repeats the action's circumstances so that the complexity of who, what, and when becomes evident: Euthyphro takes a murky situation and treats it as if it is clear. (Does the standpoint of piety tend this way, as a natural look at justice might not?) Socrates then returns to the "what is" question.[35] The pious, Euthyphro now claims with Socrates' prompting, is what all the gods love, the impious what they all hate, and what some love and some hate is neither pious nor impious.

Socrates pursues this opinion by asking whether the gods love the pious because it is pious, "or is it pious because it is loved?" He means to distinguish the independent lovability of pious or just things from their being pious or just simply because they are declared pious or just. He will suggest that things do not become lovable because the gods happen to love them; they are loved because they are pious. The holy, therefore, is other than or independent of the gods' actions.[36]

Socrates analogizes the gods' loving to anyone's "leading," "carrying," or seeing. It is not, say, our carrying something into a ceremony that makes it sacred; we carry it in because it is sacred. It is not, say, because we lead someone into a ring that he becomes a boxer; we lead him in because he is a boxer. These examples make evident that Socrates' distinction is not simply obvious, for in certain circumstances being in the ring forces one to box. Are the gods gods because we worship them, rather than being worshipped because they are divine? If we make worshipful rituals, however, does this mean that we produce the pious or holy altogether? Or, rather, do our gods and what is dear to them—say, just action—reflect what is naturally dear to us, without our simply creating what is dear to us?

The result of Socrates' argument is to distinguish piety from what happens to be dear to the gods. It therefore overturns Euthyphro's definition of the pious as what is dear to the gods.

V

Socrates now asks Euthyphro to define the pious again, from the beginning. Euthyphro, however, has no further resources because, he claims, his definition always keeps going around; whatever is said is unwilling to stay in place. Socrates has shown Euthyphro some of the complexity in piety, which the "fastidious" Euthyphro overlooks or still wishes to ignore.[37]

Socrates then resurfaces piety's connection to justice.[38] He asks whether all the pious is just, and all the just pious, or only part of it, and claims that justice's relation to piety is the same as fear's to awe and odd's to number: all awe is part of fear, but where fear or justice is there is not everywhere awe or piety. Socrates ignores the possibility that fear and justice are broader but not necessarily higher than awe or piety. Awe of the gods, after all, is more consequential and contentious than fear of thunder. Perhaps, however, justice is in some ways both broader and higher than piety. Socrates reminds us that he (ostensibly) seeks Euthyphro's teaching in order to deal better with Meletus: Meletus accuses Socrates as much to preserve democratic justice as to preserve piety.[39] In any event, Socrates' argument splits the identity of piety and justice.

VI

Euthyphro now says that the part of the just that is reverent and pious concerns tending gods; the rest of justice concerns tending human beings. (This opinion still does not tell us what justice or piety is.) Other types of tending are types of knowledge: What is piety's knowledge, Socrates now asks, and what is it for? Tending, moreover, benefits the one tended: Does piety make gods better? Socrates' examples here—horse, dog, and cattle tending—suggest that although tending is at first good for the animal groomed it is ultimately good for the groom, or the owner.[40] Do we make the gods or carry them forward for our own good? This impious possibility is, of course, not pursued; the notion that we might improve the gods is shocking enough to Euthyphro. Socrates has restored his awe, at least momentarily.

If piety does not improve the gods, what is it for, and what does it know? Euthyphro claims that it is the tending that slaves owe masters. Euthyphro's piety has now revealed itself to be an excess of fear in which he tries to save himself by fastidiously separating from others. Just as Socrates tried to moderate the self-righteousness produced by Euthyphro's belief that he can imitate the gods, so, too, will he now try to moderate piety's tendency to produce excessive obedience and dread. He pursues Euthyphro's statement by using three examples: physicians, shipwrights, and house builders. We know the work they produce. For what, however, do we serve the gods? What work do they produce? Euthyphro cannot answer, but he can say that the pious man uses prayers and sacrifices to gratify the gods. The pious things, sacrifice and prayer, he now claims, "preserve families and communities of cities."

Socrates then introduces but does not pursue still another aspect of piety: the lover follows "the beloved wherever he leads—again, what do you say the pious and piety are? Isn't it a certain kind of knowledge of sacrificing and praying?"[41] Requesting (praying) and giving (sacrificing), he suggests, are artful or "correct" commerce. While what we receive from the gods is clear (all the good things), what do they receive from us? They do not benefit from prayer and sacrifice because they have no needs. Euthyphro claims that perhaps they receive honor, respect, and gratitude. So, he is again saying that the pious (as gratifying) is beneficial or dear to the gods; the argument has moved full circle. Socrates' circles are not vitiating circular arguments, however, but, rather, clarify the elements of the phenomenon being questioned. To set in motion a hypothesis or opinion about something, as Socrates does here with piety, is to display much of the phenomenon that underlies it.

Socrates concludes by suggesting that their argument either was ignoble before or is incorrect now. He will not give up voluntarily, out of cowardice, until they learn. Euthyphro should now tell the truth and not dishonor Socrates. For, if he did not know piety plainly, he would have feared before gods and been ashamed before men of risking prosecuting his father. Euthyphro declines to begin again from the beginning; he is in a hurry to go somewhere.

VI A

The dialogue concludes by contrasting Socrates with Euthyphro. Socrates' courage in continuing to examine piety differs from fearful obedience. Perhaps, indeed, as Socrates' remark about following the beloved suggests, rather than accepting as holy what some say the gods demand, his continued questioning shows proper reverence. Socrates' inquiry imitates what is highest (something that Euthyphro unsuccessfully attempts) by making it visible through his speeches. A statement "is not more pleasing to me unless it happens to be true."[42] While Euthyphro's excess leads him to act impiously against his family, moreover, Socrates defends the justice and piety that protect the city and family. At the same time, he differentiates piety and justice, enabling public life to be freed from piety's cold hand.

The contrast between Socrates and Euthyphro also helps to explain why the *Euthyphro* does not mention virtue or the soul. The soul's true reverence for itself is its questioning examination of the most important things. What looks closest to this individual height in Euthyphro is a fastidiousness that leads him to separate himself improperly from family and city. Socratic piety of soul, however, seeks an understanding that we can share. The soul is most itself when it is least directed to itself. Socratic reverence, therefore, is also restrained or moderate, even if it can appear manic.[43] Nonphilosophic private piety is, perhaps, always excessive or deficient, that is, never a virtue simply.

Courage

The *Euthyphro* could lead us to discuss justice—because the pious belongs to the just—or moderation—because of piety's link to shame.[44] We choose, instead, to turn to courage (with which the *Euthyphro* concludes) because of the apparent difference between Socrates' courage in inquiry and Euthyphro's ignorant and piously slavish obedience.[45]

I

The *Laches* is Plato's most extensive discussion of manliness, and it refers explicitly to virtue and the soul, as the *Theages* and *Euthyphro* do not. Plato names the dialogue after Laches rather than after its other chief character, the more prominent general Nicias, because Laches defends the animal immediacy of courageous action in contrast to the subtlety of speech.[46] Nicias, who says he loves to talk and learn, proves to lack sufficient spirit. Philosophic questioning must be courageous and must also account for brute courage.

The *Laches* begins with the request for advice I discussed in the first chapter. Lysimachus and Melesias ask Nicias and Laches whether training someone to fight in armor (as Stesilaus is displaying it) is for the best. They agree to give their counsel, and bring Socrates into the group. Nicias argues, with several reasons but no examples, that the training is worth studying and that it will make the student "more courageous and confident than he is" because he will appear "well formed and therefore terrible to the enemy." Laches, however, argues that it is not worth studying because he has seen Stesilaus in action and he is ridiculous. Besides, such supposed knowledge would only embolden a coward and bring his cowardice to light or subject someone courageous to slander, envy, and ridicule "unless he were wonderfully greater than the others in virtue."[47]

Socrates refuses to break the tie and suggests that they should not be persuaded by a vote but by whomever has studied, practiced, or been taught. Indeed, they do not even know what they seek: For what purpose might they need to study Stesilaus' art? Socrates claims that they are looking "for the sake of the soul of a youth." Just as one must know what sight is to improve the eyes, so one must know what virtue is to improve the soul and advise "how to possess it nobly." But, Socrates continues, they should not look straightaway at the whole of virtue, but at the part to which fighting in armor seems directed, namely, "what the many opine to be courage."[48]

II

Socrates thus asks Laches what courage is.[49] Laches replies that if someone is willing to stay in the order to repel the enemy and not flee, one knows he is courageous. What of one who fights while fleeing, Socrates asks, as the Spartans turned around and fought like cavalry against the Persians in Plataea and won victory? Socrates wishes to hear about those courageous not only in arms but also in the whole class of war, and not only in war but in sea perils, illness, poverty, and the political, and not only in pain and fear but also about those who fight cleverly against desires and pleasures. Some have somehow acquired courage in all this, some cowardice.[50]

Socrates then helps Laches see what he intends. If someone asked what "quickness" is in, say, running, cithara playing, and speaking, he would answer: quickness is the power that in less time accomplishes much. Socrates asks Laches to discuss courage this way: What power is it that is the same in all of which they speak?

Laches replies that it is some endurance of the soul, if he is to tell of "the natural concerning courage through all." Socrates knows Laches believes courage to be noble, however, and while endurance that follows prudence is noble and good, following imprudence it is harmful and mischievous.[51] Thus, Laches cannot say that all endurance is noble.

Perhaps, then, courage is prudent endurance? But, Laches would not call courageous someone who spends prudently in order to possess more. Nor would he say that a man who prudently endures in war knowing that he will be assisted, and that the other fighters are weaker, is more courageous than one in the opposite camp who is willing to stand and endure. Laches also agrees that the many who are willing to dive into a well uncleverly and endure are more courageous but more imprudent than those who venture such a deed artfully.[52] Socrates and Laches had said that imprudent daring and endurance are base and hurtful, however, and that courage is something noble. They are thus speaking ignobly; the deeds and their words do not symphonize.[53] Perhaps, Socrates concludes, they will endure in the search, so that courage itself does not laugh at them for not being courageous in searching for it.[54] Laches replies that a love of victory takes hold, and he is truly irritated not to be saying what he understands.

II A

Socrates at first shows narrowly the inadequacy of Laches' opinion that courage means standing in place: direction is irrelevant. We sometimes need to break the conventional infantry order to achieve victory; Laches forgets the relation of courage to winning. He loves victory, but his love clashes with his view of courage, which disassociates it from success in war; the knowledgeable general is, for him, not courageous.

Socrates helps Laches by giving him an example. Why does he select quickness? Quickness is connected to courage because courage is related to boldness. Laches is inclined to see the rash as the courageous; Nicias will understand the rash as a defect that masquerades as courage. Courage thus has two vices, rashness and cowardice. As a virtue, it must account for the power that rashness exemplifies; it must be a form of daring quickness as well as stolid endurance. Socrates' example indicates what Laches misses in his definition (which is based on endurance) but somehow grasps in his understanding (which points to boldness).[55]

Socrates' definition mentions accomplishing much in less time. It does not account for the too quick and too slow, however, the quick as measured by what fits. It is as if we could measure quick harp playing with no reference to the beauty of the music we produce. Socrates' definition deliberately abstracts from the measure of appropriate speed, although the examples he gives suggest it.[56] Laches' understanding makes a similar abstraction; he does not properly connect courage—the stolid or the bold—to what is fitting in a particular time and place—say, prudent victory.[57]

Laches says that he speaks of the natural concerning courage, by which he means what is untaught or not artificial. He also mentions the soul: courage is a natural power of soul. Nicias' understanding will speak of knowledge and the fearful but not of soul. Socrates' refutation of him centers on animal courage and virtue's parts, that is, his refutation is related to the soul's characteristics. Although courage is only part of virtue, however, the *Laches* does not connect it to a part of the soul and, indeed, does not mention the soul's parts. Here and later in the dialogue, Socrates also refuses to differentiate the virtues in terms of their different objects (say, fears versus pleasures). So, if virtues are not differentiated by objects and if the soul does not have parts, why does virtue (the soul's perfection) have parts?[58]

Laches has also not attained the intellectual realm where courage serves courage: the courageous search for courage belongs to this realm. Its flight or escape is *the* danger that we must boldly and enduringly overcome. Speech about courage may exemplify it better than deeds because search is most fully oriented to courage as such. Plato suggests (without developing) the height or virtue of knowledge, not just its utility.

III

Socrates asks Nicias for help, and his inviting Nicias to assist them silently teaches Laches that help need not detract from courage. Nicias suggests that Socrates has not been separating courage nobly.[59] He has often heard him say that each of us is good as he is wise and bad where he is unlearned. If someone courageous is good, clearly he is wise. Courage, Nicias says under Socrates' prompting, is knowledge of the terrible and of those things about which one should be confident, in war and all others.

Laches asks incredulously if Nicias is calling courageous physicians and other craftsmen who have such knowledge in their arts. Nicias asks in reply if Laches believes that physicians know whether health is more to be dreaded than sickness. Does he believe that the same is to be dreaded by those who are to live as by those for whom death is due? Laches replies that Nicias is calling the diviners courageous, for who else knows who would be better alive than dead? Nicias replies that the diviner only judges signs of what is to be, not whether it is better or not to suffer it.

Socrates and Nicias then agree that Nicias is saying that someone is not courageous if he lacks knowledge of what is to be dreaded and of those things about which to be confident. But, Socrates continues, this means that Nicias is saying either that lions, leopards, and boars know, or that lions, deer, bulls, and monkeys are naturally alike in courage. Nicias replies that he does not call courageous beasts or children who through mindlessness do not fear; rather they are fearless and moronic. The fearless and the courageous are not the same. What Laches and the many would call courageous, he calls bold, while the courageous are prudent.

Socrates and Nicias agree next that they are looking at courage as part of virtue, there being moderation, justice, and other parts, and that the dreaded are expected evils and that those things about which one should be confident are future goods. Generalship forecasts nobly about war and knows that it should rule the diviner's art because it knows more nobly what is becoming and what is to become in war. The law orders that the general rule the diviner, not the diviner the general. It also seems to Socrates that there is not one knowledge of how something became, another how it becomes, and still another how it would most nobly become, but that these are the same.[60] Courage, therefore, professes to know the happening and the having-happened in all, not merely future good and evils. Nicias thus agrees that he separated only a third of courage. Is something lacking, however, in the virtue of someone who knows all the goods and evils? Nicias has thus described all of virtue. They had said courage is only one part of it, however; they have therefore not discovered it.

III A

The chief difficulty with Nicias' opinion is that although he believes knowledge is important, he is unclear about it. He does not say precisely what kind of knowledge virtue is, if it is not an art. On what grounds is death "due" (or not), and how do we know what they are? Nicias, moreover, does not treat knowledge as good for its own sake, and Socrates does not discuss with him knowledge of what never becomes, for example, courage itself.

Nicias' horizon is belief in gods and concern with the afterlife, not love of wisdom. He wishes to know what is to be dreaded and about what to be confident in order to secure his own fate. He separates himself too drastically from other Athenians, from the "many," as well as from the few such as Laches. Indeed, Socrates must remind him that the law commands generals to rule diviners. Nicias' courage falls short because it is too private, as it is with Laches, but for different reasons; Nicias improperly separates courage from victory, and he ignores the city's good.

Socrates sees that Nicias makes courage indistinguishable from justice, moderation, and piety. This seems a gain, for we now apparently learn what all virtue is, namely, knowledge of good and evil. But this benefit is illusory. Failure to see parts as parts makes our grasp of the whole indistinct and imprecise.[61] If courage is a virtue of soul, we must see how it perfects the soul's powers. Reason is not the soul's only power; if it were, we could not understand animals to be gentle or fierce. A life devoted to knowing would need perfectly to express the powers of endurance and quickness, as well as reason. Yet, because any enduring exists only within a more complete activity, its perfection (courage) must be similarly dependent. Endurance cannot be considered fully excellent in war if it is not directed by the victory of the whole.[62] We can call such ordering or directing "prudent" or knowing endurance, especially when the whole to which endurance or risk contributes is a self-sufficient or independent good. Socrates' suggestion that there is courage in searching for courage indicates the possibility of a knowing that deals with permanent good and best uses the soul's natural powers. He does not develop this suggestion, here, however, for the *Laches* does not analyze the soul's powers systematically and leads up to but does not mention philosophy.

The conversation concludes when Socrates agrees to come to Lysimachus' house the next day to consult about the best teachers for themselves and, later, for the boys.[63]

Moderation

Courage proves to involve quickness and endurance, suitably measured by a comprehensive good, the good of the city, soul, or mind. I turn next to moderation because moderate rule of desire seems the twin of courageous restraint of fear.[64] To study self-control, moreover, is to explore more completely than we have so far the soul's self-knowledge. The dialogue Plato devotes to moderation is the *Charmides*, which Socrates narrates, as he does the complete *Republic, Lysis,* and *Lovers,* and the bulk of the *Protagoras* and *Euthydemus.* In the *Charmides,* this allows him to show us his moderation, as Laches had attested his superior courage, Demodocus and Theages his reputation for wisdom, and Euthyphro his special piety.[65] Socrates apparently has the ordinary virtues, indeed, outsized versions of these virtues.

I

The *Charmides'* opening is especially beautiful or apt. Socrates returns from battle at Potidea and goes the next morning to Taureas' wrestling school across from "the temple of the Queen."[66] He recognizes many there but not all. His unexpected entrance is greeted from several places. Mad Charephon leaps from the greeters' midst, and he and others pepper Socrates with questions about the battle. Socrates answers and then asks how it stands with philosophy and whether any youth is outstanding in wisdom, beauty, or both. Critias tells Socrates that he soon will see about the beautiful ones, "for these entering happen to be heralds and lovers of the one who is reputed to be the most beautiful right now."[67] This is Critias' cousin, Charmides. Socrates sees him; he appears to Socrates to be especially wonderful and supernaturally beautiful, although Socrates says he is no measure (a "white line") because all youths who have just become mature appear beautiful to him. The others become confused when Charmides enters; Socrates notices that none looks anywhere else, but all are "contemplating him as if he were a statue."[68]

Socrates asks Critias if Charmides' soul is of good nature, and they agree to contemplate it by stripping it in conversation. Critias calls his cousin over, and Socrates agrees to pretend to have a drug to cure Charmides' headaches. When Charmides arrives, others on the bench ludicrously push, shove, or fall off; he sits between Critias and Socrates, and a circle forms around him. Socrates claims to be perplexed and without boldness about how to proceed. He is inflamed by catching a glimpse inside Charmides' cloak. Socrates "was no longer in control of myself." When Charmides asks Socrates if he knows the drug, however, "with difficulty I answered that I had knowledge of it."[69]

I A

This opening shows in the flesh what Socrates seeks in thought. Charmides' beauty stands for the ideas. He is gazed on as a statue.[70] He is both loved and observed. His presence disorders the crowd and then reorders it into a circle. Charmides is the living presence of the permanent, orienting, beauty whose attraction first disorders and then orders us.

Between permanent or truly supernatural beauty and the fading looks of the one "who is most beautiful now" stands the good nature of the soul, which we can observe in conversation or inquiry. Plato previews philosophic search through the questions Socrates asks and answers in the opening scene, and by what he indicates in using the terms *knowledge, measure, moderation, boldness, love, wonder, laughter,* and *perplexity.* We usually know by recognizing, as Socrates recognizes most but not all the people present. We ordinarily trust eyewitness accounts, such as Socrates gives of the battle. Our normal questions are spurred by concerns and the unexpected, as Socrates' appearance here; the unexpected is both odd and familiar, something surprising here and now. Socrates seeks knowledge of "ideas" that is equal to everyday knowledge, arrived at through questions and answers as reliable as ordinary inquiry, and spurred by wonder and concern.

Socrates also seeks the "super" natural in things. To see or measure this is to know it. Socrates' measuring, however, is not bloodless. It attempts to preserve the attractive in what attracts. Ordinary perplexity about how to proceed in love, or loss of confidence in battle, becomes in Socrates' philosophic quest the dizzying perplexity caused by the power and incomprehensibility of the ideas or basic causes one seeks to grasp. Yet, their compelling presence is also always familiar. Continued (but not frozen) perplexity transforms one's own ignorance (which masquerades at first as knowledge) into Socratic recognition of ignorance, incompleteness, and uncertainty. Philosophy begins in wonder, in recognizing or "loving" the unexpected or surprising in the expected and ordinary, in seeing the unexpectedly ordered or beautiful, or in glimpsing one's connection to what is more permanent and complete. It continues in perplexity, in recognizing and enduring the (unexpectedly) difficult, confused, restricted, and obscure, or one's separation from what is complete.

The *Charmides'* opening also indicates these points through its suggestions about laughter and love. Charmides' presence causes laughter. Is it the laughter of high spirits, of ridicule, of recognition, or of self-knowledge? Our pursuit of the extraordinarily beautiful is laughable, perhaps most clearly in our pretentious claims to deserve it. Plato's understanding of the path toward the beautiful, wonderful, and perplexing recognizes the ridiculous and stands up to ridicule.[71]

When Plato speaks of lovers, he sometimes means followers, supplicants, protégés, or admirers.[72] Nonetheless, the erotic element in philosophy is always present, here obviously. Moderation is an apt theme when eros and wonder are a dialogue's opening subjects. Socrates asks to stay in the middle; Charephon leaps from the other greeters when he first sees Socrates. Socrates also is immoderate, however, asking almost immediately about philosophy and claiming to be no measure at all in the face of ordinary beauty. As Socrates proceeds to examine Charmides and Critias, however, the eros and beauty of the *Charmides'* opening fade. There are versions of measuredness (Charmides) and of the excess that high moderation controls (Critias) but without love, beauty, and wonder as their explicit goals or forms. The opening prefigures, but the dialogue does not achieve, philosophy's moderate extremism and extreme moderation.

II

Socrates tells Charmides that the headache drug requires a Thracian incantation.[73] Physicians say that to treat part of the body they must treat the whole. Just as one cannot doctor the eyes without the head and the head without the body, so one must not treat the body without the soul.[74] If the whole "is not in beautiful condition, the part is not able to be in good condition." Everything starts from the soul; the incantations with which we treat it are beautiful speeches from which "moderation" comes to be.

Critias tells Socrates that Charmides is already the most moderate of his contemporaries. But, Socrates asks Charmides, can he do without the incantation? Is his nature sufficient in moderation and other respects, or is he in need? Charmides blushes. As we said, one cannot answer Socrates' question decorously, for it is shameful both to claim moderation and to lack it. Socrates' solution is to investigate in common; if moderation is in Charmides, it "furnishes some perception from which you have some opinion as to what" it is.[75]

II A

The action or movement here is to replace piety—incantations and Thracian gods—with Socratic questioning and examining. Charmides does not show his moderation by repeating homilies. For, trust in the gods may lead to the extreme self-righteousness of a Euthyphro, and fear of the gods may lead to the extreme hesitation of a Nicias. How does one know when trust and fear are virtuous, not excessive? We need to understand moderation naturally to determine whether actions go too far or not far enough.

We should recognize the peculiarity of Socrates' proposed procedure. We test Charmides' soul to see if it is moderate and thus beautiful. We discover this by questioning: if Charmides is moderate, he can say what moderation is. But does his inability to describe it prove his immoderation? It would only if virtue and knowledge are inseparable. The ordinary sources of virtue—habit, opinion, experience, and law-abidingness—would then be given short shrift. Socrates intends to explore not just how the soul may rule but how knowledge may rule the soul.

Socrates' lovely statement of the priority of virtue is extreme, designed to appeal to the ordered whole of a beauty such as Charmides.[76] For, anyone can see that we can set a broken arm for a man who can barely hear, that courage can be dangerous to health, and that moderation is not sufficient to cure all headaches.[77] Socrates draws a picture of the ordered dependence of parts on wholes as if the healthy soul rules a healthy body, which lacks any independence. Moreover, he bypasses the soul's relation to a further whole—say, the city— and the several virtues' relation to a class ("virtue") to which they belong.

III

They now begin to investigate moderation. Charmides claims, after hesitating, that moderation is a certain quietness. Socrates defeats this sensible view by showing that while moderation is among the noble things, the quick, vigorous, keen, and easy (not the slow, quiet, and decorous) are noble in activities such as writing, reading, "all works of the body," and in learning, teaching, recollecting, readiness of mind, comprehending, inquiry, and taking counsel.

Socrates' sleight of hand is clear on reflection: that quiet things are noble, as Charmides suggests, need not mean that all or only quiet things are noble. We know from the *Laches* (and *Statesman*) that courage calls to mind the swift and keen. If quiet things are sometimes noble, however, then the swift are also not always noble. Perhaps there are two nobilities of soul, moderation and courage?

Socrates skips questions we might raise about the connections among opinion, the moderation inside one, and moderate actions. Charmides may merely believe that moderation is noble and that men call certain actions moderate. He then generalizes from the actions, but the generalization (the opinion) does not directly govern his actions, which might be caused by habit, softness, law-abidingness, or the wish for a good reputation.[78] Socrates also does not suggest here that moderation involves prudence.

IV

Charmides tries again, "courageously" looking at what sort of person moderation makes him. The unstated bias of this procedure—he must already "know" what moderate action and moderation are, or are said to be—continues. Moderation, he says, is awe; it makes humans ashamed.[79]

The link between quiet, decorum, shame, and awe is obvious but not easy to clarify. The link is causal. Not the characteristics that distinguish, say, moderate learning and action (quiet or decorum), but one of their causes (shame) and its cause (awe) are now central; the moral or pious element in moderation becomes visible. Of course, this element can block investigation or training and, therefore, may also cause ignobly slow learning and action. Indeed, Socrates uses this point to defeat Charmides. If moderation is noble, he suggests, it must be good. But awe is not always good (and, therefore, not always noble) because, as Homer says, it is not good for the needy. We note that not only vanity prevents us from seeing and meeting our needs, but shame, too. We require courage as well as moderation, or we must resist what frightens as well as what attracts.

Socrates' sleight of hand is again clear, on reflection. That awe is good need not mean that it is always good or that nothing else is good. Both courage (swiftness, irreverence) and moderation (quietness, awe) are noble and good.

Proper awe or reverence allows us to elevate ourselves and not remain self-satisfied, but improper awe or reverence is self-belittling. We need both courage and moderation, proper quickness and patience, if we are to view and propel ourselves correctly.

V

Charmides is soft. He looks inside but defends his opinion with little vigor. He wants his desires to be satisfied easily. He bows quickly to authority. He wishes to be amused. He is demanding but insufficiently bold, quick, independent, or self-motivating. His third effort to answer Socrates, therefore, is something that he has heard from "someone," whom Socrates immediately claims is Critias.[80] Moderation is "doing one's own things."

Socrates challenges this opinion, too. Producing through art is doing something, but a city is ill managed if each weaves his own cloak; moderate management is good management, so each doing his own is not moderation (because not good). Socrates again acts as if Charmides must be claiming that each instance of doing one's own is moderation, though he may only mean that some are. Critias, not "enduring" Charmides' prodding and, according to Socrates, angry with Charmides "just as a poet is with an actor who recites his poems badly," then agrees to take over the argument that "moderation is doing one's own things."[81]

VI

Critias saves his argument by distinguishing among making, doing, and working: those who do and/or work their own are moderate but not those who make their own. Moderation is doing or working good things "and only such · as these are kindred to myself."[82]

Socrates then asks whether the moderate are ignorant of being moderate. Critias does not believe this but agrees that the moderate benefit others and themselves. He then dismisses Socrates' suggestion that the physician who cures (that is, who benefits) without knowing how is moderate yet ignorant of his moderation, and moves to his next definition: moderation is, almost, recognizing oneself.

Socrates claims not to know if this is moderation; he is still investigating. Other knowledge, however, produces something different from itself (as do house building and weaving) or is of something other than itself (as are calculation of the odd and even, and weighing.) Critias replies that moderation is "not similar in its nature to" and "differs from" other knowledge, because it knows itself and all other knowledges. "Moderation, and oneself recognizing oneself are knowing both what one knows and what one does not know."[83]

VI A

Critias' opinion marks a turn in the *Charmides* similar to the turn Nicias' opinion effects in the *Laches*. Both identify virtue with knowledge, aping the Socratic view we will see in the *Protagoras*, and Critias imitates Socrates' statement of the link between (self) knowledge and ignorance.[84] Both dialogues move from discussing an opinion about a virtue's substance to its status as knowledge. A similar development occurs in the *Euthyphro*'s move to the question of the knowledge involved in tending the gods and in the *Theages*' move to the question of appropriate teachers.

Critias' complicated-sounding view may simply mean that to be moderate is to know one's resources, skills, or limits, as a student knows which subjects he has (or has not) mastered, or a wealthy man knows that he needs to use lawyers and accountants. A moderate man neither boasts about his skills nor thinks too little of them. In any event, Critias does not clarify what kind of knowledge self-recognition is, what its place is in virtuous action, or how what is akin to oneself can also be common, as knowledge is. It is also unclear how Critias' view fits with shame, awe, or eros; we can glimpse their connection to moderation as knowing what one lacks or where one falls short, but Critias does not develop this connection.[85]

VII

Socrates now wonders if it is possible "to know what one knows and what one does not know, that one does not know it."[86] Even if this knowledge is possible, it is not moderation unless it is "beneficial and good." He begins by indicating that it is impossible because he claims, and Critias agrees, that something similar is impossible in analogous cases. Other things do not have their own power in relation to themselves. There is no seeing that sees itself but not color, and no hearing that hears itself but not sound. There is no "kind of perception of perceptions and of itself that perceives nothing of what the other perceptions perceive."[87] Indeed, there is also no "kind of desire that is a desire of no pleasure but is of itself and other desires," or wish that wishes nothing good but itself and other wishes, or love that loves nothing beautiful but itself and other loves, or fear that fears no terrible thing but fears itself and other fears.

VII A

We begin by asking about Socrates' knowledge here. What does he grasp that enables him to argue as he does? He may not "see" seeing, but he understands it. Indeed, can one know that one sees a color if one does not recognize what color is in advance? Does seeing see only colors, moreover, or does it not also see shapes?[88] We have similar questions about Socrates' remarks concerning desire, wish, love, and fear. We sing of falling in love with love or say that there is nothing to fear but fear itself. Perhaps this love or fear is itself beautiful or fearful? One can be disposed to do the "right" thing without knowing what the right thing is.[89] If shame is not useful for a needy man, should one be ashamed of it? Do we not hear and see or, at least, perceive, not only sound and color but also fearful, pleasant, or beautiful things, as Socrates sees the beautiful Charmides? Can we not wish for pleasure (rather than just desire it) if we believe it to be good? In sum, Socrates abstracts from the variety of approaches to (and ignorance of) things in our perceptions and desires. He brackets what is common in these approaches in order to moderate Critias by making the knowledge of knowledge so perplexing.

Critias tries to make himself the sole anchor of his efforts: moderation is knowing one's own. Such self-reference is complicated, however, by the many things to which we reach out erotically. One cannot try to be noble without going beyond oneself to what is good not only for oneself, that is, without being, and risking being, incomplete.

VIII

Socrates continues, "It seems we assert that there is a kind of knowledge of nothing learned, but is a knowledge of itself and of the other knowledges."[90] But, greater, double, heavier, lighter, and older cannot have their own power with regard to themselves, for their being and power would contradict. If heavier is heavier than itself, it is also lighter than itself. With sizes and quantities this is impossible.

Socrates then adds motion (and heat) to the list. (Do the motions—the shrinking and yearning—in fearing, loving, wishing, and desiring, however, in no way move themselves?) "Some great man" (not Socrates) "is needed who will draw this distinction powerfully in everything": whether nothing "has itself by nature its own power with regard to itself, except knowledge" or whether some others have it, including moderation.[91]

Socrates is now perplexed. Critias is too, but he is ashamed to admit it because (Socrates suggests to us) he is concerned about his reputation. Critias does not see, nor does Socrates show him, how recognizing and investigating perplexity is a knowledge of nonknowledge, a path to better understanding, and a being humbled but not shamed. He does not show how philosophic moderation participates in seeking to know what moderation is. Critias wants to know not in order to know but, perhaps, better to use, master, control, or gain repute.

IX

Socrates now continues the discussion by supposing that knowledge of (non) knowledge is indeed possible. At most then, however, one who knows knowledge alone would know that he knows, not what. Only a physician, say, could know about health and disease, not someone who knows knowledge but not what it knows. How, then, could moderation (understood as such knowledge) be useful? It would not greatly benefit the household manager or governor of cities, for they would turn things over to those who do things correctly and beautifully, and be happy. Critias now claims that moderation knows the good and bad. But of what use is this, argues Socrates, if in any instance we do not call for moderation but for the relevant art?[92] Charmides and Critias conclude that it would be moderate to submit to Socrates, that is, to the superior knower of ignorance.

Socrates uses an argument he employs elsewhere.[93] What does a statesman know (what good is his knowledge) if we would always use an expert in any particular case? The possible replies—the statesman ranks and orders ends, or assures that artisans act justly—seemingly are unavailable here. For, Socrates has so arranged things that the moderate man knows nothing of subjects or ends, and does nothing.[94]

Perhaps, however, we can transform Socrates' argument usefully. Moderation keeps desire, love, and wish in their proper place by knowing which good things to pursue, when, for oneself, or one's city. It (and other virtues) thus "rule" the arts, as Socrates half-suggests.[95] That this guidance must include some "knowledge" of the arts' objects is necessary. But it need not be an artisan's knowledge. Not only physicians but laymen, too, can discover fraudulent doctors because they can recognize health.[96] In the last analysis, indeed, virtue knows nonknowledge as well as knowledge because the philosophic quest surfaces our perplexity about the goodness and nobility we normally take for granted.

Justice

Plato discusses justice thematically in the *Gorgias, Republic,* and *Cleitophon,* and explores it often elsewhere, as we saw in the *Euthyphro*.[97] It is the most political virtue and, seemingly, the most comprehensive one. Consequently, the *Gorgias,* to which we turn now, brings out more fully than our previous discussions the links among virtue, the soul, and the city. It also explicitly questions the relation between philosophy and politics; this question becomes the heart of the *Republic*.

I

The *Gorgias* is lengthy, so I present its arguments en masse and then examine their implications. Its three chief interlocutors, Gorgias, Polus, and Callicles, stand, respectively, for distortions of what the *Republic* describes as the three parts of the soul—reason, spiritedness, and desire.[98] The *Gorgias'* overall perspective is to examine justice in terms of Gorgias' wish that rhetoric dominate. Plato indicates what would need to happen for rhetoric or speech to rule, namely, the identity of something true and its image, and persuasion's success in replacing punishment. He also displays the difficulty or impossibility of achieving this and shows how this aim can be realized more fully when transformed to Socrates' philosophic activity. For, there, speech is dominant and directs the soul.

Plato follows a similar practice in other dialogues. He displays how Euthyphro's individual piety could dominate only if (impossibly) all gods were fully assimilated to his piety, or if he alone were honored, and indicates how the purity of philosophic reverence might allow gratitude for the gods to be assimilated to human distinction. The *Laches* shows how philosophic courage alone permits the harmony that Laches wishes between deeds of risk and endurance and speeches about them which, on his own terms, would require an (impossible) separation of action from its end, or from mind. The *Charmides* displays how moderation as quiet self-control, self-knowledge, or self-containment is impossible, or cannot be good, apart from the independence of other things, and shows how Socrates' openness or yearning allows a better or more complete self-mastery.[99]

Gorgias teaches rhetoric, so the *Gorgias* examines justice in terms of Gorgias' hope for rhetoric. After a short opening, Socrates indicates the difficulty in saying what rhetoric is. He shows Gorgias that although rhetoric is, as he says, about speech (*logos*) and is effective through it, this basis in speech does not distinguish it from, say, mathematics.[100] Gorgias then claims that rhetoric crafts "the greatest good" and causes "freedom for human beings themselves and at the same time rule over others in each man's own city."[101] He agrees with Socrates that rhetoric produces belief, not knowledge, and that it crafts persuasion in souls, and in "law courts and in other mobs . . . about those things that are just and unjust." "Rhetoricians" such as Themistocles and Pericles counsel the city, and they, not artisans "victoriously carry their resolutions" about walls and troops. Indeed, Gorgias says that he can persuade the sick to take drugs while his brother, a physician, cannot.

Socrates forces Gorgias to concede that he teaches justice to his students, although Gorgias had said earlier that they sometimes use their rhetoric incorrectly. Polus then intervenes: Gorgias contradicted himself because he was ashamed to say that he does not teach the just, noble, and good things.[102] He then asks Socrates to say what rhetoric is. Socrates claims that it is not an art but, rather, an "experience" of the "production of a certain grace and pleasure." It "belongs to a soul that is skilled at guessing, courageous and terribly clever by nature at associating with human beings; and I call its chief point flattery."[103] Cooking, rhetoric, cosmetics, and sophistry are the four parts of this pursuit, "directed to four kinds of business." Rhetoric is "a phantom of a part of politics."

Gorgias does not comprehend. He agrees with Socrates that there are good and seemingly good conditions of body and soul. Politics, Socrates then argues, is the art directed to the soul; it splits into justice and the legislative art. The art of the body also has two parts, medicine and gymnastics. Each cares "in accord with the best." Flattery, however, pretends to be each of the four and "guesses at the pleasant without the best."[104] Cooking pretends to know the best foods and, among the thoughtless, wins the contest with the doctor. Its guessing is experience, however, not art, because it lacks a reasoned account (a *logos*) about "the things it administers, of what sort of things they are in their nature; and so it cannot state the cause of each thing." As cooking is to medicine, Socrates continues, rhetoric is to justice, and as cosmetics is to gymnastics, sophistry is to the legislative art.[105] Sophists and rhetoricians are closely related, but the soul sees this natural difference.

II

Polus now defends rhetoric by suggesting that rhetoricians "have the greatest power in cities." For Socrates, however, they have the least if "having power is something good for him who has it." Rhetoricians, like tyrants, do little of what they wish "although they certainly do what seems to them best." For, they do not wish "what they do on each occasion" but wish to have that "for the sake of which" they act. We wish to slaughter and steal only when it benefits us.

Polus suggests, nonetheless, that Socrates would envy whoever killed or confiscated as seems good to the killer. Socrates claims, however, that someone who acts unjustly is wretched, for doing injustice "happens to be the greatest of evils." Socrates does not wish to suffer injustice, but were it necessary to do or suffer it, he would choose the latter.[106] Polus then claims that any Athenian would agree that the murdering and illegitimate tyrant Archelaus is happier than if he justly had remained a slave.[107] Doing injustice is "more shameful" but not worse than suffering it, for the noble and good differ. Polus, however, then agrees with Socrates that bodies and laws are beautiful or noble only with reference to use or pleasure.[108] If doing injustice is more shameful than suffering it, it must therefore surpass it in badness, pain, or both. It does not surpass it in pain, so it must surpass it in badness. So, doing injustice is worse than suffering it.

Because just things are good, moreover, someone justly punished is benefited. He is released from the greatest evil, badness of soul. Judges release one from injustice, as physicians do from sickness, and moneymaking from poverty. Rhetoric is perhaps useful for bringing out injustice in oneself and one's friends, so they will pay the penalty and their souls not fester. Although this position is strange, Polus says, it agrees "with the things said before."[109]

III

Callicles now claims that Socrates says things that are not beautiful by nature. For, by nature, suffering injustice is shameful and worse; doing it is more shameful only by convention. The many weak establish conventions for their own advantage; they are content with an equal share.[110] By nature, however, it is just for the better, more powerful, and stronger to have more than, and to rule, the worse, less powerful, and weaker. We do this according "to the nature of the just" and "by Zeus, according to the law of nature." Socrates will know this when he lets philosophy drop, Callicles continues, for a man who philosophizes into old age becomes inexperienced and ridiculous in political action. Philosophy is noble, fitting, and liberal for a lad's education but ridiculous for the older, who become uncourageous, "never to give voice to anything free or great or sufficient."[111]

Socrates then asks Callicles to help him pursue the "noblest" investigation: What sort of man ought one to be, and what should one pursue, and how far?[112] Callicles agrees that the many are stronger than one and thus (by his own argument) superior and noble. The many hold that justice is having an equal share, however, and that doing injustice is worse than suffering it. So, Socrates concludes that, according to Callicles' view, the many's view of justice is just by nature, and nature and convention are not opposed.

Callicles accuses Socrates of speaking drivel and irony. By superior (and stronger) Callicles means not the mightier but the more intelligent. One intelligent man should indeed rule ten thousand who are not, and by nature he justly ought to have more—but not, as Socrates leads Callicles to see, more food, drink, or clothing, as if a shoemaker should have the biggest shoes. Callicles then says that by *stronger* he means those most intelligent in the city's affairs and "also courageous, being sufficient to accomplish what they intend" (say, through tyranny) and not soft in soul.[113]

IV

Socrates next asks Callicles (to his confusion) about ruling oneself, moderately ruling one's pleasures and desires.[114] Callicles says that it is noble and naturally just that one who will live "correctly" let his own desires be great and unrestricted.[115] Socrates suggests, however, that such an insatiable soul's desire would be like a leaking, perforated jar that we must fill painfully. For Callicles, nonetheless, to live pleasantly and happily is to keep "as much as possible flowing in." To need nothing is to live the life of a stone or corpse. Socrates shows him, however, that if the good is "rejoicing" in all ways, shameful things follow; someone whose life is the continued scratching of itches, or a catamite, would be happy.[116] He then points out still other difficulties in identifying the pleasant and good. If, for example, knowledge, courage, and pleasure differ, knowledge and courage would not be good, if the pleasant and good are the same.[117]

Socrates and Callicles continue after Gorgias urges the reluctant Callicles to answer "for our sake too."[118] They agree that cowards and fools rejoice equally with their opposites, so if good things are pleasures, the good (the intelligent and courageous) and the bad (the fools and cowards) are equally good and bad. Callicles then claims to consider some pleasures better and others worse. The beneficial ones, Socrates argues, produce something good, that is, health or strength. The end of all actions is the good; things are done for its sake; it is not done for theirs.[119] Do rhetoricians aim to make citizens as good as possible, or do they strive to gratify them for the sake of the rhetorician's private good? Some rhetoricians say the best things for citizens' souls; others do not. Socrates disputes Callicles' suggestion that either Themistocles, Cimon, Miltiades, or Pericles "turned out to be a good man."[120]

Artisans such as painters, Socrates now says, choose and apply materials "into a certain arrangement." They compel things to fit and harmonize "until they have composed the whole as an arranged or ordered thing"; they make what they are "working on to have a certain form." The soul, too, is useful when it has "arrangement and a certain order." Health and strength come into being from the "healthy," the body's arrangement and order. The soul's arrangement and ordering is called the lawful and law, from which it becomes lawful and orderly: "these things are justice and moderation." The artful and good rhetorician always asks how to have virtue arise in souls: "being punished is better for the soul than intemperance."[121]

Socrates thus suggests that we are good "when some virtue comes to be present," and that a thing's virtue comes to be present "by its assigned arrangement, correctness, and art. A certain order arising in each thing—each thing's own order—makes each of the beings good."[122] A soul with its own order is an orderly and moderate one. "The moderate soul is therefore good," and the foolish, intemperate soul bad.[123] Moderate men act fittingly concerning men and gods; that is, they act justly and piously. They are also courageous because a moderate man flees, pursues, and is steadfast as he ought. Indeed, the whole of heaven, earth, gods, and humans is (according to the "wise") held together "by community, friendship, orderliness, moderation, and justness."[124] Geometrical (proportionate) equality, not taking more, "has great power among gods and humans." The moderate man is blessed and happy.

It is worse and more shameful for someone to do injustice to Socrates than for him to suffer it, Socrates says again. To suffer little injustice one must rule tyrannically or "be a comrade of the existing regime."[125] A tyrant's friend must be "of the same character" and be "willing to be ruled."[126] He will not be done injustice, but he will do injustice. His imitation of the master will ruin his soul. Callicles now calls it "infuriating" that the base man will, if he wishes, kill the noble man who will not imitate him. Socrates reminds him, however, that one should not prepare to live as long as possible by practicing the arts (such as rhetoric or swimming) "that always save us from danger."

There are two aims, Socrates recapitulates, caring and fighting for the body's, or the soul's, being as good as possible. Socrates "alone of the men of today" puts his "hand to the true political art" by speaking with a view to the best, not the most pleasant. He has done nothing unjust, and, therefore, as he recounts in a long "logos" about life after death, he will be happy, both while living and when "he comes to his end."

Let us now summarize the major results and implications of the *Gorgias*.

Virtue

Socrates' standpoint in the *Gorgias* is the unity in the soul of the good, the noble, virtue, and knowledge. The good is the soul's excellence, not the body's pleasure. It is naturally noble to aid the good, not to take more. Justice and moderation are true virtues, not shams. Courage and intelligence do not properly serve the body's pleasure but are allied with the other virtues. The common source of virtue is the soul's order. Speech is indeed primary, not as rhetorical guessing and experience but, rather, as art.

Socrates does not visibly differentiate philosophical from moral or legal virtue, however, so some of his statements seem naïve or incredible. He does not explore the limits that the body places on the soul's excellence and on politics.[127] If we consider the soul's virtue when it seeks to know philosophically, however, Socrates' paradoxes about doing and suffering injustice (and his linking the good, noble, and fittingly ordered) are less peculiar than when we consider ordinary goods. For, self-satisfied ignorance—philosophic injustice—is both done to and suffered by oneself.

Socrates does not explore justice dialectically in the *Gorgias*, but he does bring out many of its elements. It is a virtue of soul, the soul's lawful order, or what this order brings. It is connected to each thing's being its own, to the relation between doing and suffering, and to punishment. It is a kind of equality, rather than taking more. It is better to suffer unjust loss of possessions or death that to do such injustice, although better still neither to suffer nor do it. Socrates also subtly indicates that it is better to have justice done to you (especially by yourself) than to do it to others.[128] Overall, the place of proportion is important, but it is not analyzed.[129]

The presence of justice indicates the presence of the other virtues, especially moderation, but Socrates does not examine precisely how the virtues differ. (He is showing us how things look when we are defending justice rhetorically.) Moderation is self-rule, and limit in satisfying desire. Courage is seen as endurance (by Socrates) and risk (by Callicles.)

Good

Part of Socrates' rhetorical success in the *Gorgias* comes from his interlocutors' confusion about the connections among goodness, nobility, justice, truth, and happiness. Socrates treats them as if to have one is to have the others; any differences require that they be in no way alike. (This is how matters look to rhetoricians, and Socrates exploits them through his superior understanding.)

He also, however, indicates at least three ways to connect what is different without obliterating difference. The first is at the start of his discussion with Gorgias, where rhetoric is distinguished from other types of speech, yet is still speech. The second is in Socrates' proportion between rhetoric and justice, and sophistry and legislation. Rhetoric is justice's semblance; that is, it differs from but is not wholly unlike it. The third is in his discussion of order and fit, where different parts and actions can belong to one unity or whole. As with other issues in the *Gorgias,* Plato explores these matters more fully elsewhere, although still inconclusively.[130]

The *Gorgias* also indicates elements of what counts as good, again without examining it as a problem. The good is the "for the sake of" or end in terms of which actions and arts are beneficial. Ends have semblances, as cosmetic beauty resembles true beauty. The true is the object for which the semblance wishes, but pleasure intercepts desire. Pleasure can lead to satiety or oversatiety.[131]

The good is also something's order. But what if something has several orders, as men wish for health, beauty, strength, virtue, and intelligence? The lower orders are used by the superior ones, yet are their own orders. Socrates downplays possible conflicts between body and soul, and he does not detail all that the soul orders. By doing this he can treat the "lawful" in the soul as comprehensive. He in a sense identifies the lawful and natural even more radically than Callicles does by acting as if he can overcome the difference between philosophy's quest for truth and politics' service to ordinary pleasure and nobility: Socrates claims to be the only true politician.

Pleasure

Socrates shows that maximum pleasure is not our end because some pleasures are too base or trivial to be good, because (bodily) pleasure is never free from pain, need, or desire, and because pleasures may displace goods such as health. Socrates ignores (here) purity, intensity, and other ways pleasure could be good. Because pleasure is not the good, it is not good.[132] Socrates' extreme split between the body's pleasure and the soul's good is part of what makes his argument seem incredible to Callicles, if not to us.

One modification here to Socrates' argument is what he says about his pleasure in refutation, what Callicles says about gratifying Gorgias and his own pleasure in argument, and Socrates' suggestion that rhetoric (and, thus, pleasure) can be useful. He also suggests in his concluding story that there are those so incurable that their punishment after death for injustice features the most painful sufferings. That is, their punishment is not the opportunity to continue to exercise their disordered soul.[133] Plato suggests, but does not explore, these adjustments to his argument because his immediate purpose is to dispute pleasure's excessive claims.

Philosophy

Socrates defends philosophy explicitly, outrageously (in the scope of his claims about himself), and moralistically or popularly. He is a philosopher and also Athens' only true statesman, because he alone seeks to improve citizens' souls. He first posits, but then retracts, the difference between politics and philosophy. Socrates reduces usual politics to pleasure and injustice, and occludes (while displaying) philosophy's threat to political virtue or patriotism.

In the course of Socrates' discussion, he suggests without exploring several elements of philosophical activity. He divides and combines phenomena to help his interlocutors arrive at understanding (of, for example, rhetoric); seeks clarity and correctness, that is, tries to make manifest the subject proposed in the argument; suggests the need for precise rational accounts, especially of causes and natures; always says the same about the same; distinguishes being from seeming; attends to geometric fit; is unashamed; and deals with a "common good."

None of these suggestions is unambiguous. Socrates calls his concluding myth about the afterlife a logos, plays with the connection between intellectual and penal correctness, does not clarify the elements of "nature," leaves unclear the meaning of order and the links among semblance, being, and proportion, and does not explore precisely the place of experience, guessing, and routine in his own conversations.[134] These ambiguities both indicate the (impossible) identities that the rule of rhetoric or the equating of philosophic and ethical virtue require, and are spurs to true reflection.

Politics

Socrates' discussion of politics in the *Gorgias* is complicated. Its chief feature is to establish the soul's good as politics' aim and to act as if the soul's virtue could dominate all. He downplays political urgency and immediacy, and does not make clear that bodily goods sometimes need separate attention, even if they ultimately serve the soul. Yet, he subtly lets us see the limits to his standpoint. True superiority differs from bodily strength and numbers, even though this strength sustains law and convention. Persuading many differs from persuading one, even if rhetoricians claim that there is no difference.

Socrates also covers over the clash among the soul's goods. He occludes the split between common and individual good, as if what is good for oneself, one's friends, one's city, and all cities is the same. He evaporates the distance between political or ethical virtue and philosophical virtue. The effect is to transform competition over scarce goods to conversation about thought's common and inexhaustible objects. Socrates ignores individual reputation and fame, or assimilates them wholly into justice, while Gorgias' own standing and Callicles' list of statesmen points to this fame. Unjust excess is condemned, but the just excess that one needs for leisure, nobility, or rule is bypassed.

Speech (Rhetoric)

Plato also indicates, through his portrait of rhetoric, the possibilities and limits of the soul's dominance of the body. Gorgias and Polus apparently believe they can persuade anyone of anything, but, in fact, they bow to the conventions and practices of the stronger, serve democratic natures, and produce pleasure. The sheer power of the many and the force they wield require that they be persuaded, but these also show why speech cannot simply dominate.[135]

The rhetoricians are also aware of, but do not truly grasp, the natural justice that ennobles the superior. One truth they miss is that bodily strength and numbers limit natural excellence or superiority. Another is that the ignobility of saying certain things in certain circumstances—Gorgias' unwillingness here to claim not to teach justice—arises not only from convention or fear of the strong but also from our openness to the high and the limits that reverence for it impress upon us. The political question is how far we can elevate our legal conventions to true natural excellence, given the strength of the many and the necessary importance of ordinary goods such as health. (The individual question is how far the soul's virtues can be elevated to natural intelligence). The legal and conventional can to greater and lesser degrees follow nature, but no full natural order of superiority and strength exists in the flesh.[136] Socrates seeks here to persuade us to believe in a politically just order simply, a salutary belief, but, as the omissions and distortions show us, not an altogether true one.

Virtue

Our discussion of the five virtues leads us to wonder about the connections among them and what virtue is as a whole. This issue arises in each dialogue that we have discussed. Plato considers it directly in the *Meno* and *Protagoras*.

Meno

The *Meno* begins when Meno asks Socrates if virtue is teachable.[137] How could one say, however, if one does not know what virtue is? Meno claims that a man's virtue is to carry out the city's affairs in a way that benefits friends, harms enemies, and does not lead to harm for himself.[138] A woman's virtue is to manage the house well, by preserving its contents and obeying the man.[139] Children and slaves also have virtue: "the virtue belonging to each of us is related to each task appropriate to each action and time of life."[140]

This discussion, however, does not show us the same, single form of virtue. After all, one health and strength exists for men and women. What, however, is the one "virtue?" When Meno becomes tongue-tied, Socrates gives him an example. Shape, whether round or straight, is "that which alone of the beings happens always to accompany color."[141] Meno thinks this naïve: What if one is perplexed about color? So, Socrates now says that "shape is the limit of a solid," and, when Meno "insolently" continues to ask him, says that "color is an emanation of shapes commensurate with sight and hence subject to perception."[142] Meno, but not Socrates, believes this to be better than the first answer.[143]

I

Socrates once again asks Meno "what virtue is as a whole."[144] His answer is that virtue is "for one who desires the noble things to be capable of providing them for himself." He then agrees that to desire noble things is to desire good things. Virtue, thus, is "the capacity to provide the good things for oneself."[145] But if one provides good things unjustly, immoderately, or impiously, Meno and Socrates agree, the provision is not virtuous. To say that virtue is just, moderate, or pious provision, however, is again to give only part of virtue, not virtue as a whole.

Underlying Meno's opinion about virtue is his view that real men courageously rule the city to accumulate wealth, and that virtue in others belongs to the means (e.g., slavery and obedience) one uses for one's own ends—pleasure, or wealth itself. Socrates' questioning suggests implicitly that Meno improperly understands the varieties and importance of ends, wholes, likenesses, and limits. To subtly point this out is one reason Socrates defines shape as he does. Perhaps virtue is connected to the soul as follows: as shape is the limit of body, so form is the (beautiful) limit of soul. As shape is always accompanied by color, so virtue is always accompanied by prudence, perplexity, or opinions about virtue that allow the soul to see or look at itself.

II

Meno now admits that he is perplexed and reminds Socrates that in another city his reputation for perplexing others would lead to his being jailed as a sorcerer. Socrates claims to make others no more perplexed than he is himself. Meno then asks how one can search for what one does not know and know when one has found it. Socrates reports what priests and poets, and "both men and women wise in divine matters" say: the soul is immortal, and knowledge is merely recollecting what we once knew. Because all nature is akin, moreover, if we learn one thing here and courageously examine it, we can discover all else.

Socrates then tries to demonstrate the truth of recollection by bringing out from a slave some mathematical truths and characteristic errors. The slave must especially come to see that he does not know what he thinks he knows. There is no attempt to know before one becomes perplexed and before one longs to know.[146] Socrates suggests that when the slave answers correctly, he is recovering or recollecting opinions he always had (or was taught in another life) which, when stirred up, became knowledge. "The truth about the beings is always present for us in the soul."[147] "By supposing one ought to inquire into things he doesn't know," Socrates tells Meno, "we would be better and more courageous and less lazy than if we should suppose either that it's impossible to discover these things that we do not know or that we ought not to inquire into them."[148]

Perhaps the most natural way to grasp Socrates' argument about recollection is to see that once we begin to think, look, move, or inquire, we notice what is general, not only individual. We always find ourselves within some articulation; we always have some understanding. We can attempt to uncover what is congealed and perplexing in our understanding, what makes our articulation or opinions possible, and what is reasonable in them. To grasp these matters fully is to "recollect" fully. Such discovery of what is (say, what virtue is) differs from learning a skill or art, or being taught to be virtuous by exercise or habit, or becoming virtuous spontaneously (or "naturally").[149] These are the possibilities that Meno has in mind when he asks if virtue is teachable.

III

Meno returns to his first question: Is virtue teachable, present naturally, or attained in some other way (e.g., by habit)? They agree that virtue is good, that what is good is advantageous, and that health, strength, beauty, and wealth are advantageous if used or guided prudently. So, the soul's neutral virtues—confidence, moderation, docility, its undertakings, and its endurance—are advantageous only if guided by, or as, prudence or intellect. Virtue is prudence either in whole or part.

Socrates apparently equivocates between virtue's being knowledge and its being several neutral powers, motions, or elements in the soul.[150] His point is that knowledge allows these powers to be well used and, thus, to be worthy of being called virtuous.

To the extent that virtue is prudence or intellect, it has teachers. Who are they? Socrates now asks Anytus, Meno's host in Athens, and the future accuser of Socrates, to join the conversation. With other arts, he and Anytus agree, we can pay a practitioner to teach us, although Anytus vociferously disputes that sophists are those we pay to teach us virtue. He has not experienced them but knows them. We can learn virtue from any good Athenian citizen, he claims, as they did from their predecessors. Yet, Socrates makes clear, those among the best—Themistocles, Aristeides, Thucydides, and Pericles—taught their sons many things, but the sons are not eminent for virtue.[151] (Socrates does not mention the possible inferiority of the sons' nature or their fathers' rivalry with them.) Anytus cannot dispute the facts but dislikes the conclusion: "Socrates, in my opinion you speak ill of people lightly. So I would advise you, if you're willing to be persuaded by me, to be careful: perhaps it is not easy in another city to harm people or to benefit them, but in this one it is very easy indeed."[152]

If neither gentlemen, sophists, nor poets teach virtue, how, if at all, do men become good? The answer, Socrates now suggests, following what is implicit in Anytus' view that good citizens teach each other virtue, lies in reexamining whether we truly require prudence to guide our affairs advantageously. Perhaps all we need is correct opinion. True opinions, however, do not stay put in our soul; a "calculation of cause" is needed to tie them down to make them noble so they can accomplish good.[153] That is, true opinion must become knowledge. Socrates may be guessing this, but he knows that correct opinion and knowledge differ.[154]

We possess neither true opinion nor knowledge naturally, however, and prudence apparently is not teachable. Nor does it arise from chance. Those who guide cities well (e.g., Themistocles), therefore, do so by right opinion that is divinely inspired. They speak many true things about great matters without knowledge, as do soothsayers and diviners.[155] Virtue is present by divine allotment—it is neither by nature, nor teachable, unless someone with virtue's true substance can make another skilled politically. But we will know this only when we inquire into what virtue is "itself by itself."[156]

The *Meno* thus concludes by subtly pointing to alternatives to Meno's standpoint about acquiring virtue (that it is natural or is "prudence" taught by sophists), namely, philosophic inquiry about causes, and (divinely inspired) law. The central problem remains: We cannot know how virtue comes to be unless we know what it is.

Protagoras

We continue our discussion of what virtue is and whether we can teach it by considering the *Protagoras*. Socrates "gratefully" relates a conversation, on request, to a nameless audience just after it occurs. He had been awakened by Hippocrates, a young man who wants Socrates to accompany him to Callias' house, where the famous sophist Protagoras is staying. Hippocrates wishes to learn from Protagoras how to speak cleverly. He proves unsure, however, about which subjects sophists teach. What is it that they know?[157]

Protagoras claims that he will help Hippocrates improve in "good counsel concerning [his] own affairs," managing his house well, and becoming most powerful "in carrying out and speaking about the city's affairs." Socrates doubts that one can teach the "political art" and how "to make men good citizens."[158]

I

Protagoras tries to show that virtue is something teachable, by telling a story.[159] (Socrates and Protagoras implicitly identify having the political art with being able to teach virtue or, indeed, having it.) Its upshot is that while only a few can advise about virtue (excellence) in arts, everyone shares in "political virtue, that must as a whole follow the path of justice and moderation."[160] Even the unjust must pretend to be just. Political justice is not natural, however, but belongs to us through care, practice, and teaching. "The noble things and their contraries" are present "by nature and through chance," so we do not punish the ugly, weak, and small.[161] But we do become angry with and admonish the unjust and impious; that is, we believe justice and piety can be taught.

Men, especially the powerful wealthy, teach the very young what is just, noble, and pious. They send boys to teachers where they learn to emulate the good men in poetry, learn moderation and become gentler in soul from music's rhythms and harmonies, and improve their bodies through training "so they will not be compelled to be cowards" in war.[162] After this, the city requires that they rule and be ruled under laws from a good legislator. "Reciprocal justice and virtue are profitable."[163] There could be no city without virtue, none conceals it, and all generously teach it.

II

Socrates then asks Protagoras whether virtue is one, with justice, moderation, and piety its parts, or whether these are merely names of the same thing. Protagoras says they are parts, leading Socrates to ask how parts are parts. They agree that the parts of virtue are like parts of a face, each with its own power, not like the parts of gold, which differ only in size from each other and from the whole.

Socrates now explores virtue's parts and drives toward the conclusion that the different virtues are in fact merely names for one thing. Protagoras is especially sure that "many are courageous but unjust, and there are those who are just in turn but not wise."[164] Socrates forces him to concede that justice and piety are the same or "as similar as possible," and that wisdom and moderation also must be one because foolishness is their single contrary. Protagoras stops Socrates' questioning in the midst of Socrates' next step, which is to explore the relation between moderation and justice, and he makes a speech about the multiplicity, complicatedness, and variety of the good. Olive oil, for example, is good for human but bad for animal hair and, sometimes, for human ingestion.[165]

Protagoras is now unwilling to converse through short answers.[166] A discussion ensues among the other listeners and sophists; its unannounced theme is justice, or justice and wisdom. Does justice in conversation require that each speak as he chooses—here, making long speeches or asking and answering questions—as Protagoras and Alcibiades (defending Socrates) now claim? Or, as Socrates says, should the more capable or stronger concede to conduct himself as the less capable chooses or on equal grounds? Or, as Prodicus says and Critias indicates, should the conversants through friendly good will do what is right for the listeners, arriving at common ground that allows them to listen but to gain more delight from the wiser? Or, as Hippias suggests, are the present conversants and listeners natural kin who are not subject to legal tyranny, and who should display their wisdom about nature, giving speeches neither as long as Protagoras' nor as short as Socrates', but as an arbiter measures? As Socrates remarks, however, the umpire will either be inferior to the discussants, the same (and therefore superfluous), or better. He then suggests a compromise (favorable to him) that wins the company's support and Protagoras' reluctant consent: Protagoras can ask Socrates questions; Socrates will then ask Protagoras questions.[167]

II A   Socrates thus gives an example of rule of the wiser (himself), that is, an example of winning the consent of the less wise; he arranges through his compromise, and by rising to leave after Protagoras' speech, a continuation of the discussion that looks even-handed but favors his way. He plays on Protagoras' vanity and shame, and the others' desire that the conversation continue. This Socratic triumph, however, occurs only in these apparently special circumstances: the discussants believe themselves to be students of nature and natural kin beyond law. Indeed, would Socrates have prevailed even in these circumstances without the support of Alcibiades who, says Critias, "always loves to win?" Even a kind of natural kinship cannot produce community without rule of the wise and its alliance with desire and spiritedness. Justice is naturally good or necessary in a community of such discussants, not as law or tyranny, but as rule of the persuasive best.[168]

III

Protagoras now asks Socrates to discuss virtue "transferred to the realm of poetry" because educated men should be "terrific" at giving accounts of what poets say. The immediate result of Socrates' reply, in which he shows how such interpretation contrasts with "investigating thoroughly the things I myself am continually perplexed by," is that Protagoras, "ashamed in [Socrates] opinion" agrees to let Socrates question him.[169] Socrates summarizes their previous discussion: each of the five virtues has its own power, each has its own being and thing underlying it, and they are dissimilar to each other, and to the whole of which they are parts, as are a face's parts.[170] Protagoras now says that although each is part of virtue, courage is "very different from them all." Many are courageous, yet very unjust, impious, licentious, and unlearned.[171] The courageous, in Protagoras' view, are confident and advance toward what many fear.[172] He then agrees that the whole of virtue is noble, that knowers (e.g., skilled cavalry) are more confident than nonknowers, and that confidence without knowledge is not (noble) courage but (shameful) mad overconfidence. Nonetheless, Protagoras does not agree that wisdom is courage; not all the confident are courageous any more than all the powerful are strong, although all the strong are powerful.[173] Courage (and strength) arise from nature and proper nurturing of souls (or bodies), but confidence and power from art, spiritedness, or madness.[174]

Socrates next begins another line of inquiry designed to show that courage and wisdom are equivalent or, indeed, that all virtues are equivalent, with wisdom being the element of that equivalence.[175] Many say that knowledge serves (say, spiritedness, pleasure, pain, eros, or fear) but does not rule. If we all choose voluntarily what is good, moreover, only ignorance could lead us astray. This is clear, Socrates contends, if pleasure is what is good.[176] If I choose a present pleasure that will lead to greater future ills, I am measuring incorrectly; I am taken in by the apparent large size of the near and small size of the far.[177] Courage is advancing toward what one is confident about (not what one believes is terrible), namely (here), the pleasant things. Only ignorance of the terrible, ignorance about what merits confidence, leads the bold and cowardly to advance toward the shameful and bad. So, courage is wisdom about what is terrible or frightening. This means that virtue can be taught, because the art of measuring pleasure presumably can be taught—Protagoras is correct about virtue's teachability, and Socrates wrong! The dialogue concludes as Protagoras declines Socrates' offer to continue to investigate virtue, which concerns Socrates "for the sake of my own life as a whole." At this point, indeed, all that remains to show that the virtues are one is an argument that equates justice or piety to one of the other three virtues, say, the unfinished argument connecting justice and moderation.

III A   This discussion is suggestive in several ways. It indicates that search issues in discovery, and that to discover is to make manifest: to see truth is to clarify and reveal.[178] It is also to measure correctly; measuring involves calculating, but it first depends on distance and, therefore, on seeing clearly. Moreover, to grasp the cause of apparently being overcome by pleasure and, therefore, of choosing poorly, one must (Socrates claims) first understand the experience of being overcome.[179] To properly see what is is, thus, the central step in knowing. Yet, one cannot see what something is apart from the (proper) whole to which it belongs, as one cannot grasp any virtue without seeing its connection to other virtues and to virtue as a whole. The problems of measuring, perspective, and wholeness that are indicated here are elaborated in Plato's discussions of images, Protagoras, and virtue's wholeness in the *Theatetus, Sophist,* and *Statesman.*

Socrates chooses pleasure as the good in this discussion because this appeals to Protagoras, but we cannot help noticing the questions about pleasure that his argument begs.[180] We remember that Socrates shows in the *Gorgias* (and elsewhere) that pleasure is not the human good. For, who, including Protagoras, does not distinguish among pleasures?[181] Who would choose a life of pleasure with no intelligence or awareness?[182] Does calculating pleasure use reason sufficiently to allow reason's full expression? (Calculation may help to choose pleasures: Is it central in enjoying them?) Are the good, noble, and pleasurable always the same even if they are sometimes the same? (Is death in war pleasurable, or to be justly imprisoned, noble?) Courage properly endures or risks the fearsome—for example, death—for the sake of nobility or victory (freedom). Does this nobility make the terrible pleasant, even if courage has its own pleasure? What assures that my ranking of pleasures is the same as yours, or the city's? (Whose pleasure, then, should govern?)[183] In general, moreover, Socrates flattens measuring what is good to mere calculation, where virtue's parts or the human good become more and less of the same.[184]

The argument also begs questions about weakness of will. It is reasonable to say that at the moment I give in I often incorrectly judge what is good for me, whatever I claim to believe. But one cannot say this simply, because it is unclear that we can ever know fully what virtue requires when it deals with the usual, fleeting goods with which Protagoras is concerned. Socrates, after all, roots his argument in a view—that pleasure is the good—whose truth he neither demonstrates nor unequivocally believes.

In any event, incorrect judgment is not the only truth about the will's weakness. One can be overpowered physically by a killer, while struggling for what one knows is the better end of one's survival. Is nothing of this sort true among one's own desires, pleasures, pains, risks, and fears? Do not different degrees of spiritedness and desire differentiate some—say, Alcibiades—from the rest of us, allowing them a nobility too daunting for those with less nerve to carry it off? Still, even when one seems too tired, discombobulated, enflamed, angered, or overwhelmed to continue to endure, or to stop what one is doing, giving in (usually) seems best, then and there. The times when one simply loses strength or control are few, and close to the incurability Protagoras mentions earlier. In any event, it is the virtues displayed philosophically that best support Socrates' suggestion that virtue is knowledge. We elaborate this question in the book's next two parts.

Conclusion

It is useful to summarize some of what we have learned. Virtue combines knowledge with action and with the soul's passions or motions. It is not action or passion alone, because the risk, endurance, quiet, delight, acquisition, and distribution we see in courage, moderation, and justice lack excellence if we misunderstand their purpose, timeliness, and degree. Socrates' interlocutors may not see this at first, but he does.

Although virtue is not passion alone, it is connected to the soul's movements. Courage, for example, is a proper pushing away of fears (and pleasures), not being taken over by fear in the sense of not being overwhelmed or scattered, that is, enduring, or not being cowardly. It is also not being excessively stymied or blocked by fears. Here, courage takes proper risks by jumping over or pushing aside, by going forward and mastering, expanding, absorbing, or imperializing (or by being properly restricted). It does not merely endure but is confident or bold. Moderation is a proper yielding to pleasure (and fear), a proper joining, or refusing to join, as expansion or modesty. It is neither being submerged by or falling into pleasure, or improperly eschewing it. Such move-ments of soul are central in both ethical and intellectual excellence.[185]

The soul's movements are not virtue unless they are proper, and the sub-stance of what is proper is connected to knowledge. Nonetheless, virtue is also not knowledge simply, although Socrates shows knowledge's importance. We need knowledge to tell us that ethical virtue, or a particular act, is good, but knowledge alone does not make it good. Knowledge may discover what in-creases pleasure, but it does not cause or exclusively experience pleasure. Cour-age requires naturally arising fear or boldness, even when knowledge properly directs them. Self-knowledge proves in the *Charmides* to capture moderation insufficiently. Speech cannot completely direct the passions because they are spontaneously, although imperfectly, inclined to their good. Knowledge can cultivate but not altogether replace them.

Knowledge's complexity also makes it difficult to clarify its relation to vir-tue. Is the knowledge that is connected to virtue a form of art, opinion, rheto-ric, law, calculation, measuring, or philosophy? Is it recognition of what virtue is or of how to achieve it? Is it knowledge that activates or that acquires? These vary. We cannot split courage from the city, for example, but law is not knowl-edge simply.

We note further the variety of occasions or places for virtue. There is pos-sible virtue in the soul, city, home, and in philosophy. Virtue is not "absolute." Courageous actions on the battlefield differ from courageous actions in seek-ing the good of one's soul. Prudent risk and endurance in thought may be harmful distractions or excessive caution in war. One can say generally what the virtues are—one can find an "idea"—but the idea is unintelligible, and its causal power not grasped, until one explores the full, sometimes contradic-tory, powers it organizes, and the places in which it organizes them.

Because the virtues take on meaning from the activity or substance in which they are expressed, any general statement about, say, courage or moderation implicitly has in mind risk, endurance, or decorum in a city, body, or soul. What makes endurance proper endurance does not exist apart from its home. An "idea" forms or causes a range of phenomena that are indispensable for discovering it and giving it meaning. Its sameness in these phenomena is the sameness of presence, likeness, and aspiration, however, not of definition. Ultimately, an idea is what it is only together with others in a proper substance or whole.

This is true of virtue itself, not just the separate virtues. Socrates in the *Gor-*

gias connects the virtues to the soul's proper order. The differences between courage and moderation, and their unity as proper or prudent, suggest that virtue is not a generality still emptier than the specific virtues but, rather, the greater concreteness and cause of the experience of their unity. This concreteness, moreover, is inseparable from virtue as noble or good. When Socrates seeks in the *Protagoras* to show the identity of the virtues, he chooses a way in which each and all appear to be noble and good. Because each virtue deals with all goods, each can seem to be virtue simply. Courage and moderation can both deal with pleasure and pain. Justice is the soul's or city's full order. Prudence is a necessary condition of each virtue. Piety is in truth subordinate to justice but can easily appear to be virtue entire. This breadth or pretense is characteristic of anything taken as independent or as a whole. Nevertheless, the virtues differ from each other and from thought.

To see that this is so we will need to examine more carefully the variety of motions in the soul and the status of thought and its objects. Before doing this, however, we should consider virtue at work in politics and better grasp Plato's understanding of politics itself.

CHAPTER 3

Virtue and Politics

The *Laws*

We pursue our study of virtue by considering more fully Plato's understanding of its place in politics. His thematic discussion of politics occurs in three dialogues, the *Laws,* the *Republic,* and the *Statesman.* As we have seen, moreover, political ambition stimulates many young Athenians and is a prod to inquiry in several conversations.

It is useful before we discuss the *Laws* in this chapter, and the *Republic* and *Statesman* later, to identify the elements of Plato's understanding of politics that differ most from our own. These differences sometimes prevent us from taking his arguments seriously. They are also sometimes bypassed by those who believe that Plato highlights political truths we foolishly disregard today. After all, how many current Platonists would actually choose to live under the regimentation he apparently favors? For them, rather, Plato's practical use comes from seeing how good elements from his regimes can be insinuated into our own. So, while calling Plato "totalitarian" is a foolish and dangerous overstatement, we should recognize that few now could abide, say, the *Laws'* regime, whatever our pretensions.

Our current view of the proper limits to political control, however, also helps us to grasp Plato's intention. For, he suggests, and he is the first power-fully to demonstrate, how much of political life can and should be liberalized in a naturally reasonable direction. He also indicates what restricts this possibility. To "see" tyranny in Plato (rather than more virtue, ritual, and piety than most of us prefer) is to ignore his liberalizing and rationalizing, and the Socratic enlightenment generally.

The Scope of Politics

The political ambition we notice in so many—in Meno, Alcibiades, Critias, and Glaucon—does not result from their drive alone. For, why should that drive find its satisfaction politically? Even figures less gifted than Alcibiades—say, Hippocrates or Theages—have politics in mind. Political ambition is central because the scope of politics in the city is vast. Easy references to the differences between all ancient cities and the modern state, however, do not fully grasp this issue. The Athens that allows the conversation of the *Symposium* is different from the Sparta that a sophist such as Hippias must circle warily.[1]

The great scope and control in Plato's regimes is, from our viewpoint, visible in four ways. First and most obvious is religion or piety, for we see no religious license or formal toleration in these regimes. The *Republic*'s opening scene and Socrates' indictment for introducing new gods, however, indicate that religious innovation existed in Athens, and that it was questionable. The proof in Book X of the *Laws* of the gods' existence and their care for us, moreover, occurs in the light of doubts about their being. And, Euthyphro's piety leads him to depart from traditional practice. So, the monolith of belief developed and encouraged in the *Laws* strengthens actual belief and practice, even in Sparta and Crete. Cleinias begins the *Laws* by subtly distinguishing what is said about Crete's divine origin from what is so.

This heightening, nonetheless, arises from what is, for us, a tall base. Many dialogues occur at or near Athenian religious temples. Religious festivals belong to everyone's everyday life.[2] Socrates observes the usual practices; his last words are that he owes the god Asclepius a cock. Euthyphro's excess takes place amid his concern about pollution. The poetry the interlocutors discuss and examine abounds with examples from the gods. Oracles, divination, interpretation, and prayer are present constantly. This religious presence and unity is concentrated in the *Laws*, but it is much more powerful even in the

Republic than in liberal democracy. In the *Statesman,* too, which demotes priests, persuasive mythology and "divine" bonds are present.[3]

The most obvious example of the tie between politics and unitary religion is in the dogmas taught in these regimes, and in festivals and choruses that sing about and honor gods. These dogmas are not matters of private belief, nor are the choruses and festivals private events, with attendance optional. Plato's best and better regimes are suffused with ritual and belief, and the rituals do not belong to a variety of different faiths.

The pervasiveness and unity of ritual, dogma, gods, and temples is the most obvious way that Plato's better regimes differ from our democracies. Religious life is not private but public, not optional but legally compulsory, not a matter of study but of dogma and ritual. It is characterized by piety and observance, not toleration or indifference.

We can overstate matters and fail to notice the rationalizing direction of the dogmas in Plato's regimes, his concerns about debilitating piety or awe, the radical nature of philosophy, and the looseness in Socrates' Athens, as Plato portrays it. But we would be wrong to ignore what is before our eyes. Piety, ritual, and dogma are political matters directed by legal authorities and intertwined with every other activity. Politics is oriented to piety, and Plato then tries to orient piety and ritual to virtue, or to the divine naturally understood.

A second way the pervasiveness of Plato's politics differs from our regimes is in music, painting, architecture, and "culture" generally. The *Laws* and *Republic* are filled with directives about songs, rhythms, and harmony. These directives are often quite precise. The *Laws'* Athenian Stranger talks at length about proper motions in children's dances, for example, and about choruses for various stages of life.

Socrates' Athens was open to traveling poets and sophists. Yet, even there, rituals and prescribed practices guided the way and times that drama was presented, and, as we saw with Anytus, sophistic visitors were not universally welcomed. In Sparta and Crete, poetry was more controlled. The *Laws* (and *Republic*) follow this degree of Spartan control, although not its purpose. The Athenian in the *Laws* is worried about what is good for the city, not what is good for the arts. Buildings are political implements, not architects' statements. The city is planned as legislators see fit, not according to design school whimsy. The issue is not so much censorship as prior restraint, and the restraint is bred into men and enforced by law for political purposes. "Art" belongs to politics, or virtue.

Does this mean that art is subsumed by politics, that Plato's regimes are totalitarian ("fascist"), that he does not understand beauty? Although art belongs to politics, we must distinguish good from bad regimes. Plato subordinates art in the *Laws* and *Republic* to regimes that he believes to be prudent, virtuous, and just. Not any politics, but, rather, virtuous politics, may properly subordinate art to law. This subordination is onerous but not stultifying if opportunities for pleasing elevation are broad, or if artists' and poets' talents do not outstrip the city's way of life but find their place in it. Was the art of Bach, Dante, and Michelangelo (that needed to display its service to Christianity) inferior to our own? Plato does not justify art as the independent product of the freest souls but places artists' talents within the self-mastery and legal guidance of political virtue. That this restricts artistic choice, as it does other licentious freedom, is clear. That this restriction need venally distort the use of talent is not. The beauty of art finds its place within the nobility of virtue.

Art can also teach us about moral nobility, however, because image and likeness is for Plato the true description of most things. To understand objects and qualities is to see how they are more or less like their perfect or usual models. No courageous action is courage itself; no single tree is "tree"; love is striving, not completion. The varieties of images are clues to the varieties of being.[4] Someone who seeks to understand must therefore grasp production and imitation in poetry and art. The path from art to understanding and, therefore, art's liberating power is especially apparent in the *Republic*'s images of knowledge, and even in its discussions of poetry, read with care.

Education is a third area where Plato's politics extend beyond our tolerance. Statecraft is soul-craft, we are told in the *Gorgias* and *Laws*. Both the Athenian in the *Laws* and Socrates in the *Republic* prescribe in detail the education of the young, from letters to musical instruments to geometry to gymnastics. Whatever is not in the curriculum is apparently not to be taught at all. The variety that we crave and permit is absent. We also mandate education, however, test frequently, and determine much of the curriculum. The mutual public concern with education is an obvious place where the natural power or common sense of the range of Plato's better regimes is evident, even to us. In the most important matter, one's own or one's children's souls, public understanding takes precedence.

A fourth area where Plato's regimes intrude more than ours is the family and marriage. Men and women dine publicly with others of their sex, not privately with their families. Marriages are directed. Control is greatest for the

Republic's rulers and the *Statesman*'s citizens. It is somewhat less intrusive in the *Laws*, where boundaries are more permeable between congealed custom and enforced statutes. Marriage, in the *Laws*, should have in mind producing children whose virtue will best serve the city. Confirmed bachelors are fined heavily. Women should marry between sixteen and twenty, men between thirty and thirty-five. Attraction and some choice are not irrelevant, but they are not dispositive. Nor is increasing one's family's wealth or standing a central concern; in the *Laws* men are asked to marry (slightly) down. The natural attraction of like to like must be overturned so that the courageous and moderate marry each other.

The steps from these prescriptions to our own are not vast. We overtax the single and still encourage marriage. But, our encouragement is mild, our regulations weak, our concern with procreation much more private than public, and our strictures concerning divorce tepid. Even our dealing with homosexuality differs from how it was practiced in actual Greek cities, several of which allowed it without relieving citizens of the obligations of marriage and fatherhood. The interlocutors in the *Laws*, to whom homosexuality was evident, will have none of it in the city they found. Although we see the path from Plato's better regimes to our own practices, therefore, a gulf exists between them and our view that romance (or sexual preference) should dominate.

A final place where Plato's cities are more intrusive than ours is the economy. Nothing in the *Republic*, the *Laws*, or the *Statesman* is oriented to economic growth based on unleashed acquisitiveness. The *Laws*' wealthiest families can be only four times richer than the poorest, and land holdings and numbers of citizens are limited. One must have a city and country home, whose locations are strictly controlled. The city's location should be far enough from the sea that the corruption that arises from excessive trade and variety should not infect it. In the *Republic*, the rulers have no private wealth. In the *Statesman*, the political scientist's art and his citizens' character have little to do with economic gain.

At the same time, Plato is concerned with justice in contracts and markets. Several of the *Laws*' magistracies regulate economic matters such as weights, measures, and roads. This regulation is not altogether different from ours. Moreover, the desire for wealth and the prevalence of trade are visible in usual cities throughout the dialogues, and in the character and hopes of current and future tyrants and oligarchs. Liberality (or generosity) is a significant virtue. Furthermore, Plato treats household management and statesmanship as identical arts in the *Statesman*. In the *Republic* and the *Statesman*, moreover, the root of politics in meeting bodily or economic need is obvious. The *Republic*'s discussion of cities begins with the city of pigs, which is the true city, and soldiers become necessary because excess requires expansion.

These practices belong to the economic similarities between Plato's better regimes and ours. Quite different, however, are his directives about degrees of wealth, his limiting the city's size to what enables citizens to support each other and to defend themselves, his omission of any discussion (other than of weights and measures) that connects generating wealth to mathematics or science (our "technology"), and his extreme view of virtue's ability to bring us external goods. The *Laws*' city is oriented toward virtue, not growth, and to the character and conditions for using well, not the character and conditions for accumulating. Something of a standpoint we can still (barely) recognize—the standpoint of the gentleman—shines through.

War

The scope of political control is the first element of Plato's better regimes that differs markedly from ours. A second is the importance of war—educating, training, and legislating from the point of view of fighting and winning wars. Defending one's own independence, or one's elementary freedom, is a present and forceful necessity that Plato's better regimes serve.

This importance of war is visible in the *Laws*, the *Statesman*, and the *Republic*; its presence is clear in those dialogues such as the *Laches* and *Menexenus* where one might expect it, and in those such as the *Theatetus* and *Charmides* whose subjects seem not to require it. At the *Laws*' beginning, the Athenian elicits Cleinias' view that all Cretan institutions exist for the sake of war or have victory in view; the laws' goal is courage. In the *Laws*' own regime, the goal is expanded, but training for war remains vital. The *Statesman*'s regime seeks a proper balance between courage and moderation so that defeat comes from neither weakness and timidity nor extreme boldness and risk. The rulers in the *Republic* have war as their first function, and their conduct of it concludes Plato's discussion of the city prior to the rule of philosophers.

We may wonder whether courage and prudence can keep free a city as small as that described in the *Laws*. Innovation in weaponry seems necessary, once one gets wind of it among one's enemies. Although we may sometimes require innovation, however, it is not sufficient to achieve liberty. Cities will not be

free without courage and discipline. Plato's better regimes, therefore, are always centrally concerned with virtue in war and with training for war, even if
their goal is a more complete virtue. Moreover, they permit or encourage innovation, but only innovation that is consonant with virtue. The radical
equalizing of women that we find in the *Republic,* and to a lesser although still
remarkable extent in the *Laws,* occurs in the context of military necessity and
its attendant political requirements. In a small place always under the gun,
one cannot waste half one's talent. Although Plato subordinates war to peace,
his better regimes are organized for war much more completely than are our
own. War is needed to protect one's own; to a degree it substitutes for acquisition and growth.

With war, as with religion, family, education, and economics, the differences between Plato's cities and ours highlight natural facts about politics that
are at once the basis for comparison and a standpoint for mutual criticism.
Our regime is not oriented to war—it is not an armed camp—or to courage.
Yet, part of our regime (the military and much of our technological innovation) attends to it. Its remaining significance is evident.

Virtue

The importance of war and courage are a second element differentiating Plato's good regimes from ours. More broadly, virtue, generally, accounts for these
differences, for it is also the ground of Plato's greater political control. His better cities are oriented toward the necessity of virtue or toward happiness understood as virtue.

Virtue also allows us to understand the absence of individual rights in Plato's regimes. Our current looseness in culture, economy, and religion is not
caused only by our view that these work best with little control. Rather, it is
because of our desired ends that we wish these institutions to conduct themselves freely. These ends center on securing individual rights and advancing
individual wealth and comfort. Securing rights and expanding material goods
depend on cultivating new virtues—tolerance, industriousness, considerate-
ness (niceness), and responsibility—and permitting traditional ones to grow.[5]
These new virtues, however, serve primarily to support the effective use of
rights. Effectively employing rights, and supporting men's equality as holders
of these rights, requires a large realm of individual choice. It suggests broad
areas of government reticence. Regulating unfair economic advantage is for us

a more just use of government than is Platonic-style intervention to shape character. In the *Laws'* eighth book, Plato legally restricts each foreigner to one art and limits citizens to cultivating virtue and citizenship, not allowing them to practice the crafts at all. Although the scope of our own intervention can be surprisingly large, we do not subscribe to such restrictions.

Our occupational mobility, romantic marital choice, and educational expectations are all linked to advancing equality in rights and to exercising effective responsibility in using them. The abilities of the excellent are checked by competition, which limits their excesses, yet still makes them useful politically and economically. Our purpose is not to support well-defined virtue restricted to a few, but to allow the free expression and economic satisfaction of many. So, the virtues that we need to make freedom widespread yet effective are connected to social, religious, and professional practices that are more open than Plato's in the *Laws* and the *Republic*. And, it is not these virtues, but freedom, that is our chief goal.[6]

Equality

These points are connected to the next difference, political equality. Democracy is the best of the bad regimes in the *Statesman,* the actual home of philosophy in the *Republic,* and its factual home in Plato's dialogues and in Greece generally. Some degree of popular rule is necessary in any actual regime, moreover, because of the majority's strength. Even decent ancient democracies rest on slavery, however, and its absence now shows that our liberal democracy is based on a new justification for popular rule, namely, equal rights.[7] We justify government in terms of an end (equal freedom) that virtuous rule cannot simply supplant. Following one's choice (and developing the character to do so) is the central point. Exercising one's own responsible prudence and freedom is our motivating principle and goal.

This new ground and degree of equality leads our liberal democracies to choose political institutions that differ from those in the *Statesman, Laws,* and *Republic*. Those three do not promote separation of powers, political parties, or representation. The *Laws'* discussion of magistracies and other institutions, moreover, is less significant to it than is the discussion of institutions in, say, Locke or *The Federalist;* an analysis of institutions is largely absent from the *Republic* and the *Statesman*. Magistracies are arranged in the *Laws* to honor the claim to govern based on virtuous prudence and numerical strength, and to give virtue an advantage. Magistracies do not clash with each other; if they do it is harmful, not useful, as it is with our separated powers today. Democracies, oligarchies, and tyrannies are, when compared to the *Laws'* best regime, mere "factions" that rule over involuntary subjects.[8] Subjecting a good regime to faction or civil strife is a crime almost as serious as crimes pertaining to the gods. Indeed, the gap between outright rebellion and ordinary dispute is not terribly great. No competing parties legitimately contend for office; differences among the virtuous and strong, or rich and poor, are managed in advance in a unified structure of offices. Because government is not limited to securing equal individual rights, the internal clashes that we validate and institutionalize today in separation of powers and party splits are harmful for Plato. Comity and unity are superior to internal war.[9] With our present-day liberal democracies, however, mild internal conflict is beneficial, given our goal of securing rights, enhancing and expressing the character that uses them, and limiting the scope of government and public religion.

For the same reasons, we see no representative government in Plato. Our representation is not caused by size but by trying to make democracy intelligent by encouraging deliberation and prudence. Foolishness and majority tyranny are democracy's enemies. Representatives stand for us when the common result of our individual actions would be something that, on reflection, we would not choose. In Plato, however, all offices are linked to the limited number of true citizens. Measures that restrict and define eligibility and enhance the opportunity for excellence, rather than forms that dilute rule, are used to bring about just action, as best one can. Although rule in Plato's regimes is more immediate than representative, however, it is also (in the *Laws*) more subject than ours to citizens' direct intervention and audit. At the same time, the absence of clashing institutions, the large number of social matters determined in advance by law and custom, and the strictly defined duties of magistrates mean that Plato's better regimes put beyond political contention much that we include in endless policy debates today.

Founding

These institutional differences point to the question of founding. In the *Laws,* the *Statesman,* and the *Republic,* individual nobility is restricted. Their regimes' orientation to excellence of character and prudence is not directly an orientation to magnificently individual political exploits. Magistrates have some choice in the *Laws* about education, market regulations, and punishment, but the Athenian's regime sets down in advance much more than, say, our Constitution. The virtue and prudence of the citizens in the *Laws* do not make one think of, say, Pericles.

What occurs, instead, is that Plato directs outstanding virtue to political founding, or philosophy. The excellence of the Athenian and Eleatic Strangers (and of the *Statesman's* political scientist) who found regimes is greater than that of the rulers in the regimes they found. The better members of the *Laws'* nocturnal council at most begin to approach these founders' grasp. Young Socrates' dialectical training is a counter to, and more comprehensive than, the education of the *Statesman's* rulers. And, of course, the *Republic* culminates in the education of philosophers whose characteristic action is thinking, not ruling. Plato's basing politics on virtue points to lives that go beyond, or hardly involve, ordinary statesmanship.

Our contemporary politics are not based on virtue. Yet, we too recognize the special excellence of our founders, and of the Lincolns and Roosevelts, who act as if they are founders or refounders. Their actions require more than mediocrity. Political life devoted to virtue and freedom points to a nobility and education beyond politics that statesmanship cannot encompass fully.[10]

These many differences between Plato's regimes and our liberal democracies should not blind us to the familiarity of much that he recommends. In the *Laws* in particular, his strictures about murder and property differ in detail from our laws but are similar to them as a whole. The piety, comprehensiveness, and virtue of his laws notwithstanding, the substance of his criminal and economic law, his intention to educate, and his basic description of the powers of the human soul are more familiar than strange. A significant bedrock of natural similarity exists among men and governments that are open to reason and seek to honor it.

The *Laws*

Plato's *Laws* develops a regime in speech, many of whose institutions could plausibly exist in the flesh. It differs from the *Republic* because it is not directed to producing philosophers. It differs from the *Statesman* because it does not describe immediate rule by the political scientist.[11]

These differences make the *Laws* an appropriate culmination of our discussion of virtue, to this point. For, although in the conversations we have just examined Socrates indicates how virtue opens to philosophy, he is more visibly exploring in those discussions how virtue shapes practical affairs and directs ordinary goods and passions. The *Laws*, too, intends to bring out moral or political virtue's natural height or reasonableness. Its goal is to found a regime grounded on what in laws "constitutes correctness and error according to nature."[12] Plato adjusts the ordinary political dominance of pious belief by showing how we can make "divinity" correspond to natural height. Indeed, he visibly infuses reason into law by presenting preludes or prefaces to the laws that he outlines. He does not merely pronounce authoritative codes.

I

The *Laws'* structure is complex. Its first two books address and relax the standpoint of readiness for war from which political communities must begin. This standpoint is also a barrier to open discussion. The Athenian Stranger (the *Laws'* chief interlocutor) introduces peace, moderation, and music in order to loosen or improve political life and to soften his interlocutors' rigidity. Consequently, the *Laws* begins at once piously and impiously.[13] The Athenian asks a Cretan, Cleinias, whether a god has founded Crete and Sparta.[14] Plato then immediately indicates the difficulties of simple belief in a divine founding by mentioning poets (for we wonder if all stories of divine origins are concocted by Homer and others), pointing to the unclarity in founding stories even if believed (for they need interpreting), indicating how easy it is to make up tales about the gods to fit our wishes (for the Cretans are said to create a story about Zeus to justify their homosexuality), and showing us Cleinias' doubt (a god has laid down Crete's laws, he claims, "to say what is at any rate the most just thing," i.e., not necessarily a true thing.)[15]

The Athenian next asks why Cretan law ordains common meals and gymnastics. Cleinias claims that all Crete's laws have war in view—courage is thus a central virtue—for without victory one's goods are taken. Therefore, cities' warring against each other is natural. As the Stranger points out, however, not all victory is good: when an unjust majority enslaves a just minority, the city is inferior to itself. Moreover, friendship (say, the willing subservience of the inferior to the rule of the superior) is also good. Courage is the central virtue only if all we should do is to overcome enemies in and outside the city and ourselves. This is unclear, because war is for the sake of what happens in peace. Mere friendship and peace, however, are also not the full goal; neither war nor peace alone sustains full excellence.[16] A divine lawmaker refers to the whole of virtue, not only a part.

The Athenian advances this discussion of law's purpose by suggesting that correct laws make one happy by providing good things, of which four are human (health, beauty, strength and other bodily motions, and wealth that follows prudence) and four divine (prudence or intelligence, moderation of soul, and justice, which arises from these two mixed with courage, the fourth). By nature, these four rank above the human goods, which depend on and are guaranteed by them. The Athenian is here subtly equating divine goods with natural virtues, identifying virtue, goodness, and happiness, and demoting courage.

The interlocutors next discuss how institutions can promote virtue. We care for citizens by correctly apportioning their honors and by guarding pleasures, pains, and other experiences of soul. We properly direct them by praising and blaming according to law, by teaching what is noble, and by observing justice. The Athenian then asks the Spartan Megillos, the *Laws'* other interlocutor, how Sparta's practices—such as the common mess, gymnastics, and hunting—promote courage. He suggests, moreover, that overcoming pleasure belongs to courage as well as to moderation; one half endures pain, the other pleasure.[17] He therefore indicates, without analyzing, what we explored in the previous chapter—how difficult it is to specify virtue's proper parts and definition.

In the first book's next section, which continues into the second book, the Athenian examines drunkenness and symposia (or banquets). Sparta and Crete's difficulty is that they do not educate well in how to experience pleasure or in moderation. Well-ruled symposia serve education (as war serves victory) by promoting moderation, shame, or proper fear of a bad reputation.[18] Indeed, when a legislator calls shame awe or reverence, it can replace courage and moderation.[19] (We may note, how, despite the Athenian's suggestion, awe differs from courage, because courage also involves confidence or boldness, and how it differs from moderation, which encourages, and does not merely contain, proper love and desire). Drinking during symposia tempts one to shamelessness. When symposia are properly regulated, they are thus able to advance moderation by permitting a safe experience of the intoxicated boldness of eros, anger, and other passions.[20] Indeed, they afford a safe way to test men. "The knowledge of the natures and the habits of souls" "is of the greatest use for that art whose business it is to care for souls . . . politics."[21]

To regulate symposia according to nature, we need a clear and sufficient account of what is correct in music and in education generally. What, then, is education and its power? Whatever a man intends to become good at should occupy him when he is young: future carpenters should play with miniature tools.[22] Education draws children's souls to love what they must do to excel in their jobs, and it makes one desire to be a perfect citizen who "knows how to rule and be ruled with justice." Education leads children to love being virtuous citizens, understanding virtue now as obedience to laws. Law is primarily correct reasoning about what is better and worse, when this becomes the city's opinion: reason cannot rule without law's compulsion.[23]

II

Book II continues the discussion of education and symposia. Its goal is to make virtue, pleasure, goodness, correctness, and beauty mutually dependent. Plato especially impresses on one the possible links, through art and play, between virtue and pleasure. Virtue remains the standard by which the interlocutors judge the utility of symposia and choruses.

Education teaches children by correctly arranging pleasure and pain in their souls. When passions that are consonant with reason affirm the correctness of habits, we have virtue in its entirety.[24] Humans are pleased by order in motion—by rhythm and harmony. This leads us to combine song and dance in choruses, which are beautiful if the songs and dances are beautiful.[25] Correct education brings about delight in the noble, for the postures and tunes that belong to the virtue, or images of virtue, of soul and body are beautiful. Differences in our natures and habits, however, often lead us to praise what we do not in fact enjoy. Taking pleasure in base performances, in ugly singing and dancing in choruses, harms us even if we still praise only beautiful things.

The Athenian next considers music education generally. He praises Egypt's ten-thousand-year-old practice of sacralizing certain beautiful songs and positions, and permitting no deviation or innovation.[26] We have seen, however, that good cities also need the irreverence and frankness of symposia, not to mention philosophy. Performances must please, and pleasure is one attraction of change. The Athenian thus relaxes the strict Egyptian standard. He nonetheless makes clear that older men's judgment about pleasant performances should dominate. Poets should be persuaded or compelled to create correct poetry that depicts "the postures and songs of moderate, courageous, and wholly good men."[27] Indeed, the Athenian continues, good things (such as health, wealth, and the tyranny and immortality) that the many call good are good only for just men but bad for the unjust. The lawgiver will seek to persuade everyone that the unjust life is the more wicked and unpleasant, as well as the more shameful, even if this is a lie or if some such as Cleinias do not agree.

The Athenian then returns to choruses, primarily the "Dionysian" chorus of older men, those between thirty and sixty. To show their beauty, he again digresses. In things accompanied by charm, what is serious is the charm, correctness, or benefit. Pleasure is the charm in food, for example, and healthiness the benefit or correctness. Pleasure is learning's charm, but truth its benefit or correctness. So, pleasure is not the correct criterion of what produces benefit, and we should not judge music by it. Serious music "contains a resemblance to the imitation of the beautiful." (Here, this imitation is legal virtue.) A prudent judge of an image must know the being of the thing imitated and how correctly and well it is imitated.[28] Poets, however, create mishmashes in music by harmonizing, say, a free man's posture with the rhythms of a slave. The older singers must thus become educated in harmonies, rhythms, and, especially, the noble, the virtuous, so that the young will be able to "hear an adequate incantation on behalf of virtue."[29] Drinking in symposia enables reluctant older men to be easily led in choruses by the good lawgiver who has the knowledge and ability to mold souls. His laws can make the sanguine bolder and the ignobly bold justly fearful or awed.

III

The first two books establish politics' natural purpose—virtue—and connect the noble as virtue to the noble as beautiful music. They also establish an atmosphere conducive to discussion. Accordingly, Book III presents a new beginning: to understand virtue (and, especially, justice), we must better understand cities in which we find it and link cities to their needs.[30] The Stranger thus replaces Books I's beginning in divine lawgiving, war, and courage with another start that contains a natural genealogy of the material of political life and a genealogy of governments.

Cataclysms such as floods destroy the cities that already exist. The simple, virtuous, naïve, truthful men who remain lack arts but in time develop skills such as hunting, herding, weaving, and molding, and characteristics similar to Homer's Cyclops. (Waging war is not the only way to meet necessities.) Eventually, the clans of these men come together, and some choose among, or combine, their different orderly and courageous ways. These legislators rule until the aristocracies and monarchies that they fashion begin. Still another story concerns Sparta's and Crete's origin and returns us to the beginning of Book I. Sparta's government proved defective when its laws did not have prudence, friendship, and freedom in view, and succeeded when its institutions attained "due measure." Indeed, political decline generally comes from people's failure to obey intelligent rulers. Each human "desires to have things happen in accordance with the commands of one's own soul," but our wishes are not always prudent.[31]

How, then, can those who at best have right opinions (the unwise) obey the wise? The Athenian develops this question by discussing seven titles to rule. The most important are those of the wise and the strong. Government needs to be both wise and strong, but these qualities rarely coincide: strength resides in the majority; wisdom may reside in one. We see that the three traditional titles—the rule of parents, the well born, and the older—"reflect the principle of wisdom," and that the usual rule of masters over slaves, and of one chosen by lot, reflect the principle of strength.[32] This is why democracy and monarchy are the mothers of all regimes: the intellect and the body exist in every city; the highest title must be modified by the other titles. Measured rule is superior either to slavery or to complete freedom among the ruled, as the Athenian attests by discussing Persia under Cyrus and his successors and Athens when it opposed Persia. When despotic or free regimes are "limited within measure," "affairs [go] outstandingly well."[33]

IV

Starting with Book IV, the interlocutors found their own city. Their founding takes the form of advice that the Athenian and the Spartan Megillos give to Cleinias, who is helping to found a Cretan colony. He and the nine other founders from the city of Knossos may use Knossian laws in the colony but also better foreign laws if they discover them. Cleinias may therefore make use of their construction in speech. The standpoint of the interlocutors remains what advances virtue. In producing his city, the Athenian subtly combines the leading subjects of the first three books (virtue, forms of government, and the material of politics) and keeps in mind what he has effected there: the expansion of virtue from courage to moderation and prudence, and the broadening of institutions that encourage virtue from the military to those that educate in beauty.

They first discuss the conditions of good laws, such as territory, resources, and population. The Athenian worries about too close proximity to the sea, with the untrustworthiness this causes. He considers the difficulties involved when colonists all come either from one tribe (it is hard to give them new laws) or many (it is hard for them to be friendly.) This leads him to call founding cities and lawgiving "the most perfect of all tests of manly virtue."[34] The best city arises most quickly from a naturally moderate, magnificent, courageous, and smart tyrant who chances to come together with someone who is by nature a true lawgiver. When there are more rulers—say, in a democracy or oligarchy—the change is less swift and easy. The great difficulty is to find powerful rulers who have divine love for justice, moderation, and prudence.

The Athenian turns next to determining the new city's regime. Megillos and Cleinias are not sure if Crete and Sparta are democracies, tyrannies, oligarchies, monarchies, or aristocracies. The Athenian suggests that all these rule unjustly for their own advantage; a just regime legislates for what is common, and it is not the rule of partisans. Not strength, but the rule of law and of those most obedient to law will be paramount in the city that they are founding.[35]

The interlocutors now begin to act as legislators who address the colonists. They will, in the general prelude they offer to the laws, try first to produce in their citizens a standpoint conducive to obedience to the gods and, thus, to virtue.[36] They will advance citizens' moderation by persuading them of our likeness to gods and by promoting proper sacrifice and just respect for parents and the dead. They will also use preludes to the specific laws they promulgate. The legislators will thus be like physicians for free men, who investigate illnesses according to nature, give an account of them, learn, and command only after they have "in some sense persuaded."[37] Of course, even the citizens in this regime need punishment as well as persuasion to produce their lawful obedience.

The first law that the Athenian outlines concerns marriage. Marriage and procreation reflect natural desire and, therefore, an immediate natural beginning in a way that concern with gods does not. Marriage can become the "cause of all childbirths in the city," however, only when law elevates the body's natural desire to the soul's virtue. Immortality is at the core of the Stranger's short prelude to the marriage law, which requires all men between thirty and thirty-five to marry and fines those who do not.

V

Book V returns to the legal code's overall prelude, which the law on marriage had interrupted.[38] The prelude encourages ethical virtue that is inseparable

from the new city and its laws. The founders, therefore, do not shy from en-
joining punishment of the incorrigible, vigorous magisterial enforcement, and
self-defense; they do not demand that we turn the other cheek. The Athenian
or, as he sometimes says, their "logos" will say that, after the gods, the soul (as
it tracks down and dwells with the best) is the most divine thing that belongs
to men. The soul is "the thing that is most one's own."[39] It should honor itself
by honoring "the things the lawgiver . . . sets down as" good and noble. The
soul should "use every means" to practice these and to avoid the "shameful
and bad." It should honor virtue more than survival, bodily beauty, or gain.
Honoring moderate strength, health, swiftness, and beauty is third, followed
by moderation in wealth. Children should be shown and taught what supports "modest awe." Family ties are to be revered, one should seek "the victo-
rious reputation of having served his own laws," and strangers should not be
treated wrongly. Praise for truth, the "leader of all good things for gods" and
of all things for humans, helps make individuals obedient, by bringing trustworthiness. The prelude also praises moderation and prudence, but men
should be spirited as well as gentle, for without spiritedness they cannot punish and defend. As for justice, we should praise the man who prevents injustice
even more than the man who eschews it. "The bearer of victory in virtue is the
one who does what he can to assist the magistrates in inflicting punishment."[40]
One should not be excessively friendly to himself, moreover, because self-love
leads us to believe we should "honor [our] own more than the truth and what
is just."[41]

The Athenian concludes the overall prelude by discussing pleasure and
pain. He tries to show how prudent, moderate, and courageous actions, on
balance, give more pleasure than their opposites. That is, he again tries to
show that nature supports virtue, that, in addition to its rational height, it has
(through pleasure) an immediate or spontaneous incentive and reward. Men
are naturally limited to ways of life in which we wish for and choose greater
pleasure and less pain. Such are the virtuous lives, which bring us beauty,
fame, and correctness. Involuntary submission arises from ignorance of the
greater pleasure of virtue and from lack of self-control.[42] As with other phenomena that the Athenian discusses in the prelude, he examines pleasure
broadly enough to produce statements and laws that replace mere fiat, but he
does not examine it with the precision and sufficiency that constitute philosophic questioning or speech.

Once the interlocutors finish the general prelude, they outline specific laws:

the scope of Plato's discussion makes clear, for the first time, law's full natural range. They begin with property and the size of the citizen body, although the "two fundamental parts" of a regime are "the laws that are given to the ruling offices" and the appointment of men to fill them. (He will discuss these in Book VI.)[43] They allow private farming and dwellings, although the land and buildings belong to the city, which will consist of 5,040 citizens divided into twelve tribes and dedicated to twelve gods. A citizenry of 5,040 allows moderation, defense, and easy division for various purposes.[44] The Athenian outlines ways to keep the free population at this low number; his constant intention is not growth and wealth but rather what is good for the soul.

He next discusses justice and injustice in acquiring wealth, and liberality and stinginess in spending it. He tries to keep accumulation to a minimum and considers several combinations of spending and acquisition to achieve this. Too much citizen concern with wealth worries good legislators because the resultant litigiousness weakens concord and friendship. Private property, however, requires that wealth (as well as looks and virtue) be given some title to rule. So, the Athenian divides the city into four classes (with changing membership), based on differences in wealth (which cannot exceed a ratio of four to one), with distribution of some benefits and offices determined according to these classes. In general, the Athenian's emphasis on numbers belongs to his liberalizing of Spartan institutions throughout the *Laws,* for studying numbers "awakens he who is by nature asleep and unlearned . . . making him surpass his nature by a divine art."[45]

VI

In Book VI the founders' task is to constitute the ruling offices and to choose how to fill them. Justice in distributing offices (or honors) means awarding them according to what naturally fits the potential office holder. Some equality must exist, given the necessary strength in the city of the many. Nonetheless, equal distribution conflicts with distributing offices to the virtuous. The city needs to mix strength and prudence (democracy and monarchy); any mixture, however, will be imperfect.[46]

The regime's offices feature thirty-seven guardians of the laws, each fifty or older, who can rule until they reach seventy; generals and other officers who are elected by those who have fought in or are about to fight in wars; and a council of 360 that favors the more propertied. The guardians must be able to be constitutional lawgivers, for although the interlocutors' lawgiving is as sufficiently precise as they can make it now, it will need to be improved with experience, as a beautiful painting must be touched up so it does not decay after its artist dies.

The city also allows some election by lot. Indeed, this plays a special role in choosing priests, because lot and leaving decisions to divine chance are connected. Even here, however, lot is insufficient, because someone must ascertain that a potential priest's birth is legitimate and that he is ritually pure. Furthermore, priests must be over sixty, and the treasurers in charge of sacred funds will come from the most propertied class. In this way, Plato allows the Athenian to recognize the place of the sacred in supporting a regime dedicated to virtue, while containing the priesthood within natural, reasonable requirements.[47]

The Athenian discusses particular magistrates at some length, including city and market regulators, judges, and those who judge musical and gymnastic contests. Punishment for misdeeds and harsh living conditions for those who guard the land are featured, in order to remind us of our "noble enslavement" to the laws. The Athenian's description of the measures needed to guard the city against enemies and supposed friends reminds us of the central place of war and defense in political life, even when we construct a city that departs from the view that courage is the chief or only virtue.[48] In general, the more important functions have magistrates who come from the more propertied classes, with other qualifications also increasing. Law and reason will always differ because the democratic principle of equality dilutes the monarchical principle and because virtue is hard to recognize. Within these constraints, the Athenian gives the fullest rule to law guardians and the least to the poorest.

The most significant magistrate is the Supervisor of Education. "This office is by far the greatest of the highest offices in the city." The supervisor must be over fifty, and he should be the best man in the city. "In every thing that grows the initial sprouting, if nobly directed, has a sovereign influence in bringing about the perfection in virtue that befits the thing's own nature."[49] With correct education and a lucky nature, a human being becomes the most divine and tamest animal; with inadequate or ignoble upbringing, man becomes the earth's most savage growth.

In the remainder of Book VI, the Athenian turns again to marriage. Central here is the link between marriage and the sacred. Citizens should regard each of the city's twelve divisions as a sacred gift, with sacrifices and choral plays occasions both to solicit the gods and to meet future spouses. Again, the natural primacy of sex is elevated or sanctified. Although young men may choose pleasing partners, the law's prelude suggests that they choose the less highly placed and thus more measured prospect and recommends that impatient men choose the orderly and phlegmatic men the hasty. The city's needs come before natural attraction to what is similar to oneself; this attraction would cause unevenness in the citizens' characters and wealth.[50] Bachelors over thirty-five are fined and not honored by the young, dowries and wedding expenditures are limited, drinking and injustice are especially to be avoided when one engenders children, and parents and their married children's households are to be split because longing cements attachment.

Slavery exists in these households. Slaves are the first property mentioned and are discussed in conversation with Megillos and Cleinias. The Athenian recommends having slaves from different regions, with different languages, and treating them with dignity and justice. Just treatment of slaves shows one's natural reverence for justice. (The interlocutors note that although masters sometimes think slaves are unhealthy and untrustworthy, they can be superior in virtue.)[51]

After slaves, the founders discuss houses and other buildings. A city wall is discouraged, for it makes men soft and harms health. Men will eat meals in common, even after marriage; private as well as public matters must be regulated. It is also according to nature to regulate women's affairs, including mandating common meals among them. Women are eligible for magistracies (at forty, men at thirty) and military service (after their children have been born). Women's virtue as well as men's is the city's goal, and supervising the young women and men who are procreating is especially important. Both bride and groom are enjoined to "reflect intelligently" on each other—and on having children. The Athenian rationalizes and elevates the status of women here, and he breaks with tradition in the direction of equality. His discussion, nonetheless, is less radical than that of the *Republic,* whose rulers have no families of their own.

VII

Book VII's subject is educating children. Throughout it, the Athenian attends more than we do to the influence of the private on the public. Central is educating the soul: even gymnastics serves the virtue of soul as well as body, for it is a first step in subduing fear.[52] The correct way of life should neither pursue pleasures headlong nor flee pain entirely; infants too should be habituated to this "gracious" middle.

The Athenian emphasizes the importance of custom, habit, and practice as well as law in educating, and he criticizes changes in customs and poetry. He requires that children's games never be changed, for example, and that there be little innovation in music and dance. He seeks the benefit of respect for, and pleasure in, ancestral customs that (as here) he has made naturally good. (One may of course question whether he allows sufficient variety.) It seems to be a "strange dogma" to legalize or sacralize songs so that the same dispositions are always praised and blamed, citizens experience the same pleasures, and innovation is strictly limited.[53] We should inquire fully about things puzzling or strange, the Athenian claims, and he suggests that perhaps "the way itself as a whole, taken to the end, would reveal sufficiently the answer to what now is puzzling."[54]

The Athenian again emphasizes the connection between education, playfulness, and maturity. Girls as well as boys must train for war and take their meals in common because courage is so important.[55] The key point in poetry is that "the poet is to create nothing that differs from the city's conventional and just version of the beautiful or good things."[56] Ancient songs are chosen or reworked to fit the regime. By nature, a man should devote himself to "cultivating the body in all respects and his soul as regards virtue." "There should be a schedule regulating how all the free men spend all their time," from dawn until the next dawn.[57] Comedy is permitted—"for someone who is going to become prudent cannot learn the serious things without learning the laughable or, for that matter, anything without its opposite"—but it is to be performed by slaves and strangers. As for tragedy, "our whole political regime is constructed as the imitation of the most beautiful and best way of life which we at least assert really to be the truest tragedy."[58] The city will not prohibit all tragedy but will judge whether a tragedy accords with its own songs.

The Athenian discusses the rest of education, from reading through astronomy, largely as if instructing the magistrate in charge and sometimes as if conversing with himself. As matters increase in difficulty, different natural gifts require differences in education. Especially important (because especially characteristic of our freedom, liberality, and "becoming among human beings a god") are counting, geometry, and astronomy.[59] "Trying to discover the causes" "with regard to the greatest god and the cosmos as a whole" can be made coherent with this city's piety. Nonetheless, astronomy and geometry, in particular, go beyond what is merely useful for ordinary piety; law cannot fully employ or account for mathematics. Play and education are ultimately superior to war.

The Athenian concludes Book VII by discussing how the lawmaker encourages certain passions by praising actions, as well as by regulating or preventing them. His example is ways of hunting: the goal is to encourage love of victory (say, by hunting with dogs) rather than laziness (say, by setting traps.) What the laws permit and restrain in this regime continue to show the priority in it of virtue and the sacred. Even a less restrictive liberal regime such as ours must praise or encourage some actions more than others.

VIII

Book VIII further discusses festivals: daily and monthly sacrifices, choruses, and music and gymnastic contests will honor the twelve gods for whom the city's twelve tribes are named. Most of the discussion of festivals involves training for war, which the Athenian describes in detail. Practice in war helps secure peace by making one formidable. The Athenian especially describes contests in running, fighting, and horsemanship that establish bodily "keenness." Two causes prevent cities from practicing as they should for war. One is private love of wealth that turns the courageous toward piracy and housebreaking and turns the moderate toward merchandising and trade. The other is democracy, oligarchy, and tyranny, that is, the "non-regimes," or factions: fearful rulers do not allow the ruled to become warlike.

The Athenian's attention to war again shows how he modifies his initial criticism of Crete and Sparta's orientation to war, and to courage. He must counteract the possibly excessive piety or fear that could arise among the citizens because of the regime's careful attention to the sacred. Indeed, we especially need piety to control eros or sex. Crete and Sparta's pederasty is a particularly great problem: it nourishes neither "courage in the soul of the seduced" nor "the offspring of the idea of a moderate man" in the soul of the seducer. "Reason attempting to become law" will not permit it.[60] What, then, will enable them to enact a law that prohibits these desires? Incestuous desires are often quenched or controlled by being condemned "as unholy and hated by the god," an unholiness that no one denies. The legislator learns from this that condemning unnatural desires as unholy can lead us to subjugate them. Still, we also need punishment. What is unnatural can be ambiguous; the Athenian points to animals to indicate that pederasty is unnatural, but he does not do this with incest. As the discussion proceeds, moreover, he treats as unnatural not only pederasty but all extramarital sex; unnatural here means not serving sex's natural purpose of procreation. So, the Athenian's first choice for his city is a law that prohibits all sex but married sex. His second choice still prohibits pederasty but allows hidden adultery. In any event, the Athenian's central distinction is between love or friendship whose basic concern is the virtue of the beloved's soul and pederasty (or other relations) whose exclusive concern is sex.

The Athenian argues that his proposed restrictions can become actual. Young men in the new city could be convinced from childhood that happiness means conquering pleasure and could restrain themselves for the sake of such a noble victory. We are able to restrain eros through piety (i.e., through fear) but also through love of victory or honor (i.e., through legal praise), as well as through proper love of the beloved (i.e., through reason). Honor and understanding, and not merely pious fear, can overcome lack of self-control.[61]

The Athenian then turns to still other laws whose purpose is to keep citizens within their own. The goal of laws about farming is to control neighbors' disputes. Citizens (and domestic servants) are prohibited from becoming artisans because the citizen already has "a sufficient art, requiring much practice and many branches of learning," and "there's almost no human nature that is capable of laboring with precision at two pursuits or two arts."[62] The city divides food into equal amounts for citizens, slaves, and artisans/strangers; only a portion of the third part may be sold. Export and import are limited, with generals directing imports for war. The effect is to restrict or control concern with wealth. The Athenian then describes rules for the marketplace, the city's layout, and laws for resident aliens.

IX

The basic topic of Books IX through XII is penal law and its ground. Because the Athenian continues to bring to the laws as much rationality as seems possible, his conversations in Books IX through XII feature reasonable preludes to the laws, discussion of how voluntary injustice is possible, proofs of gods' existence, the nocturnal council and, even, philosophy. Punishment (i.e., strength in the form of penal law) is guided by, or elevated toward, wisdom. The need for punishment, however, shows the limits of such elevation.

The first penal law and its prelude concern crimes against the gods, such as temple robberies. The Athenian then discusses dissolution of the regime, treason, murder, and theft. He subtly rationalizes laws about these matters in several ways. Temple robbers are treated as incurable and killed, but their children are not punished, even if their father's crime is traced to an unexpiated curse.[63] Fines are limited to the excess people have beyond their landholdings. And, capital trials are to be spread over two different days. That is, passions are allowed to cool before sentencing (as they had not during Socrates' trial, when the penalty was voted on immediately after the speeches that directly followed his conviction).

The Athenian next differentiates the three interlocutors from ordinary legislators, responding to Cleinias' question about why they will penalize all thefts equally. As the Athenian had said earlier, a free man's physician converses and, as he now says, almost "philosophizes" with him, tracing his illness to its origin in the nature of bodies.[64] Similarly, they treat the citizens here not as mere subjects but as if they are legislators—as if they themselves are knowers. Their citizens' obedience will mimic the self-treatment of physicians as much as possible. Indeed, the discussion of punishment culminates in a difficulty that the Athenian arrives at by, as it were, philosophizing with Cleinias: just things are noble, but undergoing just punishment is disgraceful. The disposition to be just is noble, but how is it noble to be rightly punished?

The Athenian deals with this question by claiming that men are bad involuntarily and, therefore, unjust involuntarily. If all crimes are involuntary, however, would not penal law be destroyed? The Athenian thus discusses the question of voluntary and involuntary crimes; he will not legislate without argument, as a god. Indeed, he tells us, it is impious not to say what one believes true.[65]

We might suggest that all crime could be involuntary if all vice were ignorance alone. Punishment could then be noble as well as just if it educated us and thus brought us to virtue. The Athenian does not claim here that virtue is knowledge alone, however, as he should if vice were ignorance alone. Nor does he claim that these citizens' knowledge goes beyond correct opinion. Virtue is indeed knowledge, and, thus, teachable and fully voluntary, but it is so only philosophically, we should say: Virtue is knowledge only when the soul turns fully to truth. No city, based as it must be on law and opinion, can fully express this turn.

The Athenian, therefore, subtly relaxes his standard of voluntary crime by stating that the incurable in this city will be killed.[66] He also claims that spiritedness and pleasure (i.e., not merely ignorance) cause crime and vice. In fact, he soon distinguishes between involuntary and voluntary homicides and remarks how a particular punishment does not educate but is a concession to ancient fears. He thus indicates the necessary irrationality of this and every regime and, in effect, moderates his extreme statement. The view that all crime is involuntary is not satisfactory for penal law, or for regimes grounded in necessity as well as what is best, and for souls wracked by spiritedness, fear, and pleasure. The soul is passionate and not only reasonable. The rationality of the laws, even in this regime, must be imperfect and rest on opinion and piety. Law needs to accommodate passion and strength.[67]

The Athenian's discussion of penal law emphasizes pollution, purification, spiritedness, and the gods' vengeance.[68] He develops midpoints between voluntary and involuntary action; central is the degree of one's deliberation. Murders that are "voluntary are totally unjust [and] spring from weakness in the face of pleasure, desires, and envies."[69] To control the most impious murder, the murder of kin, we must recur to fear of gods. Divine vengeance is insufficient, however, for some do not believe or cannot restrain themselves.[70] So, humanly enforced law must supplement unwritten laws. Moreover, victims' families must prosecute crimes or themselves be penalized. The city must cultivate proper spiritedness and not permit improper mercy. We see again that it is not enough in this city merely to avoid committing injustice or to ward it off against oneself.[71]

We need law to separate us from beasts, for no human being's nature grows on its own to know sufficiently what regime benefits us, nor is anybody always willing to do spontaneously what is best. It is especially difficult to know that the true political art cares for what is common and that this care benefits common and private needs. If someone knew sufficiently that "this is the way these things are by nature," he should rule autocratically, but even he would be pushed toward the private and pleasure, ahead of the just and better. Were a human being with sufficient nature to be born, he would not need laws, for no law or order is "stronger than knowledge," and it is wrong to subordinate intelligence. It should "be ruler over everything, if indeed it is true and really free according to nature." But this does not now exist or exists only to a small extent, so one "must choose what comes second, order and law," which sees most things, but not everything.[72]

X

The Athenian begins Book X with a law that prohibits taking something that belongs to another or using what is owned by a neighbor without persuading him. "Such behavior has been, is, and will be a source of all the evils that have been mentioned."[73] He then discusses insolence, especially about the gods and sacred things. No one who believes that the gods are as the laws claim would do or say impious things. Rather, he believes that they do not exist or, if they exist, that they do not care for men or, if they care for men, that we can bribe them through prayer or sacrifice.

Cleinias wonders what to do about those with such views. He then tries to persuade the "joking deniers" by proving the gods' existence. His simple proof is insufficient, so the Athenian turns to his own proof.[74] He begins by stating the argument he will oppose, namely, that the heavens, animals, and plants are all generated through aimless and necessary motions of the elements fire, water, earth, and air. These are said to be by nature (and by chance). Arts come later and stem from men. Legislation posits the gods through art and posits a justice that is not natural; mastery over others, not justice, is naturally correct.[75]

Cleinias and the Athenian agree that because these pernicious views are widespread the legislator must defend the ancient laws by showing that there are gods. Their adversaries are wrong, the Athenian claims, because the being and power of the soul have escaped them. Soul came into being prior to bodies and governs their changes: if nature means the first things, then soul, not the elements, is more fully natural. Art and law are akin to soul and, therefore, also have priority over bodily things.

Can we prove this primacy of soul? The Stranger proceeds, first in discussion with himself and then together with Cleinias. The motion that can always move itself (and other things) is prior to the other nine motions; otherwise, there is an infinite regress. Soul is this self-moving motion; in something bodily it is "life." Soul, therefore, is the first motion of all things and has come into being prior to body.

The Athenian continues. Given their argument, body cannot cause the bad, shameful, or unjust, because soul causes all things. How account for these, then? There must be two souls, one causing noble and the other base things. Soul's motions—wishing; investigating; supervising; deliberating; opining correctly and falsely; feeling joy, pain, confidence, fear, hatred, and desire, among others—drive all things, including the secondary motions of bodies. When soul takes "intelligence—god, in the correct sense—for the gods, it guides all things toward what is correct and happy."[76]

The Athenian suggests that the virtuous soul rules heaven and earth: the cosmos' motion has the same nature as the intellect's invisible motion. It moves according to one proportion and order, in one place around the same, toward the same, and in relation to the same.[77] The soul itself is invisible and can be grasped only by intellect and reasoning. All things are full of gods—are moved by soul—whether or not something is alive, that is, whether or not its soul dwells in its body.

We note that the Athenian is perhaps less certain of his argument than is Cleinias.[78] For one thing, the proof that gods exist because soul exists obfuscates the differences among god, soul, and human soul. Or, it suggests loosely that gods are the intelligent soul, and man the base, or partly intelligent and partly base, soul. But, has the Athenian explained the nature of intelligence and its link to the rest of soul and to virtue?[79] Moreover, his suggestion that the first motion is soul—because this is the definition to which we give the name *soul*—does not prove that soul's other characteristics are equivalent to, or belong to, this first motion.[80] More broadly, is soul truly the cause of everything that is? The Athenian says nothing about things that do not move and change, but soul would seem to act only together with these or their images. Intellect is oriented toward truth.

In any event, we can see that the Athenian's argument fails to prove the gods' existence, as gods might usually be understood. Has the demonstration of soul's priority to body established the existence of thinking gods, with permanent, yet changeable, shapes?[81] Do the souls of heavenly bodies fear or hate? Are we not assuming that we know what virtue is and that gods (as causing noble things) are guided by it? Do the virtues or their forms perhaps precede the soul? Could the "virtuous" soul that is guided by prudence, together with what is not soul (rather than bad soul) be "the cause of all things"?[82] In general, the Athenian's attempt to defend a "first" cause (understood as the efficient cause of what comes into being) leads him to downplay what he nonetheless alludes to partially—nature as the fitting, common, formal, and complete, and intelligence as grasping this nature.[83]

The Athenian next tries to prove that the gods care for men. The heart of his proof is to compare gods to human artisans and rulers. He makes matters easy by arguing at the same time with someone who denies divine care and with someone who believes that the gods can be bribed, that is, that they do care.

The Athenian's proof of the gods' humanly pleasing care is also faulty because it assumes that the gods have put each of us in the right place, as we desire it; it assumes the coincidence of our wishes and our being parts in the common (here divine or cosmically common) order. The Athenian does not demonstrate this coincidence.[84] It is unclear whether our benefit is similar to or clashes with the gods' benefit from their property (us).[85]

The Athenian next establishes the third dogma, that the gods cannot be bribed. His argument is again persuasive but faulty, for it asserts without proving that their virtue is immune to the bribes that pilots, charioteers, or other guards might take. One wonders, in particular, whether the gods might not compete and, therefore, take more than is just from impious men.[86]

Book X ends with the laws about impiety to which this theology had been a prelude. These laws include harsh penalties for impiety, and the prohibition of shrines in private homes. The central issue concerns what constitutes impiety. Is it belief in, say, cosmic gods but disbelief in Olympian ones? Is private atheism that does not ridicule believers impious? The Athenian suggests implicitly that the threat of punishment would keep in check the frankness of naturally just nonbelievers, or "ridiculers." It is, rather, the "ironic" men who are especially dangerous. It is from these that arise diviners, magicians, tyrants, generals, and sophists.[87]

XI

Book XI returns to crimes against neighbors' property and continues with laws about buying and selling, adulterating merchandise, and retailing. The Athenian begins by reminding us to honor "the acquisition of justice in the soul before that of wealth in property." Retail trade is beneficial because it makes wealth commensurate to needs, but it is regarded as ignoble because so many choose to gain insatiably. Only resident aliens or strangers, therefore, are to engage in it. In this regime, one is to avoid excess in seeking wealth or in piously shrinking from it.[88]

The Athenian turns next to regulations about orphans and their guardians, and to a discussion with Cleinias about property and death. Men wish to give their property to whomever they want, but the law takes precedence. The legislator cares for the whole and cannot fill each individual desire. Perfect correspondence of whole and part is impossible. Even divine providence can more easily be asserted than proved to perfectly unite them.[89]

Death demonstrates our limited control over our property and bodies, and requires that they be sanctified. Such sanctifying is visible in the Athenian's discussion of sacred duties to orphans and their assignment to the law guardians as fathers.[90] What is sacred extends or elevates the natural love of one's own.[91] The existence of defenseless orphans shows both the failure of providence and the need for pious support of human law. It reminds us of parents' natural care and the limits to that care.[92]

The next section of Book XI concerns dissension between parents and children, and between spouses. It recalls the sacred duty to honor aged parents. Their possible senility also suggests the limits to identifying what is old and good. In general, the *Laws* explores the complex connections among the naturally good and permanent things, the sacred and legal things, and the things (old and young) that are most one's own, including one's soul. One's own must be sacralized in order to be or to remain good: the soul's self-regard is truly protected only if it is elevated to virtue's restraint. What is good, however, needs the sacralizing of one's own to become or to remain powerful: virtue is active only together with one's own, properly elevated, dignity or pride. The Athenian attempts, as best he can within the limits of law and necessity, to connect the intelligent, just, good, beautiful, natural, honorable, and divine.[93]

The Athenian concludes Book XI by discussing laws that concern or refer to poisons, spells, diviners, the madness of untamed spiritedness, ridicule, and testimony at trials.[94] He apparently means to control fraudulent signs of (and acts toward) the divine and to protect those who are subject to comic ridicule. Comic poets will not be allowed legally to lampoon citizens, whether their intention is playful or angry. The Athenian also seeks to limit the number of lawsuits and to prohibit rhetoric or sophistry, which he describes but does not name. Citizens' lawsuits for money (and second lawsuits from mere love of victory) result in exile or death.

XII

Book XII, the final book, continues to show us how the Athenian's understanding moderates Sparta, and moves it toward a city that fosters individual education, political prudence, and virtue generally. He measures what is reasonable in Sparta and Crete so that it may fit within a more completely reasonable or natural community. Natural virtue and evidence supplement or replace justice, that relies on oaths and other practices that depend on caring, observant gods.[95] Despite the Athenian's efforts, however, the law cannot fully overcome the gap that will always exist between reason and strength or consent.

Most of Book XII concerns public matters such as military service. Its central regulation is that a ruler must always exist in a man or woman's life, in peace as well as war.[96] To whom, then, are the magistrates subject? They are subject to auditors, who judge them after their term has expired. After discussing these auditors, the Stranger considers foreign travel. "By nature," the intermingling of cities mixes dispositions. This is better for bad than for good cities, but one cannot ban all travel. Besides, good reputation among others is significant. The interlocutors thus turn to regulating "observation" missions and ambassadors.[97] Those between fifty and sixty may travel if the law guardians approve. This helps the city improve its laws by better knowing them. The observers accomplish this improvement by gaining experience of bad as well as good human beings and by conversing with the few divine human beings who "do not by nature" "grow more frequently in cities with good laws than without them."[98]

When the Athenian discusses the observer or spectator, the *theoros,* he obviously is alluding to a more purely theoretical observing. When an observer returns, he must report to the council of those who keep watch over the laws. The council, which meets at dawn, is composed of current and former education supervisors, the ten eldest law guardians, those ("priests") who have won the prizes for virtue, and a young man (aged thirty to forty) each supervisor chooses. The council discusses the city's laws, whatever they have learned elsewhere that clarifies them, and what learning "seems to contribute to this inquiry."[99]

The Athenian interrupts his discussion of the council to outline still other topics: strangers who visit the city, searching homes, pledging securities, disputes, witnesses, judicial procedures, offerings to gods, and funerals. Only a measured amount should be spent on funerals, for "the being that is really each of us" is the soul; the body is a semblance.[100] This point leads the Stranger to discuss again lawfulness in the soul or safeguarding the laws by "naturally implanting irreversibility in them."

We should note that the council falls short of intellect simply, for its composition depends to some degree on age and visible virtue, which are at best markers of intellect. Its members go beyond mere opinion, but neither the travelers nor council members need be, or are likely to be, philosophers.[101] The Athenian, indeed, subtly points to the problem of the connection between intellectual and ethical excellence by raising an issue we noticed previously and will see again: There are four kinds of virtue, so each is one; each is "virtue," so they are one. How do they differ, and how are they one? He discusses this with Cleinias. Courage differs from good sense (prudence) because there is no good sense without reason, but beasts (and men) have natural fear and courage. The city needs animal virtue, moderation, and courage because it consists of many as well as few. In it, therefore, true excellence must be diluted. Indeed, meeting the city's necessities and promoting the virtue of its citizens often require different actions from statesmen.

The members of the nocturnal council require precise education, although some on it may lack the fullest ability. The education described reminds us of the Eleatic Stranger's and Socrates' remarks in the *Statesman, Republic,* and other dialogues. It is training to see how different things can comprise one idea (as they consider here the unity of the diverse virtues.) They will learn to look from many and dissimilar things to the one idea and to order everything from this standpoint. All in this city is designed for virtue, but we do not know the virtues precisely until we grasp their unity. This comprehension includes knowing whether virtue is "one, or a whole, or both of these or however it is by nature."[102] Such philosophical questioning or knowledge is necessary if the city is to be well secured. The regime that the Athenian founds will at some point require someone such as himself.

The council members must also study the noble and the good, although the Athenian does not connect these directly to virtue. "The guardians of the laws" must be able to judge "by the standard of nature what things come into being in a noble fashion."[103] Their third subject is the being and power of the gods. Again, the Stranger does not connect this immediately to the previous two subjects. We do hear that the guardians must try to acquire full proof about the gods. Assurance about the gods and the possibility of revering them is based, as we saw, on grasping that the soul is the oldest of the generated things and that the intellect regulates the whole. Such piety differs from the piety of the usual citizens, who are still dedicated to the Olympian gods. Nonetheless, it is not clear that the council members' education goes as far as the Athenian's must have gone for him to conceive the proofs he did. Again, the members are not (all) philosophic. This is among the reasons the Athenian does not discuss education in the detail that Socrates does in the *Republic.*[104] The question of knowing is, nonetheless, central, for the *Laws'* regime of virtue fails without the council, and the council ultimately will fail without philosophy. Plato's discovery of the connection between politics and philosophy is, thus, the theme of our next section.

Part Two
Politics and Philosophy

CHAPTER 4

The Roots of Philosophy

Socrates' conversations are motivated by the concerns we discussed in the first chapter. These concerns issue in admonitions to continue to deliberate or to be virtuous. What virtue is, however, proves to be elusive. Several of its elements are reasonably clear, of course, and we see that a city governed by virtue will look something like the regime of the *Laws*. Yet, some of virtue's elements are hazy, especially because the virtues involve knowledge. It is here that obscurity is most obtrusive because the range and power of knowledge is unclear. What differentiates and connects the *Protagoras'* calculation, the *Meno's* recollection, and the *Charmides'* self-knowledge? What, moreover, are the elements of soul that virtue orders? What are its parts and wholeness? What are the true connections among the pleasures, pains, benefits, and nobility with which it deals?

These questions point to philosophy, for philosophic understanding is knowledge about such matters. They also point to the philosophical way of life, the use of our powers to attempt to know. As we have seen, Socrates suggests that philosophical activity perfects political virtue or more fully reflects its aims.

Although philosophy perfects political virtue, it also radically shakes it. We

see this disturbance in the *Gorgias* and *Euthyphro,* despite the surface recon-
ciliations they effect. Radical philosophical questioning walks along the path
of justice and ethical virtue, but it also lingers at the start in a way that uproots
the path's origin and transforms its conclusion. The philosophical life originates in questions and experiences more telling or general even than fathers'
concerns for sons, and it concludes in an order more general but less restrictive
than legal justice and piety.

In this chapter I make a new beginning by discussing four experiences and
phenomena at the center of Plato's understanding of philosophic inquiry. He
devotes a dialogue to none of these subjects, however, although in some cases
he offers a central or core analysis.

Nature

Socrates often claims to be searching for something's nature.[1] When he examines justice, he seeks what is naturally just; when he or the Athenian and Eleatic Strangers consider forms of government, they look for regimes that are
naturally best. We may say provisionally that what philosophy seeks to know
is nature and what is natural.

Plato's approach sets the course of political philosophy, for its central question is the question of natural justice or right.[2] Hegel, who turned the question
of justice away from nature, still designated his political work with the traditional name. Even those who claim today that natural differences between,
say, men and women are, in fact, constructed, must first have in mind what
would constitute a natural as opposed to a merely conventional difference.

The intellectual turn by Hegel, Nietzsche, and Heidegger away from nature
is not made so completely in practice. The United States is founded on a Dec-
laration that defends our independence by appealing to natural rights, and we
continue to conduct political and legal discussion in their terms. (Of course,
we more frequently clamor for our rights than call them natural.) The Catholic Church and American Catholic intellectuals, moreover, have rediscovered
the natural analysis of politics and ethics that Thomas Aquinas adapted in the
thirteenth century from Aristotle. Questions of abortion, marriage, death, and
genetic engineering have thrust nature and natural right into the foreground
of contemporary political debate.[3]

Nature, natural rights, and natural law, are, therefore, still present in our
politics and in the understanding that underlies our way of life. It is, thus,

especially useful to consider what Plato has in mind by nature. Indeed, natural law was the standard term through the nineteenth century for the truths sought by physics and economics; "physics" transliterates *physis,* the Greek term for nature. So, Plato's quest for the natural is at the core of science or philosophy generally.

Our difficulty is that Plato does not discuss what he means. He wrote no dialogue "On Nature" to rival Aristotle's *Physics.* Nor do his characters examine nature systematically in any dialogue. So, to the usual difficulty of extracting Plato's teaching from the conversations that embody it, we must add the fact that we have no explicit conversation from which to start.

I

I begin by indicating briefly how Plato's view differs from our own everyday notions. First, while we speak of natural rights, Plato thinks about what is naturally just.[4] So, while natural justice may involve serving natural rights, the two differ. In Plato (as we have seen) natural justice does not mean securing the individual rights, or unique authority, of each individual, ignorant or not.[5]

Second, when we discuss "nature," we think primarily of the birds, the bees, and the environment. In Plato, however, the natural as the subhuman is not central. He concentrates on these no more—and indeed, less—than he does on the human.

Third, much of today's discussion concerns birth and death. What is the natural beginning and end of life?[6] Is the difference between men and women natural? Plato is also concerned with natural differences between men and women, and with the training appropriate to them; as we have mentioned, he sees a smaller gap between us than do most of his contemporaries.[7] While some today, under Aquinas' influence, discuss these questions as matters of natural law, however, Plato does not. Natural law is a term Socrates never uses.[8] It is almost contradictory because one element of the natural is to be opposed to the legal or conventional.

II

I turn now to Plato's own, closely related, uses of nature. I consider what he has in mind by bringing together various meanings from several dialogues, attending as necessary to their context, and working toward his leading conceptions.

The natural is distinguished from the artistic, conventional, legal, forceful, violent, and habitual, and from what occurs because of practice and rearing. "You men who are present," Hippias tells Protagoras, Socrates, Alcibiades, and the others in the *Protagoras*, "I hold that you are all kin and relatives and fellow citizens—by nature, not by law. For like is by nature akin to like, but law, being a tyrant over human beings, compels many things through force, contrary to nature."[9] Alcibiades tells Socrates that if those "who practice the things of the city" were educated, one who competed with them would need to practice in order to face them. Because they are so little prepared, however, "why is it necessary to go out of one's way to practice and learn? For I know well that, where nature is concerned, I will get the better of them by far."[10]

The natural, here, is the original or inborn, that which grows, happens, or is present on its own. This self-origination is the quality that most obviously distinguishes natural from artistic and legal things: these result from human producing, making, or establishing. Socrates believes that young Charmides "is not to be withstood" if, in addition to beautiful looks, "in respect to his soul . . . he happens to be of a good nature." "Surely it is fitting," Socrates says, "for him to be such, since he is of your family."[11] He asks Alcibiades whether "it is likely that better natures should come to be in well-born lines or not." "Each person," he tells Phaedrus, "picks out from the beautiful ones his love after his fashion; and he constructs and adorns for himself a sort of statue of that one, as a god for him to honor and celebrate. So, then, those of Zeus seek someone heavenly in soul to be the one loved by them; therefore they look into whether he is in his nature philosophic and capable of leadership."[12]

We can extend this sense of the natural as the inborn and original to the natural as what is already present or, even, always present. "Parmenides, here's how it really appears to me to be," a young Socrates tells him, "these forms stand in nature like patterns."[13] It is primarily this sense, indeed, that leads us today to view nature as the surrounding environment of plants, animals, rivers, rocks, and streams. "Many and great were the floods that occurred in the space of 9,000 years," Critias tells Socrates, Timaeus, and others, "and during this succession of natural disasters the soil was washed down from the high places."[14]

Another sense of the natural is something's unimpeded direction or tendency, its easy motion. What is natural is its normal, undistorted activity or, even, the completion to which unimpeded it is directed and flows, or in which it unfolds. What is natural are the guideposts and (sometimes) guiding ends of activity; what is natural are a thing's own limits. "So if the One hasn't grown by nature, against nature," Parmenides tells Aristotle in the *Parmenides*, "it would have come into being neither before nor after the different things, but at the same time."[15] "All body, indeed, to which being moved comes from outside is soulless," Socrates says to Phaedrus; "but all body to which being moved comes from within itself to itself from itself is ensouled, seeing that this is the nature of soul."[16] "And I myself," he also tells Phaedrus, "am a lover of those dividings apart and bringings together, so that I might be capable of speaking and thinking. And if I consider someone else to have the power to see the things that have naturally grown into one and toward many, I pursue this man."[17]

A third meaning of nature is what characterizes something, what is central, dominating, basic, or essential to it, what the thing is in its very own. "The very nature of the One," Parmenides tells Aristotle, "is surely not the same as the Same." "Could the One have come into being against nature, against its own nature, or is that impossible?" "The one who doesn't pay heed while being punished and taught," says Protagoras, "must be cast out from cities or killed on grounds that he is incurable; if this is so, and given that he is such by nature . . . "[18] "Do you assert," Socrates asks Protagoras, "that this very thing [piety] is by nature of such a sort as to be such as the impious or such as the pious?"[19] "Is anything else the case," I said, "than that nobody willingly advances towards the bad things or towards things he supposes to be bad, nor is this, as seems likely, a part of human nature, namely to be willing to go toward things one supposes to be bad instead of the good things?"[20] "Motion will rest and rest in turn will move, for in the case of both, whichever one of the pair becomes the other, it will compel the other in turn to change into the contrary of its own nature, inasmuch as now it does participate in its contrary."[21]

We can also grasp Plato's complex understanding by considering his statements that something is through or from (*dia*) nature, according to (*kata*) nature, and by (*para*) nature.[22] They reflect nature as an origin or unchanging presence from (or within) which things take place, nature as the basic characteristic according to which something is (or can be) as such, and nature as that by which something moves or develops unimpeded on its own.

III

The next characteristic of nature follows from the main three: nature as a general or pervasive quality that many share, or that binds individuals into one species, class, or type. Something's origin, direction, and, especially, dominant characteristic define and unify: a "nature" is a dominant characteristic or direction that makes things alike or similar. When Socrates asks Laches what courage is, he finally replies, "In my opinion, then, it is a certain endurance of the soul, if one must say about courage what it is by nature in all cases."[23] Protagoras' myth in the *Protagoras* recounts how Epimetheus distributed different powers to different "mortal species." "To some he gave weapons; to those he gave an unarmed nature, he contrived for them some other power to preserve themselves."[24] Being unarmed is an original quality that all in the species share.

Nature's next attribute is (often) to be the correlate of rational understanding. In both medicine and rhetoric, Socrates says in the *Phaedrus,* "one must divide up nature . . . not only by routine and experience but by art." Can one "understand the nature of the soul, in a manner worthy of speech," however, "without the nature of the whole?"[25] In the *Cratylus,* a correct name is one that follows and (thus) speaks or brings out the nature of what it names.

IV

These meanings present several perplexities, especially because they may appear to contradict. The natural, we suggested, differs from art, law, practice, and habit. Yet, art can be guided by nature, education can enhance it, laws and regimes can (to different degrees) imitate natural justice, and while virtue is a natural end, it is rarely fully present.[26] So, what we distinguish from nature need not oppose it, and a nature is not uniform, but allows distinctions of better and worse. Natural characteristics originate without art, moreover, but we also discuss the nature (i.e., the basic characteristics) of any art. The natural development or unimpeded direction of say, man, furthermore, may be what is usual or average for us (say, health, pleasure, and procreation) or what re-emerges after reasonable control weakens (say, tyrannical desire). Yet, the average cannot be the natural simply, because the average often falls short of what is excellent or completes our development (say, strength and beauty, virtue that overcomes pleasure, and immortality that we seek through understanding or fame).[27] Someone, moreover, may have several natural characteristics. Which of them is central, essential, or defining?[28] As we have just seen, our unimpeded (free) direction (say, to seek pleasure) may differ from our truly guiding or basic limit or end (say, virtue and reason, which require education). Nature as reason's object, moreover, differs from that in nature which seems impervious to full rational mastery or comprehension, for example, environing nature, generation, and pleasure.[29]

V

Does Plato have in mind an overarching meaning of nature? One candidate is the natural as one's own or what is most completely one's own.[30] Something's nature is there from the origin, so it is most unavoidably its own, even when it is perfected, perhaps even when one tries to overcome it. A thing's natural course is its very development, what is inherent in its own action, unimpeded or undistorted by what is outside it, that is, by what is not its own.[31] Something's essential or dominant characteristic separates it most fully from what it is not; it defines or contains it most fully as its own self, not as something else. Justice, as the *Republic* tells us, is each thing's doing its own or what nature suits it for.

This view, however, is complicated by the conflicts among the elements of one's own. Nature as origin need not be identical to nature as unimpeded or complete development, or to nature as basic ("essential") characteristic. My original nature as someone who is orderly or rash, for example, is suitably developed toward prudent calm or due speed, that is, toward proper character. It is not natural if it remains merely as it starts. My essential nature as reasonable is fittingly directed to the intellectual life. Although political and intellectual virtues guide my actions as their proper ends, however, they are rarely completely present. The propensity to seek pleasure must be taught to be virtuously controlled by reason; the possibility of true understanding expands and elevates the calculating tendency that is present originally.[32] Even a horse's or sheep's nature, there from the beginning, can be improved (through human training) in speed or strength. What is usually fully present by nature in members of a species, moreover (say, health), differs from what can exist by nature in a few. This difference is most obvious in human intelligence, which defines us as opposed to other animals but is not there fully from our beginning (as our bodily shape is), is more developed and dominant in some men than in others, and would not progress sufficiently were it unimpeded. What most of us are as our very own falls short of the reason and virtue that are also our very own.[33]

If the natural as the original, unimpeded, excellent, and usual (or normal) differ, nature appears to be an ambiguous guide. Indeed, it is an ambiguous guide in still another sense: If someone's nature is to be incorrigible, his nature should be eschewed, not followed or, even, redirected. If a flood's nature is to destroy, we should impede it.

VI

These difficulties point to resolutions or to guidelines that direct us to resolutions. If something's nature is connected to its origin, to what is always there in it even if unrecognized, what is most natural is what is most original, what is everywhere and always present or unavoidable. If something's nature is its unimpeded motion, the most natural is what is most spontaneous or most completely accomplished and independent. If something's nature is what is most basic, essential, dominating, defining, or pervasive in it, the most natural is what is most essential simply. Nature would then be what is most original or ever-present, most independent or complete (or the source, cause, or measure of what is most complete), and most essential or defining. Nature in the fullest sense is not only or primarily the "natural" in each and every fleeting thing, but the most natural things—the most original, pervasive, complete, independent, and dominating (distinct) things. These are the sources of the natural in all things, to the degree that they are present in them.

The elements of something's nature are not obviously coherent, as we just suggested. In the *Meno,* however, Socrates mentions the kinship of "nature as a whole" and in the *Phaedrus,* the nature of the whole.[34] The essence of the whole, the whole as such or on its own, would be (or include) the natural things, taken as a whole.[35] These characteristics of the natural set the direction for what philosophy seeks: cause, form, completion, and power. We can understand something's dominant or pervasive characteristic as its capacity to affect or be affected, or as its limiting form, shape, or look.[36] We can see its origin as its causal genesis.[37] We can see what is always in something as its form, or as its material base.[38] We can see its inherent or unimpeded motion as its effective power, or, in light of its destination, as the goal that sets the limit and path of its genesis, the end that measures and orders it. Forms (looks), fitting measures, limits, ends, and powers especially recommend themselves to Plato as ways to clarify what things are in their natures; a thing's nature is its distinct, pervasive order or form, its articulated causal power, its fitting or unimpeded motion to its completing end.[39] Form, limit, measure, and cause become Plato's objects because they show us what things are and how they occur, naturally.[40]

Wonder

Theatetus tells Socrates (in the *Theatetus*) that he "wonder(s) exceedingly" and "truly get(s) dizzy" about contradictory or impossible statements about a thing's being at once larger, smaller, and equal, and our measuring it. "The reason," Socrates replies, is that "this experience is very much a philosopher's, that of wondering. For nothing else is the beginning of philosophy than this."[41]

If wonder is truly the beginning of philosophical exploration, we would like Plato to examine it. To grasp wonder would be to grasp the origin or principle of philosophy. Plato, however, never subjects it to extended analysis. Philosophy studies nature, but we apparently never find nature apart from particular natures or natural things. Does wonder, similarly, indicate characteristics that can set investigation in motion, while not being found apart from some longing or something questionable?

I

It is useful to begin by discussing our current view. One meaning of the wonderful is the very good or excellent: we speak of wonderful performances, paintings, dinners, events, and times; sometimes we do so ironically. Although we could speak of a wonderful criminal, moreover, we do not. "Wonderful" refers to a very good instance of something desirable or attractive, that is, to something excellent.[42]

Our examples suggest, further, that "wonderful" often indicates a rarely seen excellence, the unusually or exceptionally good. The wonderful violinist is exceptional, as a wonderful meal is not. Indeed, "wonderful" may indicate the rare, remarkable, or unusual even if not desirable, as with an eclipse.

The wonderful can also be impressively large or magnificent, as are the seven wonders of the world. It need not be so vast, however, as wonderful proofs are not. A wonderful proof, rather, is precise and fitting. The impressive and fitting suggest beauty or nobility's connection to the wonderful. Alternately, this connection need not always exist, for a "wonderful" (very good) meal need not be impressive, and a magnificent mountain range may be neither (very) good nor bad.

We also think of a baby or child's development as wonderful. The facts of learning and curiosity, the fit and interrelation of the baby's actions, are wonderful. The very existence of what happens (and the very existence of the child's birth) is wonderful. Here, what is wonderful is the fitting. Moreover, the fit is also wonderful as remarkable. What is remarkable here is the repetition of the fit and development among humans, the presence of this fit when compared with chaos and chance, and its unique existence as one's own, the singular.

The wonderful, thus, is the excellent, the magnificent or perfectly fitting, and the remarkable (or unusual), rare, or unique. The unusual also suggests the wonderful as the surprising, inexplicable, or unaccountable. One asks of the exceptional musician: How did he do that? Or, we think of the return of the seasons as miraculous, or believe it miraculous that one should have this wonderful blessing, this child. The wonderful as remarkable in these cases seems to defy explanation or cannot be captured by it.[43] Perhaps this is especially true of perfection in its singularity here and now.

The wonderful occasions wonder, so we can learn more by considering their connection. To wonder means, first, to be amazed or surprised at the unusual or extraordinary. It is also to admire the excellent (as distinguished from enjoying it.) Surprised admiration points at observant gazing, not using—hence wonder's connection to the theoretical. The pleasure of wonder itself is, like the pleasure of virtue, different from joy in wonderful things that are also excellent. The element of pleasure or attraction in wonder means that it differs from terror at the terrifying.[44]

One wonders not only at something's unusual fit but at its powers, at what it can do.[45] Consider a baby's observing that and how a ball rolls, that and how the amount of one's pushing affects it, and so on. (And, consider our considering.) Here, the wonderful is the surprising power or ability of something as you learn about it by seeing what it can do (sometimes as you affect it). One admires and observes powers one does not take for granted.[46]

We may develop our analysis by exploring further wonder's connection to observing. The thing observed can draw one in, keep one looking. It is fascinating, magnetic. Wondering is simply, compellingly, and admiringly observing and learning about—opening to—the unusual, unexpected, and newly discovered. The unusual here is, especially, an unusual fit (perfection), excellence (power), or singularity. Such wonder can also be at a newly discovered, surprising regularity, as a baby or child wants the same thing shown or read again and again; what is delightfully unusual or unexpected is the predictable fit and similarity.

Wonder as observant recognition of the unusually excellent, impressive, fitting, or singular is connected to reason, for in wonder one sees or hears.

When recognition is uplifted by excellence or beauty, it can be loving or erotic and also, at first, self-forgetting. One can then return to oneself as uplifted (in philosophy or love) but not to possess, use, or control the wonderful. Wonder is not pride. The experience of wonder is an outgoing and (often) uplifting lingering and observing, and the wonderful as the unusual draws (compels) observant exploration and lingering.

Another meaning of to wonder is to question. I wonder why the sky is blue, where she is, how to succeed on the examination, what car to buy, how he does that, how to get there, who is at the door. Here, wonder is: I am not sure, I am asking for help or information, I am curious. Wonder seeks an answer; that is, it seeks an ending of uncertainty, a closing off. Wonder is directed at the unclear or, even, the unaccountable.

How is wonder as questioning that seeks clarification linked to wonder as wide-eyed observing, or lingering in the beckoning unusual? Although ordinary questioning is about the unclear, not about the wonderful in the full senses we are discussing, the unclear or uncertain is a version of the unaccountable or inexplicable. True or full wondering, thus, explores the fully remarkable. Indeed, questioning is not primarily doubting but an impetus toward discovering or, indeed, exploration itself. (Let me continue my questioning, I might say—i.e., my exploring and investigating.) The point is usually to know things better in their own terms or on their own path, not to give an explanation from outside. Even doubting (as not believing) means, let us not stop here, but let us continue to look; there is more to see; we are not at the end. Wonder as questioning can mean exploring, incredulity as seeing more to describe rather than as continuing to be stunned.

To wonder as to question means to explore the unclear, unusual, surprising, unaccountable, or "impossible." Yet, why does one want to know? It can be in order to help, punish, use, and so on. But, one may also merely be curious, as when we wonder what is behind a door or as we see it in a baby's learning. Here, wonder simply seeks to grasp (to explain or clarify in the sense of seeing and describing further and more securely) the unusual. Indeed, wonder may simply seek to grasp something unusual that is also excellent, impressive, fitting, or striking. This is the purest wonder, and also the fullest, if it is about the most wonderful. One wants to see fully, to have missed nothing. This wonder is a clue to, or is, what philosophy is, and reminds one of loving observation of a beloved. It is to explore observantly the highest or most wonderful beings, the most excellent, beautiful, and unusual. Philosophy is considering or knowing these, as such, in their singular, impressive, natures and powers.

II

What can we glean about wonder from what Socrates and others say in the dialogues? Plato's characters mention both the experience of wonder and its object, from which we discern several meanings. They agree with the account we just offered of our understanding, but they do so with different emphases.

Wonder is surprise at the unusual, exceptional, or extraordinary. It also is surprise at the impressive or spectacular, that is, at one instance of the unusual. (For, one can be unusually stupid or cowardly.) Especially here, wonder gapes at or is astounded by the magnificent and, perhaps, admires it. Wonderful things can also be contradictory, odd, or unclear, that is, unusually or surprisingly unaccountable. To wonder, here, is to be struck by the inexplicable. Connected to this is the wonderful as the questionable and wondering as questioning. This is the fourth meaning,

Let me give instances of these observations. When Socrates first sees Charmides, he says: "But especially then he appeared wondrous to me in both stature and beauty, and, indeed, at least in my opinion, all the others were in love with him . . . Now this was not wondrous on the part of us men; but turning my attention to the boys I noticed that none of them . . . looked anywhere else, but all were contemplating him as if he were a statue."[47] When Socrates tries to avoid spending time with Theages, he says he happens "to know so to speak nothing, except a certain small subject of knowledge: what pertains to eros. As regards this subject of knowledge, to be sure, I rank myself as wondrously clever beyond anyone, whether human beings of the past or of the present."[48] Charmides is wondrous, exceptional, perhaps extraordinarily so, in beauty and size; Socrates is exceptional in his knowledge of love. As Alcibiades says in the *Symposium,* "I and many others have been affected in such ways by the flute songs of this satyr here before us. But as to the rest, hear me tell how he is like those to whom I have likened him, and how wonderful is the power he has."[49]

We see especially from Socrates' statement about Charmides, and Alcibiades' about Socrates, how wonder at the extraordinary can shade into wonder at the impressive. "Now one could praise Socrates for many other wonderful things; but whereas for the rest of his pursuits—one might perhaps say the like about someone else as well—what deserves all wonder is that respect in which he is like no human being, neither ancients nor those of the present day . . . unless one were to liken him in himself and his speeches to those I say—to no human being but to silenuses and satyrs."[50] "Why Socrates," Hippias tells him, "you know none of the beautiful things about this. For if you knew how much money I have earned, you would be filled with wonder."[51] "And it is in wonder at these things," Socrates tells Gorgias, "that I have long been asking what in the world the power of rhetoric is. For it manifestly appears to me as a power demonic in its greatness, when I consider it in this way."[52]

Wonder at the unusual, extraordinary, great, impressive, and singular—wonder as being surprised, stunned, astounded, amazed, or (sometimes) admiring—is both connected to and different from the wonderful as the contradictory, or remarkably false, odd, and mistaken. "But what an altogether wondrous speech, if it strips the god of knowing," a young Socrates replies to an argument Parmenides makes about Socrates' suppositions about the ideas.[53] At the end of the *Protagoras,* Socrates creates some "human being" to accuse them of a strange reversal in their argument. "For if virtue were something other than knowledge, as Protagoras was attempting to say, it clearly wouldn't be something teachable. But now, if it will appear to be entirely knowledge, as you are urging Socrates, it'll be a wonder if it isn't teachable."[54] Socrates tells Protarchus in the *Philebus* about an argument that is "wonderful" "by nature" "that just now came up incidentally. That the many are one and the one many is a wonderful utterance, and it's easy to take a stand on either side against anyone who posits either one of them."[55] "By Zeus," Socrates exclaims in the *Phaedo* to Cebes at the end of his life, I

don't even allow myself to assert that whenever anyone adds a one to a one, the one added to the one that was added to has become two, or that the one that was added and the one to which it was added become two by the addition of the one to the other. Here's what I wonder about: When each of the two was separate from the other, then each was one and the pair were not two, but when they come close to each other, this then becomes the cause of their becoming two . . . Nor again can I be persuaded that if somebody splits a one apart, this—the splitting—has in turn become the cause of their having become two. For then this cause comes to be the contrary of the former cause of their becoming two.[56]

As Socrates had said near the *Phaedo*'s start, as he was rubbing his leg while sitting up on his jail bed, "How absurd a thing this seems to be, gentlemen, which human beings call 'pleasant'! How wondrously related it is by nature to its seeming contrary—the painful—in that they're not both willing to be present with a human being at the same time, but if somebody chases the one and catches it, he's pretty much compelled always to catch the other one too, just as if the pair of them—although they're two—were fastened by one head!"[57]

Wonder, here, is at the contradictory or seemingly contradictory and, more generally, at the unusually unclear, what is difficult to know or explain, such as contradictory and diverse statements about similar matters. As we also see, these problems can spur questioning. Echecrates in the *Phaedo* reports that "we kept wondering why, when the trial took place so long before, he apparently died so much later. So why was that, Phaedo?"[58] To "wonder" is to question—the wonderful is the unclear, surprising, or difficult to believe. "Just satisfy my soul about this point that I wondered about in what you just said," Socrates tells Protagoras, namely, "whether virtue is some one thing, and justice and moderation and piety are parts of it; or whether these things that I was just now speaking of are all names of it, being one and the same thing. This is what I still desire."[59] "Do you know then, Theodorus, what I wonder at in your comrade Protagoras?" Socrates asks in the *Theatetus*. "What sort of thing?" Theodorus replies. "All the rest of what he has said pleases me a lot, that that which is the opinion of each this also is for each. But I've been in a state of wonder at the beginning of his speech that he did not say in beginning his *Truth* 'Pig is the measure of all things' or 'dog-faced baboon.' "[60]

We should not force these uses into one meaning, or one leading meaning, but should consider matters patiently. It is significant that wonder ranges from unusual but not extraordinary occurrences, such as the delay in Socrates' execution, to his own extraordinary speeches and actions. It is significant, too, that one wonders at or admires impressive wealth, the impressive colors of the earth, the impressive happenings in a Platonic myth, and the impressive claims to complete knowledge of characters such as Euthydemus. The wonderful as the unusually impressive, moreover, is not identical to the wonderful as the contradictory.[61]

III

We can better understand Plato's view by gathering additional uses. Just after the passage I quoted from the *Philebus*, Socrates distinguishes explicitly between popular and true wonders. Protarchus asks, "Do you actually mean this [about one and many] . . . setting down the same [me] as tall and short, heavy and light, and thousands of others?"[62] "Well Protarchus," Socrates replies, "you have spoken of the popular wonders about the one and many, but virtually everyone . . . has conceded now that one ought not to fasten on things like that." Rather, "whenever . . . someone sets down—not the one as we just now spoke of it, which is of the things that become and perish . . . but whenever someone tries to set down human being as one and ox as one and the beautiful as one and the good as one," Socrates says, " . . . it's in the case of these that we dispute whether there are such monads." These, not the popular wonders, "are the cause of every kind of perplexity" if we do not agree on them.[63]

The intention of Socrates' statement is also visible in the *Symposium.* "Whoever has been educated up to this point in erotics," Socrates recounts Diotima's telling him, "beholding successively and correctly the beautiful things in now going to the perfect end of erotics shall suddenly glimpse something wonderfully beautiful in its nature, that very thing . . . for the sake of which" the "prior labors were undertaken," something "always being and not coming into being, or passing away, something not beautiful in merely some respects at some times to some people . . . but as it is alone by itself and with itself, always being of a single form . . . while all other beautiful things share in it."[64]

So, there can be true wonders, and a nature can be wonderful, here wonderfully beautiful, and, indeed, wonderfully good. "I'm aware of no one yet whose nature is as wonderfully good" as Theatetus', Theodorus tells Socrates. As Socrates says of himself, to Hippias, "I have this one wonderful good that preserves me. I am not ashamed to learn, but I inquire and question and am very grateful to the one who answers."[65]

IV

If we connect these points to our earlier ones, we discern a unified understanding. Wonder, at its peak, would be at or caused by what is at once the most excellent, extraordinary, fitting, magnificent, question worthy, and unaccountable. Such would be the beauty and forms of the *Symposium* or *Charmides,* the limits of the *Philebus,* and the duality of one and many and good and bad of the *Phaedo* and *Philebus.* Wonder at the highest things is an arresting gazing at them and, at the same time, a questioning, an exploration, set in motion by the naturally unusual or deeply contradictory in them—questions of many and one, of the being together of different or opposite things, and of the being or cause of these extraordinary things. Socrates' wonderful good of not being ashamed to learn, of gratefully inquiring and questioning, is itself, as the object of questioning admiration, the key to philosophy and human excellence.[66]

Perplexity

Another phenomenon Plato employs to describe the root of philosophy is perplexity (*aporia* and its derivatives).[67] Perplexity names the experience of confusion, unclarity, or being stymied that demands investigation and continues alongside it.

I

As with wonder, Plato does not discuss perplexity thematically but highlights its importance once explicitly. Meno tells Socrates that "I used to hear nothing else than that you are perplexed and make others perplexed as well. And now . . . you're . . . casting a spell over me so that I've become full of perplexity. In my opinion too you are in every way—if I may be permitted a little joke—in form and other aspects most like that well-known stingray" who makes those who touch it numb, "and I feel a numbness in both my soul and my tongue, and I can't give you any answer." Socrates replies, "I don't make others perplexed while I myself am free of perplexity but above all else I myself am perplexed and in this way I make others perplexed too."[68]

We see from this exchange that to be perplexed is to recognize that one does not know something, in this case, what virtue is. Yet, recognizing one's ignorance does not always inspire inquiry. Perplexity is ignorance in which one initially is numb, but, as opposed, say, to frightened awe, it is ignorance in which one is able to continue inquiring, as Socrates does in the *Meno*. How? By backtracking through a maze and walking through rejected options, by starting again from the beginning, by looking for likenesses or more recognizable instances of what one seeks (as one recognizes in a small word letters hidden in a large one), by experimenting with new opinions about one's object, by thinking about its place within new settings or classes (such as the political community or soul), or by trying to clarify perplexity about perplexity itself.[69] What we do not know is, nonetheless, still present to us in opinions, images, and what we take for granted. So, we always both know and do not know, and can "recollect" and reexamine our beginning on the path that led us to perplexity.

II

Let us now glean what we can from Plato's other uses of perplexity.

"When I was younger," the Eleatic Stranger tells Theatetus in the *Sophist*, "whenever anyone spoke of this present perplexity, that which is not, I believed I understood it precisely—but now you see where we are in the perplexity about it." "Perhaps then," he continues, "with regard to 'that which is' we have no less taken into our soul this same experience, and we say we understand and are not perplexed by it whenever anyone utters it, but this is not so about the other, though we are in a similar state in respect to both."[70]

Perplexity here is the soul's experience of not understanding or knowing.[71] More directly, it is being confused, unsure, stymied, or having a question one cannot answer. "Recently," Socrates tells Hippias, "someone threw me into perplexity during an argument when I was censoring some things as ugly and praising others as beautiful. 'Tell me, Socrates,' he said, 'from where do you know what sorts of things are beautiful and ugly? For, come now, could you say what the beautiful is?' And I, because of my poverty, was perplexed, and I could not answer him properly."[72]

The perplexed numbness Meno reports means to be unable to go forward, to be impeded, to lack the resources to advance. "Aporia [perplexity] is an evil as is likely, that hinders motion and progress," Socrates tells Hermogenes in the *Cratylus*. "So you want us to summon Nicias to the hunt [for courage] if he is in some respect more resourceful than we," Socrates asks Laches. Laches agrees, and Socrates then asks Nicias to "deliver us from perplexity."[73] "And I at least, Hippias," Socrates tells him after a failed argument, "no longer have anywhere to turn, and I am perplexed." Plato presents similar examples in other dialogues.[74]

Perplexity as not understanding (as lacking an answer), and as being without resources to go forward, also is experienced as (or issues in) dizziness, being tongue-tied, or being aimless, inconclusive, wandering. Socrates seeks arguments that do not wander and that can discover the immovable. But the arguments must ultimately stand still alertly, not numbly.

Socrates recounts his own wandering to Hippias: "Some demonic fate, as seems likely, has taken hold of me so that I wander and am always in perplexity, and by exhibiting this perplexity of mine to you wise ones, I am in turn bespattered by you in speech whenever I exhibit it."[75] "Perhaps what is truly a friend escapes our notice," Socrates tells Menexenus in the *Lysis*, "and it may be . . . [that] whatever is neither good nor bad may thus at some times become a friend of the good." "How do you mean?" Menexenus asks, and Socrates replies, " 'Well, by Zeus,' " I said, I don't know, but I am really dizzy myself from the perplexity of the argument."[76]

III

What is perplexity about? What causes it? How do things appear or present themselves so that I do not understand them, can proceed no further with them, wander aimlessly but can eventually go forward?

The first such appearance is contradiction. Socrates is perplexed when friendship seems to be neither of good with good (like with like) or of good with bad (like with unlike). How, then, is it possible? "Do you see then how you are coming around to the same thing?" Socrates asks his comrade in the *Hipparchus.* "Gain appears to be good, and loss bad" (the opposite of what the comrade believes true). "Well, I don't know what to say," the comrade replies. "Not unjustly are you perplexed," Socrates suggests.[77] "For to appear and seem but not to be," the Stranger tells Theatetus in the *Sophist,* "and to speak some things but not true—all these are forever full of perplexity, in former times and now."[78] Indeed, perplexity can be caused by contradiction with convention, as Lysis is perplexed about how to satisfy his desire to join the older Socrates and Ctessipus in conversation.[79]

Perplexity also occurs when an outcome is unacceptable, even if not strictly contradictory. Friendship seems to Socrates and Menexenus to be neither of like for like or unlike for like. This is a difficulty, however, only if friendship in fact exists and there are no possibilities other than these two. As it turns out, Socrates surfaces a third option (a friend may be neither good nor bad); he must do so because friendship's not existing is unacceptable. Socrates and Hippias reach a point in their conversation about beauty such that "the beautiful is not good and the good is not beautiful." But this "is the least satisfactory of all the arguments they have spoken." With the failure to show that the "useful and the powerful to do some good are beautiful," "we no longer have anywhere to turn," Socrates tells Hippias, "and I am perplexed." They are blocked from further movement because they cannot accept something—the disjunction between the good and the beautiful—that might in fact be correct, or illuminating. In any event, because of Socrates' desire to know and ability to suppose, he proves as usual to have more to say.[80]

Contradictory (and sometimes unacceptable) outcomes often involve matters of division and combination that cause perplexity because they present unclear or unsayable distinctions and connections. Dionysodorus asks Socrates in the *Euthydemus* whether he has ever seen a beautiful thing, and Socrates replies that he has, many of them. Are they "different from the beautiful or the same as the beautiful," Dionysodorus then asks. I was altogether "perplexed," Socrates tells us; he replies that they differ from the beautiful, although "each one" has some of it present. Dionysodorus asks how this can be; I do not become an ox by having an ox present. "Are you perplexed?" asks Socrates. "How would I not be perplexed?" Dionysodorus replies, "I and all other men, at what is not."[81] Obscure or nonexistent differences and similarities are the basis here of the unclarity correlated with perplexity. Indeed, Socrates' proposed first step away from Dionysodorus' perplexity is to see that the beautiful is beautiful, the ugly, ugly, the same, same, and different, different.

If one is impeded to the point of numbness or dizzy wandering, one is perplexed. What first leads one down a path that may issue in perplexity? Generally, it is a practical need or an "intellectual" desire to understand. More directly, it is a wish for something good, and the attempt to obtain it. Plato gives several examples of practical perplexity. Crito tells Socrates in the *Euthydemus* that he is perplexed about what to do with his son. His immediate recourse is to consult Socrates, who tells him not to judge philosophy by its paltriest practitioners.[82] Epimetheus, in the myth that Protagoras tells in the *Protagoras,* is perplexed about what to give men so they may defend themselves against other animals. Lysis, as we said, is perplexed about how to join the conversing Ctessipus and Socrates. Perplexities emerge because of a good that is desired or needs to be secured.

These examples point to deeper desires and impediments that underlie their initial expression. Lysis' perplexity is caused by convention (the inappropriateness of the young interrupting or approaching the older), the shame or bashfulness it causes, and a natural reticence it enhances. He overcomes his reluctance through his friendship with Menexenus, who is both bolder and (conventionally) more able to join Socrates and his cousin. Crito "always" experiences perplexity and concern for his son; this perplexity belongs to the ever-present question of how best to live, and the worth of education and philosophy. Seeking something good but elusive causes perplexity about how to achieve it and, then, perplexity about what the good ends truly are. Ends confuse us not least because it is so difficult to discern the difference and unity of the virtues, and the line between philosophic and other education.

IV

Perplexity also has political import. "When Critias heard this and saw me in perplexity," Socrates recounts in the *Charmides,* "then, just as those who see people yawning right across from them have the same happen to them, so he too in my opinion was compelled by my perplexity and was caught by perplexity himself. Now, since he is well-reputed on every occasion, he was ashamed before those present, and he was neither willing to concede to me that he was unable to draw the distinctions I called upon him to make, nor did he say anything plain, concealing his perplexity."[83] Meno, we remember, suggests to Socrates the danger that may come from his sorcerer-like appearance as a numbing stingray. Perplexity is at once a shameful appearance of weakness and a shameful appearance of doubt about things of which one should be certain. Does Socrates truly want Meno to report that Socrates does not know what virtue is?

At the same time, however, not admitting perplexity and, thus, seeking to overcome it dooms one to ignorance and mistake. One believes one knows what one in fact does not and lives half asleep. The merely yawning life leaves no room for the questioning one. Or, one recognizes perplexity but is too ashamed to admit it to oneself, or (as with Lysis) too modest or fearful to overcome it.[84]

V

To clarify one's perplexity about significant matters is to revere the high by seeking to follow or track it truly, and thus to know it. Clarifying perplexity can also be irreverence toward what is believed to be high, for one examines rather than merely obeys. It thus requires courage.[85] When Cleinias blushes at Euthydemus' question about whether the wise or the foolish are learners, and in his perplexity looks toward Socrates, Socrates tells him to be confident and "answer courageously." Lysis interjects and then blushes when Menexenus becomes perplexed in his discussion with Socrates; Socrates' view is that what Lysis said "fled him involuntarily because of his applying his mind intensely to what was being said."[86] Socrates and Laches ask whether Nicias can help them in their perplexity about courage. For, Socrates had just told Laches, "let us remain persistent and enduring in the search, in order that courage herself not ridicule us, because we do not seek her courageously, if perhaps endurance itself is often courage."[87] Courage in inquiry is central to overcoming shame at being unconventional and shame at one's ignorance, for "the good hunter must pursue and not give over."[88] We need intellectual courage to dwell in perplexity and to separate and safeguard what we discover, just as we need it to steel ourselves against fear of conventional reproach and against vanity about what we believe we know.

VI

The clearest response to perplexity is inquiry itself, searching or hunting for what answers the question, resolves the impediment, or reaches the end one wishes. Socrates deals with practical perplexities by stimulating discussion of the goal that drives the question, by defending ordinary justice or developing a higher version of it, by debunking frauds, by seeking teachers, and by encouraging or defending philosophical inquiry as such.[89] Most of these procedures involve further inquiry, and it is especially in Socrates' own philosophical explorations that we see how he deepens and responds to perplexity.[90]

Inquiry in the face of perplexity finds ways around or through impediments but does not pretend that they are absent. Without "digressing and wandering through all things it is impossible to possess a mind that's hit upon the True."[91] Socrates shows impressive, not to say incredible, resourcefulness throughout the dialogues. The *Lysis* concludes with a characteristic example. Socrates sums up the apparent failure of his attempt to discover what friendship is. "I want to count up all the things which have been mentioned, as those who are wise in the law courts do. For if neither the loved ones, nor those who love, nor those who are like, nor those who are unlike, nor those who are good, nor those who are akin, nor as many other things as we have gone through—for I, at least, don't remember any more because of their multitude—if nothing among these is a friend, I no longer know what to say." "But as I said these things," he continues, "I already had in mind to set in motion something else."[92] This display of Socratic resourcefulness is interrupted by the arrival of his interlocutors' attendants, who drunkenly refuse to be driven away.[93]

In general, Socrates deals with a perplexing subject by observing it from all sides, in all ways, and, therefore, beginning to grasp it by seeing its appropriate range, limits, independence, and interdependence.[94]

Laughter

Laughter is another phenomenon central to Plato's understanding of philosophy to which he does not devote a dialogue. What is remarkable about laughter philosophically is that to laugh at things is to know or recognize them, in a certain way. Laughter (as is true of wonder and being perplexed) stems from intelligence, or "noetic" understanding. What, then, does laughter recognize? And, what are we such that we can recognize it?

I

Let us begin with a story that Laches tells about Stesilaus, the man whose art the characters in the *Laches* are observing. "This Stesilaus, whom you saw . . . putting on a display amid so great a crowd and saying the great things about himself that he said—I have seen him elsewhere truly putting on a finer display, albeit unwillingly." When Stesilaus' ship was attacking a transport vessel, he used his distinctive weapon, a combination of a scythe with a spear.

> As he fought, it somehow became entangled in the ship's tackle and held fast. Then Stesilaus pulled on it, wishing to free it, but was not able, and the one ship was passing by the other. So for a while he ran along on the ship, holding onto the spear. And when the one ship passed beyond the other and dragged him along, holding the spear, he let the spear pass through his hand, until he was holding fast to the end of the handle. There was laughter and applause from the men on the transport vessel at the figure that he cut, and when someone threw a stone on the deck by his feet and he let the spear go, then indeed the men on [his] trireme too were no longer able to hold back their laughter, seeing that scythe-spear hanging from the transport vessel.[95]

In Laches' opinion, Stesilaus' study is not worth learning, "for if someone cowardly thought he knew [it], he would be more clearly revealed for what he was," and if courageous he would receive great slanders "if he made even a small mistake . . . for the pretense of such knowledge evokes envy, so that unless he is distinguished from others in virtue to a wonderful degree, it is not possible that someone who claims to have this knowledge should escape becoming ridiculous."[96]

Laches description of Stesilaus' plight shows us most of laughter's central elements, as Plato understands them.

First, laughter is at the pretentious, especially what claims to be better or higher than it is.[97] We laugh at the exposed clay feet of what believes itself high, or at its inadvertent likeness to something it thinks is beneath it.[98] Such pretense, indeed, is the heart of Socrates' brief discussion of laughter, in the

Philebus. He is discussing with Protarchus the possible blending of pleasure and pain, say, in comedies. Envy is a pain in our soul, he suggests, but the envious take "pleasure in the evils" of their neighbors, such as their ignorance. Socrates and Protarchus can on this basis "look at the ridiculous and see what nature it has." Those who are ignorant of themselves opine that they are richer, superior in body, or better in virtue than they are. Of those with such a false opinion, some are strong, some weak. The weak "are incapable of taking revenge"; they are laughed at and ridiculous. Those who can take revenge are frightening: their ignorance is hateful and ugly. So, "in our eyes, weak ignorance has taken as its lot the order and nature of the ridiculous." When we laugh at our envied friends' harmless seeming-wisdom or seeming-beauty, we take pleasure, but our envy is painful. So, Socrates and Protarchus conclude, such laughing blends pleasure with pain.[99]

Laughter is the safe or pleasant recognition of pretense. We recognize it only because we can differentiate true and false, real and fake, and high and low. Laughter recognizes the difference between being and not being wealthy, beautiful, virtuous, or skilled. To recognize pretense, moreover, is to notice that things may seem to be what they are not. We can expose pretense once we see the mere likeness to what is high of what believes itself high. We laugh at the short man whom we discover to be wearing elevator shoes.[100]

Laughingly exposing pretentious attempts is possible only because we recognize imitation and gradation, what seems to be but is not fully. Much that is comic is mistaken identity.[101] Indeed, pretending can be pleasant, as Charmides gracefully and laughingly agrees that he must "persuade" Socrates, that is, pretend that they are equal. We laugh at someone poor who puts on the airs of the rich.[102] Socrates also suggests that someone ridiculous does not know that he lacks what he believes he has.[103] When I laugh at your pretense, I know, and you are ignorant.[104] Laughter depends here on my seeing (and your forgetting) the gap between what is and its imitations or contraries.

We should see that gentle laughter may also involve pretense.[105] It amuses us when a baby toddles awkwardly when learning to walk. He looks like an imitation adult or an as yet incomplete adult. He shows himself as what he tries to be but is not yet. His imperfect attempt is necessary for him to become the real thing. Our laughter here is at the imitation or pretense in an attempt that will soon be successful.[106] We see something similar in the rivalry of young friends, as Lysis and Menexenus laugh about who is more beautiful, and in this way recognize beauty's height or elusiveness even as they seek to claim it.[107]

Does the toddler believe that he is walking fully, not toddling? The young girl who dresses up in her mother's shoes and makeup knows she is only imitating, but we smile or laugh at her encouragingly. Perhaps here we also smile at her seriousness, that is, at the times she seems most to forget she is only playing. She (and the toddler), however, laughs at herself too. Can we not laugh at our own shortcomings or pretenses? Or, even then, are we not also laughing at our self-forgetting, our momentarily ignoring that we merely pretend?[108] Laughter is not merely at what is visibly pretentious (as are Stesilaus and elevator shoes) but also at the self-forgetting (the ignorance) of pretense implicit in so much that we do, and do "seriously." The would-be philosopher should recognize the absurdity in the pretentiousness and self-forgetting of his own pursuit.[109]

We treat the toddler gently because we wish him to succeed. We do not wish to break his spirit or damage his pride. Some laughter encourages, rewards, or stimulates self-knowledge. Ridicule, however, discourages or punishes.[110] Laughing at pretense, indeed, can be close to scorn.[111] This is also important in Plato's understanding. Socrates is afraid he will be ridiculed for studying as an old man the cithara, usually studied by the young.[112] Philosophers generally are mocked for their inexperience in political and judicial affairs and their hapless pratfalls in everyday life.[113] Is such scorn only a punishment for exhibiting pretense or an incentive to overcome it? Ridicule at the arrogant philosopher's pretension is, indeed, properly exercised when he falls into a well while gazing at stars. Socrates' studies, however, seem to be humbly odd, not arrogantly so. They are different more than they are threatening. Different from what? Different from the expected and conventional. Laughter, especially scorn, is not only at what pretends to excellence (and at ignorance of being pretentious) but also at the unconventional (and at ignorance of being so). The outstanding example in Plato is the laughter Socrates knows will be invoked by his suggestion that women should train together with men in the nude. His notion appears ridiculous because it is so unconventional.[114]

Perhaps, however, Socrates' suggestion is ridiculous not just because it violates convention but also because it ignores nature's unruliness? Laughter also occurs when what is natural erupts into the conventional, when we see that the emperor wears no clothes, hear burps and belches from the immaculate and bejeweled, or notice that we can easily mistake a part for a whole, as so often happens by Socratic design.[115] Laughter may even occur at the irruption of the conventional into the natural, when, for instance, people dress dogs in winter fur.[116] Ctessipus ridicules Hippothales for writing (conventional) love poetry that praises Lysis' family, but says nothing distinctive about Lysis himself.

Laughter at the discrepancy between the natural and conventional depends on, and recognizes, the difference between them.[117] Irreverence often intuits the natural and, hence, the limits of the conventional. It is an irruption prior to reasoned argument. Adolescents are capable of reason but not thoroughly conventionalized, so they may be closer than adults to the naturally ridiculous (and erotic)—the cosmopolitan.[118]

The laughing recognition of the difference between nature and convention (and of the merely unconventional) does not mean that nature is always high and convention low. The ridiculous may be the irruption of a natural that is lower than the conventional, that is, lower than the natural height that the convention is conveying—for example, laughing or burping at weddings. Elegant decorum is higher, not lower, than the raucous natural gobbling of the untrained human animal. We may laugh at someone unfrightening who dresses unconventionally simply because he looks strange, but also, perhaps, because he foolishly and pretentiously acts as if he (or humans generally) can do without (one's own) conventions. Sex without the elegance of love is ridiculous or ugly in ways we make more attractive by practicing, observing, or describing it with human refinement.[119] Laughter is often at the unusual on behalf of the naturally or conventionally average, not only on behalf of the fully accomplished as it puts the imitation, the weak, fraudulent, or average in its place.[120]

Laughter at the unconventional is also at conventions other than one's own, the unfamiliar, or simply different. Ridiculing the different is a way to notice and point it out, and also a way to protect one's own. Laughing at something makes it stand out in the peculiarity of its difference, as, say, Stesilaus stands out. But in the ridiculous Stesilaus, we also see what is beyond convention, or transpolitical, in laughter and its objects. Both friend and foe laugh at him. The exposed pretension of his presumed expertise, the comic indignity or ignobility of a pratfall that shows the pretense that lurks in human nobility or independence, transcends the foes, and unites them even as they fight. The visible foolishness of affectation illuminates something beyond convention.[121]

Our ridicule of the unconventionally different suggests the complexity of laughter as recognition. As we suggested, an unusual practice—say, Socrates' continuing childish studies at an advanced age—may be naturally higher than the convention that ridicules it.[122] Recognizing in laughter the emergence of the natural, however, may also see only what is naturally ordinary, lower than many conventions and the natural reverence that these conventions some-times convey. The stupidity of falling into a well shows that it sometimes is good to look down, not that it is best never to look up.[123] Laughter at the pre-tense of exceptional knowledge may mistakenly substitute its own vulgar lim-its for the natural excellence that is the truer standard that shows the pretense to be ridiculous.[124] Even the pretense we expose when we laugh at ourselves may link us more firmly to convention than to nature, when, say, we laugh-ingly expose our incompetence in seeking conventional rewards.[125]

In short, then, laughter is at the pretentious, unconventional, or inept, the usually hidden shortcoming that is now, often suddenly (sometimes surpris-ingly, sometimes expectedly), exposed. Laughter makes difference, ineptitude, or novelty stand out clearly.[126] It is a way we recognize the difference between the real and fake, what is and what imitates, high and low, cosmopolitan and local, unavoidable and conventional, and us and them. This variety in what laughter recognizes mirrors the variety in what we know, and foreshadows philosophical clarifying of what things are. Irreverence allows us to glimpse the natural versus the conventional but does not as such distinguish the natu-rally average, low, and unavoidable from the high, or the absurdity of mere convention revealed by natural disruption (the belch) from the absurdity of nature revealed by a beautiful convention naturally disrupted (the belch), or either from the absurdity of the merely different revealed by clashing conven-tions. Although much laughter deflates or punishes, some also encourages and rewards, because the pretense may not be fraudulent simply but, rather, imi-tatively on the way to excellence or sufficiency, and the difference that amuse-ment notices and protects may be a natural pleasure or grace.

II

Socrates also suggested to Protarchus that we do not laugh (publicly) at the strong or threatening. Our safety in laughing belongs to laughter's being pleas-ant or to the fact that what we see is pleasing. Some ridiculous actions or con-versations please because they are playful; that is, they do not intend to satisfy the serious desire that set them in motion.[127] Playful as well as scornful or gentle laughter exists, for we are amused at the intentionally playful and sometimes (but not always) at someone who unwittingly treats the playful seriously. Con-sider the pratfall that does not actually break the actor's back. Playful actions are those that are not intended to reach their usual end, unlike serious ones, which are. They are also actions we do not perform to meet necessities. They may be frivolous sideshows (or even make-believe attempts) in a serious context—joking while building a house, or threatening victims; usually, they are actions in a context where reaching the usual end is not the point, such as child's play. What is playful as (un)intentionally unserious reveals, and is based on, discrepancies among means, efforts, and ends, that is, on various ways in which we are inept and fall short.[128] Were Stesilaus' weapon the last line to prevent defeat, his pretentious ineptitude would not amuse his shipmates.

Especially ridiculous are actions designed to achieve the opposite of their usual end.[129] Socrates mentions the typical comic device of sneakily pulling out someone's chair, so that he falls rather than sits.[130] (This reveals the pretense in our decorum.) But it is also ridiculous, perhaps even more so, when someone politely pulls out someone's chair, pretending to help her sit comfortably, and then intentionally pulls it out a bit too far, so she flops like a fish.[131] Not only her indignity but your play is funny, as long as there is no real pain or you cannot be punished.[132]

What if you helpfully try to pull out the chair to just the right degree but miss your mark, and your guest goes tumbling? You and he are both laughable, but you (also) are embarrassed or ashamed because you need not and should not have been inept. The father's ineptitude in trying to put a bicycle together by following obscure instructions is funny as inept or pretentious effort, funnier still when someone adds to his ineptitude by designing a piece that cannot fit and we watch him struggle, and funnier still when what looks finished falls apart once driven (because the ineptitude is more complete and the momentary pride—pretension—at success more absurdly punctured.). But if someone is hurt riding the shoddy bicycle or trying to construct it, or if the bicycle suddenly proves necessary but collapses on a trip to a hospital, our reaction changes. The father's failure to assemble the bicycle may cause not only the father's amusing (to us) anger and the mother's amusing (to us) contempt but also the child's tears at failure. If the person at the dinner table is injured in the fall, then the jokester's and audience's laughter is (usually) stilled or turns to anger or regret. Inept or pretentious failure to accomplish the usual goal, and revelation of the pretense of dinner-table decorum, must not be overwhelmed by what (one believes to be) harmful consequences, if pleasant ridicule or laughter are to dominate, rather than anger, chagrin, or shame.

Laughter recognizes the difference between being and seeming, and the eruption of one into the other. It makes manifest what often is hidden or unknown, from many or one. It thus shows us to be both more and less than we hope or are. The human openness it often encourages is lost, however, unless we can preserve what it recognizes. We need reasoned reflection to secure what it reveals. Such reflection requires that we can see much laughter as good or just, not merely as conventionally cruel and surely not as illicitly irreverent.[133]

Conclusion

The four experiences or phenomena that I have discussed here belong to the possibility of philosophy and the philosophic way of life. They display our ability to understand, to see the difference between what is and what appears, and to experience the attraction and, often, the majesty of what is. Dwelling in them, and what they reveal, following them through to the end, distinguishes philosophy from other activities and is central in uncovering the elements of knowledge that we discussed earlier. Knowledge is clarity, precision, and adequacy or sufficiency in the face of, or amid, the wonderful and perplexing.

These phenomena and what they show also appear, in different degrees, in the everyday or co-philosophic world. What is is linked to what seems to be, and does not stand fully apart from it, as laughter shows. What is most completely is linked to other things that are only partially, as we see in the perplexities into which Laches, Charmides, and Meno fall. When the phenomena at the root of philosophy set us on the path of seeking to know simply, they also uncover the pretence and limits to the knowledge that belongs to the arts, virtues, and ordinary calculation.

We examined in Part 1 some of the similarities and differences between philosophic and ordinary understanding of virtue and between philosophic and political, or everyday, aspiration and activity. We now continue this discussion, on the basis of our fuller exploration of the roots of philosophy. In chapter 5, we consider beauty or nobility, a phenomenon we have seen to be at the heart of the unity of the virtues and of their connection to speech, education, and play. Yet, beauty is not itself a virtue. We then explore these unities and differences still further, from the standpoint of the *Republic*'s emphasis on the good, and its understanding of the connection between the philosophical and political ways of life.

CHAPTER 5

Beauty and Nobility

To develop our understanding of Plato's view of philosophy and of virtue, we will turn to the question of nobility or beauty. For, virtue is above all noble, and philosophic wonder has the magnificent and fitting among its objects.[1] The phenomenon of beauty is a central link between intellectual and ethical excellence.[2]

The *Greater Hippias*

Beauty is central in several dialogues (the *Phaedrus* and *Symposium,* for example) and discussed revealingly in others. Only in the *Greater Hippias,* however, is it explicitly Socrates' chief subject. I therefore begin with the *Greater Hippias* and then consider Plato's view of beauty generally.

I

Socrates starts by exclaiming to the "beautiful and wise" Hippias that it has been a long time since he has come to Athens. Hippias replies that he has had no leisure; his city Elis always sends him as an envoy, most often to Sparta.

What, then, caused those named wise in the past—Pittacus, Bias, Thales, on down to Anaxagoras—to hold back from politics? Hippias replies that they lacked the power and prudence to succeed sufficiently at both the common and private. By Zeus, Socrates concludes, the sophists' art has progressed, just as have the other crafts: Bias would be as ridiculous today as Daedelus.[3] Hippias agrees, although he claims that he usually praises past men more than present ones, fearing the envy of the living and the wrath of the dead.[4] Socrates finds Hippias' thinking and naming to be "beautiful." "Gorgias and Prodicus too," were public envoys, made display speeches, associated with youths as Protagoras did, and earned more money than any craftsmen. The men of the past, however, neither earned money nor exhibited.

Hippias replies that Socrates knows nothing beautiful about this. He has earned more money (which he gave to his father, who was filled with wonder at it) than any other two sophists. That Hippias earns so much money while Anaxagoras lost his, Socrates replies, is a beautiful proof of the wisdom of today's men as opposed to their predecessors. But, "tell me this": "from which city have you earned the most money?" "Clearly it is not from Sparta where you have gone most often?"[5]

I A

Unlike conversations others force on Socrates, he initiates this one. Why? One reason is to learn something from Hippias. What could this be? Perhaps Socrates also wishes to teach Hippias, to perplex or deflate and thus neutralize him as a rival for students, and to control the political dangers that flow from his naiveté.[6]

Socrates' question about Sparta bypasses other topics he easily could have discussed. He might have asked whether money not used well is worth possessing.[7] Perhaps, however, Hippias loves money too much to question its worth. He might have asked what makes an art an art or what constitutes progress. This question may be too general for Hippias. Socrates therefore asks a question whose answer proves to upset Hippias' assumptions about the easy accord among private benefit, public benefit, and progress in sophistry.

II

The "wonderful" fact is that Hippias earns no money in Sparta despite his frequent visits there. No one buys or allows him to sell. Why not? Hippias agrees with Socrates that his wisdom improves virtue, that the Spartans desire virtue for their children, that they are wealthy, and that (in Hippias' view) they cannot educate better than he. Nonetheless, he cannot persuade them that he, rather than they, could advance their sons' virtue. "It is against ancestral tradition for the Spartans to change their laws," he says, "or to educate their sons contrary to what is customary."[8] Is it, thus, against their tradition to act correctly? No, Hippias replies, it is not lawful for them to employ foreigners.

Hippias agrees that law is set down to help cities but harms them if set down badly. So, are not the law and lawful mistaken when the good is mistaken? Hippias concedes to Socrates that this is true in "precise" speech but not in the many's customary usage; he and Socrates agree that those who know the truth consider the beneficial to be the more lawful. If Hippias' educating is more helpful than the local one, therefore, it is more lawful for Sparta's sons to be educated by him than by their fathers. Hippias agrees, "for you seem to be stating the argument to my advantage, and there is no need for me to oppose it."[9]

Socrates continues. Why do the Spartans praise and listen to Hippias? They do not put up with talking about "the things which you know most beautifully, matters concerning the stars and events in the heavens," geometry, and calculations "since many of them, so to speak, don't even know how to count," or about the "harmonies and letters," which Hippias "among human beings knows how to distinguish most precisely." Rather, Hippias says, they enjoy hearing about the generation of heroes and human beings, the founding of cities, "and, in sum, the entire account of ancient things." So, Hippias has "been compelled to learn completely and practice all these sorts of things." He recently "gained a great reputation there regarding beautiful pursuits by describing in detail what a young man ought to pursue." He has "a beautifully constructed speech" that he shortly will exhibit in Athens.[10]

II A

This remarkable conversation shows us the gulf between science or wisdom and law or tradition, and indicates Hippias' ignorance of this gulf. Law is truly lawful only if it is good. But legislators do not (always) know what is good. Some or most laws, therefore, are not true law. Such precise knowledge of what is truly lawful, however, differs from customary use. For, in practice, we treat as legal whatever a city promulgates and enforces. Knowledge progresses, moreover, but law is ancestral. A Hippias who learns about numbers, shapes, letters, and harmonies is cosmopolitan, furthermore, while those pleased to hear stories of ancient foundings favor local custom.

Socrates does not press Hippias about this gulf. He does not explore the difference, say, between merely knowing what is good and securing it through enforced law.[11] Rather, he hints at force by suggesting that Hippias, who is "compelled" to practice what Sparta wants (for, Elis needs to send envoys there), would recite the list of Athenian archons if Spartans happened to enjoy this.

Hippias does not see that artistic progress puts in question not just old techniques but also ancient laws and foundings. He does not reflect about Sparta's striking contempt for the liberal arts. And, he reduces to a matter of "precision" the difference between what we customarily treat as law and truly beneficial law—that is, he treats them as fundamentally equivalent.[12]

One reason Hippias does not wonder about these splits is because he is so conventional or pious.[13] He does not recognize a difference between Spartan virtue and the virtue he himself teaches "beautifully." Although he laughs at the old sophists, he gives his money to his father. He believes the good is what is advantageous for him or his own. He thinks that what is wonderful about money is having large amounts of it.

Hippias is not perplexed by the gaps between Sparta and the sophists, the ancient and the beneficial, and law and advantage. Perhaps, then, it is fruitless to explore these questions with him. About what, then, can he be questioned? How might Socrates arrange that Hippias' obtuseness remains harmless? Socrates fastens on the noble or beautiful. Hippias sees that the Spartans are preeminent in virtue (nobility) and also capable of hearing beautiful displays. The "beautiful and wise" Hippias does not understand his "wisdom" and its political effects. Perhaps however, he understands the "beautiful."

III

Socrates turns the conversation by mentioning a perplexity into which "someone" threw him.[14] Socrates praised some things as beautiful and blamed others as ugly. When asked "what the beautiful is" he was perplexed; he could not answer. He expects that the wise Hippias can teach him sufficiently and precisely "what is the beautiful itself," so he will not be ridiculed.

Hippias argues that this will be a "small" piece of learning and agrees to let Socrates, imitating this "someone," ask questions and raise objections to what Hippias says. They agree that the just are just by justice, the wise are wise by wisdom, all good things good by the good, and all beautiful things beautiful by the beautiful, as something that is. So, what is the beautiful? Hippias answers that "a beautiful maiden is beautiful." Yet, are there not beautiful mares (as even a god says) and lyres? Hippias agrees but objects to Socrates' spokesman's next example, the pot. The man is "vulgar, taking thought for nothing but the truth." Nonetheless, Hippias sees that if a pot is smooth, round, beautifully fired, and molded by a good potter, "even this utensil is beautiful when it is beautifully made."[15]

"As a whole," however, the pot is not beautiful compared to the maiden or mare. As Socrates quotes Heraclitus, 'the most beautiful ape is ugly compared to the class of humans.' The most beautiful maiden or wisest man, however, would appear like an ape when compared to the class of gods. So, when asked about the beautiful, Hippias answers with something no more beautiful than ugly. Hippias agrees that none would contradict that "the most beautiful maiden is ugly when compared with the class of gods."[16]

Socrates reminds Hippias that his answer would have been correct had he been asked "what is both beautiful and ugly." "But what is the beautiful itself by which all other things are adorned and appear beautiful whenever this form becomes present in a maiden or mare or lyre?" This leads Hippias to his next answer: the beautiful is gold.

III A

Socrates' question about beauty is strange because it presumes a similarity or identity among beautiful things other than their name, "beautiful."[17] If girls, mares, pots, gods, and monkeys are so far apart, however, why should their beauty be similar or identical?[18] Socrates' question is also odd because by asking for "the beautiful" itself he rejects the possibility that beauty consists of all beautiful things, or all outstandingly beautiful things. Ordinarily, however (before one becomes sophisticated), one might answer a question about what "the beautiful" or beauty is by pointing to someone pretty, as one indicates what a tree is by pointing to several of them or to one that stands out. (Hippias initially sees no difference between saying what is beautiful, i.e., pointing out beautiful things and saying what the beautiful is.)[19] If Socrates pestered someone about pain, the temptation would be great to twist his arm. Why does the beautiful face that launched a thousand ships not tell us what beauty is, or bags of money what wealth is? Socrates looks for a "precise" answer, but Hippias' answer is in its way quite precise. It is a precision, moreover, that anyone can accomplish, because Hippias does not claim special knowledge. Socrates apparently seeks a "beauty," however, that is precisely visible to a knowledge that is not ordinary. What kind of knowledge can this be?

III B

Looking at someone beautiful surely is a clue to discovering beauty. For, what could beauty be without beautiful instances? Nonetheless, what Hippias does not see is that calling the beautiful a beautiful girl overlooks what distinguishes her beautiful characteristics from her other features, and that it fails to connect her beauty to other beauties.[20] The beautiful is what is distinctively beautiful in everything beautiful.

Socrates' discussion with Hippias also suggests the significance of the difference between the generally and the outstandingly beautiful. Hippias' view that pots are less dignified than women or horses and, therefore, less beautiful is, within limits, compelling; after all, a museum director who saves his prettiest pot in a fire while letting his homely secretary burn is mad. Yet, to risk only his own life to save his exquisite pot is almost noble. Hippias' definition shows that in grasping beauty we must account for outstandingly beautiful things, and Socrates' "vulgar" example shows that we must also grasp the beautiful even in the low. Indeed, Socrates unobtrusively points out general characteristics that make a pot beautiful. Beauty is or accounts for both the most beautiful and most generally beautiful things.[21]

Hippias implicitly distinguishes what is whole—a girl or mare—from what is not—say, something we use only for an external purpose. Indeed, a pretty girl is not (only) pretty for some use or because she is beautifully made but is beautiful as herself and, thus, not so far from "the beautiful." Is the beautiful itself a whole, or is it something partial and dependent? Is beauty present in what we use only because it is present in the beautiful whole to which use belongs? In what way is beauty a cause, that is, that "on account of which things are beautiful?"[22] Hippias readily agrees that we can rank species, with the most beautiful girl appearing ugly when compared to the gods. If beauty itself is, how does it permit its "appearance" so that a beautiful girl can appear both beautiful and ugly? Hippias is ambiguous (when he ranks what is beautiful) about whether he is comparing classes to classes or classes to individuals. Can the most beautiful pot be more beautiful than an ugly girl, or the wisest or most beautiful human wiser or more beautiful than some gods?[23]

IV

Hippias' second answer to the question of beauty is gold: a thing that had appeared ugly is "made to appear" beautiful when adorned with gold. They agree, however, that although Phidias is a good craftsman, he made Athena's face from ivory, not gold, and the middle of her eyes from stone. These, too, are beautiful; stone is beautiful "whenever it is fitting" and ugly whenever it "is not fitting." Hippias agrees that "whatever is fitting to each thing makes each thing beautiful" but does not quite concede that ivory and gold must be fitting to be beautiful. They do agree, however, that a ladle made from fig wood is more fitting for a pot of soup than a golden ladle is.[24] If the fig-wood ladle is more fitting than the golden one, however, it is more beautiful, so gold is not more beautiful than fig wood.

IV A

Hippias' second answer declines from his first: gold has neither the soul nor the independence of the beautiful girl. His answer is not altogether foolish, however, for he takes literally Socrates' suggestion that they are searching for "the beautiful itself by which all other things are adorned and appear beautiful whenever this form becomes present."[25] Hippias allows us to see the common sense or literal meaning of some characteristics of Socrates' ideas. Whatever the beautiful is, it can be present in what we make and adorn; that is, it can be added to or brought out from this.[26] Although Hippias includes adornment and appearance here, he forgets what Socrates has said about form and in-itself-ness.

Hippias is reluctant to reduce gold and ivory's beauty to their being fitting and useful. Indeed, can we not see that gilding beautifies furniture's appearance even if it adds nothing to, or detracts from, its use? We do not smash lovely old china merely because it is not dishwasher safe. The beautiful cannot be reduced to the useful, or what is fit for use. It is also not equivalent to what is fitting for (or pleasant to) our sight; this view of beauty does not capture a whole that stands beautifully alone. The beautiful girl's parts may fit, but her beauty (her looks) also belongs to her striking independence, completion, separateness, form, and vivacity, the whole that shapes and contains the parts. Seeing her as useful, moreover, is not the only or most immediate way of seeing her. Gold is formless and obviously not the only beautiful thing, but it, too, strikes and pleases independent of its use, and often independent of its fit. There is a reason we use gold and ivory when we make beautiful things.

V

Hippias now tries again: "You seem to me to be seeking . . . some sort of thing that will never appear ugly to anyone anywhere." "Certainly Hippias," Socrates encourages him, "and now you comprehend beautifully." Hippias' answer is that it is "most beautiful" for a healthy, wealthy, and honored old Greek who has beautifully celebrated his parents' funeral "to be beautifully and magnificently buried by his own offspring."[27] Socrates praises Hippias for his good intention—unlike the clownish sophists Euthydemus and Dionysodorus, the foolish Hippias is earnest—but claims that his unyielding objector will mock them and beat Socrates.[28] (Athens penalizes unjust beating, so Hippias will, without a trial, accept Socrates' account of this beating's justice.) For, they are asking about the beautiful itself that inheres in everything in which it becomes present such that the thing—stone, wood, human, god, every activity and all learning—is beautiful. They are asking what beauty itself is, what is beautiful for all and always—past and future, too. And, despite Hippias' claim, Achilles and others born from gods were in fact buried earlier than their forbears. Hippias claims that such talk (perhaps even in response to another's question) is disrespectful. He then says that he does not include in his answer gods, their children, and some heroes. For them to bury their forbears would be "terrible, impious, and ugly." So, it turns out that the burial Hippias said was beautiful is sometimes ugly, and is not beautiful for all. The objector's reproach is just: Socrates has not said what beauty is.

V A

Hippias' third attempt to say what is beautiful fails "even more laughably" than the first two, perhaps because it is the most pretentious. Yet, his example also advances the discussion, for he is now considering what is noble or reputed to be noble, not only what is pretty. He himself, however, does not distinguish virtue from the actions (proper burials) associated with good reputation. Is not, say, courage always beautiful, even if courageous actions vary, and courage is not the only beautiful thing? Indeed, some beautiful things (say, virtues of character) come closer than others to being beautiful in all times and circumstances, although they are not everything that is beautiful, nor (as human) "always." The beautiful is beautiful for all beautiful things, the beautiful is always beautiful, and the beautiful is beautiful and nothing but beautiful or, at least, never ugly.

Plato subtly develops these points in the colloquies about Athens' justice and the gods, as they bring to mind the earlier colloquies about Sparta. Justice is perhaps treated as a virtue, or as a source of virtue, but Hippias does not call virtue beautiful, let alone "the" beautiful.[29] Virtue as a cause of reputation, not virtue itself, is Hippias' horizon. He believes that those with wealth, health, and honor deserve a beautiful and magnificent burial. Indeed, Hippias does not call the soul noble or even mention the soul, although it is an obvious link between just punishment, burial, and reverence.

Hippias again shows us his fear of the gods or of a reputation for irreverence. He does not question gods' characteristics, as Socrates does through the alter ego who interrogates him.[30] Socratic punishment for, and anger at, foolish answers—his self-punishment for believing he knows what he does not—replaces punishment for impiety. Beauty is always; it replaces or supplements the gods, and searching for it vaults the nobility of the soul beyond Spartan nobility. Hippias falls far short of this.

VI

Hippias has exhausted his inventiveness or Socrates' patience by giving such "naïve and easily refuted answers," so Socrates now tells him that his alter ego sometimes takes pity and makes suggestions: Is the beautiful (or anything else he inquires about) such and such?[31] Did they, perhaps, catch hold of something when they said that gold is beautiful for the things it fits? They should "consider whether this very thing, the fitting, and the nature of the fitting itself, happens to be the beautiful."[32]

They do not, however, directly explore what the fitting is. Rather, Socrates asks whether the fitting makes things in which it is present appear beautiful, or be beautiful. After saying "both," Hippias chooses appearance, for suitable clothes make even the laughable appear more beautiful.[33] The fitting, however, would then deceive about the beautiful, Socrates says, and he reminds us that they seek that by which all beautiful things are beautiful, just as all large things are large by what exceeds, "whether they appear so or not."[34]

Hippias then suggests again that when the fitting is present it makes things both be and appear beautiful. It is impossible that beautiful things not appear so "when that which makes them appear so is present." Yet, Socrates reminds him that really beautiful laws and pursuits are neither reputed nor always appear to be beautiful to everyone. Privately and in cities, strife and battle are "most of all about these things." So, if the fitting makes things beautiful, it does not also make them appear so, and if it only makes them appear to be beautiful, it is not what Socrates and Hippias are seeking. "The same thing would never have the power to make things both appear and be either beautiful or anything else."[35] Given the choice, Hippias again says that it seems to him that the fitting makes things appear beautiful. So, they once more have failed to recognize the beautiful.

VI A

Socrates elevates the conversation by suggesting that the beautiful is general, not something particular, such as a girl or a burial. His choice of the fitting as a central element of the beautiful is not arbitrary, for it stems from Hippias' earlier remarks about gold.

We are so used to generalities such as "the beautiful" that it is easy to forget their oddness. The fitting and, especially, the "nature" of the fitting, however, are commonsensically less beautiful or desirable to a lover of beauty than the beautiful girl, golden portrait, or Mozart symphony that he immediately pursues or enjoys.[36] Socrates does not suggest here (and only indirectly suggests earlier) that "the beautiful" is itself the most remarkably beautiful of all. If it is not, however, how could its presence beautify the most beautiful things?[37]

This issue of the being, or beauty, of beauty underlies Socrates' distinction between making things be beautiful and appear to be beautiful, and the complexity of this distinction. If beauty does not make things look beautiful, after all, how could we recognize it? In what way, moreover, could it cause the beauty of the visible, or even what is beautiful to the mind's eye? It is difficult to conceive a "beautiful" face that never appears beautiful. Indeed, Socrates has said earlier that the beautiful is that "by which all other things are adorned and appear beautiful whenever this form becomes present."[38]

Perhaps, however, true beauty can appear but need not, as a dark room or veil hides a naturally beautiful body, not only a cosmetically improved one. The appearance of the true is impossible without the true but not guaranteed by it; lighting and perspective are to some degree relative to us. We can blot the large sun with the small thumb. But, then, what appears may be truly, not fraudulently beautiful, even though it appears dimly. The distortion is not caused by what is but is inseparable from (knowing) what is, in all but the truest light, if even there.[39] Indeed, it is unclear how anything could appear beautiful unless it presents something of the truly beautiful. Cosmetics must know enough of what it imitates to make the face or body appear to be what it is not.[40] Even the merely apparent beauty of "beautiful" things may draw us to them or beautify us, as the mind or heart is (somewhat) ordered or elevated by the apparently beautiful girl, piece of music, or good reputation. The beauty that arises from exercise and health is better than what arises from cosmetics and adornment, but it is better (truer) mostly because it is healthier (more truly caused and connected to other goods) and more lasting, and not so much in terms of the immediate instance of beauty itself. Yet, seeming to be healthy but in fact being ill, is far from health. Beautiful clothes can adorn an ugly body. The noble reputation for virtue—fame—is for a while outstanding even if on false premises, but it does not form the soul nobly or assure noble action. The truly and seemingly beautiful are different, a difference more basic as one moves from body to virtue (soul) to thought, but they are closer than the seemingly and truly good. The closeness of seeming and being is one reason the noble is so contested.

We may explore this matter in another way. When something beautiful appears to the eye, ear, or mind, it seems complete, but, especially to the artist or trainer, its shortcomings or imperfections are also evident.[41] A beautiful girl is and is not beautiful. Beautiful things—noble things—are contentious because they show themselves in practical affairs, where merely being reputed to be excellent brings the external rewards of being excellent.[42] Nobility cannot be in practical affairs without being distorted, and because beauty has much of its power practically, it will indeed be distorted. "Beauty" can perhaps appear in its plain truth to the mind's eye, but its plain truth involves appearance, complexity, and distortion.[43] The total disjunction of the true and false is false.

VI B

We should examine further why beauty and the fitting differ, because, despite Socrates' discussion, fit, proportion, and suitability may seem to us to define beauty adequately. One difficulty is that a beautiful or noble fit differs from the fit of just acts; it is fitting but not (always) noble to be punished, and suitably keeping contracts is too ordinary to be beautiful.[44] So, not all that fits is beautiful.

Moreover, not all that is beautiful can be captured by how things fit. A well-proportioned roach is not beautiful. The balance, suitability, or lack of excess in something's parts—what we see as its beautiful fit—belongs to but does not altogether define the thing's power, form, independence, and end. The parts' own powers, not just their fit, contribute to the whole: the independent or striking beauty of gold is necessary for gold to be applied fittingly. As we have said, the well-fitted parts of the pretty girl do not fully capture her striking and containing shape, limit, form, vivacity, or independence. The beauty and action of the whole contains, forms, brings out, and awakens the (excellent) parts: to be beautiful is not simply to be well fitted. "Beauty" does not merely fit things together but brings them forth in their active presence.[45]

The perfection and completion of the usual beautiful whole, furthermore, is not fully independent of an end or good external to it.[46] Beautiful girls are destined to belong in couples, and well-contained teams are oriented to victory. The fit in something beautiful is set in motion by its ends, and if the end is trivial or base, something's fit and, indeed, the whole that contains it, is not beautiful. The precisely organized burglary is not noble. The nature of the fitting, furthermore, does not directly account for the element of splendor and magnificence in what is beautiful, for the magnificent action fits together resplendent powers. The beautiful involves a certain splendid excess, parts that strain beyond their fit, or a resplendent whole whose independence is itself beyond mere fit or use.[47] The parts of a flea fit together, so in seeking to understand beauty the flea is no more to be sneezed at than the smooth pot of perfectly peppered soup. But the flea is not splendid, magnificent, pleasurable, or choiceworthy.

This discussion does not tell us fully why the fitting is Socrates' example here of the gulf and connection between being and appearing to be beautiful. Perhaps what fits is easier to counterfeit, undetected, than the simplicity of beautiful gold, or even a beautiful woman. The complexity of the fitting may permit deception and mistake more easily than does the directness of what is striking.

We sum up as follows. The fitting is not equivalent to the beautiful because much that is fitting is not beautiful; the fitting as beautiful needs to be distinguished from the fitting as (merely) useful, just, or precise. There can be little beautiful about a key that fits the lock to a jailer's cell, or a justly applied dose of hemlock. Moreover, the beautiful is not only the fitting. The beautiful as fitting also needs to be aligned with the beautiful as resplendent, magnificent, uplifting, striking, independent, rare, grand, and pleasant—what Hippias may have in mind with his beautiful girl, and, surely, with his magnificent burial.[48] More generally, the beautiful as the fitting leads us to wonder how the beautiful can be present in, and therefore connect as beautiful, everything beautiful, and at the same time allow beautiful things to be distinct in their independence or attractiveness.

VII

Socrates still hopes "that whatever the beautiful *is* will become completely *apparent*."[49] Hippias claims that he could tell it to Socrates "more precisely than total precision" were he to "go into seclusion for a short time and consider it by myself." Socrates claims that Hippias' talking big will cause the beautiful to be angry and flee still more; "yet there is nothing in what I am saying. For you (Hippias) will find it easily when you are alone. But, before the gods, find it in my presence. Or if you wish seek it with me as we were doing just now and if we find it that will be most beautiful."[50]

Before Hippias can agree or disagree to "contemplate now what the beautiful seems to you to be," Socrates (not his alter ego) suggests another hypothesis. "Let this be beautiful for us: whatever is useful." Beautiful eyes "are not those that seem to be such yet do not have the power to see, but those which do have that power and are useful for seeing." With whole bodies, running or wrestling, living things, utensils, vehicles, instruments, pursuits, and laws, we call beautiful the useful one, for "how," "in relation to what," and "whenever" it is useful, looking at "how each of them by nature" is made or established. Hippias agrees and is especially vehement about Socrates' next assertion, that "the useful, more than anything else, happens to be beautiful." Power is beautiful and its lack ugly, because a thing with the power to produce something is useful. Politics especially bears witness to this, Hippias claims, "for in politics and in one's own city the powerful is most beautiful of all, but the powerless most ugly of all."[51] And "because of this," Socrates continues and Hippias agrees, wisdom is "most beautiful of all and ignorance ugliest."

The first difficulty now emerges. We do many more bad things than good. Surely, the power to produce what is bad is not beautiful. Perhaps then their "soul wanted to say" that the beautiful is "the useful and powerful for doing something good," that is, that the beautiful is the "beneficial." There is a difficulty here, too, however. What does something is the cause, so the beautiful would be a cause of the good. The cause, however, differs from what it causes. What does something is one thing, and what is done by it (e.g., that which comes into being because of it) is another. The beautiful is "in the form of some sort of father of the good," and we are serious about beautiful things such as prudence because their offspring, the good, is serious. But, then, as the cause is not the caused, or the father the son, the beautiful is not good, and the good is not beautiful. This is unsatisfactory: Hippias and Socrates (he says of himself) are once again perplexed.

VII A

What are we to make of this argument? It begins by saying that the useful is beautiful, acts as if this is equivalent to saying that the beautiful is the useful, and concludes by treating the useful and powerful as altogether different from the good and, therefore, (presumably, although unsaid) as not the beautiful. Earlier, we heard that gold could not be the beautiful because it is unfit for a useful ladle. Here, Socrates begins by implicitly taking this reduction of fit to utility and generalizing: the useful is (the) beautiful. On reflection, Socrates' view is strange, for is not the lovely but useless rose more beautiful than the manure that helps it to grow? Not everything beautiful is useful, and not everything useful is beautiful. Socrates himself, however, does not proceed by directly bringing out the limits (and suggestiveness) of the view that the useful is the beautiful. Rather, he proceeds indirectly, by considering cause and caused, means and end, and power and result.

We should note that Socrates emphasizes utility as function. (An eye is "used for" seeing in the sense that its power is to see. It functions beautifully or virtuously by seeing well.) He does not here differentiate such use from utility considered as a means to a good end (as a needle helps to sew a coat.) Rather, he basically treats the beautiful as a power in a thing or action, the hammer's hammering or nailing, not its being a means for the chair it helps build. We also note that, on this understanding, the same entity could be both good and beautiful, both end and power, or means. Pace Socrates, running, and the healthy whole body (his beautiful means) could cause good in each other (depending on which is the end), as virtuous acts and habits cause each other. Moreover, an eye that sees perfectly (and therefore may cause a good such as success in war or a hunt) might, nonetheless, look less beautiful in one face than another or look less beautiful than another eye that also sees perfectly. Plato's discussion suggests, but does not work through, the complex connection between the beautiful and the good, and their assimilation to and separation from each other. He especially hints at but avoids the duality of wisdom and politics, for prudence may serve politics, but using the mind beautifully may be its own end.

Another feature of this section is to recall again the earlier discussion of Sparta. Nothing useful can be fully beautiful unless it secures the truly good. Are wisdom, wealth, reputation, tradition, or strength the truly noble means, or is one the true end for which we use the noble? Hippias perhaps thinks that wealth is the end and that the means or powers that cause it can plausibly be split from it.[52] In many of Socrates' examples, however, the goods or ends are not merely produced by externally useful means but also inhere in the functioning or activity that beautifully brings them about. Law is a useful external means to some ends, such as wealth, but it also establishes, belongs to, or helps form the vivacity of others (such as justice). The whole body is involved in running, and the mind belongs to (and is not a means separable from) its active thinking or discovering.

As Socrates does when he discusses the fitting, he promotes confusion and perplexity by separating and combining plausibly, but tendentiously. Something we use to produce what is bad is called ugly, but why should this be if (as he claims here) cause and caused can be split so completely? If they are not split, however, how can we determine the beautiful on its own, apart from the good?

Hippias is not satisfied to say that the beautiful is not good. He does not notice the differences between the claims that some beautiful things are good (or some good things beautiful) and all beautiful things are good (or all good things beautiful), nor does he examine the relation among such things and "the" beautiful (and "the" good), the object of their search. Rather, his dissatisfaction is caused by disjunctions he believes false among (his own) "wisdom," power, reputation, and wealth. But, he again has nothing to say, so Socrates must "come up with something" to turn them away from their perplexity.

VIII

"If we should give this answer to that bold fellow [the objecting alter ego]—'O well-born one, the beautiful is the pleasant that comes through hearing and through sight'—don't you suppose we could check him in his boldness?" "Whatever makes us delighted [through hearing and sight] is beautiful." Hippias agrees: "you are saying well what the beautiful is."[53]

Socrates asks whether beautiful pursuits and laws "are beautiful by being pleasant through hearing and sight" or through another form. Hippias suggests that it is through another form. Socrates then tells him that the objector is "the son of Sophroniscus" before whom he is ashamed to pretend, to say things without examining them, and to say that he knows what he does not. Socrates, nonetheless, presses the original argument: it also will prove perplexing.

Food, drink, and sex are pleasant, but humans (and Hippias) are ashamed to call the pleasure of sex beautiful, because it is ugly; we do it so no one sees us. So, it is (indeed) the pleasant things through sight and hearing that are beautiful. Yet, these do not differ from other pleasures in respect of pleasure itself, nor because of hearing or of sight as such (which can be unpleasant.)

What, then, is the "beauty" that differentiates the pleasures of the senses so that each one and both of two (hearing and sight) are beautiful, but the others are not?

Socrates then, in his own name, begins to discuss commonality.[54] Hippias agrees that "the pleasures of sight and sound have something the same which makes them be beautiful, something in common which exists for both of them in common and for each privately." But, he says, only someone inexperienced in the nature of things would believe Socrates' suggestion that both are (or are affected by) that which neither itself is (or undergoes). Socrates, however, sees many such things "before his soul." These do not appear to Hippias, or Hippias is intentionally deceiving him. Socrates agrees that these things are not being just, healthy, wise, and so on. Hippias now angrily admonishes him: Socrates and his customary conversationalists do not "consider the whole of things" but cut up each thing that is and "do not notice the naturally large and continuous bodies of being." Socrates gives Hippias an example of what Hippias believes impossible, namely, two, neither of whose component ones is two, and each of whose components is odd, while two is even![55]

Socrates then returns to the pleasures of sight and hearing. He plays with various referents of pleasure, sight, hearing, both, and each, and with our commonsense understanding, to show that it is impossible for the pleasant through sight and hearing to be beautiful because "in becoming beautiful it presents one of the things that are impossible" for it, that is, a both without an either or an either without a both, while it appears illogical to us that beauty should not cover each singly, as well as both together.

Perhaps, then, pleasure through sight and hearing is the best pleasure because it is the most harmless? The beautiful is differentiated from other pleasures by being helpful pleasure. If so, however, we repeat the difficulty of the chasm between the beautiful and the good that vitiated the discussion of use.

Hippias replies that all these things together are only scrapings of speeches divided into bits. The alternative is better and more beautiful: to compose a speech well, and beautifully to persuade courts, assemblies, or any rulers, and save oneself, one's money, and one's friends.[56] Socrates, however, cannot give up what Hippias thinks are his "exceedingly intelligent" babblings, for he wanders and is in perplexity about what Hippias "knows"—what a human being ought to pursue. Whenever he is persuaded by Hippias and other wise ones, the refuter in his home (and others) "asks me if I am not ashamed at daring to converse about beautiful pursuits when I am so manifestly refuted concerning the beautiful because I do not even know what it itself is."[57] How can he know whether a speech or activity is beautiful if he does not recognize the beautiful? "It is necessary to submit to" Hippias' reproach, for it seems to help him. Socrates knows what the proverb means that says "the beautiful things are difficult."

VIII A

Why does Socrates bring out the issue of each and both, or whole and part, or members and composites, through a discussion of pleasure? We might have expected him to discuss this when he discussed the fitting, and to discuss being and appearance when he discussed pleasure.[58] In fact, each issue on which he concentrates in the three definitions pertains to each (and all) of the phenomena he discusses. If pleasure is beautiful, is it good?[59] Can beauty and benefit each be affected separately as cause and caused without in any way being together? Does one know clearly (as Socrates had suggested), the difference between the beneficial and what is useful for the bad, that is, between true and apparent good? Is not the question of what "fits" a question of how the being or nature of the whole inheres in the parts? One of the lessons Socrates wishes us to learn, one of the perplexities with which he keeps us awake, is this range of problems, this unity in multiplicity.

The special connection between beauty's being a couple and the senses is that the senses grasp commonly what none sees in particular.[60] Together with the mind they grasp men, horses, pots, boats, and laws, and beautiful, useful, and just men, horses, pots, boats, and laws. This common seeing also affects pleasure, for shame affects pleasure. The connection of virtue and the noble also brings this out, for the just is linked to what we hear, through reputation and persuasion. The beauty of the speeches that the Spartans enjoy hearing from Hippias is tied to the pleasure they give, and this pleasure is tied (although not limited) to the nobility of what they say.

Pleasure (and attraction) is obviously connected to beauty, so a discussion of beauty must account for it. The ugly and shameful are, as such, not pleasurable. Pleasures of taste and smell seem too petty to count as beautiful, and Socrates dismisses in advance the sexual pleasure of touch by reminding us of sex's ignobility when visible to others. Pleasure in what is presentable, visible, reputable, seen, and said, not hidden and unsaid, is what Socrates has in mind here as beautiful.

Socrates does not attempt to find an element of pleasure—say, purity—that fits better with noble sights and sounds than with other sights and sounds, for similar purity could belong to some tastes and smells that are sweet but not beautiful. Moreover, perhaps we cannot simply split the pleasure of virtue, of moral beauty, from fearful awe. In any event, it proves hard to differentiate pleasure-sight and pleasure-hearing from each other, or to combine them. Perhaps the pleasure in virtue and virtuous actions combines seeing with hearing about invisible noble forms and is not limited to sensible pleasure. Yet, one should not dismiss pleasure's connection to sensual beauty: beautiful things or bodies give pleasure. And, pleasure is not limited to pleasure in the noble.[61]

These points suggest that beauty is best found in a combination of the fitting, good, and pleasurable, generously understood. What fittingly or precisely belongs to (is used for) beneficial purposes, stands out more or less independently, and is seen and heard in its pleasing resplendence is beautiful. Although beauty as an object of theoretical understanding is not identical with beautiful appearances, it is connected to them as their measure and as allowing the mind fully to enjoy its powers. In this way beauty is what is most beautiful, not merely an intellectual afterthought or a set of nominal generalities.

VIII B

Socrates concludes by differentiating his activity from Hippias'. Hippias is soft. He likes to wear attractive things.[62] No problem looks too hard for him. He has no intellectual curiosity. He gives people what they want, and from them he wants the wealth that it is easy to give. Hippias tends to run together what is good, beautiful, powerful, public, and private. This allows him to make things easy for himself. Everything can be smoothly connected to wealth or to the conventions of the powerful. When he does see the recalcitrance in things— say, in Sparta or in assemblies that need persuading—he does not think about the independence that makes them recalcitrant. Rather, money and pretty speeches work well with almost all. Sparta's conventions or traditions may be unaccountable, but they can be accommodated. Only Socrates provokes his anger and (some) questions. And when he does see the rank in things—pots, horses, girls, gods, and beautiful funerals—he splits them fully from each other, not seeing their likeness.

Hippias' views fit his theoretical statement that Socrates does not notice "the naturally large and continuous bodies of being." They also fit his belief that he can talk more precisely than total precision, that is, that his talk is the cause of precision. Matters such as beauty always, for Hippias, inhere in some body; bodies as "wholes" can have different degrees of power, strength, and size, and what is beautiful is what is useful for a powerful body (say, Sparta) or what it believes or establishes as fitting or reputable.

Socrates (and philosophy) differs from Hippias in these characteristics. He desires to know and does not rest content with ignorance. Speaking truly or correctly is an end, not a means. Knowledge, not wealth, is his goal. "Beautiful" speech is not merely useful speech but fitting and good speech. The soul is oriented toward knowledge of the invisible, not service to the body. Socrates is noble by being himself in defending his own.

While Hippias is unthinkingly overconfident and does not know he is being foolish, Socrates is truly bold because he overturns for himself thoughtless conventionalism. Hippias seeks to look resplendent, while Socrates deals with the truly highest things and subjects himself to them. Socrates' boldness, however, goes together with the cautious precision of seeking to know. Hippias believes he can be more precise than precision itself; Socrates seeks to know what precision is.

Socrates

Socrates' unique boldness and caution in the *Greater Hippias* should modify or broaden the sometimes overly erotic view of him. As he tells us in the *Theages, Theatetus,* and *Symposium,* he knows only erotic things. He is his mother's son; at best he can help others deliver their own thoughts. We see here, however, that Socrates is also his father's son; on the surface he is more loyal than Hippias, who gives his father wealth that one fears may corrupt him. Plato mentions Socrates' father, a stonecutter, in several dialogues. In the *Alcibiades I,* Socrates suggests his link through his father's art to Daedelus and through him to the god Hephaestus. He plays with his own divinity in order to humble Alcibiades. But, in fact, he subtly suggests a divinity beyond the gods of his father. In the *Euthydemus* Sophroniscus is mentioned as part of Euthydemus' ludicrous argument that makes everyone everyone else's father; the result, however, is hardly different from Socrates' own *Republic.* In the *Laches,* Sophroniscus is mentioned to bring out a link between Socrates and Lysimachus. Socrates knows, however, that Lysimachus has ignored him, the son of his supposed friend. Yet, he is himself not his father's son in any conventional way or, apparently, an especially good family man. Socrates is true to his father on the surface of his arguments, untrue in the life he lives, and true again at root.

Sophroniscus is the father of both Socrates and his objecting alter ego, that is, himself in another guise. Socrates does not merely seek knowledge by erotically following the good through the beautiful. He also sees what is perplexing or difficult in the beautiful and punishes himself for resting with what he does not know.[63] He pushes himself to go forward. Daedelus created statues famous for moving.[64] Socrates is as endlessly inventive as Daedelus, setting up hypotheses when none is forthcoming and setting them in motion when they seem dumbly fixed, all to explore the truths or goods that his intellectual statues imitate or set to work.

The hard side of Socrates is connected to the hard side of nobility. The beautiful things are difficult, not easy as with Hippias, or, more precisely, they are difficult as well as soft and smooth, yielding.[65] Beauty can become angry at them, as courage ridicules Laches and Socrates. This anger stems from the problems' unyielding recalcitrance, about which Socrates teaches Hippias (and himself). Socrates seeks to separate the noble, to set it apart as a whole from other wholes. As separate, it is in a sense impregnable, unmixed, difficult, defensive, protective. Nobility, indeed, is the source of our pride or dignity. As set apart in speech, however, beauty can also be opened to and combined with the other things we know through speech. It beckons, just as it stands apart. The difficulties of Socratic separating and combining, of recalcitrance and fit, of the briskly independent and the attractively yielding, are not easy to escape or to think through. But these difficulties open worlds beyond the grotesqueness of the "naturally large and continuous bodies of being." The highest things are perplexing: the noble is disputed, not accidentally because of our stupidity but necessarily because of the complexity of its simplicity, and of ours.[66]

Beauty

We can supplement or validate what we learn about beauty from the *Greater Hippias* by considering Plato's characteristic uses of beauty in other discussions.

The beautiful or noble sometimes means what is high, free, rare, grand, lavish, or not petty.[67] The soul's concerns are more beautiful than the body's. Socrates in the *Phaedo* faces death nobly. The gentleman is the man who is noble and good.[68] An element of this view exists in Hippias' opinions, as we indicated, but the suppositions that Socrates tests and finds wanting in the *Greater Hippias* do not directly consider the beautiful as the high, grand, or lavish.

The beautiful is also the fitting, as it is in the *Greater Hippias,* and it contributes to what is well formed and complete.[69] Related to this is what "beautiful" means when Socrates or an interlocutor praises an argument. Beautiful sometimes stands for what helps move the argument along. It (also) means what is sufficient, or at least adequate, to make the needed distinction. Well-made distinctions that move the argument forward are beautiful, even when the subject is coarse.[70]

Related as well, although more general, is the beautiful understood as the good, useful, functional, easy, and sufficient, a prominent use in the *Greater Hippias,* as we have seen.[71] In Diotima's speech in the *Symposium,* one loves the beautiful in order to cause the good. The loved beautiful being is impregnated with the good and seemingly eternal. With proper orientation we leave it behind for what is still more beautiful and better. One steps from considering beauty in a body to the beautiful in all beautiful bodies, from a beautiful soul to the beauty in all beautiful souls, and thence to beauty itself, in order to impregnate the soul with the good and eternal. What is beautiful acts or attracts to secure or deliver something good.

Plato also uses the beautiful to mean or to designate the simple presence of what stands as striking and attractive, what shows forth as good-looking, harmonious sounding, or pleasant. Socrates distinguishes an attractive bodily bloom from beauty of soul and what the soul understands. The ugly Theatetus is beautiful in soul; to be beautiful in body is to stand out in being well-formed.[72] This use is connected to the discussion of the pleasurable in the *Greater Hippias.*

Related to this (and to the noble as free) is the beautiful used to stand for what is separable, what stands on its own, as its own. Sometimes speech is praised as beautiful in this way.[73] The beautiful is thus tied closely to the pure and the precise.[74] Hippias seeks to grasp beauty itself precisely; his first examples of beauty are the independent girl, or horse. Connected to these uses, finally, are the particular things that interlocutors call beautiful: the virtues, various imitations, bodily forms or faces, arguments and answers, and beauty itself.[75]

I will attempt to unify and clarify these views, keeping in mind our discussion of the *Greater Hippias.* Something beautiful is the thing as it stands out on its very own, within its limits. Its beauty, its nobility, its dignity (its height as unity) is its independence, or separateness. Its ugliness is its corruption, its coming apart, its flabbiness. Something that stands out on its own, however, also stands out in the nature or essence it shares with others. The beautiful girl or mare is a girl or a mare, and beautiful. Courage and moderation are each virtues, that is, noble, separately. But, neither is virtue simply, or all that is noble. (They must come together to achieve a fuller virtue or nobility.) Because of such incompleteness (and other insufficiencies), moreover, beautiful things need or call for defense, protection. Their beauty is always contestable because it is not simply or fully beautiful or independent.

Something beautiful, although independent, may prove to be complex, because its powers are complex. Once set in motion, the height, distinctiveness, and freedom of its powers may vary with their use. A body could be strong, swift, or simply lovely to look at; gold may be lovely, comforting, a fitting part of an attractive, expensive, and useless portrait or piece of old furniture, or useful for the machines that win wars. The independence of a figure such as Shakespeare's Coriolanus is noble, but in the play this independence becomes useless and harmful; that is, it transforms itself, although never fully, from nobility to the ignobility of the traitor.

In these ways, something's beauty is not altogether separable from its use, or good. Things are beautiful as they are at work, as they exercise their powers. When a power cannot be exercised alone, when it is dependent, as the eye is on the body for its health and on the soul for its vistas, moreover, its beauty is connected to its appropriate fit within the whole activity or object it serves—its not being too large to be accommodated with the resources at hand, or too small to work well.

Beauty as fit is especially connected to cause, as the beautiful tool does its job or serves its function, the beautiful chord stands in its necessary place, or the noble war helps win freedom. A chain of argument that leads to a failed result is not beautiful. This connection to cause, however, and the subtle question of sufficiency and insufficiency in fit and function, show the openness, instability, complexity, perplexity, and contention involved in the beautiful as the fitting. For, what causes is independent enough from the caused that it is never encapsulated in it. Harmonies exceed their use in this piece, noble pride exceeds its use in this battle, the power of seeing exceeds this or that sight.

The caused, in turn, sometimes appear to be more causing than caused, as the good result inspires the beautiful or useful action that comes into being because of it. And, the multiplicity of causes or beautifully fitting capacities is too complex for any to have full sway. A house cannot be filled with rooms decorated singly according to a designer's dream, as if each room were the only one, without the overall effect being garish, making the house hard to inhabit. A beautiful face is not composed from each feature manifested in its maximum force, taken on its own. Any fitting whole, therefore, points to the limited presence of the power of its parts and, therefore, of its own limits as the thing—statue or soul—that it is. Socrates suggests these issues in the *Greater Hippias* through the paradox that completely splits beauty and good as cause and caused, and by connecting the discussion of the fitting to the issues of being and appearance.

Something beautiful is independent (separate) and good (fitting). It is also attractive, striking, stunning, resplendent, and uplifting, something compelling that stops one short.[76] (The attractive and uplifting distinguish the beautiful from the awful, frightening, and deflating.) Hippias' beautiful display speeches are meant to be like this, as is something beautiful in its golden beauty, its full blossoming or harmony.

This third meaning ranges from the fleeting to the more permanent. We can see how it completes the first two by considering the resplendent and perfectly appropriate action or argument, the perfectly complete and striking composition, the admirable city, and the fully attractive outward form or shape that fits parts together and completes them. Plato suggests or employs this sense in his discussion of pleasure or enjoyment, in Hippias' example of the beautiful funeral, and in the way that Hippias attempts to be—and Socrates ironically treats him as—perfect in beauty and wisdom. What is beautiful in this third sense also usually stands in its own imperfections and perplexities.

The beautiful itself, thus, is the (problematic) stunning or radiant presence and form in what freely or uniquely (e.g., this love, this whole) attaches together *these* fitting and useful elements. None of these components is beauty alone or always beautiful, but beauty is all of these, as one.

CHAPTER 6

Philosophy and Politics

The *Republic*

We have now discussed several experiences that are at the root of philosophy, and a phenomenon, beauty, that helps to define both ethical and intellectual virtue.[1] It is therefore reasonable to turn next to Plato's *Republic*. For, beyond any other work, the *Republic* explains and defends the philosophic way of life, and charms and attracts us to it. Moreover, it examines at length the relation between philosophy and politics, and culminates politically in the claim that philosophers should rule—not law, as in the *Laws*. It employs Socrates' rational force to explore justice, a subject that concerns every honorably ambitious man or woman. Each of its explorations turns us to the ceaselessly disturbing question of happiness, or the best way of life.[2]

The *Republic*

We have four chief goals in considering the *Republic:* to expand our understanding of justice, to see better the connection between philosophy and politics, to explore more fully the question of what is good, and to continue to examine Plato's view of the human soul.

The *Republic*'s subject is justice, and the subject is oriented thematically to the literal title, the regime (or form of government). What is the most just form of government? Plato shows what would need to be true for justice to be fully encapsulated within politics and why this is impossible.[3] He then examines the way of life, philosophy, that comes closest to justice. The political community's bodily existence and the necessities with which it deals, however virtuously, restrict its excellence. We can more justly satisfy ourselves by experiencing what is good as philosophy seeks it. Philosophy and politics are, nonetheless, inseparable, because thought depends on the leisure, and explores the opinions, that are present in (some) political communities, and because every community is governed by an understanding of what is good. The *Republic,* therefore, also attempts to uncover the natures or natural limits—the defining enclosures, unmade by man—that let politics and philosophy be what they are.

I

Justice first comes to sight in the *Republic* in three opinions that Socrates refutes in Book I. Cephalus suggests that justice is telling the truth and returning what one owes, that is, that justice is honesty. Polemarchus claims that justice is helping friends and harming enemies, that is, that justice is acquiring, producing, or distributing good things for one's city. Thrasymachus asserts that justice is the advantage of the stronger, that is, that justice is obeying rulers, or the law.

Socrates refutes each opinion in ways he links to the others. By doing so, he shows that there is truth in each one. Honesty might lead to bad results; it is not just to return a knife to a friend who has since gone mad. Justice, therefore, depends on knowing what is good. Obtaining a good, such as health, from someone who secures it, such as a physician, however, is not guaranteed by his art alone. It also depends on the physician's honesty or friendship, or on legal force. The legal force that helps to secure honesty serves common or private goods genuinely, however, only if rulers truly grasp what is good and reward those who serve it.

The central of these three opinions is Polemarchus' claim that justice is helping friends and harming enemies, and we can uncover Plato's intention in Book I by concentrating on it. Socrates refutes Polemarchus by showing that to procure any good one would prefer an expert to a just man.[4] Sick people seek physicians. Horse buyers seek trainers. Justice, therefore, seems useless.

Perhaps it is useful for safeguarding, Polemarchus suggests. But someone who knows how to protect may also be an excellent thief; knowledge as such does not guarantee proper use. The physician is the potentially best murderer, the trainer the best positioned to make an old nag look young and spry, and so on. What, then, helps ensure that the physician, guard, or trainer uses his skill properly and helps bring us the good that we seek from him? We would normally say his honesty, law-abidingness, fear of being caught, good character, "morality"—in a word, the justice Cephalus already mentioned. This is inadequate as a full understanding of justice, as we saw, but so, too, is justice understood as bringing people good things through art. For, no knowledge guarantees that it will be used properly.

Honesty helps us to see how an art can be well used. Still, an honest physician is more useful to a sick man than is someone who is honest but ignorant. So, can we find a way to support Polemarchus and show that to be just would indeed be to know what is good and not merely to be honest? The examples Plato uses—horsemanship, medicine, war, and others—lead us to a suggestion.

Physicians know better than the rest of us how to restore health, but they do not know better what health is, why it is good, and when we should prefer it to other goods.[5] War is an apposite example of properly overriding medical concerns and risking health for another good—freedom or victory. A trainer knows better than others which horse will be quick over short distances, which strong, and which calm and stolid. But, we know as well or better than he which end we want the horse to serve. Knowing what is good about things that we desire, knowing how ends rank and which we should serve when, does not belong to any ordinary art's knowledge. We find it, instead, in the judgments we use to order our lives and, especially, in the laws and customs that form and direct these judgments. Rulers' grasp of justice leads to choices that determine what we should and should not do.

Can such matters indeed be known, however, or do we at best have opinions about them? Justice understood as the virtue that forms a whole community, regulates our participation in it, and directs the order of priority of various ends and the arts that serve them is a dominant opinion that Plato thinks can become a form of knowledge. Justice is seeing or doing what is good as a whole; to know it is the substance of the statesman's synoptic science. This view of justice's breadth serves as the backdrop for the *Republic*'s political discussion. It is also essential individually, because the order of our purposes and goals is central to our happiness.[6]

II

Because justice is the heart of a good political community, to explore it is to explore the merits of different forms of government.[7] Whichever comes closest to true justice is best; we rank them by their nearness to it. Every community is composed of many parts, many jobs or functions. We should practice these jobs with skill and good character if we are to help our fellow citizens. A community's central tasks are those directed to its benefit as a whole, not merely to its citizens severally—its central tasks are war and legislation, say, not shoemaking.[8] From this viewpoint, therefore, some jobs are more important than others. The superior activities or ways of life are those that most fully benefit what is common. So, the *Republic* studies not only the best form of government but also the best way of life, and the connection between the two.

Plato outlines the best political order, the one closest to justice, in Books II through V. This community proves to be one where each citizen does precisely and only what fits his nature. This means that it is government by those suited to rule and defended by those with the requisite combination of spiritedness and gentleness. This combination occurs only when sufficiently spirited men are trained properly, musically and gymnastically. The city must especially bend its efforts to directing music—poetry, drama, and associated melodies—and the religious dogmas these bring to life.[9] As in the *Laws,* art does not exist for its own sake, but for the common good. When training succeeds, spiritedness is made courageous, with the soldiers "preserving" "the lawful opinion as to which things are terrible and which are not."[10] When each accepts his place as ruler or ruled, all are moderated. When rulers understand how to implement and safeguard a community governed by those devoted to the common good, they are prudent or wise. The justice of the whole is that each minds or does only his own job. The best political community is the just one, where each, and especially the rulers, enjoys the virtue or combination of virtues, the moderation, courage, and wisdom, to act well.

Because training and habituation are insufficient to guarantee the rulers' dedication to the common, however, the just city must further reduce the opportunities for selfish errors. As Plato describes the best community, therefore, it allows its rulers nothing private—neither the property to satisfy luxury or greed; the lovers, husbands, and wives that distract from common devotion; nor the children one is tempted or, indeed, impelled to help beyond their merit. If there is no family, however, a woman's job cannot be to raise her own children. Perhaps, then, women's work is to raise children collectively? Women with brave hearts and minds, however, are better suited than men without these to defend the community and guard its laws. Men and women equal by nature should be equally trained, whatever customs and conventions suggest to the contrary; this means that the best women cannot stay at home.[11] The weakening of the private family that is required by devotion to what is common in Plato's just city is also a consequence, there and everywhere, of the equal "professional" treatment of women.

It seems remarkable today that Plato thinks that not only the most just community but also the best way of life (here, the rulers' lives) should be devoted so completely to what is common. Yet, all he does is to follow unforgivingly what each of us hazily understands, namely, that being just means doing what is for common, not individual, advantage, and that those most devoted to the common good are most worthy of respect. Occasional devotion in war, or the habitual law-abidingness required by good economies, is insufficient. Rather, in Plato's just city each poem, exercise, or dogma is always judged by its contribution to a character in love with serving the public. This discipline, indeed, is not only remarkable to us but, also, despite our grudging sympathy, repugnant. At the least, the *Republic*'s notion that our job encapsulates our happiness and worth seems to us to restrict too much the pleasures of freedom and well-roundedness. Our job is too limited to provide happiness, especially if it is only a craft, not to speak of tasks so routinized and narrow that Plato considers them slavish.

One reason that it discomfits us so to call one life better than another is that we ground happiness on equal independence. Plato, too, is compelled to recognize that no good political community can completely blend private and common concerns.[12] Care for the community and spiritedness in defending it are linked to an irreducible or ever-present pride in one's own and love of what is good for it. Even the most public-spirited ruler seeks honors and praise, and Plato's just city is forced to grant these.[13]

Less nobly, we can recognize irreducible selfishness, and, therefore, better grasp Plato's self-criticism of the possibility of a fully common political life, by noting that Socrates' presentation of the most just community begins with an outline in Book II of what he calls the "true" city. The true city serves only the needs of food, clothing, and shelter, although it has four groups of artisans— shoemakers, in addition to farmers, weavers, and builders. Glaucon calls this

a city of pigs or sows; it turns out that a wish for "luxuries" beyond these ordinary goods leads willy-nilly to the need for conquest and the presence of
crime. War and defense require a new artisan (and a new type of training),
namely, the public-spirited soldier-guardians we have just discussed. It is only
with this public-spirited city, and not in the city of mere needs, that ethical
virtue emerges.

It might thus seem that public spirit and moral virtue are accidents because
the wish for luxury beyond basic needs is not necessary, that is, is accidental.
This is not so. That the wish for "luxury" is unavoidable becomes evident if we
consider the true city's original needs. For, need as such knows no natural
limits: What could be "enough" for me if many are gathered together on limited land in harsh conditions?[14] Moreover, who can say simply which are the
true needs and which the mere luxuries? Socrates adds shoemakers to the
ranks of the other three artisans to subtly but clearly make this point. Shoemaking also makes us wonder how naturally precise the fit can be between
men and jobs, both in the true city and in the just city that builds on it. For,
who is born with "shoemaker" rather than "weaver" branded on his fore-
head?[15] In one way or another, moreover, resources in the true city will be
contested. More than one artisan will claim control over the same things—
plants and animals that supply materials for food, clothing, and shelter, for
example, and people's time and attention.[16] The "true" natural needs, that is
to say, do not appear to furnish a standard for ranking themselves. Would we
not require someone competent in all their purposes to judge among them?
Must one not go beyond the apolitical "true" city even to achieve the true
city's ends?

For these reasons, the luxurious or feverish city and its guardians are less an
accident than an inevitability. As Plato describes the true city, moreover, it
lacks sex, poetry, education, statesmanship, and philosophy. This shows that
the true city is unlikely or undesirable and leads us to see that once these new
activities appear, what we must know to do our jobs, or to be virtuous, becomes especially complex. As we have said, the guardians need competence in
at least two arts—music and gymnastics; indeed, some must have more than
one job, because they must rule as well as fight. This complexity then makes
it easy to choose or desire the wrong thing in the wrong way at the wrong time
with the wrong people. Indeed, once rulers and other citizens notice the multiplicity of jobs and arts, they may wish to do something for which they are ill
suited or not wish to do what the community believes they do best. Not every

gifted young Catholic boy in an Italian village, let alone on the streets of Man-
hattan, wishes to be a priest, however forcefully he may be encouraged. A
"noble" lie must be told to the occupants of Plato's just or "beautiful" city to
convince them that a perfectly natural fit exists between jobs and workers (we
are born with metallic souls that suit us only for this or that) and that common
and individual good are identical (we are all literally born from this soil.) That
the lie is a lie displays the inevitable presence of the disjunction between private and public.[17]

All these considerations show the limits of political justice and common
devotion, as Plato experiments with them. Conflict, selfishness, and an imperfect fit between jobs, talents, and desires occur even in this most public-spirited
of cities. From these difficulties, however, neither we nor he can conclude that
individual independence is superior to just functioning. Nonetheless, it might
be, and Plato deals with this issue throughout the *Republic*. His analysis culminates in his description of rare philosophers, whose excellence we cannot reduce to any political work. So, in a dialogue devoted to excellence as just
participation, the inevitably independent philosophic life emerges as best. The
Republic is for this reason the work that first inspired the world to the truest,
most complete, most natural, and least conventional liberalism or individualism—the philosophic life. But, it is this liberalism, and not every "liberty," that
is best.

III

Plato's *Republic* thus presents two outstanding instances of the good or best
life: the moderate, courageous, prudent ruler and the philosopher. Socrates
describes both lives, in the course of seeking justice. So, to say why they are
good, we must now examine more deeply what Socrates claims in Book IV to
discover about it. Justice is each thing's minding its own business, having or
doing its own, doing the job or function for which its nature fits it. In the just
city, rulers rule wisely, soldiers defend courageously, artisans work moderately,
and all acknowledge the rulers' priority. In the soul—which Plato parallels to
the city in order to determine whether the just or unjust man is happiest—reason rules wisely, and spiritedness courageously supports reason in moderately
controlling eros or desire. In fact, Socrates is sufficiently satisfied with this
discussion of justice that he is ready to prove that the just man is happier than
the unjust.[18] Only because Polemarchus wishes to hear more concerning what
Socrates briefly said about having wives in common is the discussion inter-

rupted by Plato's magnificent description of the philosopher. Up to then, to be "philosophic" was to be musical, gentle, or not simply spirited. The interruption indicates, of course, that the description of justice in Book IV cannot be as complete or transparent as it seems.

To say that political justice is each thing's minding its own is to equate the singularity of the city's members with the nature that best serves their community. It is as if no split exists between being as and for oneself, and functioning for the common good. This can be true politically only if one's own could be completely reduced to one art or skill and if skills mesh perfectly. Otherwise, we and others will not have completely and solely what belongs to us. This equation of one's own and the common good is paradoxical, indeed, because it is usually on account of our "own"—that is, our private, selfish, selves—that we wish to receive more than we deserve as functionaries. We are rarely satisfied simply to be or do what from the common point of view we do best. As we suggested earlier, even the rulers in Plato's just city desire and receive the private advantage of honor, recognition, and choice burial. Our own and what is good can, in fact, never completely fit politically. This is why the noble lie and communal property and families become necessary.

To treat justice as each doing its own shows us that "justice" is essentially the virtue that places or fits one into something common and, consequently, that restricts one's activity. From the point of view of what is common, one is not independent but is useful, good, or functional in some way; one has a useful nature. The difficulty here and the reason, indeed, why acting justly is not automatic (i.e., why it is not natural in the sense of always spontaneous) is that what I wish or need for myself is rarely identical to what my community needs from me. My being just is my limiting myself by fitting into the common enterprise; politically, this is not completely possible, which is why no community can be altogether just. Plato extends as far as he can the notion that minding one's own and participating in the common good can be one; he intends to show the limit to political practice at the same time that he determines its nature.

We must pursue this question further. Why, indeed, should anyone limit himself justly or be forcefully persuaded to limit himself? We see one reason in Socrates' claim that justice somehow causes the other virtues. Without it, wisdom, courage and moderation would not actively exist.[19] How, then, can each doing its own (justice) be the cause of the others? What might this mean? Let me mention two possibilities. The interlocutors' search for justice in the

Republic causes the city that they construct in speech; without their quest, nothing would have happened. And, potential citizens' wish to enjoy what is good might bring about and sustain the city that Socrates describes, or any other city we might make. "Justice," that is to say, names the virtue by which each of us does what he does well in this place, in this community and common enterprise. Without it there would be nothing politically common. Therefore, none or few of the goods that most want could in fact be produced or enjoyed. For, there would be no active exercise of the natures that can succeed only when they belong to something political. Justice names the connection and, therefore, the possible openness, of each part in a whole—here, a political community—that enables its work to serve the community and enables the community to achieve what is good. It is what makes each part good for the whole and is, therefore, needed for each part actually to do its work well. In this sense, justice causes the other virtues.

This analysis also explains how justice in Socrates' city differs from moderation and from knowledge of the arts. For, having an art, as we have seen, does not as such guarantee that it will be used well, that is, in a way that fits together each skill and purpose by connecting it to the others. This is what justice does. Justice is a necessary condition for the other virtues and skills to be present and effective, to be virtues here and now. This is why it sometimes seems identical to them, because to be good the other virtues will also be just, and when we do our job well in a good community we do our job skillfully as well as justly. A good football team needs fleet running backs and strong-armed quarterbacks, but unless they limit and connect their skills—unless they achieve the right proportion of run and pass—they will not win many games. Similarly, it is only when the soul operates as a whole with each part open to the others that its powers are self-limiting or self-adjusting and, therefore, may achieve their end.

Of course, that we need justice for parts to achieve their good as parts of a whole, that we need justice for a whole to be good, does not tell us what is truly good or which whole or community should take precedence. Socrates argues that whatever else we want, we want what is good. Even when, in the course of proving that our souls have parts, he laboriously distinguishes desires for things from desires for things with certain qualities—thirst for drinks, say, from thirst for cold drinks—he claims that thirst is always for good drink. The priority of what is good is the horizon within which Plato conducts the *Republic;* hence, he considers justice primarily in the way it is good, and is required by what is good. But, he still needs to explore the full dimension of what is good. This exploration occurs in the sixth book and follows Socrates' introduction of philosophy. He introduces philosophy for the reason we mentioned earlier; it is the activity of the complete, independent individual. In the terms we are discussing here, it is the activity of the just soul.

The just soul obviously differs from Socrates' city, whatever their similarity. It also differs from the soul of the ruler in the just city. There, the ruler's reason is subordinate to defending the community. The just city is an image of the fitting together of singular parts into a good whole. But it is only an image of this, because its parts never fit simply in their purity and fullness as themselves—as we have emphasized, citizens are communal but cannot be only communal—and because the good they serve is always linked to piggish desires. Courage, moderation, and, especially, prudence or reason are not simply goods in themselves in Socrates' city and, therefore, in the ruler's soul. Can there, then, be a just whole whose members can more fully be themselves while still fitting together? Can there be single souls that more completely fit their parts together, for a fuller good, than the city or its rulers? The city and its members are images of the "ideas" that fit together in a good whole. It turns out that a philosopher is someone who seeks to understand this whole. The philosopher, the ideas, the good, and the links among them become the next subjects of the dialogue.

IV

Plato's presentation of philosophy as the most just way of life is somewhat different from Socrates' discussion of philosophic education in Book VII, and from philosophic activity itself. For, the presentation intends to defend philosophy and inspire us to it in terms that are connected to ordinary concerns. It arises to help explore the question of justice. It is not a bare discussion of the possibilities of knowing. We can be inspired, however, only if philosophy's objects are brought into view, because philosophy's own beauty and scope depend on what it mirrors. Socrates' discovery of philosophy as the life to which the aspiration to justice actually leads must, therefore, be interspersed with discussions of philosophy's objects and of philosophical education.

Philosophy's attraction in the *Republic* comes to light in terms of its importance for the city, its being the activity that most completely uses the powers of the soul, and the depth of what it seeks. I begin with the second point.

The just soul, we have learned, is one whose desire, spiritedness, and reason each does its work well. It is moderate, courageous, and wise. But, can the prudence of the just city's rulers satisfy reason's full possibilities? Socrates shows in his just city that artisans' knowledge is subordinate to rulers' judgment. He even tries to show how to subordinate poets' imagination politically.[20] But, we can use the mind in ways that we cannot subordinate to prudence, because the mind is oriented to natural concerns beyond politics' proper direction. The mind as mind cannot be satisfied by thinking about politics as politics. The most just soul in the city, therefore, cannot be the just soul simply, because its reason is too truncated.

To say that philosophy may be the just activity because it exercises reason more fully than does political prudence is initially plausible to us, if not obvious. It becomes more plausible if we follow Socrates in including or subordinating mathematics, physical science, and poetry to philosophy, and in distinguishing it from impostors. But, how could philosophy also perfect eros and spiritedness or, at least, involve a courage and moderation not inferior to that of courageous rulers and decent, hard-working, law-abiding citizens? How can the selfish cloistering of the life of the mind equal, or, indeed, replace in perfection the bold valor of the hero who defends a just city?

We find the answer in the objects of philosophy's quest. Philosophy, Socrates says, seeks to understand the permanent objects, those that are always, and that cause or account for the substance of what becomes. It seeks to articulate these ideas and show their interconnection. Any beautiful thing, for example, pales before the permanent beauty that gives it its startling moment of splendor amid inevitable decay. Beauty itself attracts a longing to grasp and know it that is deeper, purer, and more fulfilling than any ordinary attraction. The magnificence of a fleetingly beautiful sunset, lover, or painting is less than the magnificence of the permanent beauty in which they share and to which they lead. The longing to know and be together with the proper objects of thought—the perfect ideas or forms—is, when directed by reasoned understanding, shaped into a "moderation" grander than the moderation of moral virtue.

In what way does philosophic courage perfect spirited pride in a manner equal or superior to courage in battle, or in dealing with ordinary fears? After all, as we said, when Socrates earlier mentioned philosophy colloquially, its synonym was to be gentle, not harsh. Socrates speaks of the courage to risk opprobrium, to question convention. Virtuous pride fears above all the lie in one's own soul. It directs its unforgiving spirit to overcome that lie. Fear of punishment by the powerful, fear of losing the benefits of more ordinary pursuits, fear of the ridicule wielded by convention, lose their terror. The courage of the intellect is measured at first by the chains it breaks and, finally, by its appropriate defense of what is true and natural.[21]

This kind of courage and attraction do not tell us fully how eros and spiritedness operate together with philosophic reason. It is at least clear that love at once combines and separates, and that defensive pride and courageous risk do so, too, albeit along a different path, with a different kind of motion.[22] The passionate adjuncts to philosophic reason can belong to philosophy's own work; they are not only its aides in the movement up and away from convention.[23]

It is also clear that whatever the magnificence of philosophic love and spirit they do not simply replace more conventional courage and moderation. (To a degree this incomplete substitution is also true of philosophic reason vis à vis political prudence, professional knowledge, and economic management.) Risking death is like but not identical to risking outrage or ridicule. Proper love of permanent truths is like but not identical to sensual pleasure in loving communion. Nonetheless, Socrates has said enough about philosophy to make it visibly and compellingly attractive, the "individual" answer to the question of the best or happiest life. The subtleties and complexities of what philosophy actually discovers do not put in question its justified height.

Socrates broaches the issue of the connection and rank among the noble ways of life primarily as the question of philosophy's relation to politics. He answers it here with the claim that philosophers should rule.[24] After all, the just city's founders (the interlocutors) have looked at matters beyond the citizens' ordinary sight.[25] Moreover, philosophy is linked to the other (just) uses of eros, spiritedness, and reason. Nonetheless, philosophic rule is a great paradox because philosophers seek to live in the truth simply, while the political community cannot.

This paradox is most visible in the necessity for the noble lie. Part of Plato's intention is to develop each institution of the just city in an extreme form that makes clear what every community must practice to some degree if it is to be just. The extremism shows both the nature and limits of politics. The noble lie brings out such necessities with special clarity. Whatever the community, its citizens must believe their place in the social order to be proper—the result, say, of divine plan, ancient practice, or equal opportunity—and they must believe that their connection to these people here and now is so strong that they properly enjoy their goods together with them and should, if they must, die for them. To say the least, neither the order of talent and standing nor the link among citizens could ever be so perfect and complete. Some always receive more or less than they deserve or want. Cosmopolitan or private friendships inevitably interfere with political fraternity. The full force of the noble lie seeks to overcome these stubborn facts as completely as one can; this, indeed, is why it must be a lie.

More than the citizens' dislike of philosophers or the philosophers' wish to be left alone to think (although, perhaps, as the cause of both passions), it is this distinction between truth and lie that makes the justice of philosophic rule so paradoxical. Socrates suggests that we all seek what we actually believe is good. (We would not rest easy with a false version of what we think is good even if we are wrong about what in fact is good.)[26] So, there is a link between what is and what is good. Socrates also suggests that what is most to be feared is the lie in the soul. If, however, what is good in the just city requires a lie, there is a disjunction in it between what is and what is good. The just city prior to philosophic rule (as Socrates discusses it through Book V) does not seek knowledge. To explore this problem further we must now, therefore, turn to the questions of the good simply, and the good of knowledge.

V

What makes the philosophical life the best way of life for man is the completeness of its use of our powers of reason, spiritedness, and eros. Only when our powers participate together in the search for knowledge is the soul perfected and its parts well exercised.[27]

This excellence of philosophy points toward the good simply. Rather than analyzing the good directly, however, Socrates approaches it through three images—the sun, the divided line, and the cave.[28] The divided line and the cave are images of the relationship between knowledge and opinion.[29] The sun is the good's direct analogue: as the sun's light makes knowledge of visible things possible and helps to generate them, so does the good make knowledge of intelligible things possible, and help them be.

From the viewpoint of ordinary experience, what is "good" has several meanings, powers, and substantive qualities; considering these briefly will help us to understand what Plato has in mind. "Good" means useful, helpful, profitable, advantageous, suitable, sufficient, complete, satisfactory, beneficial, enjoyable, desirable, and admirable. We desire to furnish a war hero whom we admire with a drug that is useful and sufficient to restore the benefit of his health. Good things, moreover, have the ability or power to guide, direct, or form us, as knowledge is a goal or end that orders our efforts in learning or study. Such guiding ends, finally, can be seen in many aspects or have several qualities; among the ends or the true ends for man are pleasure, honor, holiness, moral and political nobility or excellence, and wisdom.

When we consider in the light of these ordinary characteristics Plato's statement about the good's making knowledge possible, we may say the following. By ordering and forming our efforts or perspective, an end or goal enables certain things to stand out as, say, useful, suitable, or sufficient to a purpose, and to come to sight in the qualities that make them useful, suitable, and beneficial. What is good helps matters to be articulated, to be noticed, differentiated, and connected and, therefore, to be known, and, in a way, to be. The measure provided by the end enables us to see how the separate powers of things need to be limited and connected to achieve this end. It then enables us to allow them to be themselves, or mind their own, within these limits. The overall good or purpose—say, a team's victory—provides the measure by which the arrangement and, even, discernment of the team members' abilities becomes possible. It therefore enables an expressing through limiting of those abilities, a justice among them, that will secure the common good of victory, provided that the skills are sufficient.

Justice is good in this sense in several ways. As the end or goal of the interlocutors' search, it brings into being a more or less sufficient and interconnected use of the interlocutors' (and our own) powers: it makes our souls philosophic. As that within a community or soul that is said to cause the other virtues and to be each part's working well, justice places qualities together beneficially so that their own powers may actually meet their end: spiritedness is courage and not brutality only when defending prudence, moderation, and the political, educational, and economic practices of a city that secures them (and itself). As admirable in itself, justice stands as a possession worth having and imitating, whatever the consequences.

Although justice is in these ways good, it is not the only good. Its own goodness, indeed, is hard to specify apart from other goods. An artisan in the just city cannot work well without justice because, as we have argued, his art alone does not guarantee its proper use. An honest artisan, however, is not necessarily a competent one. Moreover, although justice may mean that, say, a physician will use his skill to secure health, not disease, justice is not itself health or security. The city comes into being not only for its justice but also for its other goods. Nonetheless, to the degree that these goods and the skills that help secure them occur only when ordered to each other, the goodness of the city is most generally or characteristically its justice.

As we have emphasized, one shortcoming of the political community is that the good of the parts is not completely satisfied by just participation. The ordered relation of ends and occupations gives some of them short shrift. In even the best city, basic ends, say, health, are subordinated to other ends, say, victory in war. They are not all given full sway. Yet, unless ends and occupations are open and ordered to each other, they cannot work well. Socrates tries to overcome this problem of partiality by making all goods politically common goods; Plato means to teach us that he cannot fully succeed.

It is in philosophy that all human goods most easily become common goods, because nothing of the admirable, attractive, sufficient, excellence of reason, spiritedness, or eros seems unaccounted for in the passionate quest to know. Each can fully be itself in the just order that seeks or reflects the inexhaustible good of knowledge. Yet, as we have said, love of learning and courage of the intellect are like but not identical to all bravery and moderation. Moreover, searching for knowledge is not equivalent to having it. Full wisdom is unlikely or impossible; at the least, one could hardly grasp or present it all at once.

The perfection of philosophy and, indeed, the just city, comes from imitating the whole of things. To know is to liken or reflect in the mind what can be known and the order of what can be known. The deepest questions about the good and what is good occur when we consider this order. These questions are linked to Socrates' discussion of what the philosopher seeks to know, the "ideas," a term that we have seen Plato use at various stages here and elsewhere to (among other things) articulate a gathering or assemblage into a class or constraining form that nonetheless is problematic enough in its definition to spur a discussion forward.[30] An idea is the single class character, shape, or look that yokes together many instances, the beauty, say, in all beautiful things.[31] An idea is itself and nothing but itself; one way beauty differs from beautiful things is that unlike them it can never be ugly—it cannot be marred by any characteristic that is not beautiful. For it to be marred by nothing ugly, beauty must never decay. As independent and incorruptible—as self sufficient—the idea of beauty could hardly exist fully in beautiful things; it causes their beauty in the sense that they imitate, rely on, or are attracted to it. An idea is the self-sufficient shape, form, or limit that defines as what they are those that participate in it.

If each idea is an incorruptibly independent form that attracts our intellectual desire and is the ground for everything that participates in it, then each idea is good. Justice is good, but it is not the only good. If the ideas are all good, however, they must share this quality in common; they cannot be themselves only. Each idea is not only itself but is also good, beautiful, unchanging, separable, countable, and so on; it seems that they cannot be themselves fully by being themselves alone. In fact, the ideas are surely open to each other; if not, how could a city or soul be wise, courageous, moderate, and just? A central question about the ideas, therefore, is how they can be fully themselves and yet also combine justly with each other in a manner that brings out their interconnections but does not restrict (and perhaps enhances) them. The good would in this sense be the end or forming measure in terms of which they fit. It would allow them to fit by giving an end and a form ordered to that end—that is, a wholeness—that would also enable an apparently whole substance such as the city to connect instances of the ideas. How this programmatic possibility might actually be is, to say the least, difficult to grasp precisely. The possibility is easier to discern in the images of the whole—the city and the soul—than among the ideas themselves. But this is because the city and soul are imperfect, and because their parts are never fully independent or unified.

This unclarity is one reason that Socrates treats the good from such a distance and by using images. Another reason is that the good is not the only good thing; after all, justice and courage are good too, and they are also themselves. Socrates calls the good beyond being, but he also calls it the idea of the good. This may mean that we can describe or discuss the whole of things only under different aspects or from the point of view of different ideas taken as the defining end. Even what is good can or must come to light in terms other than itself—order and measure, for example, can come to light in terms of justice or wisdom. Moreover, we can discuss the ideas (or any defining point of view) not only through each other but also as "beings," "natures," or "causes," as well as ends. One might even wonder about the relationships among these characteristics and the ideas themselves.[32] In any event, however profound these questions, they do not disrupt the clarity of Plato's argument about the desirability of the just city, or philosophy; on the contrary, they are inspirations to further thought.

VI

Socrates' descriptions of philosophy and the ideas do not tell us precisely how philosophers proceed or what they study. He must, therefore, discuss the philosopher's education. His presentation in Book VII also serves as a prelude to the *Republic*'s final three books, in which he outlines various communities and ways of life, various images of justice and philosophy. Because the *Republic* concludes with a myth about the afterlife, the conclusion is itself a prelude to the work's start, for it begins as Glaucon and Socrates, returning to Athens from praying at and observing a festival, are pressed into going with others to Cephalus' house, where his concerns about approaching death lead to the view of justice we discussed earlier.

Socrates' plan for teaching philosophers is not a dead letter. Rather, it sets in motion the liberal education that has dominated the West from his time until ours. This education centers on mathematics but is directed ultimately to an understanding that does not rest on hypotheses or sense experience. Rather, it seeks to uncover what these are based upon, namely, the objects of dialectics (such as the ideas). True freedom is an education that liberates, so liberal education is coherent with political virtue, the virtue of the free, not the slavish.

The very great unlikelihood of philosophic rule and complete communism leads Socrates to discuss democracy and other forms of government in Books VIII and IX. In doing this, he begins—and so telling and comprehensive is his analysis that he nearly completes—the scholarly study of politics, describing the meaning or goodness, the central practices, and the inevitable motion or decay that characterize every regime. Moreover, in also outlining the purposes, practice, origin, and decay of the human type or soul associated with the regime—the democratic, honor-loving, oligarchic, and tyrannical men—he begins, and almost completes, practical psychology, that is, the description of human beings from the standpoint of how we organize ourselves to achieve what we have come most to love. Socrates' rich outlining of human and political types goes far beyond his ostensible need to show that the most unjust man—the tyrant—is the unhappiest. For, in a dialogue devoted to the best way of life, he must consider all the competitors to the throne. Moreover, he helps demonstrate that political and philosophic justice are true human goods by showing that the other ways of life that seem good are in fact good to the degree that they imitate them. As we have said, being and seeming are linked.[33]

Plato teaches that human souls and political regimes are characterized chiefly by what visibly rules them, not, as we so often say today, by unconscious drives or historical inheritances that push us along ineluctably. What rules us in practice is some combination of the spontaneous (and in this sense natural) path or tendency of our eros and spiritedness, and the shaping of that path by paternal persuasion (enforced by shame and patrimony), law (enforced by punishment), poetry (supported by musical charm), the arguments of friends and acquaintances (supported by ridicule and dizzying sophistry), and true education.[34] That is, what chiefly shapes us, together with our immediate tendencies, is some type of speech or reason. But, it is speech that employs fears and hopes to appeal to our nature. We are what we are in practice because of the way that reason—in the form of a teaching about right and wrong, for example—works upon our spontaneous tendencies, shapes them, brings them forward, and allows them to shine through. Speech or talk alone, without being connected to natural attraction and spiritedness, is mere convention or empty poetic embellishment, easily forgotten. Nature alone, as it first seems to rule in us, looks to be only one's thoughtless and spontaneous way, a tendency to gentleness and laziness, or to firmness and harsh stubbornness. Convention apart from nature is rebelled against by nature; our natural tendencies alone, without reasonable and beautifying conventions and forms, are flighty, destructive, pointless, and often vulgar, and they leave nothing stable behind. The *Republic* seeks to elevate speech to nature by showing how true speech is about what, in the fullest sense, naturally—unavoidably and spontaneously—is. And, it seeks to elevate natural spontaneity to speech by taking our and our communities' gentleness and harshness (our eros and spiritedness) and elevating them beyond animal immediacy, mere calculation, occupational flowering, or, even, ethical but conventional virtue, to allow them their proper use and fullness in philosophy.

The practically good political communities shape what is natural into a reasonable order and allow desire and, especially, courage and honor, to flourish within that order. However high, this shaping is no longer philosophy as such, or the precise rule of the wise. It is, rather, the result of whatever reasoning can be embodied in the rule of intelligent law; law is never fully reasonable because in it reason inevitably becomes somewhat congealed, or inflexible.[35] Law and prudence in the service of reasonable, although not philosophic, excellence characterize the actual regimes of city and soul that in ranked order we are likely to see—the regimes that are devoted to honor (timocracies), wealth or money making (oligarchies), and satisfaction or spending (democracies).[36] Plato's political legacy is not only liberal education but also the sanctifying, through law, of the rule of reason, whatever the limits of law.

These limits are most obvious in Socrates' ambiguity about democracy, which is considered only the fourth best regime in order of virtue but is also the place where we can learn most about human variety. What is best for philosophers, that is to say, is not normally what is best for most of us. The best regime in the soul almost always requires in practice an inferior regime in the city; the two wholes do not simply fit. Yet, what the philosopher learns about justice is the condition for the good laws that are necessary for most human happiness.

VII

Plato concludes his *Republic* by showing, in Books IX and X, philosophy's superiority in terms of pleasure, where it is apparently at a spontaneous disadvantage, and in terms of poetry and myth, whose attractive speech apparently shows dry philosophy's verbal disadvantage.[37] His strategy here and throughout the *Republic* is to demonstrate philosophy's superiority to other activities by showing how it provides a fuller version of what they seek for themselves.

The clue to his procedure is always to keep in mind outstanding examples—the pleasure of philosophy, say—when describing the general phenomenon. Pleasure (or justice) is usually a truncated version or imitation of the perfection it imitates; the standard is the excellent, not the ordinary. We can truly understand pleasure (or justice) not by averaging its instances or adding them up but by narrowing down from its richest presence. The idea or nature that holds classes together is not always something that they share equally or identically, but, rather, imitatively as likenesses; an idea's members are both it and less than it, as a man's shadows both are and are not him.

Plato understands pleasure to be neither repose—because this stands between pleasure and pain—nor relief from pain (e.g., satisfying thirst)—because this merely moves us to repose. Some pleasures, moreover—such as smelling sweet jasmine in the garden—strike us directly, without filling any prior lack. The heart of pleasure is a completion and suitability, a burgeoning satisfaction, a fitting fullness. Tyrannical pleasures—which we all know from our dreams unless reason controls our dreams—merely relieve from pain, are never completed, or are unsuitable. Philosophic pleasures, however, belong suitably to the satisfactory exercising of our mind; they are superior as pleasure.

To make his point Plato must ignore for the moment the labor of learning that is so often required to enable us to experience the pleasure of understanding. He must also ignore for the moment the effortless pleasure of looking at beautiful things. Calling attention to these facts would bring the philosopher down a peg and make tyrannical collectors of large homes with nice views on the outside and pretty art and people on the inside a bit too compelling for rhetorical simplicity. Yet, just as the soul is more complex than the eye, so, too, is the pleasure of understanding more complex and refined than sight (not to say smell), more suited to our capacities, and better able to use them and complete us. Perhaps it is also in some manner more concentrated and intense, a type of fullness that Plato does not discuss as such here, for the intense concentration of the mind lasts longer and ranges wider than the intense concentration of the body.

Plato's next topic (which begins Book X) is the superiority of philosophers to poets. With the telling but ludicrous unfairness that characterizes comic poets themselves, Socrates assures us that poets are more ignorant than the simplest craftsmen, let alone philosophers. Why? Because they imitate imitations. A painter paints the couch made by the craftsman, who imitates the idea of the couch made by the god. In the heart of the dialogue, however, ideas were said to be always, that is, never to be made, even by a god.[38] Throughout the dialogue, moreover, gods are constrained by necessities; what could these permanent self-sufficient constraints be but the ideas themselves? Socrates, who obviously is aware of these difficulties, therefore subtly shifts his argument and suggests that use and the requirements of the user are what the couch's craftsman obeys. On reflection, we see further that a couch's use is not isolated but depends on a whole order of proper use. The moderate man's couch meets requirements different from what pleases the lascivious man; the common meals of the guardians require and permit simple tables different from the elegant private places where rich democrats count their money and take their meals. If the poet indeed imitates something already made, it seems most reasonable to say that he imitates such an order of use, or imitates the statesman whose laws set in place such an order.[39]

The turn from copying to using, however, poses its own paradoxes, because the copied table looks like a table, but the use to which we put a table does not directly copy the way its user looks. Indeed, the correspondence between look and purpose tends to blur as the thing used becomes more complex (a whole house, say, vs. a suit of clothes) and as the purpose that the user has in mind becomes more subtle. Form and end or use are not evidently identical. When the end or use of something is its working completely well, however, its self-benefit as it were, then its function and its look or shape may come close, as the soul's proper understanding mirrors what it sees and perfects the soul's powers. The priority of philosophy is visible among other things in this unity.

Poets seem to us to know too much to be treated as Plato treats them, yet it is also true that they imitate artifacts, nature, and political events that they do not make. Perhaps the best way to square our view with Plato's, and square Plato's statement with his appreciation of poetry here and elsewhere, is to suggest the following. The poet—Homer, Sophocles, or Shakespeare—in fact knows more about human use than the craftsman or almost all users; when Plato introduces use rather than mere copying as the lodestar for making things, poets rise in estimation. Who knows more about the use of beds than the author of *Romeo and Juliet?* Indeed, who most inspires us to that use, either to indulge an unformed "romantic" nature or to master or elevate passions to exquisite "courtly" propriety? Bad poets too are in a sense teachers of what to admire and desire.[40] But, even the best poets do not as such—as such because Plato and others can be both poet and thinker—know strictly what is good, just, or courageous for man, how these human qualities imitate what is simply, or how they fit together. What we can learn from poets is relevant for founding and securing political orders, but it is not knowledge simply, which is the serious meaning of Socrates' denigrating them as mere imitators of imitators. Poets do not demonstrate the way that mathematicians do. Sculptors cannot explain themselves well enough. The full dimension of the problem of specifying and then connecting the things that truly stand on their own is beyond the poets' concerns. Yet, it is the hidden heart of their power.

Indeed, even the most compelling stories are beyond poetry, because the most compelling stories concern life after death. That is, they rely on a view of the immortality of the soul, choice, reward, and punishment that poets as such do not have. Plato concludes the *Republic* by discussing these very topics. His discussion serves several purposes. The obvious one is to secure the happiness or rewards of the ordinarily just by showing that the link between being and seeming to be just holds true not only for philosophers who fear the lie in the soul but for the rest of us, at least in the eyes of a god who sees our intentions. The less obvious one is to address the link between body and soul, an issue that clearly affects the strength of Plato's proof of the soul's immortality. If the soul cannot exist without the body, it cannot be immortal, because bodies are corruptible. The problems of immortality, and of reward and punishment, take us back to the concern for life after death with which Cephalus nearly began the *Republic*. With unobtrusive poetry, Plato completes his circle.

Conclusion

The *Republic*'s examination of justice in a sense concludes our basic discussion of it. Justice, as we said, is each part's doing its own, and this accords with the *Gorgias*. Still, we do not yet adequately understand the full powers of the parts of the soul or the city, the full place of knowledge in recognizing and implementing justice, or the good at which such wholes aim. Socrates tells us explicitly that he is discussing the good only in terms of what is "most similar to it" and that "there is another longer and further road leading" to the soul than the ways they have taken.[41] There is more to say about Plato's view of the human soul, the human good, the place of knowledge in politics, and the possible connections among parts and wholes. To these questions we will now turn.

Part Three
Politics and Knowledge

CHAPTER 7

Pleasure and the Soul

We begin our discussion of politics and knowledge by developing our understanding of Plato's thoughts on the human soul and the human good. Indeed, unearthing the soul as the heart of man and his political life is one of Plato's emblematic achievements.[1]

The Soul

Plato first distinguishes the soul from the body.[2] If souls are immortal (as the *Republic* suggests), they flee the body.[3] If we understand something immaterial—something we cannot reduce to our senses and what they sense as such—we understand it through the soul.[4] Pleasures and pursuits of the body are inferior to pleasures and pursuits of the soul. In Socrates' boldest statements of the difference between body and soul, the body is an oyster's shell that we shuck in death, a prison, not a passageway.[5] Less extremely, the body's pleasures, pains, and perceptions are linked to the soul and experienced by it.

I

If soul actually differs from body, its core is speech, mind, or intelligence. Discussions of virtue become discussions of speech and knowledge because the heart of human life is our soul, and the defining element of our soul is mind. Soul is not identical to mind, however, but is its house, or something that necessarily accompanies it. (Nonspeaking animals apparently have souls.)[6] Soul, indeed, sometimes stands for life, or is "life" when it is together with body. It makes bodies live, and it accompanies mind. The soul is the source or origin of self-movement or, indeed, the very power of self-movement. It also passively receives and perceives.[7]

Socrates understands our soul to rule our body, to use and direct it.[8] The body's distinctive ends are health, strength, and beauty, although the connection of these ends is ambiguous.[9] Often, however, we need the physician's and trainer's arts (i.e., mind) to produce or secure these ends. The body's goods, moreover, serve the goods of the soul—virtue, prudence, and understanding. The soul leads us, either by calculating the body's pleasures or by shaping and directing its own perfection.[10]

Naturally, if the soul directs only by calculating the body's pleasures, it does not rule simply. Nonetheless, intelligently choosing means to the body's ends and opportunities for enjoying the body's complex pleasures seems necessary to experience them fully. The soul governs even when it does not altogether rule. To the degree that moral virtue is the noble or beautiful stance toward fear, awe, pleasure, and attraction, moreover, prudence shapes the passions and their objects. But it is then still oriented to them and, therefore, does not rule purely.

II

Although the soul differs from the body, it is related to it subtly. Plato indicates this in several ways: the status of error and opinion; the place of sensory perception, and the common sensing of whole objects; the connection of thought to pleasure; the relation of passions (such as love) to their goals (such as love for beautiful things), and of these goals to speech (such as speaking beautifully), and the form these all share (such as beauty); the possibility of images; the soul's ability to measure and fit; and the presence of causality.[11] Because of these subtle relations, Plato approaches important matters dialectically. The things his characters say are imperfect and incomplete to the degree that full knowledge is unavailable to them, and the things they say about the soul and its objects are relative to each other.

A relevant example here of the soul's relation to the body, and of the dialectic between the soul and its objects, is Socrates' analysis in the *Phaedrus* of love of beauty. Socrates presents there a story about the soul. It culminates in a picture of the connection between body, soul, and love of beauty. We begin by loving one beautiful body that we see and then move to loving the beauty in all beautiful bodies, the beauty in a soul that learns, and, then, beauty as such, as we can understand it. Beauty is immaterial, but it shapes the material. Love is for this beautiful one but also stretches to and experiences the general. The soul can rule the body because what one seeks through the body is perfected and caused by the objects of mind. The soul can love or seek both what it perceives and understands.

Socrates' picture of the progress of the soul rationalizes the story in the *Phaedrus* that precedes it. Only a few love beauty as such, and only they are attracted to others whose souls learn beautifully. Such beauty reminds some most resplendently of the pure bodiless sights above the heavens that they glimpsed when they followed their god. Philosophers followed Zeus and, therefore, dwelled most with the pure ideas. Others followed different gods and saw less above. This accounts for their love of warlike and kingly, political, gymnastic, prophetic, poetic, craftsman-like, sophistic, or tyrannical souls. The philosopher's love of a young potentially philosophic soul reminds him of the simple beauty to which he tries to lead the beloved, that is, his protégé. The protégé, in turn, comes to love the lover, the teacher; in fact, he is loving himself, or the possibility of his elevated soul, as he sees it in his lover's eyes. Love is self-love, but self-love is love of one's beautiful soul and, finally, beauty simply, to the degree one's soul reflects or approaches it. Love loves what is alike, in the unlike.

Plato complicates this picture in the *Phaedrus'* other, earlier, image of the soul as a charioteer and team of horses. The charioteer is reason or prudence, one horse being obedient and the other not. The obedient horse is similar to the *Republic*'s spiritedness, reason's ally in controlling desire.[12] The disobedient horse is an image of unruly desire; it has sex in mind even in the most refined love. Training, punishment, persuasion, and shame can control desire, but only philosophic eros keeps it fully in line. Desire differs from love of the beautiful, but its arising together with love also shows their similarity. Because the place of rhetoric in controlling desire, or elevating love, is the *Phaedrus'* explicit theme, we are reminded again of mind's intrinsic connection to the false as well as the true, and of the soul's orientation to a range of things, high and low. The soul is passion, reason, and self-direction (choice) infused with each other, with reason the distinctive power. Its essence is the movement connected to thinking, eros, and spiritedness (combining and separating) as reason activates and guides them.

III

This discussion brings us to the next element of Plato's understanding of the soul, its parts. He gives no exhaustive list of these parts. Best known is the admittedly incomplete discussion we just encountered in the *Republic* of the soul's three parts— reason, spiritedness, and desire.[13] At times, as the *Phaedrus* suggests, Plato differentiates eros, or love, from desire. Eros' object is the beautiful, and desire's is pleasure. Socrates also speaks of wishing for what is good. One therefore hates the ugly, flees the painful, and fears the bad or harmful. We also hope for pleasure if we believe it good, however, and are confident or bold in seeking it. And, we fear doing something shameful or ignoble and being justly punished for it. The picture of the soul and the focus of its different passions is complex.

Part of this complexity arises because beautiful things can also be good, good things pleasant, and ugly or shameful things harmful or painful. Moreover, Plato does not confine himself to rigorous terms, notably in the connections between love and friendship.[14] And, when he speaks of love of wealth or gain, he speaks of something that may look beautiful or attractive but is intrinsically more useful than noble. His experiments with making all matters of virtue matters of knowledge, furthermore, also have the effect of eradicating some of the differences among the soul's actions.[15]

Part of this complexity also comes from the difficulty of the phenomenon of spiritedness. It differs from desire, yet it is hard to speak of several of its objects in terms different from love—we mention love of victory and love of rule as well as anger and indignation. Plato discusses spiritedness as such only in the *Republic,* and refers to it infrequently. It does not appear in the *Laches* and *Protagoras* (despite their discussions of courage) or in the *Statesman,* where, as we will see, the difference between courage and moderation proves significant.[16]

The passions that spiritedness groups, however, are mentioned often enough: anger, competitiveness (or love of victory), puffed up pride, rashness, and strength of soul.[17] When Plato assimilates the objects of these passions to those of desire, eros, wishing, and hoping (and to knowledge), he treats, say, boldness, as hope or confidence in attaining good things.[18] The more one knows, the greater the confidence and the smaller the risk. Is this confidence still courage? If it is not, is courage foolish? But, boldness or rashness is also an element of unthinking movement, and although anger may be caused by thwarted desire or injustice, it is not itself a need we fill or a proper distribution we make.[19] Unlike eros, anger and the other phenomena of spiritedness seem, rather, to punish, push away, separate, guard, protect, defend, endure, and to overcome, dominate, master, and destroy. These phenomena may ultimately be oriented to something noble that we love, such as our country, not only to necessity and one's immediate own. As such, however, unlike eros, spiritedness does not seek to join together. (The painful things we flee, bad ones we fear, or ignoble ones we hate are primarily things we try not to be with.) At their extremes, the phenomena with which spiritedness deals do not call for ecstatic merger but for fanatical fastidiousness or mastery. Spiritedness and courage are one's freedom and security, or one's possible rule, and the increase of one's imperial separation as one is. "Mad" eros or desire, and self-knowing or moderation, on the other hand, are phenomena of openness, transformation, reaching up and embracing, not thrusting away and pushing back.[20]

We should not draw unbridgeable distinctions between the erotic and the spirited or suppose that there is in every circumstance a fixed order of the soul. The punishing or guarding carried out by the *Republic*'s spirited soldiers can serve freedom, understood as proper or moderate assimilation to the beautiful. The "true" city of desire is elevated to the city of spiritedness. Overcoming fear and shame is necessary for one's own philosophic search for knowledge. What is especially fundamental intellectually, however, is to follow the true guidance of things that are not one's own. The soul's passions are the seat both of the enclosedness, rationally understood, that spurs the self-attention that we require to improve ourselves, and of the openness, rationally understood, that can grasp what counts as "improvement."

Plato also deploys several elements of mind that belong to soul: perceiving, remembering, calculating, thinking mathematically, dividing, combining, measuring, speaking, and recognizing (seeing and understanding) images, things, and rational forms.[21] The core of speech or reason is noetic understanding or recognition, and the dividing and combining associated with it. In the *Republic*'s image of the objects of knowledge as a divided but connected line, imagination sees shadows or images, trust sees animals and artifacts, thought grasps mathematical objects, and understanding (*nous*) sees ideas.[22]

Perception, memory, and opinion are the elements of the soul's knowing and learning that Plato connects most to the body. Perception through the senses is often, but not always, mistaken. Opinion can be false, but also true. The soul houses the mystery of error and image, the heart of man's status as in between pure body and pure reason. The developed soul is passionate reason, or reasoned passion. To understand it, therefore, we must understand its actions and goals, not its parts alone.

The *Philebus*

Our next step is to examine further Plato's understanding of the good. I base my discussion on the *Philebus,* which is explicitly about the human good, "the state and disposition of soul capable of supplying to all humans a life that is happy."[23] Its central topic is the worth of pleasure and thought.[24] Its purpose is to defend thought and, as much as possible, to assimilate pleasure to it. The *Philebus* also introduces to our analysis Plato's understanding of measure, standards, and limits, and offers further reflections about how to divide and combine things. These subjects are especially significant for the *Statesman,* Plato's dialogue on political science, which we will discuss in chapter 9.

I

The *Philebus* begins as Socrates is inviting Protarchus to continue a conversation that Philebus is giving up: Protarchus agrees to take over Philebus' argument that "pleasure . . . is good for all animals." Socrates' stand is that prudence and thinking are "better than and preferable to pleasure." They agree that if something is superior to either, both are "defeated" by it. If it is akin to pleasure, pleasure wins; if akin to thought, thought wins.[25]

Socrates "knows" that pleasure is complex: "beginning from it . . . we must examine and reflect on what nature it has."[26] He suggests that pleasure takes on shapes "in some sense unlike each other," for the immoderate and moderate take pleasure, but it looks mindless to call them alike.[27] Protarchus, suggests, however, that they are not contrary qua pleasure but that their pleasures arise from contrary things. Yet, Socrates replies, color is like color, but black and white are contrary.[28] There are contrary pleasures, although the pleasant things are pleasant. While Protarchus calls all pleasures good, Socrates asserts that some are good, and most bad.

II

Something that is "amazing and somehow or other wonderful by nature," Socrates claims, "came up incidentally" in what they just said. "That the many are one and the one many is an amazing utterance." Protarchus' example is that he is one by nature, yet has many contraries—he is heavy and light, and so on. For Socrates, however, this is only a popular wonder because it is about things that become. What he finds wonderful concerns "whenever someone tries to set down human being as one and ox as one and the beautiful as one and the good as one." Are there monads of this kind? Among what comes to be and is unlimited, one must, apparently impossibly, set down a monad "as pulled apart and become many," or "as a whole apart from itself" "it comes to be one and the same simultaneously in one and many."[29]

There is a way out, Socrates asserts, "of which I am always a lover," although it often escapes him and leaves him perplexed. "Whatever the things are that are said to be, they are out of one and many, and have in themselves an innate limit and limitlessness." So, we must "always set down on each occasion a single idea about anything and go on to search for it." After we find one idea, we must examine two, "three or some different number and see how many each of these ones is, not just that it is one and many and unlimited." We must glimpse the entire number between one and unlimited, that is, "the middle things."[30] Pleasure is unlimited, unless we differentiate it by classes. If we do not differentiate pleasure and thought within themselves, moreover, and equate each with goodness, each pleasure or art becomes equally good. We discover, indeed, that Socrates proceeds not by classifying pleasures directly by different substances—sex, music, and the like—but, rather, by classifying in terms of criteria such as purity, expectation, and restoration. This enables him to differentiate pleasures as such and not claim only that different pleasures arise from contrary things.

Socrates clarifies with the example of letters: what proceeds from our voice is one (say, sound) and a multitude (say, many sounds), but we are skilled only if we "know how many and what kind [the sounds] are."[31] We understand no letter, moreover, unless we understand all.

Socrates also is suggesting here the importance (and restrictions) of thought in articulating things. The articulation of letters results from voice or sound, that is, it carries its own sensory articulation. But enumerating, classifying, and linking these sounds and voices so that each is a letter only if all are is an act of mind. That we can articulate notes, harmonies, and rhythms numerically suggests that we can express mathematically what pleases in music. Yet, the pleasure of knowing the numbers is not identical to that of hearing the pleasing song.

III

Socrates now turns to speeches that say that neither pleasure nor thought is the good but, rather, "a third, other than but better than both." They agree that the good is perfect, sufficient, and pursued and desired without "a thought to anything else." Neither pleasure nor thought taken alone can really be good, Socrates then suggests, because each is needy (i.e., insufficient). Protarchus claims, however, that if he were already enjoying he would not need to calculate future needs. But Socrates shows that he would still need mind, for without it he would not even opine that he is enjoying or remember beyond the moment what he enjoyed. Protarchus is speechless; he clearly would not choose what he agrees would be a jellyfish's thoughtless life. He should not be soft and cowardly, Socrates tells him. For none would choose mind with no share in pleasure, "but altogether unaffected by all things of the kind."[32] Everyone would choose the life "mixed together from both and a partner in both." Neither of the pair is "sufficient, perfect and choosable for all plants and animals."[33] Socrates will still be arguing, however, that mind is more akin to "whatever that thing is, in the taking of which this (common) life has become as choiceworthy as it is good."

III A

Socrates shows easily that no one chooses utterly mindless pleasure. To say that we choose a life that mixes pleasure and thought because pleasure needs mind, however, suggests only that we minimize pleasure if we cannot remember, hope, plan for, or recognize it. What if bursts of pleasure brought with them their own discrimination from other things, however, so that we notice them, although we do not recognize them as "pleasure" and, therefore, do not connect them to other pleasures? What if, moreover, one were passively guaranteed pleasure so that forethought was unnecessary and memory irrelevant?[34] Mind would then be unnecessary for pleasure, unless one called any disconnected discrimination mental.

One might then still argue that a life that mixes mind with pleasure is best, because the mind's pleasures are especially powerful. If we choose the life of the mind just because it is pleasant, however, or because it helps us see and calculate other pleasures, we are not choosing the life of the mind as mind. We see, therefore, that Socrates has not yet shown that in mind's possible combinations with pleasure it is the senior partner in their mixed goodness nor explained just what is good in mind as such. Nonetheless, because no one in fact chooses or can choose a life of completely dumb though guaranteed bursts of enjoyment, Socrates succeeds in commonsensically vindicating mind over the absence of mind.

This section's other major part is its brief portrait of the elements of what is good—to be desired, sufficient, and perfect. What are the differences and connections among these elements? If we choose what is desirable but insufficient, we must select more, for choosing what is sufficient leaves us happier. What, however, distinguishes sufficiency from perfection? The sufficient is missing no part. But it need not, as such, be ordered fittingly or do the job well. Even a baseball team with nine stars plays well only if coached, or organized, well. Fit is the "perfection" here; the team is better if it is well ordered. It is better still if each part excels, that is, if sufficient goes beyond adequate, for the perfect or complete organization of nine mediocrities also is not good enough; good enough to do the job does not do it well. What is perfect fits the task by using available powers to the fullest. What is truly perfect as well as truly sufficient is completely satisfactory for the task—the perfect gift, meal, or team. A perfectly sufficient weapon in the hands of a tyrant, however, is hardly good. The good must also be choiceworthy; that is, the task or action that the implement serves must itself (sufficiently and perfectly) satisfy the fuller ends to which it belongs. It must ultimately be choiceworthy in the full sense, that is, truly be pursued and desired "without a thought to anything else." Tyrants' weapons do not serve freedom and virtue.

IV

Socrates now begins to consider if mind is more alike than pleasure to what is good in their mixture. He starts by dividing "all beings now in the whole," into three species, the limit, the unlimited, and a mixture. He then adds a fourth, the cause of the mixing.[35]

What Socrates means by the unlimited is the more and less that go on without stopping—to use his examples, the endless extremes of hot and cold, dry and wet, or quick and slow. (He does not say what accounts for the differences among the three pairs.) His discussion of limit is more hesitant. Limit is connected to "measure" the way that 98.6 degrees is a healthy temperature and unlimited heat or cold are not. Number makes these "commensurate and consonant." He also suggests that the wickedness and hubris of limitless pleasures are limited by law and order and that beautiful things (such as the seasons) in which there is measure are produced by mixing limit and the unlimited. Here, Socrates is alluding to the measure of too much and too little. Just right, and not too quick or slow, expresses a limit that allows a noble deed or beautiful composition to stand forth.[36] The limit alone, however, does not supply the deed or the notes, the "material." In this sense, limit and unlimited are a pair; the unending more and less can be brought into various productions (and become visible) through the possibility of limit.

V

They are now to "perfect most beautifully" the decision about whether the second prize for human happiness belongs to pleasure or thought. Given what they have just said, something other than "the nature of the unlimited" must supply "some part of good to pleasure."[37] There is an unlimited and a satisfactory limited in the so-called whole "of the cosmos, sun, and so on." "No inferior and shallow cause" presides over them, ordering and arranging years and seasons. "It has to be spoken of most justly as wisdom and mind," which "would never come to be without soul."[38] Mind rules the whole and causes all things.

Although we might have expected Socrates to assign mind to limit, mind appears instead to recognize the intelligible and to cause its mixing with the unlimited. "Limit," then, is not equivalent to mind. Rather, mind sees the intelligible and can recognize or bring it into being as limit in some bodies or things, causing them to be measured.[39] By connecting pleasure so much with the unlimited, however, Socrates arranges that it cannot cause all or most of what is good in the mixture of pleasure and mind, for what is good is sufficient and perfect as well as desirable, and sufficiency and perfection are allied more with limit than with the unlimited.

VI

None of this sufficiently clarifies thought and pleasure. Socrates begins by looking at pleasure. He claims first that we cannot taste it sufficiently apart from pain; the pair "come to be by nature in the common genus."[40] When the harmony in animals is dissolving, nature dissolves and pain is generated. When a nature "is being fitted back together again and is returning to its own nature," pleasure comes into being. Hunger is dissolution and pain, and eating is filling up and pleasure. When an ensouled species comes to be naturally from the unlimited and limit, corruption is a pain and going back to its being a pleasure. This is "one species of pain and pleasure." The soul's expectation of pleasant things is pleasant and confidence making, and its expectation of painful things is painful and frightening. This expectation, which occurs in the soul itself, is another species of pleasure and pain. Animals who are neither being corrupted nor restored are neither in pain nor taking pleasure. We can live the thoughtful life in this third disposition—according to Socrates and Protarchus, this life might be the most divine of all.[41]

The pleasure that belongs to soul comes to be "through memory." What occurs "in common in a single experience and in the joint motion of the soul and body" is sensation. Memory preserves sensation, and the soul "recollects" when it resumes what it once experienced with the body.[42] This helps clarify "vividly" and "precisely" the pleasure of soul and desire apart from body. Hunger, thirst, and others, are desires: What "is that same thing we look at" in calling them by a single name? In thirst, one experiences emptiness and desires its contrary, fulfillment. One can be in touch with fulfillment either by sensation or memory, but (in this example) the body is empty, so it is the soul, by memory, that is in touch with fulfillment. Protarchus thinks the bodily experience of emptiness together with the soul's longing or expectation would be doubly painful, but Socrates claims that in hoping for fulfillment one rejoices: the "singly double" pain is emptiness and hopelessness.

VI A

We see that Socrates does not begin with pure pleasures but with the pleasure connected to pain, in the sense of dissolution.[43] His thrust is to connect even such pleasure to mind, because of the importance of hope. Pleasure is the filling, or the expected filling, of emptiness. He for the moment ignores the pleasure of taste apart from quenching thirst and the trainer or general's directing diet for purposes beyond satiety. He is trying to show mind's importance even in the simply natural bodily pleasures and to show, too, that a steady disposition is possible that is not a cycle of pleasure and pain.

Socrates' move to mind is obvious in his second species of pleasure, namely, confidence or hopefulness about satisfaction. He does not picture desire as emptiness alone but directs it toward remembered fulfillment. He can therefore say that longing with hope is pleasant; he does not even say that expecting remembered fulfillment is less pleasant than sensed fulfillment.

Socrates leaves open the precise nature of desire's movement, memory's touching, actual fulfilling, and the harmony whose dissolution is pain. The connections among mind, limit, a fulfilled state, desire for fulfillment, and pleasure in becoming fulfilled are tantalizingly present but out of reach or undeveloped. Clearly, however, Socrates has sufficiently intellectualized desire and pleasure that his next topic, his discussion of false pleasure, does not sound as bizarrely contradictory to us as it does to Protarchus.

VII

Socrates now considers whether pains and pleasures are true or false. Protarchus concedes that opinions can be true or false, but not pleasures, fears, or expectations. For Socrates, however, this is a perplexity that has held him "in complete and continuous wonder." After all, if pleasures cannot be false, no one—dreaming, mad, or distracted—ever imagines that he is enjoying when he is not. Now, opinion opines something and pleasure takes pleasure in something. Opinion really opines (whether rightly or truly), and pleasure really takes pleasure. So, why is pleasure characterized only by truth, but opinion by truth and falsehood?

Choice, Socrates continues, arises from memory and sensation. When someone sees an apparition unclearly at a distance, he might luckily say to himself that it is a human or mistakenly say it is a statue. He may state this to others or hold the opinion within himself. Our souls resemble books; when memory and sensation coincide, the writer, as it were, writes true speeches. When he writes false things, untruths result. After the writer, a painter in our soul paints images of the things once opined and said. Images of true opinions are true, of false, false.[44]

They had earlier linked the soul's pleasures to anticipatory enjoyment. Throughout life, we are always full of just and unjust hopes. Our hopes are speeches and painted apparitions in which, say, we see ourselves enjoying extremely. For the good, these pleasures are mostly true, and for the bad, false. So, there are "false pleasures in the souls of human beings." They are "imitations of the true pleasures with more laughable results, and pains likewise."[45] Just as we opine things that are not, were not, and will not be, and produce false opinion, so, too, is it possible to rejoice at things that are not or have not been, and "perhaps most often and repeatedly at things that are never going to happen."[46] This same speech applies to fear, rage, "and everything of this kind."

VII A

To prove that there are false pleasures, one might try to show that some pleasures are more connected to pain than others. "False" pleasures would be unable to free themselves from the dross that we must experience with them. They would be like unclear perceptions. Or, one might think of false pleasures as incomplete. The pleasure may fade as quickly as a filling meal, or it may fade because the activity that brings it about is soon boring, that is, because it fails to engage the mind or senses sufficiently. A pleasure would thus be "false" if it is insufficiently plain or intense, fades quickly, or is cloying. Not just the activity, but the quality of the pleasure connected to it, would be inadequate.

One could ground these observations by suggesting that pleasure is complex. If pleasure is composed from longing and (expected) resolution, and also from fitting concentration (or intensity), depth (or resonance and reverberation), and purity (or distinctiveness), it would be false when it is incomplete, insufficient, diluted, short-lived, thin, cloying, or indistinct. This falseness would not be mere talk but would belong to experience or sensation.[47]

Socrates may have much of this in mind, but he does not take this path directly.[48] He still wants to demonstrate that false pleasure exists while considering phenomena such as eating, drinking, and sex. Hence, the place of madness or daydreaming in his attempt to show that pleasures can be false; we remember or expect that a sensation pleases which in fact did or will not, and thus we project an expectation of false pleasure.

One still wants to say that in all cases something in the pleasure taking is true. A "pleasure" that could not be false would need to be the pleasant feeling itself, stripped from any results or comparisons—taking pleasure would itself be true pleasure.

Such "true" pleasure may exist, but it would not make false or merely imitative pleasure impossible—"falseness" understood as in fact not filling emptiness (and therefore being falsely expected to do so), in fact not quenching thirst (as saltwater would not), or the other possibilities for falseness I suggested earlier. (I feel it satisfies, but it does not, and I often feel its inadequacy even as it partially satisfies.) More clearly for the question of happiness, moreover, the elements of pleasure one might say are prior to falsification—say the smooth movements or staccato bursts of dissolution and repletion—do not have much to do with what is good. In what sense are they sufficient, perfect, or even choiceworthy?[49]

Let us consider a final example. In hoping for or daydreaming about a pleasant afterlife, one could mistake one's remembered fulfillments for the actual fulfillments of heaven and live in a fool's paradise. One's taking pleasure would, then, be false. True pleasure is fulfillment, not what merely seems to be or imitates fulfillment.[50]

VIII

Socrates continues to examine pleasure, with false pleasure as an underlying theme. While the soul desires, the body may also be supplying pain and pleasure from its experience. Contrary pleasures and pains may therefore arise. We can compare their amounts and extremes, and judge them. When we see things (very) close up or at a (great) distance, truth vanishes. So, too, when we observe pleasures and pains at a distance or close up, they may appear extreme—greater or less than when they appear rightly.

Pain results from the body's disjunctions, conjunctions, emptyings, fillings, increases, and decreases, and pleasure from restoration to one's nature. If the animal body's nature is neither being corrupted nor restored, no pain or pleasure results. We can thus set down three lives—one pleasant, one painful, one neither. People who say they are enjoying merely when they are not in pain are "opining false things about their enjoyment."[51]

Socrates and Protarchus now agree that "to see the nature of any species" (such as hardness or pleasure), one should look at "the so-called topmost and most extreme." We commonly say the greatest pleasures are bodily, for the healthy. Yet, the thirsty and shivering ill live with the greatest desire or neediness. It thus seems to follow that the extremely ill will enjoy greater, more intense, pleasure than the healthy. Moreover, the pleasures of the hybristic and senseless seem to Protarchus to "exceed by intensity" the pleasures of the moderate, to the point of madness.[52] So, as Socrates sums up this view, "it's clearly in some evil of soul and the body but not in virtue that the greatest pleasures as well as the greatest pains come to be."[53] They then consider sex and other situations in which there are "simultaneously contrary experiences in restoration and corruption," those "where pains are set" side by side with pleasure. The "flooding in of pleasure" in sex is especially connected to "thoughtlessness."[54]

VIII A

Socrates continues to suggest that pleasures and pains can be false. A truly large future pleasure can seem as small as the moon looks from the earth, and a truly small one as large as a bug brought an inch from one's eyes.[55] He does not suggest what the true perspective is, however, or how we come to know that an apparently small pleasure will in fact be large in the future.

Knowing true pleasure seems especially difficult if the end point of being pleased is unclear. If we knew we would be punished terribly, immediately, and unsurpassably, an apparently overwhelming pleasure would be easy to combat. (With sufficient immediacy and knowledge of reward, we might even endure great pain.)[56] Without such knowledge, however, or, at least, without an effective horizon that unifies (some) pleasures and allows us to calculate their relation, it is difficult to discern genuinely large and small. So, limits other than the ordinarily absent immediate calculation seem necessary—limits (as Socrates had said earlier and intimates here) that connect pleasure to law, virtue, or the good of mind—if we are to judge pleasures by their true magnitude. In the *Phaedrus* and the *Symposium,* for example, eros goes beyond the completion to which it is first oriented; it ultimately seeks philosophical understanding, our fully natural satisfaction.

Socrates also complicates and enriches his discussion by claiming that pain's corruption can occur in filling, increase, and conjunction, as well as their opposites. Presumably, then, restorative pleasure can come from shrinking or emptying, not only swelling or filling, and from pushing off, or separating from, an intruder, attachment, or obstacle, not only from bringing together what comes apart.

IX

Socrates now turns from mixing pleasure and pain in, or with, the body to mixing them in the soul. Anger, fear, eros, emulation, jealousy, and envy are pains of the soul that are also filled with "indescribable pleasures."[57] Protarchus agrees that in tragedy people weep while rejoicing, but he cannot conceive how our souls mix pain and pleasure in comedies. Socrates uses the example of envy to clarify them all. Envy is a pain of the soul. A harmless friend's seeming beauty, seeming virtue, and seeming wisdom are ridiculous and bad.[58] So, when we laugh, say, at our friend's exposed ignorance, we simultaneously mix the pleasure of laughter with the pain of envy. (We envy his wisdom or reputation for wisdom, say, even while we are exposing it as false or incomplete.) Pains and pleasure, indeed, are mixed in the "entire tragedy and comedy of life."[59] We find mixed elements in anger, longing, "and everything of that kind."

IX A

Socrates presumably uses laughter to exemplify the soul's mixing pleasure and pain because, as we have suggested, laughing is especially connected to knowing and is visibly pleasant; he sets the stage for discussing the mixture of pleasure and knowledge. Laughing is pleasure at the false or ignorant, in particular, here, at the pretentious who seem to themselves wiser and more virtuous than they are. Without ourselves being wise we can recognize pretense, just as an ugly fan can laugh cruelly at the dripping makeup of an aging star. Of course, if the drip belongs to a scene being shot with a still lovely actress, or if not laughing would have been rewarded with a bit part in the next act, the laugh is on us. False pleasure exists, although laughing is at the moment pleasant.

Socrates does not explore the pleasure in laughter itself.[60] He means, rather, to show that the soul's pains such as anger, envy, and sadness can mix with its pleasures. He presents tragedy and comedy as two sides of defending and promoting virtue. Just as one can rejoice while crying during tragedies, comedy, too, mixes pain and pleasure because envy, anger, and the like are painful. Envy defends one's own by recognizing the (supposed) injustice or accident of someone else's talents or success. Anger, too, defends one's pride or a city's justice. Anger and envy are painful because they recognize vulnerability and imperfection, wounded pride or dashed hopes. They are unjust, however, if the punishment that triggers the anger is fair or the success that triggers the envy is merited.[61]

Socrates downplays laughing at the strong, which we certainly do behind closed doors. The closed doors show our fear of revenge, but laughing at the stupidity of the strong also encourages us to attack them. This attack is just if the pretense to virtue or wisdom is far enough from the truth, for we especially think here of the strong as tyrants. Attacking the hateful and laughing at them are not far apart.[62] Socrates perhaps also has in mind reverence and irreverence toward the gods.

X

Socrates "naturally" proceeds next to unmixed pleasures, "the perceived pleasures of painless fulfillment," such as (seeing) beautiful colors, figures, and "smooth and brilliant sounds which send forth a single pure song." Straight, round, and the surfaces and solids made from them are "by nature beautiful in themselves and admit some pleasure peculiar to themselves which in no way resembles the pleasures of scratchings."[63] We can add the pleasures of learning to this species, Socrates claims, if we admit no hunger in learning or consequent suffering in forgetting. "Pure pleasures" exist apart from pain and belong to the very few, not the many.

It is simply correct, they agree, that the purest, most beautiful, truest, whitest of whites (the example they choose) is not the greatest and most extensive but the most unblended (even if it is small).[64] Socrates concludes and Protarchus agrees "extremely," that any small and slight pleasure cleansed of pain is more pleasant, beautiful, and truer than is a great and excessive pleasure.

X A

The discussion of pure pleasure redresses the distortion implicit in the conversation so far, namely, that pleasure must be connected to dissolution, restoration, and desire. The model for such restorative pleasures is satisfying hunger. Socrates suggests that what we learn can afford pure pleasure and not be preceded by hunger for knowledge.[65] A mathematical truth can strike us as immediately beautiful and correct. But, do not many such truths strike us in their correctness only when preceded by apparently laborious study? We might reply that to learn is to look and to see, and thus differs from study that helps us know by providing tools to develop our powers, as becoming habituated to virtue differs from virtuous action and its pleasure, or painful exercise differs from the pleasure of seeing, using, and displaying the body that exercise helps to perfect. Moreover, as such study progresses, it may itself involve learning or experiencing several pure satisfactions.

One might then wonder if the learning that is preceded by study is possible without first seeking to know, that is, without desire that seeks resolution. Perhaps, however, such seeking is not, or not primarily, desire that needs filling but, rather, using or activating powers (our mind), knowing or recognizing ignorance and pretence, and discovering how to see or know more and more. Such seeking to know is, in fact, not only or primarily meeting need or dissolving tension but, rather, fully looking around and observing. (There is pleasure in the hunt, even if it fails.) By looking, one can learn about, be struck by, or be pleased by what is pure. As we have suggested, search begins in wonder and perplexity, and perplexed questioning is a natural activity of the soul, an examining, a looking around to discover the ways forward. The "pain" in seeking to know is primarily a clearing away of obstacles (including one's pretence) on the path to seeing ever more clearly; it is a recognition of unclarity or the experience of the truncated use of one's powers, as, say, in one who becomes tired. The pleasure in seeking and learning, therefore, is pure, if not altogether pure.

Despite this purity of pleasure in knowing, devotion to what grants pure but puny pleasures hardly makes sense as a way of life. Who would choose to do nothing but watch white paint dry or listen to tweeting birds?[66] Is one pure sound in fact more pleasant or beautiful than complex symphonies played with many mistakes and a bit too loud or soft? Socrates elevates purity because it is a necessary part of the choiceworthiness of the intellect, and its pleasure. We have a natural experience of pure pleasure in using our reason or seeing what is true. But, one would also need to connect such purity to some experience of extent (say, wondering at the impressive) if one were fully to relate happiness to pure pleasure, even reason's pure pleasure. Purity is not in each case sufficiency, full choiceworthiness, or, even, the fitting or perfect.[67]

XI

The issue of pleasure's purity leads Socrates and Protarchus to discuss next the claim that pleasure has no being but always becomes.[68] What becomes is for the sake of a being, as shipbuilding is for the sake of ships. That for the sake of which something becomes "is in the lot and portion of the good"; that which becomes is in a different lot. So, someone who says that pleasure is a becoming is laughing at those who assert that it is good, and to choose to live only if one experienced hunger and thirst is not to choose the good. Nor, Socrates says, is it to choose the "third kind of life," that is, "thoughtful thinking, as pure as possible," with "neither joy or pain."[69] It is "irrational," moreover, to suggest that in the soul "only pleasure is good, but courage, moderation, mind, or anything else that the soul has allotted to it as good, is not of this kind."[70]

We see that Socrates' argument is tendentious even if correct because he acts as if everything that becomes is merely a means to an end. But the cycle of emptying and filling might have in view only its own pleasure, and Socrates' examples of ends here (ships and beloveds) are themselves changeable and incomplete, that is, not beings in the full sense. What we can say, however, is that whatever someone (such as Callicles) may indicate to the contrary, restorative pleasure could not in fact be a complete or beautiful end because it is imperfect, requiring, as it does, ugly discombobulation.[71] It is, in fact, not simply good, because it is unsatisfying and insufficient. The usual sense of a good man—a gentleman or virtuous man—cannot be captured by the unattractive cycle of filling and emptying. Still, Socrates leaves undeveloped here what counts finally as an end, and what as an instrument.

XII

Socrates now turns from pleasure to the intellect and, following upon his discussion of pure pleasure, explores what is purest by nature in knowledge and the mind.[72] One part of science concerns handicrafts, the other education and upbringing. The purest parts of handicrafts depend on science, the arts of number, measurement, and weighing. What remains (in handicrafts) is conjecture, exercising the senses by knack and guesswork, which we produce through practice and toil. Flute playing, music, medicine, farming, piloting, and generalship, for example, are full of guesswork that hunts down the measure, with the steady and firm part small. Carpentry, however, is more precise and uses the largest number of measures and instruments (such as the straightedge and compass) in its ship and house building. So, we set the arts down in two, those with less and those with more precision in their works.[73]

We also must set down as two arithmetic and the most precise. The arithmetic of the many counts unequal monads (e.g., two armies, or two of the smallest and largest), and the other does not. The carpenters' and merchants' arts of measurement and calculation differ from geometry and calculation as philosophers practice them. The philosopher's art is more precise, pure, clear (and true) by what Protarchus calls a wonderful magnitude of difference.[74] So, as with pleasure, there is indeed "some knowledge purer than another."[75]

Socrates claims that everyone with any mind believes that the "truest understanding concerns that which is and the 'really and truly,' and that which is by nature always in the same way."[76] Protarchus, however, says that he used to hear from Gorgias that knowledge of persuasion is the best of all arts.[77] Socrates says that he is not yet searching for the art that "excels by being greatest," best, and most beneficial but for the one that examines the plain, precise, and truest, even if it and its benefits are small. Grant Gorgias' art superiority in usefulness for human beings. They are looking "only at whether there is by nature some power of our soul to love the true and do everything for its sake."[78]

Many arts, Socrates continues, seek things that are involved with opinion. Even if someone believes that he is inquiring into nature, he is seeking the origin, agency, and being affected of *this* cosmos, that is, things that become, not those that always are. But, there is no precise truth about things that are never in the same state. We must speak of the solid, pure, true, and uncontaminated as concerned with what is always in the same state and most unmixed, and what is "in the highest degree akin to them."[79]

XII A

Socrates' approach to knowledge does not visibly parallel his approach to pleasure. He does not discuss corruption and restoration, so that knowledge would restore us from ignorance to a natural or usual state. Nor does he discuss elements of knowledge—say, noncontradiction and comprehensiveness—other than precision. Rather, he concerns himself with purity. Pure knowledge requires that knowing and what is known involve as little of the body as possible. Socrates therefore distinguishes from purity whatever uses practice, toil, guesswork, and the senses. His distinction suggests the *Statesman,* where political science is not practical, but cognitive, because it does not use the body.[80]

Protarchus and Socrates remind us here of Gorgias. By calling attention to rhetoric, which makes pleasure the good, and by separating its guesswork from precise knowledge, Socrates largely splits science from ordinary or restorative pleasure. In the *Statesman,* however, statesmen direct rhetoricians and generals, and also use a measure that ultimately depends on the "precise itself." So, knowledge of a measure that is perhaps as pure as arithmetic, if not pure simply, presumably can help to set a limit or aid in producing a common good and even find a place in it for impure pleasure.[81] Nonetheless, Socrates does not develop here the common benefit that might arise from precise knowledge or the possible union between pure and more unlimited pleasure. What links the purity of the carpenter's precision to a ship he helps build, whose purpose his art as such does not know but that the statesman knows?

Another indication that Socrates does not (yet) fully clarify here the connection between knowledge, or pure knowledge, and what is good is his discussing pure knowledge by discarding education and looking only at craftsmanship.[82] In his picture, the accountant leads the good life while calculating a carpenter's expenses. If he needs a leisured rest he can admire a perfectly planed board and set to measuring the numbers involved. But, can knowledge be good, or the chief partner in a life that combines knowledge and pleasure, if it is only of small benefit to one's soul? Hence, Socrates suggests that a power in the soul loves and is for the sake of the true, that is, that the true (as pure) is the soul's, or this power's, good.[83] Still, Plato pushes aside any developed description of philosophy as perfecting the soul so that he can bring forth pure knowing. Philosophy as directing and limiting, as perfecting the powers of reason and the other parts of the soul, and as discovering a precision that fits together the choiceworthy or sufficient, is (to this point) missing.

XIII

They turn now to mixing thought with pleasure; Socrates likens this mixing to craftsmanship. To give the second prize they must grasp the good "or else some type of it" clearly and distinctly. They have a "way to the good," for their argument shows that they should seek the good in a mixed life, as someone seeking a human "would hold it a great thing for finding the one sought if he inquired about and learned where he dwells." To come closest to what is beautifully mixed, it is safest to mix "a true pleasure to a higher degree than another" with an art that is "more precise than another art." Sciences that look to things "that are always in the same way and same state" are the truer ones.

Will a mix of these, however, be "sufficient in their blended state to supply us productively with the most satisfactory life?" Suppose someone thoughtful about justice itself has an account that goes with his thinking and thinks this same way about all the things that are. Could he know sufficiently if he has "the account of the divine circle and sphere" but is ignorant of the human circle and sphere and uses his instruments as standards (say, in house building) in the same way as the divine circles? Protarchus thinks this "ridiculous" and agrees that they must blend the "unstable and false art of the false circle and straightedge."[84] For our life to be a life we must also interpolate music, as Socrates suggests; this, too, is filled with guesswork and imitation, and falls short of purity.

They thus agree to admit to the mix all the true pleasures and also those "that are necessary and indispensable." It is "harmless or beneficial to know all the arts," moreover, and if it is harmless or advantageous "to take pleasure in all pleasures throughout one's life," these too should be blended. It is scarcely possible or beneficial for a genus to be alone and unsupported in its purity. It is for pleasure "to set up house with" as perfect and complete knowledge as possible of each pleasure, as well as of everything else.[85]

Mind and thought do not need the greatest and most extreme pleasures. These disturb "the souls in which we dwell through manic travails." The true and pure pleasures, however, are nearly their own, as are those that come with health and moderation. The pleasures of virtue can also be mixed but not those of thoughtlessness and vice, "if one wants to try to learn" in as beautiful a mixture as possible "what is by nature good in man and in the whole, and what ideas one has to divine in it."[86]

For Socrates "the present account appears to have been produced as if it were some bodiless cosmos destined to rule beautifully an ensouled body." They are now "standing at the portico of the dwelling of the good."[87] In every mixture, the cause of everything worthwhile is measure and "commensurate nature." Without it, the things being blended are destroyed and are a mishmash. Indeed, the power of good "has fled for us into the nature of the beautiful, for measuredness and commensuration turn out everywhere to be beauty and virtue." They have not tracked down the good with a single idea but comprehend it with three things—beauty, commensuration, and truth.

They then judge pleasure and mind in relation to each of these. Mind is more akin to truth, while pleasure, especially sex, boasts and lies. No being, moreover, is "naturally more unmeasured than pleasure and exceeding gladness," while mind and science are "with measure."[88] Moreover, mind more than pleasure partakes of beauty, for none sees it as shameful, but we recognize and hide the ridiculousness and shamelessness of the greatest pleasures.

So, Socrates summarizes. The first acquisition and most pleasant choice is "measure, the measured, the timely and everything of the kind"; the second is the commensurate, beautiful, perfect, and sufficient and its family; third is mind and thought; fourth, the sciences, art, and speeches of right opinions of the soul; and, fifth, the soul's pure, painless pleasures, some going along with sciences, some with sensations. Their account probably ceases "at the sixth judgment." After Socrates' summary, the dialogue concludes with Protarchus telling Socrates to continue to the end, for a "small thing remains."[89]

XIII A

Socrates compares their search for the good life to seeking for a man by looking in his home. One cannot look intelligently unless one knows where the quarry dwells. Presumably, one also cannot find the quarry unless one can recognize it.[90] Socrates indicates, as he does in each dialogue, that the knowledge he seeks involves knowing better—more clearly, purely, deeply, or broadly—what one already knows or recognizes to some extent. What Socrates does here is to consider more fully what is and is not pure in pleasure and thought. The likeness of pleasure and thought in their purity is what allows them to mix, with no third element required. That in the sensible which allows some purity or precision—the numerical within it, and those of its pleasures not preceded by pain or need—is good in it and available for mixture. Presumably, virtue's measuring of, say, wealth in liberality is a perfecting from which springs unbidden pleasure that blends with relatively pure thought or prudence. Indeed, virtue shows the power of Socrates' linking of the good to the pure. Virtue, however, also belongs to the political community in which it takes place. This allows it to serve and enjoy a common good, that is, a larger, more extensive whole than is available in what might seem to be its "pure" acts.[91]

The dialogue's conclusion makes explicit its inconclusiveness. One outstanding difficulty is that we do not see clearly how a life that mixes pure thought and pure pleasure properly incorporates, or domesticates, magnitude or excess. A second issue is to grasp more clearly the link between the carpenter's numbers, pure numbers, and the pleasures that derive from what he makes. The shamefulness of viewing sex (to which Protarchus points) needs to be squared with the shamelessness (and nobility) of the philosopher's understanding, that is, viewing, of love and, therefore, of sex. He must grasp what is impure in order to know it and its cause. If he does not rise above ordinary shame, his understanding is truncated.

Let us consider more fully the connection between purity, pleasure, and philosophy.[92] If philosophy is the fullest use of the mind and best way of life, it must incorporate as much of the human powers as possible. The best way of life should, as we see in the *Republic* and *Symposium,* speak to the full range of eros and spiritedness. In this way it must also incorporate as much of the unlimited, as much of the extreme, as we need for full satisfaction. Otherwise, its pleasure is too petty to counter other claims. Philosophy must limit or direct our soul's possible excess if it is to advance its assertion of supremacy convincingly.[93] This suggests that philosophy cannot be restricted to small but pure pleasures, or to passive equanimity. Moreover, the perplexity in philosophy seems painful, and one of its pleasures to be the relief from perplexity. As Socrates indicates in the *Greater Hippias,* not to rest content with one's own ignorance requires constant self-questioning or self-criticism. Yet, as we have suggested, perplexity is natural, not unnatural, and we can connect it to what is wonderful. From this viewpoint, perplexity belongs to reason or to the soul's activity. Philosophy's exploring involves effort, not pain; it even experiences the pleasure of seeing what is pure. Indeed, philosophy purifies the soul by directing it to thought and by seeing the measure, or what is pure, in what it observes. It considers the wonderful and elevated, and expands it.

Philosophy, thus, incorporates the extensive, if not the unlimited; the purity of its pleasure and the range of its active equanimity (as it explores the most magnificent things) is in a certain sense extreme. After all, philosophy considers the purity and breadth of pleasure itself. Moreover, to grasp the pure measures and ends as the cause of what they measure is to deal with what is extensive.[94] This is not to say however, and Socrates does not suggest, that philosophic pleasure is in all respects superior. The soul informs the body, but the body retains its independence. Knowing the extensive, or the possibility of the (un)limited, is not the same as experiencing it as such in all of its formations. Socrates does not discuss directly here how pure thinking uses and elevates eros and thumos.

Plato also indicates the restrictions of the life of the mind, once we consider Protarchus' mistaken view that no one thinks mind is shameful.[95] Callicles criticizes Socrates for the immaturity of continuing to think and babble when he should be making himself powerful and useful, and Anytus criticizes him for undercutting respect for laws, gods, and elders, that is, for undercutting the respect for old authorities within which noble actions take place.[96] How or whether pure thought can avoid being harmful, destructive, and ignoble remains undiscussed. Socrates alludes to this question at the end of the dialogue (and earlier) when he mentions auguries and gods.

The elements of what is good change subtly in this final discussion from their earlier appearance. The sufficient, perfect, and choiceworthy become the commensurate, beautiful, and true. The true and choiceworthy, the pure, or the pure as a measure, in a sense stand outside the others. Neither thought nor pleasure is self-sufficient. But the mixture of pleasure in, and thought of, the pure is also apparently not self-sufficient either, for Socrates must allow impure pleasures and sciences to belong to a satisfactory life.

CHAPTER 8

Knowledge and Illusion

The *Philebus'* concern with knowledge and measure points politically to Plato's third dialogue about politics, the *Statesman,* which considers political "science," or political knowledge, and features an analysis of measuring and precision. It is last in a group that includes the *Theatetus* and *Sophist.* To understand it we first must discuss these two.

The *Theatetus*

The *Theatetus'* subject is knowledge. It does not present an epistemology in the modern sense, however, if by that we mean an attempt to provide indubitable support for the knowledge we think we have. Rather, its question is what knowledge is, as the *Laches* asks what courage is. Because the chief interlocutor, Theatetus, looks like Socrates, moreover, we may say that the dialogue studies knowledge from the standpoint of what resembles Socrates.

The dialogue's first major topic is the difficulty inherent in the claim that each thing is utterly different from everything else, that anything supposedly uniform and stable is only conventional, that there is no common measure, and that to know is merely to sense or perceive immediately, not to reason. Socrates, together with his interlocutors Theatetus and Theodorus, counters this claim by showing its paradoxes, and by indicating counterexamples: resemblance in looks and names, mathematics, conversation and agreement, self-awareness in wonder or perplexity, inner truth and surface pretense, memory, anticipation, and the generality of what is beneficial. The dialogue's second major topic develops alternatives to this Heraclitan claim, suggested by these counterexamples. It uncovers paradoxes in these alternatives, however, and indicates the difficulties in showing that anything is uniform or true. Furthermore, it offers examples of difference, or falseness, for which claims about knowledge and truth are apparently unable to account. The result is that the *Theatetus* surfaces the elements of knowledge, but both knowledge and error, and sameness and difference, remain mysterious.

I

Plato presents the *Theatetus* as an account of Socrates' conversation with young Theatetus, which Eucleides transcribes from Socrates' narration. Eucleides first wrote down what he remembered; he then repeatedly checked his account with Socrates and corrected it, and he then removed Socrates' "he agreed," "he consented," and, presumably, even more telling remarks. He records the transformed conversation in a book his slave now reads to Terpison.[1] So, what we read resembles Socrates' conversation by at least one remove (Eucleides' rewrite), possibly two (Socrates' possible dishonesty in recounting it), and perhaps even a third, fourth, and fifth (Socrates and Eucleides' possibly poor memories, and Eucleides' possible dishonesty). Whether Socrates' conversations fully reflect his thought or the truth is uncertain, moreover, as is our ability to understand.[2] All this, furthermore, is transmitted or created by Plato. The dialogue thus at best resembles a true Socratic conversation, let alone directly recording his or Plato's internal thought.[3] The limits to knowledge are thus presented to us from the outset.

Plato's opening suggests another limit to knowledge beyond the ambiguity of conversation or transmission, namely, our mind's connection to our body. Theatetus is dying from wounds suffered in war, but he presses for home, against medical advice. Socrates claims to be more concerned with smart young Athenians than with those from elsewhere. The dialogue ends as Socrates goes to answer the charges for which he is soon tried and killed. In general, then, the life of knowledge belongs to and is affected by the body, one's own, and politics in ways that the *Philebus*, say, suggests but leaves murky. Their connection becomes the subject of Socrates' long discussion with Theodorus in the middle of the dialogue. (Theodorus is the one who introduces him to Theatetus.)[4] Socrates sketches there a picture in which "philosophy" and politics are radically or, indeed, ridiculously, separated.

II

Socrates asks Theatetus what knowledge (or science) is. Theatetus' answer mentions each and all the sciences but does not say what the single "knowledge" is in them. Socrates' example of what he wants is mud. Knowledge is not this or that science, as mud is not a potter's, furnace maker's, or brick maker's mud. Rather, mud is earth kneaded with liquid, something we must first know in order to point out mud's different types. These types vary by different amounts of water and earth, so it is easy to say what they all are or share. Matters are more complex with the arts and sciences, however, because they serve different goals, produce different shapes or orders, use different materials, and employ different procedures.[5] Yet, we also notice some minimum commonality when first identifying sciences—say, precision in producing. Socrates seeks the one (name) science that is like the one (name) mud.[6]

Theatetus does not fail because he is stupid. On the contrary: Plato next displays Theatetus' mathematical ability by showing how he groups all rational and incommensurable roots as one. Perhaps, then, Socrates can help him give birth to a thought about knowledge. For, Socrates claims that he can do no more. He is sterile himself, but he arouses perplexity in others, through which they generate their own thoughts. His image of himself as a midwife like his mother suggests a likeness of soul to body, of truth (births) to its images or lies (wind eggs), and the importance of self- understanding in knowledge.

III

Theatetus now suggests, "once more from the beginning" that "knowledge is nothing else but perception." This proves to be Protagoras' thought, however, not his own. Men measure that and how each thing is and is not. Everything for each of us is how it appears to him, as a cold wind is cold only for those who thus perceive it. This thought's source, Socrates claims, is all the "wise" thinkers and poets (except Parmenides). Their view is that nothing is one by itself but that all come to be from "motion and mutual mixing."[7] (The good is motion, which "causes that which seems to be, and the fact of becoming, and rest the fact of non-being and perishing.")[8]

Socrates proceeds to explore the extremism, or incomprehensibility, of this opinion. (Socrates' arguments in the *Theatetus,* up to the exploration of whether right opinion is knowledge, constitute the central arguments against relativism.) If it is correct, nothing can appear the same to different human beings, or to any of us at different times. What we measure ourselves against, and we as measurers, would always be altering. Yet, such variation seems untrue of increase, decrease, and equality: When is six not half of twelve? Still, Socrates is taller and smaller than a growing Theatetus, while he remains the same.[9]

Theatetus wonders and becomes dizzy about these things. Socrates suggests that wondering is the experience that "is very much a philosopher's."[10] Protagoras' hidden truth, he now argues, is that motion has two species, infinite in multitude: the power to affect and the power to be affected.[11] We cannot grasp affecting and what is affected separately and fixedly. So, to be is nothing that is by itself. Utterances that accord with nature are of becomings, makings, and perishings. It is thus easy to refute someone who rests on something he thinks is fixed.

If good, beautiful, and everything else merely become, however, how could there be any dreams, illnesses, or misperceptions? Still, if (as Socrates and Theatetus now say) I am wholly different when I taste wine as sweet when I am healthy and as bitter when I am sick, then there is indeed no (fixed) bitterness or perception.[12] If this is so, however, why does Protagoras bother to teach us at all, given that already "each of us is the measure for himself of his own wisdom?" Indeed, why does he not say that pig measures all? (This suggests that specifying men as men must modify the grounds of the view that each individual man is a fully unique measure.) Moreover, we remember what we see, yet memory is not perception.[13] So, perhaps knowledge and perception are not the same.

IV

They thus begin again.[14] The new beginning starts to develop the place of the soul in perceiving and knowing, and how this differs from perception simply. It follows the split between memory and perception, and Theatetus' suggestion that we perceive letters, but that only letter experts know what they mean. Presumably, moreover, we cannot merely perceive whatever it is that makes all perceptions "perceptions."[15]

If we set down seeing and other perceptions as knowing, Socrates suggests, we will be claiming that it is possible to know and not know what one knows, for we can see with one eye open and one closed, and so on.[16] Socrates, playing Protagoras, then lets Protagoras defend himself: the ill and healthy are both wise, because one opines what one experiences. Some, however, can change the ill to the healthy—physicians through drugs, and sophists through speeches. Things we opine in a good condition of soul are, indeed, better, but not truer, than those we opine in a poor condition.[17] Farmers make good perceptions for plants, and "wise" and good public speakers bring into being good things for cities. Whatever things are just and beautiful in each city's opinion, however, "are for it as long as it holds them to be so."[18] Cities lay down and for a time resolve the beautiful, just, and pious: "none of them is by nature with a being of its own."[19]

Socrates now develops the question of political opinion and knowledge by bringing out and appealing to the radical split between philosophy and the city, as it appears to Theodorus. In making his argument, Socrates will overstate our split from animals, or the soul's possible split from the body, and thus will ignore or downplay political philosophy and what it can know. He will act as if one could know the nature of each whole without considering how the city and, indeed, the truly philosophic soul, is only an image of what is whole, and of justice. He will also act as if one can grasp human happiness without seeing the connection between soul and body. His own practice in the dialogues, however, and the Theatetus' opening, show the link between education and opinion, love of one's own and the good, and images and truth.[20] As Socrates' discussion with Theodorus unfolds, he subtly provides the grounds for a more complex view than the one he explicitly presents, by indicating the importance of paradigms, and of similarities.

Those reared in philosophy, Socrates says, speak as free men, in peace and leisure. They speak as long or as briefly as it takes to "hit upon 'that which is.'"[21] Public speakers in court, however, speak in the press of business and necessity, like slaves. They become shrewd but small-souled, crooked, lying, and unjust. The philosophers, by contrast, appear laughable. Indeed, Socrates claims that the top ones do not know their way to the marketplace or such things as who is well or base born in the city. For, in truth, only their bodies reside in the city; their souls geometrize under the earth and stargaze, explaining "everywhere every nature of each whole of the things which are."[22]

The many laugh at their perplexity and they laugh at the many's ignorance:

the philosopher seeks, "and all his thing is in exploring . . . what [a] human being is and in what respect it's suitable for a nature of that sort to act or be acted on that's different from all the rest."[23] Indeed, when the philosopher examines what justice and injustice are, and how each differs from everything else and each other, and "of what sort of pair human happiness and misery is," and in what way "it's suitable for the nature of a human being" to acquire and avoid one of the pair, it is the small-souled man who is perplexed.

Socrates and Theodorus now turn to a view based on, but modifying, what Socrates had said in Protagoras' name about what is good: that while some say the just is the city's opinion of what it lays down, no one is courageous enough to claim that what is (merely) laid down as beneficial is (therefore) good.[24] Legislation looks to the beneficial, especially to future benefit, but does not always hit it. The physician or farmer's opinion about whether I will have a fever or whether future wine will be sweet is better than a layman's or another artisan's. Protagoras' argument that each is the measure of truth again proves incorrect.

Perhaps, nonetheless, perception and knowledge are the same, especially when one considers only present experience. But Heraclitans cannot in fact say this because (says Theodorus) they "permit nothing to be stable in their own speech or souls."[25] The Heraclitans assert that neither what affects or is affected is by itself, but "from both of them becoming mutually together, perceptions and things perceived come to be." Motion has two species, locomotion (e.g., change of place) and alternation (e.g., change from black to white). Yet, if all flows, nothing can abide, not even the white or seeing as white, let alone whiteness or seeing.[26] Every "answer" is correct, so we in fact need not concede that man is the measure (except if one is intelligent) or that knowledge is perception.

V

Socrates now continues, with Theatetus. They agree that our perceptions "strain together toward some single look (idea)," and that it is the soul that perceives through them, "as if they're tools."[27] Indeed, the soul perceives, examines, and aims at some things through itself, say, what is common to sight and hearing: (not) being, (dis)similarity, same, other, one and the rest of number and, especially, beautiful and ugly, and good and bad.[28] The soul mainly examines these things in their mutual relations, Theatetus thinks, and calculates past and present in relation to future. These calculations require education, Socrates claims, while "experiences that stretch to the soul through the body" (say, stiff and soft) are there by nature for beasts as well as men. Theatetus believes that opinion is the soul's name for "whenever it alone by itself deals with the things that are." Socrates thus proposes another beginning, and Theatetus now says that knowledge is probably true opinion—not all kinds or ideas (looks) of opinion, however, because there are false opinions.

So, is knowledge opinion of the simply true? Socrates is perplexed "before myself," however, when he is unable to say what the experience is of opining false things and how it comes to be. False opinion cannot be of what we know.[29] But it also cannot be of what is not because in it we are opining or perceiving something—some one thing. So, false opinion seems impossible.

Perhaps, then, false opining is "else-opining," where we exchange in thought something that is for another thing that is, always opining what is, but mistaking what we are aiming at. Thinking is the soul's speech with itself, its asking, answering, affirming and denying, and opinion is a determination where it "asserts the same thing and does not stand apart in doubt."[30] But does anyone assert before himself that the other is an other, that the beautiful is ugly, for example, the unjust, just, the odd, even, the ox a horse, or the two, one? No one dares: so, there is no else opining.[31]

Socrates turns to still another way out of their perplexity. He examines the previously rejected view that "it's impossible to opine what one does not know to be what one knows, and be deceived."[32] The issue is memory, imaged as a wax block larger, purer, and more measured in liquidity or stiffness for some than for others. We remember the things we perceive that have been impressed in the wax. Many cases exist where the relations between knowing, perceiving, and having a memorial do not allow false opining. This falseness can exist only when I have a memory impression of, say, Theatetus as well as Theodorus, see one inadequately from a distance, and misassign the impression. I exchange sight and seal, or right and left, as in mirror images. Those called wise learn easily and have good memories, that is, deep, extensive, smooth, and measured wax in their souls. They do not interchange seals, and they quickly assign perceptions: they opine what is true; their casts are called the things that are.[33]

If false opinion exists only in the conjunction of perception and memory, however, what of things about which we only think? Theatetus believes we would not confuse a merely thought of (and unperceived) man and horse with each other, but he then concedes that someone might believe seven plus five to be eleven, not twelve, not to speak of larger numbers.[34] So, either we can be deceived in thoughts themselves (and I can know and not know the same things at the same time) or there is no false opinion.

To proceed, says Socrates, they must be daring and shameless, willing to say "what sort of thing it is to know," although they are still seeking what knowledge is. Indeed, to converse at all they have been saying, "I recognize, know, and understand." Socrates thus now explores the opinion that knowledge is a possession (not an immediate having or using), some thing one owns as one owns a cloak that one might not be using or hunts and encloses birds in a dovecote. One places the knowledges one acquires in one's soul and seizes, holds, or lets them go again as necessary. When one reads or numbers, one lays one's hands on what one once knew and takes these up ready to hand for thought. So, we can possess knowledge yet seize a false opinion, as one might seize eleven rather than twelve, or the wrong bird in one's dovecote, as it were. Yet, it is still strange to say that it is knowledge (here, knowing seven and five) that makes us ignorant. Perhaps, then, we also have nonknowledges flying around in our souls, and to opine what is false is to seize nonknowledge. Someone who does this, however, believes he has knowledge. So, our previous perplexities would return.

V A

The difficulties here arise from the presumed gulf between knowing and not knowing, a gulf carried over from the earlier discussion of the apparently unbridgeable difference between my perception and yours. Perhaps, however, the object of a true and false opinion is the same but only in some respects.[35] We can know seven and five yet falsely combine them. Theatetus may look like Socrates but not think as he does. Theodorus could appear fuzzy or distorted from a distance when compared to the way he looks here and now. Socrates presumably had these points in mind when he discussed else-opining, distortions from memory, and the fact that the false must be about something. Working through the possibilities and varieties of likeness, "respects," difference, and combining is, of course, more complex than merely suggesting their importance. Much of the *Sophist* and *Statesman* involves this work.

VI

They therefore again ask what knowledge is, from the beginning. They now seek what "will least contradict (them)selves" and is "plain."[36] Theatetus has no new suggestions but claims again that true opinion is knowledge, and, indeed (and unaccountably), that "everything that comes to be as a result of it is beautiful and good."[37] Socrates, however, now distinguishes true opinion from knowledge. For, the "public speakers and advocates" who are great in "wisdom" persuade and make one opine what they want but do not teach sufficiently by art. Jurors who are persuaded by hearsay, not by what they see, are deciding without knowledge, for example, even when they accept true opinion and are persuaded rightly.[38] Theatetus' next suggestion, thus, is that true opinion with speech is knowledge and without speech is outside of knowledge.[39] Moreover, whatever admits of speech is knowable and whatever does not, unknowable.

Socrates asks first about the split between knowable and not knowable. He claims to have dreamt that some people say that the first things are like letters (or elements); everything is composed from them, but they do not admit speech. They can only be named, each thing alone by itself. One cannot even apply being or nonbeing to them; that is, one cannot even say that an element is, because one can apply nothing else to it if one is to speak of it alone. "It's impossible for any one of the first things to get stated in speech."[40] Not names but "the plaiting of names is the being of speech."[41] The unknowable elements are perceptible, but it is the syllables that are knowable, opinable, and sayable. In true opinion without speech (without giving and receiving an account), "the soul tells the truth but does not know."[42]

The one who said this glanced at letters, Socrates says, so we must put to the "torture" how we learned letters. SO says S + O. The letters, at least the S, are voiceless; that is, the syllable but not the letter is knowable. But, Socrates asks, "do we mean" by the syllable both or (if more than two) all the letters, or some single look (idea) that comes to be when they are put together. Theatetus says all of them. But, then, how could one know both the S and O if one is ignorant of each of the two. Perhaps, then, the syllable is indeed not its elements but a single look that comes from elements that fit together: the whole is other than its parts.

If the syllable is a look "altogether indivisible" into its elements, however, they are not its parts. But if the syllable is its elements, such parts are as knowable as it is. Perhaps, then, the elements are in fact knowable? Socrates suggests that when we learn letters and notes we try to recognize them distinctly so we may place them correctly. This may be so of elements generally, and it is only playful to say that "a syllable is by nature knowable and an element unknowable."[43]

Socrates continues to examine what it means to say that speech added to true opinion results in complete and perfect knowledge. What is speech? One thing it means is imaging one's thought, making it evident through sound. That is not what is meant here. Perhaps, second, speech (or reason—*logos*) is the capacity, when asked, to answer through the elements. But would someone who listed all the elements of a wagon know its being? Moreover, what if someone who writes correctly each letter of Theatetus writes tau (rather than theta) to begin Theodorus? He opines what is right (about Theatetus) but lacks knowledge. This is right opinion with speech, but it is not speech as "going through the whole through elements."[44]

The third species of speech is to be the sign of the difference of each thing from everything else, as we say the sun "is the most brilliant of the things that go around the earth across the sky."[45] Theatetus thinks this beautiful, but Socrates no longer "understands anything," although when standing far off it appeared they were saying something. Right opinion about, say, Theatetus, occurs only after one knows the features, say the snub-nosedness, by which he differs from others with a snub nose, such as Socrates. One does not only know that he is snub-nosed, let alone that he is human and thus has a nose. So, if speech points out by what the opined thing differs from everything else, it adds nothing to right opinion.[46] Although much has been said, therefore, they do not know what knowledge is. The dialogue ends as Socrates goes to answer the charges against him; that is, it ends where the *Euthyphro* begins.

VI A

Knowledge may be right opinion with speech, but the speech must also be correct. Giving reasons does not guarantee that the reasons are true, because we can lie in speech and make mistakes. As Socrates and Theodorus have indicated, rhetoric, not art, sometimes persuades juries and legislators. Giving reasons does not assure that we fully recognize the whole whose parts we are describing, moreover, or grasp the parts. Knowing moves back and forth among wholes and parts, recognition and analytic division, the soul's perceiving and classifying, and caused and cause.

A right opinion, indeed, may simply be a good guess. What differentiates knowledge from good guesses? Socrates in the *Gorgias,* and the Athenian in the *Laws,* tell us that physicians discuss causes with free patients. Right opinion that is grounded on clarity, precision, sufficiency, classifying, and causality is knowledge or, at least, goes beyond right opinion alone. It sees the whole and points out, dialectically, its end, shape, material, and the origin from which it comes about.

VI B

The *Theatetus* does not say conclusively what knowledge is but subtly uncovers the phenomena that are connected to it. To know seems to be to perceive. Yet, perception alone is always in motion, it is said, or at best instantaneous. We can fix in place neither the perceiving nor what is perceived. If this is so, however, we cannot differentiate or combine perceptions, split true perceptions from dreams, have perceptions as our own, or compare them to others'. There could be no measuring at all. If, nonetheless, we would still try to assert that each man is truly the measure, we would face the difficulty that we could not then recognize "man" or split men from pigs. The view that knowledge is only my perception is self-defeating.

For perception to be knowledge, therefore, we require something fixed or unified, the person or thing one's bodily perceptions disclose. Seeing this requirement, however, does not eliminate all questions. For, what is the nature of the commonality in what we perceive when, say, we see and hear Socrates, not Theatetus who looks like him? What accounts for seeing resemblances and making errors? Knowledge is primarily through the soul, because none of the five senses alone recognizes, say, a 'tree', same, being, or even Theatetus, and mathematics and memory do not as such use the senses. Seeing this, however, does not altogether dispel the difficulty of differentiating knowledge from error. The move from body to soul is vital, but it does not make knowledge transparent. The soul's seeing resemblance and unity remains a great question, as does its making mistakes, and the manner in which things can present themselves falsely. Mathematical, artistic, and self-knowledge group and divide what is intelligible. Were we able to specify all the intelligible elements in things, however, we might still not understand their combining. To know is to analyze and synthesize, but we must first, or concurrently, see things whole, or at once. Knowledge involves anticipating or expecting something that we already (imperfectly) possess, which we then examine more completely, see in a new light, or associate with new characteristics.[47]

To see things whole or at once points in two directions in the *Theatetus*, one to the identity of mud in the varieties of mud, the other to the best mud, which we could water down to suit other purposes. We know men are not pigs even if we do not truly know ourselves. But we see that some of us are closer to pigs than to Socrates.[48] Knowing and what is known occur in a context in which some things, and similar instances of them, are largely independent, and others are not but point to their completing end. Health is good and is knowable enough that few treat everyone's judgment about securing it as equally worthwhile. Even the desirability of the body's health is sometimes not the last word, however, if, say, it conflicts with virtue, the health of the soul, or a wish such as Theatetus' to return to one's own city. The sophists seem to think the good is natural—it is pleasure—but that the just, beautiful, and pious are altogether set by man, not nature. In truth, however, not all pleasures are equally good or only bodily. The political context, does indeed affect knowledge or its pursuit, but this context is not completely conventional. Theatetus, after all, lives in Athens, not Sparta, starts from theories, and meets Socrates.

This political connection is a central feature of the difference between Plato's discussion of knowledge and the analysis of today's epistemologists. It is reminiscent of—and a counter to—the links we see among politics, religion, and knowledge in Locke, or among truth, will, and history in Nietzsche and those he influences.[49] Yet, even if justice is natural and, therefore, we can properly understand this political connection, we could not reduce self-knowledge or freedom to politics. Freedom cannot exist apart from virtue and, hence, from the political community, but it also cannot exist apart from questioning virtue. We cannot be free apart from the confidence or courage that Socrates urges on Theatetus, but we also cannot be free apart from perplexity and wonder. The link between the human good and the city and between the good and the whole is crucial but difficult to discern. Knowledge and its objects are obscure because nothing stands apart transparently.

The *Sophist*

The question of knowledge proves in the *Theatetus* to be at root the question of how things are common or together and how they make themselves available for separation. To know is to know what is, and what is presents itself primarily in combination or as combining. This presentation is also at the heart of the possibility of error or deception. The *Theatetus* is thus followed by the *Sophist*, "on being," and the *Statesman*, on political knowledge.[50]

I

The *Sophist* continues the *Theatetus* by discussing falseness or error.[51] How can we know what is true if we cannot know what is false? But, how can we intelligibly say what is false, that is, what is not? On reflection, we see that things can be similar but not identical. They can be alike in some respects but not all, can be partially alike, can merely look alike, and so on. Perhaps what is false is not altogether different from what is true.[52]

Plato examines this question by seeking to understand sophists who, like statesmen, we mistake for philosophers; he advances in the *Sophist* to statements about same and other, as such. The discussion is led by a Stranger from Elea (where Parmenides was born), and he takes Socrates' suggestion that he use Theatetus as his interlocutor.[53] Their task or intention is to investigate, seek, hunt down, or pursue the sophist, and to make clear in speech, comprehend, or beautifully elaborate what he is in his work. The Stranger does not discuss how to conduct the pursuit but, rather, begins with an example, namely, an attempt to comprehend the work of the angler. The example proves relevant because, like the angler, the sophist hunts, or tries to acquire, living beings.

The Stranger's hunt for the angler indicates, without discussion, several elements of the kind of search—division, or diaresis—that he now pursues. One feature is that each new step requires us to look back at anglers. That is, the search draws out or specifies what is implicit in what we already recognize. The second is that the Stranger and Theatetus proceed by dividing in two, where each half is often preceded by grouping into one, or a "whole."[54] Thus, they begin by claiming that sophistry is an art, that we can divide arts between those that make (or produce) and those that acquire, and that angling belongs to those that acquire. The distinction between making and acquiring, however, followed upon first grouping as making (or "poetics"), farming, fabricating utensils, and imitating, and on first grouping as acquiring, learning, moneymaking, and hunting. As becomes evident with succeeding splits, however, the Stranger could have redistributed arts that he joins here. One might, for example, group farming and learning rather than (as he does) split them or group poetry and competition rather than (as he will) divide them. As with farming, true educating cultivates; it aids a natural movement that, in its case, issues in true learning.[55]

II

The Stranger and Theatetus arrive at angling by dividing acquisitions into willing acquisitions (e.g., exchange) and mastery (i.e., getting the better of someone), dividing mastery into (open) competition and (concealed) hunting, dividing hunting into hunting of the soulless and souled, dividing hunting of the souled into hunting the pedestrial and swimming, dividing hunting of the swimming into fowling and fishing, dividing fishing into striking and using fences (e.g., nets), dividing striking into torching and hooking, and dividing hooking into spearing downward with tridents and angling upwards.

We see that these divisions group and separate according to two different criteria, although the Stranger does not point this out; the criteria are methods of acquisition and characteristics of what is acquired. One may usefully consider the Stranger and Theatetus' own activity as a kind of hunting; they have "seized sufficiently the speech about the work (angling) itself."[56] What they seek (clarity about sophistry) is elusive or hidden. Philosophy not only joins or submits, it masters.[57]

After this paradigm, they proceed to inquire about the sophist, who proves, first, to hunt rich young men. Theatetus and the Stranger take humans to be tame animals. Hunting the tame is violent hunting (e.g., piracy, enslaving, tyranny) or conviction producing; conviction producing is public or private, and private hunting gives gifts (as lovers do, or as a "species of an erotic art") or earns wages.[58] When it professes to associate and earn its wage for the sake of virtue or to educate in opinions (as opposed to earning its wage by catering to whims through flattery or pleasure), it is sophistry.[59]

Sophistry is complex, and we can discuss it further. If we turn from hunting to exchange, we see that exchange involves gift giving or marketing, that marketing involves those who sell their own wares or exchange others', that those who exchange either retail in the city or merchandise from city to city, that the mercantile art exchanges what the body uses or what the soul uses, and that the soul merchandiser exhibits for entertainment (e.g., music or paintings) or seriousness (i.e., he sells "learnings," either of arts or virtue.) The sophist is therefore not only a hunter but also an exchanger who merchandises "speeches and learnings of virtue" or (a third definition) sells his own.

These first three definitions of sophistry involve virtue. We should see, however, that neither the Stranger, Theatetus, or the sophists say here what virtue is, that is, whether it is true or merely Protagorean virtue, whether it is one, with several names or several parts, or many, and what its connection is to knowledge.

Not only is the sophist a hunter and exchanger, they continue, he appears also to belong to the competitive (the open, masterful) part of acquisition. Competition is rivalry or combat; combat is body against body (the forcible) or speech against speech (the disputative); the disputative is contrary-loving public speech about the just (the forensic) or private through questions (the contradictory); the contradictory is artlessly about contracts, or disputes as a whole about the just and everything else (eristic); and of the eristic there is money-losing garrulity and money-making sophistry.[60]

III

They are still tracking the complex sophistic beast but now, as it were, they begin to follow a new direction. "Domestic tasks" such as filtering, combing, carding, spinning, and thousands of others exist, and the "art of discernment" is their single name.[61] Discernment sets apart similar from similar, or worse from better ("purification"). Purification purifies body (e.g., gymnastics, medicine, and bathing) or soul; to remove the soul's vice is to remove its illness and sedition (where the soul is corrupt because its opinions, desires, anger, pleasures, speeches, and pains are discordant) or its ugliness (i.e., its lack of measure in moving toward its target). The soul's ugliness, its disproportion, is its unwilling ignorance when it sets out for the truth.[62] As medicine treats the body's illness and gymnastics its ugliness, so, by nature, chastisement is closest to justice; it treats insolence, injustice, and cowardice. Instruction deals with ignorance, which has several genera; its largest species is to have the opinion that one knows something one does not.[63]

Education (not handicrafts) is the art that removes this folly.[64] It splits between paternal admonition and refutation, in which one shows someone that his opinions are contrary to themselves, that is, that he says nothing, although he believes he says something. The consequent shame and harshness to oneself leads the stiff opinions that impede learning to be taken out.[65] This is of all removals "the most pleasant one." The art of refutation is the greatest purification. "And one must hold . . . that whoever's unrefuted even if he is in fact the Great King if he is unpurified in the greatest things has become uneducated in these things in which it was fitting for whomever will be in his being happy to be purest and most beautiful."[66] It gives the sophists too much honor to call them the users of this art, the Stranger claims. Their resemblance or similarity to it is like that of wolf to dog, "the most savage to the most tame." The refutation that deals with seeming wisdom (doxosophia) is "sophistics noble and grand in descent."[67]

III A

The Stranger indicates that opinionated ignorance of the greatest things is the soul's greatest impurity, that is, that such ignorance is more impure than other ugliness. But he leaves unclear the connection between removing this ignorance and other beautifying of the soul, just as he leaves unclear the connection between the two kinds of soul purification, removing sedition and removing ignorance.[68] One might suggest that the refutation that removes folly sufficiently eliminates other vice. Indeed, the Stranger indicates subtly that the soul generally, not merely the mind, is involved in knowing, or in coming to know, our ignorance: He considers paternal admonition to be "softer" than refutation, and he mentions the shame that is connected to recognizing and overcoming folly. But he does not work out this connection. The soul's faculties are unexplored. Indeed, he separates courage, moderation, and justice from prudence.

Another way to pursue this question of the connection between removing sedition and removing ignorance is to ask what the origin is of the opinions that properly accord with anger and desire. Are they mere opinion, or knowledge? Vice is discord or sedition; to restore discordant elements is to restore concord or harmony. Why this concord is excellent is unclear here, however, because the Stranger does not spell out the nature of its elements. It would seem possible, for example, for outrageous desires and opinions that justified them to reach agreement. Perhaps, however, disorder will in fact emerge whenever desires are immoderate or opinions imprudent. It is safest to say that the soul that is purified ethically through punishment is ready to begin virtuous action, or to become virtuous, but is not fully virtuous. In any event, although the Stranger is reluctant to call the sophists true refuters or educators, he was not reluctant earlier to say that they sell speeches of virtue; however great their distance from moral virtue, it is apparently less than their distance from truly relieving ignorance.

The Stranger's discussion of purification is fundamentally at one with his discussion of the pure in the *Philebus*. The Stranger's discussion here enables us both to understand purity better and to raise further questions about it. To purify removes the worse, and, thus, allows the better to stand out. From what point of view, however, is the better good? It is easiest to see that it is good as means to an end, as we remove chaff from wheat we will bake or clean wool we will weave. Purifying, here, would not give the end at which we aim but would presuppose it. In the Stranger's understanding, we aim at the truth about the things that are central to happiness. Refutation is a purification that removes our false view that we already know these sufficiently. Purifying through refuting eliminates the opinionated ignorance that is ugly or dispro-portionate as measured by truth or self-knowledge. Refutation lets one face one's ignorance. This is a first step, or a necessary means, to moving toward knowledge of the greatest matters, although it is not in any obvious way this full knowledge itself. Such purification is pleasant, or more pleasant, than other relief; it is presumably in then recognizing ignorance, free from pre-tense, that one begins to enjoy the *Philebus'* intellectual pleasure of knowing what is pure.

The Stranger's discussion of purification also suggests that we are naturally or immediately on the correct path and that false opinion or discord deflects us from it. We aim to purely and beautifully achieve what is true. (Perplexity would then make it evident to us that we do not know how to proceed.) Yet, we wonder from whence arises our understanding of the true, proper, or final point of our path. What is the substance of our target? It does not seem that continuing purification alone can make our ends clear if purification leaves us only with good means for our ends, proportionate parts of beautiful wholes, or sensible concord. The purification must itself be measured by the end or whole, or by an original view of the greatest things, or those central for happiness.

Although purification would seem to presuppose the end in light of which the impure is bad or disproportionate, the Stranger also seems to suggest that continued purification can itself bring us to our end. To judge from the *Philebus,* the greatest things are themselves the purest things. In a sense, therefore, con-tinued purification is at once one's goal and one's path. As we suggested when discussing the *Philebus,* and as we just suggested in discussing ethical virtue and the soul, however, the status of the connections among the purest things themselves and the status of their connection to the full range and extension of the soul's powers and concerns remains unclear. Perhaps this range and, indeed, the substance of the end or whole by which we measure happiness is inseparable from the political community's establishing of comprehensive opinions, purposes, and actions. Some discussion of this issue occurs in the *Statesman* where "the greatest enchanter[s]of all sophists" are said to be those who deal with the political things, that is, not the mock refuters.[69] We cannot understand the *Sophist* completely on its own.

In the course of carrying out the divisions we have been following, Plato makes several points that we should draw out. We can group and regroup from different points of view the items that are available for division so that, for example, body divides from soul, yet both suffer corruption and ugliness. As Theatetus suggests, we use something as a paradigm—we make it plain—with a "question in mind."[70] Divisions are "beautiful" in light of their purpose or aim, not in light of the nobility of the things cut. When the Stranger groups purifications of body, he tells Theatetus that to display hunting, lice killing is no more ridiculous that generalship.[71] The Stranger's divisions do not visibly purify their genera. Indeed, the refuting that purifies the soul may often be advanced or accomplished through a discerning that separates like from like.

IV

These divisions leave Theatetus "perplexed" about what the sophist is and leave the sophist perplexed about whether he will slip through their speech. The Stranger first deals with Theatetus' perplexity by summarizing their results. Notably, he does not mention virtue. The upshot is that the sophist's many learnings make it difficult to see the singular feature of his art. They thus examine again, "somehow from the beginning."[72] Especially revealing for their continued search, the Stranger now says, is that the sophist is a contradictor and teacher of contradiction. Sophists promise to make everyone competent to contradict and dispute about divine things that are not evident to the many, about things evident in earth and sky, about private associations concerning being and becoming, and about laws and "all the political things and arts."[73]

Yet, how could one soundly contradict a knower without oneself knowing everything?[74] The young are willing to offer sophists money only if they contradict correctly, or appear to do so. Sophists seem to their pupils to be "wise in everything," although this is impossible.[75] In speeches (spoken images), as in painting, there is an art that enchants the young and makes the images seem true and the speaker wise.[76] The sophist is "a kind of enchanter and imitator and is in "the genus of conjurors." In the Stranger's new beginning, we see, he no longer confines the sophist to acquisition. When he began his discussion of angling, he placed imitation with making, thereby splitting it from acquisition.

To further pursue the sophist, they now divide imitation (mimetics) into eikastics, where one produces semblances that conform to the proportions of the paradigm in length, width, depth, and color, and phantastics, where one does not give back the "simply true proportions" but produces apparitions. (My standing close to the lower segments of large works and far from the upper segments, for example, makes the lower appear bigger and the upper smaller. In painting I must distort something's original proportions to make it appear proportionate, from the viewer's viewpoint.) So, a craftsman "nowadays" produces what seems beautiful, not "the proportions that are." The sophist "has some kind of art of phantastics."[77]

Their examination of the sophist as a phantastic imitator is difficult because "to appear and seem but not to be and to speak some things but not true—all these are forever full of perplexity."[78] How can one say that false things are, without being "stuck in contradiction"? How can one say that that which is not, is? One cannot even speak what is not, for in discussing it one could not properly say "something" or enumerate it. One also cannot refute this view, however, because to do so one must attach "to be" to it. So, the sophist "has slipped into a trackless region." When he asks us what, in calling him an image maker, we mean by image, he will not accept in our answer mirrors, bodies of water, "or sight altogether" "but will ask only on the basis of speeches."[79] That is, he will ask about the one "image" in all these images.[80]

An image is a semblance of that which is and, thus, contrary to it. Yet, Theatetus claims, an image still is, in a sense. It is in its being a semblance, and, thus, a strange plaiting or weaving of that which is and that which is not.[81] They will have to say that that which is not, in some respect is, and that that which is, in some point is not.[82]

V

The Stranger suggests that thanks to Theatetus, that is, to his view that semblances in some sense are, they will dare to try to refute Parmenides. They begin by investigating what seems plain, lest they agree while being confused. For, although they claim not to be perplexed about that which is, do they understand the Eleatic statements about it? When, say, we declare all things to be hot and cold, "what are we to suppose about this 'to be' of yours? Is it a third?"[83] If both are, is it not more clearly a one? This is perplexing, as is the meaning of those who say the all is one. For, it is then perplexing how something can be, can be named, and can be a whole, because this suggests that what is, is more than one simply. It proves to be "no more readily available to say about 'that which is' whatever it is than about 'that which is not.'"[84]

Those who define body and being as the same, moreover, battle with those who "force the simply true being to be some kinds of intelligible and bodiless species." The tame among them, however, are "ashamed to dare to agree" that "justice . . . intelligence and the rest of virtue, as well as their contraries, and soul . . . in which these things come to be" "are none of the things which are," or to insist that they are all bodies.[85] To refute them it is enough to show something bodiless, no matter how small. If they are perplexed about what one is looking at when saying both that bodies are and that what is naturally cognate with justice, intelligence, and soul is, moreover, they might at least agree that that which is is the power to affect or be affected.[86]

The friends of the species say that through bodily perception we share in becoming, and through the soul's reasoning (calculation) we share in being, which "is always . . . in the same state in the same respect."[87] What, however, is this sharing? They would disagree that being is sufficiently defined as the power to affect or be affected, because, for them, becoming is what is affected.[88] Yet, is not cognizing an affecting, so that being is affected or in motion when cognized? But how can this be if being is at rest? Still, can motion, life, soul, and intelligence truly not be "present to that which perfectly is, and it's not even living, not even thinking, but august and pure, without mind" and stands motionless?[89] Yet, if it does have thought, mind, life, or soul, it moves. But "that which is in the same respects and in the same state and about the same thing" could never "come to be apart from rest."[90] But, then, mind would not be or come to be. The philosopher who knows "these things" must, therefore, refuse "to accept the all" as stationary from those who speak of one or many species but also not listen to those who set 'that which is' in motion in every way. Rather, he must say "that all that is motionless and in a state of motion are both together 'that which is.'"[91]

They are still perplexed and ignorant of 'that which is.' Motion and rest are contraries, yet are, so being is in its nature neither of them. Perhaps, then, some things mix but not all? If nothing mixes, the various views that being is this or that—say, motion—refute themselves, but if all mixes "motion itself would altogether be at rest."[92] So, "some are and some are not willing to mix together." Musicians and grammarians recognize which high and low notes mix and how vowels bind other letters. Pretty nearly the greatest science, the science of the free, philosophy, knows which genera are consonant, which "hold them together through all of them" (as vowels do), and which "are causes of the division through the whole."[93] The dialectical science divides by genera and does not believe the same is another species, or the other the same.[94] The dialectician perceives one idea stretched through many that are apart, many "comprehended on the outside by one," one bound together through many wholes, and "many (ideas) set apart and distinct in every way."[95] The philosopher, he who "philosophizes purely and justly" is found in a region such as this.[96] It is hard for the many to see the philosopher because of the brilliance and divinity of his place; he is "devoted to the idea of what always is through reasoning (calculations)."[97]

They continue to look at the biggest genera, that is, not at all ideas. That which is is mixes with rest and motion, which do not mix with each other. Each is other than the two and the same as itself. Same and other must therefore be set down with the other three. For, "it's not on account of its own nature that each one is different from all the rest but on account of its participation in the idea of the other."[98] "So it is after all of necessity, in the case of motion and throughout all the genera, that 'that which is not' be, for in each and every case the nature of the other, in producing each to be other than 'that which is' makes it 'not that which is' and on the same terms we'll in this way speak correctly of all things as 'not the things which are.' And, once more, because they participate in 'that which is', we'll say they are and 'the things which are.'"[99] That which is not is other to that which is, but not its utter nihilation; that which is in itself is other than all the rest. To be not beautiful, for example, is other than the nature of the beautiful, not contrary to it, and not less among the things that are. (The not beautiful is the just or good, say, and not only the ugly.) "That which is not is one species to be counted in among the many things which are."[100] "The nature of the other both is and has been chopped into bits to extend over all 'the things which are' in their mutual relations."[101] "The pair of 'that which is' and the other has gone through everything and each other"; that is, they mix with all.[102]

V A

It is beyond our purpose to discuss being and nonbeing in detail. We should, however, make several points. First, each of the five genera or ideas is an object of soul and is not bodily. These genera refute the claim of those who deny intelligibles. The senses cannot perceive same, other, and being, as such. Indeed, we might say that the five genera are not only intelligible but conditions of intelligibility.[103] Second, and connected to the first point, we should observe that the Stranger discusses motion and rest in terms of thought and its objects, or in terms of mind and the things at rest that it seeks to know, or succeeds in know-ing. Each is—that is, not only thought's objects, but mind, too, is. Third, the nature of being, indeed, being itself, is hardly discussed. What, then, is its char-acter? "Same" is also insufficiently explored, because the emphasis is on other, given the theme of sophistry. Fourth, to grasp what the Stranger intends by pointing to "other," one should keep in mind the differences among otherness as such (as opposed to rest, motion, being, and same) something that is other than, or different from, another (as rest, motion, same, and being are different from otherness and from each other without themselves being otherness) and something as we attend to it in its being other, as opposed, say, to its own nature (as we might focus on rest as other than motion, rather than focusing on rest in its own nature.) Fifth, we notice the unanalyzed importance of nature, which seems to indicate the heart or essence of each of these genera without being yet another among them. Indeed, it is not obvious that the five genera are complete or that they are greater than ideas or classes such as beauty, goodness, the vir-tues, measure, and cause. The list is neither clearly exhaustive nor clearly of the greatest things. As we said, the five genera discussed are conditions of the intel-ligibility of what things are or (if one could be clearer about what being is) conditions of what things are. They do not as such seem to be what anything is, however, its character or substance. On the other hand, they are said to cause or produce through the whole or among the genera.[104] Sixth, how we might weave the genera is also discussed insufficiently. Same, other, and being are bonds among them all, but the nature of their binding is not transparent. Indeed, in much binding, say, in weaving itself, we can weave two together (the warp and the woof) without needing a third thread.[105] We can grasp this binding (and the five genera) better only when we more fully understand the range of natures, powers, and types of combinations among the *eide*. Still, "other" does help one make sense of participation or images and, therefore, of sophists. A shadow has the same shape as its original but different solidity and effect.

V B

The Stranger says that philosophy is the science of the free, although he does not develop what he means. Philosophy, as he had suggested earlier, requires leisure. Philosophy is the science of the free because it demands and uses the leisure that is denied to slaves and those who are harassed by the press of busi-ness. Philosophy is also the science of the free because its action is its own end. It and its knowledge are for its own sake, not for the sake of another purpose, however useful we might later discover it to be. It is also what most of all liberates. To be free is to be neither directed nor obstructed by another. Philosophy liberates from ignorance. It therefore frees from insidious control by opinion and false problems. It allows the truly perplexing obstacles to join with the purifying movement away from self-ignorance and toward the truly attractive and wonderful. Philosophy is the science of the free because it requires freedom, acts freely, and liberates.

Understanding philosophy as the science as the free, however, does not make immediately evident what the Stranger intends when he outlines dialectic by distinguishing finding one idea among many from comprehending many on the outside by one, and from one bound together through many wholes. The Stranger's practice (and Socrates' too) shows us what Plato has in mind, without our being able clearly to assign different practices to these three procedures. One might think of the first procedure as, say, grouping the things that rest as "rest," think of the second ("outside") procedure as grouping rest and motion as both "being," and think of the third procedure as seeing the various ways that being and other can mix with rest. The distinction between rest and motion would then exemplify the ideas that are "distinct in every way." Or, one might think of the first procedure as, say, grouping courageous acts as "courage," the second procedure as grouping courage and moderation as "virtue," and the third procedure as seeing the several ways that virtue can unite the specific virtues and can organize different goods. The example of virtue, moreover, enables us to see that a higher or broader idea may be richer than those below it and need not be an empty generality.

V C

We should develop more fully the Stranger's indications about being and power. Plato does not offer a full discursive treatment of power (*dunamis*), which we can also translate as ability, capacity, function, and, sometimes, as activity or possibility, where the substance of the ability is at first an acting or affecting (or a being affected or acted upon). In the *Gorgias*, Socrates tell Polus that a power that does not serve proper ends is in fact not a power at all. From the political point of view, this suggests that no neutral means exist that can serve every end or, at least, most ends, equally well. Political life is not properly the accumulation of wealth, friends, rule, or mastery. Each power is a power only when directed toward accomplishing the end for which it is a power or means. Powers are, therefore, not additively commensurable, as if each is merely more or less of the same. Plato's understanding here is similar to his understanding of the differences among pleasures, such that one could not simply add them up whatever the nature of their direction, completion, and source, and achieve happiness. His discussions of these matters in the *Gorgias* contrast, therefore, with today's tendency, rooted in the arguments of thinkers such as Hobbes, to equate all powers as neutral means for the satisfaction of equally worthwhile desires.

Plato's view of power's link to satisfaction fits with his view of its other features. A power is an ability to accomplish that is inseparable from its end and the order—say the order of activity, or the order of measuring, in which it is embedded or from which it stems.[106] Hearing and seeing are powers; seeing accomplishes vision, or good vision. Opinion is the mind's power of assent and dissent, which seeks to be knowing, or correct, assent and dissent. To connect power and accomplishment in this way is to connect a power to its virtue, its excellent acting or sufficient functioning. This excellence, in turn, fits within an order, say, a political order, or an order of the soul.

Power that is connected to accomplishment in the way just sketched, however, does not appear to be equivalent to powers that, in Plato's discussions, appear to be more neutral. Socrates suggests in the *Laches,* for example, that quickness is the power to accomplish much in little time. Mathematical roots are powers. (Indeed, we remember that in the *Protagoras* Socrates suggests a calculus of pleasure that one might take to be an attempt to add up amounts of identically enjoyable or worthwhile pleasures.) Powers in this sense are connected to the numerical measure of more or less of the same that, in the *Statesman,* the Stranger will distinguish from the measure of what fits. Quick is not the same as too quick. Even here, however, a power is not separated from what it accomplishes, although what it accomplishes is easier to distinguish from using well and the power is not a part of a fitting order. Even powers such as quickness are not simply fungible with all other powers, moreover, although their basis in counting tends in that direction.

The connection between this sense of power and the first sense belongs to the question of the relation between the two types of measuring. It also belongs to the question of the relation between the average and the excellent, the degree to which, say, one can recognize and discuss eros apart from its virtue, or good sight apart from any further order or use. We will explore these issues in chapter 9. In any event, power is not the equivalent of being or nature, because it is not simply equivalent to form and end. A power's defining movement is unintelligible apart from what it accomplishes or tries to accomplish, but the movement is not identical to what allows it to be complete. Opinion is not right opinion or (only) its own object. A thinking and choosing soul attempts to know and, in this sense, is moved by or attracted to what guides, orders, and allows us to separate and combine.[107] We might even speak intelligibly of activating ideas through our choices and actions. Indeed, one might speak of the power of the ideas: the Stranger mentions the power of the ideas to share in each other. What is, however, is not simply such movement, activity, and capacity.[108]

VI

Speech, the Stranger now suggests, comes about because of the weaving of species with each other. If that which is not mixes with speech, then false speech, opinion, deception, images, semblance, and appearance can come to be. The sophist is therefore wrong to claim that one cannot speak falsely.[109] Some sounds indicate actions, some those doing the action. Some sounds spoken in succession fit together in making something plain; some do not. Nouns or verbs in succession do not make the things that are clear. Rather, speech weaves names and verbs, makes plain, puts a limit on something, and is always of something.[110] As the Stranger says, "Theatetus, with whom I am now conversing, flies," is about Theatetus, but it says "other things than the things which are" about him.[111] It is a false speech. Thinking is speech (conversation) within the soul before itself, without sound. Opinion is assertion and negation in speeches. An experience of something present through perception is appearance—appearance mixes perception and thought.[112] So, some of these (thought, opinion, appearance), as congeners to speech, can be false. False speech and false opinion are possible.

Although the Stranger's argument tells us what error and falseness are—the mixture of speech with that which is other—it does not clarify this at length. It at most suggests that because of combining and negating (differing), falsehood can exist because it is partial but not completely nugatory.

VII

Having attempted to clarify falseness, the Stranger and Theatetus again pursue the sophist. Because false speech is possible, so too are deceiving, imitating, semblances, apparitions, and images. They proceed by dividing making, and arrive at divine and human imitation, which they then discuss. (While we at first saw the sophist among apparitions of acquisitive arts, we now continue to find him among the producers.) Some things are said to come from nature by a divine art, rather than by spontaneous cause. The gods make men, animals, and those from which natural things, such as fire, come to be. There are also "demonically" contrived images of these—apparitions, dreams, and shadows. Men make things and images too—say, houses and paintings of them.[113] Making images phantastically can also involve using one's body in a simulacrum of another. This is imitation, where one can either know or be ignorant of what one imitates.[114] Many are ignorant "of the figure of justice and virtue in general" but opine and try eagerly to make it appear "as if it were possible in deeds and speeches." One can fail to be just yet seem to be just. The sophists are opinion imitators rather than "historical" (i.e., knowing) imitators. The sophist, indeed, is an ironic imitator, because he fears he is ignorant of the things he embodies, not a simple one who believes he knows the things he opines.[115] The public speaker, not the statesman, is "capable of being ironical before the multitude in public and with long speeches," and the "one who in private and with brief speeches compels his interlocutor to contradict himself" is not wise but an imitator of the wise, and receives the derivative name, sophist.

The Stranger's view of the links among speaking, politics, and sophistry remind us of Socrates' understanding of rhetoric in the *Gorgias*. Sophists do not transcend opinion, however ironically they imitate it, and remain in thrall to a conventional view of virtue. At the same time, the sophist fears his ignorance but does not act courageously in the face of this fear. He remains impure. In contrast, Socrates and the Stranger encourage their interlocutors and themselves. By falling short of self-knowledge, we fall short of virtue, both moral and intellectual.[116] We accept or ignore more pretense than is necessary. The Stranger exemplifies the issue of irony and education here by trying to persuade Theatetus to agree that plants and animals are made by god rather than being naturally generated "from some kind of spontaneous cause that grows without thought," and indicating to Theatetus that he will in time arrive at the Stranger's opinion because Theatetus' "nature" is such "that it by itself will advance to this view."[117]

CHAPTER 9

Knowledge and Politics

The *Statesman*

The *Statesman* directly follows the *Sophist*. Its purpose is to define the *politikos,* whom we may call the statesman, the political man, the political scientist, or the political knower.[1] It means especially to explore the place of knowledge in political life—in human life—and the ways to combine things, politically and more generally.[2]

The *Statesman*

The *Statesman*'s opening prefigures much in the dialogue.[3] Socrates rebukes Theodorus for suggesting implicitly that sophist, statesman, and philosopher "are of equal worth," for "in honor they stand farther apart from one another than according to the proportion of your art." Later in the dialogue, proper measuring becomes crucial, and throughout it the Stranger's classifications seem to ignore honor or rank.[4] Socrates says that the two young interlocutors are his kin, because Theatetus "appears similar to me in the nature of his face," and young Socrates "has the same name." The connection between members of a pair, and between nature and convention, is later central to the discussion of virtue. Finally, the Stranger chooses that the "pair of us" now seek the states-man (not the philosopher) because "it is necessary, it appears to me." Unexplained choice that accords with necessity prefigures the rule of the knowing statesman over ignorant but willing citizens.[5]

I

The Stranger and young Socrates begin to search for the statesman by agreeing that he is characterized by knowledge or art. What, then, defines his art as opposed to other arts? They first divide all knowledge into practical and cognitive science, and, surprisingly, place the statesman in the cognitive half.[6] Practical arts such as carpentry "possess their science as if it naturally inheres in their actions," completing through their actions new bodies. Cognitive arts such as arithmetic furnish only knowledge.[7]

This classification means that the Stranger conceives statesmanship, as such, apart from molding or acquiring political bodies, that is, apart from, say, the ruler's own persuading and warring. The Stranger, therefore, also says that the advisor who knows how to rule is as much a political scientist as the ruler himself.[8] This further means, as the Stranger develops his point, that states-men do not differ from kings, tyrants, or slave masters. (If rule is cognitive and only cognitive, nonknowers have no claim to participate in ruling through, say, election or heredity.)[9] The Stranger even suggests, further, that political science and household management are the same, because "the figure of a large household and the bulk of a small city" do not differ in point of rule.[10]

Statesmen may not be practical, but they are also not geometers or other mathematicians. What is the difference? We can divide cognitive artists into those who merely discriminate (or judge) the things they know and those who, having "made a discrimination," are not finished but "charge each of the workmen with that which befits them, until they've produced whatever's been charged to them."[11] Statesmen, like master builders, belong to the injunctive or commanding branch of cognitive art.[12]

Cognitive commanders include more than statesmen. How do we separate them, so that we continue to isolate the statesman? The next step is to split those who issue their own commands from those who transmit others' commands, such as interpreters, coxswains, diviners, and heralds. Kings issue their own commands; they are in this respect like gods.[13]

Up to now the Stranger has divided arts by differences in knowing but not by differences in subject or material.[14] He now completes his first definition of political science by moving in this direction. As opposed to other cognitive commanders, the statesman's commands enjoin for the sake of what has a soul, not other things that become. Of these ensouled things, he deals with herd animals, not single ones, and of these, animals who are landed, pedestrial, hornless, breeders only with their own kind (featherless), and two rather than four footed. The political scientist or royal ruler issues commands that concern nurturing human beings.[15]

I A

The chief meaning of these further divisions (and of the hesitations, peculiarities, and corrections with which young Socrates and the Stranger make them in the conversation itself) is to show with ever-greater specificity what humans must be to be ruled completely by someone else's knowledge. Plato experiments with the notion that we are simply tame herd animals with nothing divine in us who, therefore, are deservedly ruled by a god or statesman who is wholly beyond us. The Stranger says of the soul, for example, only that we have one, and he then quickly identifies being ensouled with being an animal.[16] He brings out no distinguishing eros, spiritedness or, especially, reason, but treats us merely as animal bodies of a certain type—we have two feet, no feathers, live on land, and so on. Men are apolitical and thoroughly slavish or economic.

Plato's second purpose here is to suggest subtly the complexity of human beings, even when we consider ourselves merely as animals. For, reflection shows that we fit within each part that the Stranger rejects in his divisions, as well as in each part he accepts. We do live on land, as he says, but we also can be taught to swim and sail; we do reproduce only with our own bodily kind, but we also unite different natures and qualities to make artificial products; we do lack natural horns, but we create defenses for ourselves; we are indeed bare, but we learn to cover ourselves with animal skins, and so on. The Stranger later takes up these possibilities explicitly: weaving is an art that furnishes defenses, and a good regime mixes moderate and manly people. Indeed, the remarkably malleable human body fits not only the rule of a divine or knowing shepherd but also our own free, rational soul. We can improve our bodies by arts that steal and learn from the other animals.[17]

I B

The *Statesman* is also characterized by Plato's treating education as a counterpoint to politics. He often stops the proceedings to have the chief interlocutor (the Stranger) give the student (young Socrates) lessons. Teaching a single student to inquire is the parallel to governing humans in common. During this first set of divisions of the arts, for example, the Stranger pauses to instruct young Socrates about how to divide properly. His explicit statement is that when they cut, they look for species: they divide a previous genus or species into two more. Indeed, they seek to cut evenly, for doing so makes it more likely that they will cut species, not mere parts. When they are cutting, moreover, they look to find "natural joints." So, from the standpoint of this first division, what one seeks is a species to be found by seeing double, as it were, and progressively cutting at natural joints to separate the thing into two parts that are as equal as possible.

We can better understand the Stranger's divisions by considering the connection between finding species and cutting at natural joints. One would think from this juxtaposition that he is dividing natural species from each other. Yet, he divides classes that are not self sufficient, such as horned versus hornless. (A living or working horn is only part of this or that animal; it is not a naturally independent whole.)[18] Moreover, the Stranger also does not divide here self-reproducing species. At most he finds two at the end of his analysis, pigs (featherless quadrapeds) and men (featherless bipeds). If natural species are self-reproducing or self-sufficient, the Stranger does not seem to be discovering them. Indeed, despite the importance of natural joints, the Stranger does not say what counts as "natural."

Let us pursue this question. If a natural cut splits self-sufficient species, the species that the Stranger divides are not natural but dependent. What he cuts and groups is visible, however: we recognize horns and feathers, even if they cannot function well apart from the animal to which they belong. In contrast to such visible but not self-sufficient features, the Stranger will later divide what he calls "protections" and "defenses." These seem to be only invisible generalities. Even in these early divisions, however, something similarly abstract occurs. Kings who issue their own commands differ from heralds, diviners, coxswains, and interpreters who do not, but no ordinary name groups these arts, and we do not see this class in ordinary experience, as we do plants and animals. As with defenses, however, this generality (issuing one's own commands, not another's) does pick out a common, nonarbitrary, characteristic. Indeed, on further reflection, we see that defense is a natural function or need. Natural classes here sometimes involve spontaneous (natural) needs or powers we do not create that cause and direct our actions, where these needs are not connected only to self-sufficient species but, rather, are common among them.[19] The common quality of being "pedestrial," for example, may tell us more about human locomotion than do our own two human feet simply. We should consider here, too, the Stranger's later linking of courage to quickness in all things.[20]

Once we begin to compose species by common qualities that are not self-reproducing or self-subsistent, however, the interrelation among qualities becomes hard to understand properly. An animal's grazing for food, and need to procreate, limit and direct his natural horns. When we treat horns or defenses apart from their user, however, we may "perfect" them to the point where they are useless or consume too many resources. When we look at powers separately, their function as part of a whole is missed or ill defined, and the experts or artisans who handle them run amok.[21] The Stranger suggests this issue when he claims that the split between noncloven and cloven-hoofed animals is the same as the split between the animals who interbreed (horses and donkeys) and those who do not. For, either cut allows us to take one more step to discovering the "man" whom the statesman rules. These qualities, however, obviously differ from the standpoint of a species' self-subsistence. Plato conducts profound inquiries in the *Statesman* into species and nature, but the connections and mutual limitations among these inquiries are not often explicit.[22]

The effect of the Stranger's first set of divisions is to explore statesmanship as the nurturing of "human" bodies that lack spiritedness, eros, or intelligence.[23] The species he discovers, including the human species, are simply bodily. They are cuts of genera whose members are equal, and where the cleanest cut is a cut in half. Human beings' unity is herd unity, that is, one where class members are equal, not ranked, and where their oneness is treated as an equality in bodies or bodily parts. Every class the Stranger cuts here is of this sort.[24] He (or the statesman) acts as a godlike fabricator of merely quantitative material.

II

Once the Stranger completes these divisions, he tells a story or myth to deal with the error he now surfaces, namely, that for men, but not for cows and sheep, the ruling nurturer—the statesman they just defined—has competitors. Merchants, trainers, farmers, cooks, physicians, marriage brokers, and midwives all would deny his singular claim to be man's sole caretaker or nurturer.[25] The true circumstance in which humans are directed by a sole nurturer would be one where a single god is assigned to rule us. Only a god who rules nonconsenting beings could be the statesman they just defined.

The Stranger's myth is replete with fantastic happenings in which the cosmos reverses its spin, we grow young instead of old, are born from the earth, can talk with other animals, and the like. The Stranger makes clear that under the god's care we want for nothing and need no arts and sciences.[26] Whether such a life would be excellent, however, depends on whether we would use our leisure to philosophize, discussing with other men and beasts the various things each of us knows.[27]

The effect of the Stranger's tale is that a god who cared for us so perfectly that he left nothing to chance or art would, in effect, rule us tyrannically, not through force but by nurturing animals without eros and spiritedness, and the energy and need to think. (If we remembered better what cowherds and shepherds do to their flocks, we would look more suspiciously on the hackneyed metaphor of the shepherd as the just ruler.) Given the Stranger's account, we wonder how human consent, freedom, or voluntary choice could be compatible with the rule of knowledge, let alone with rule by a god as different from us as a goatherd is from goats.[28]

II A

The Stranger's immediate solution to falsely identifying the statesman, cowherd, and god is to say that they should have divided herd tending or herd caring, rather than herd nurturing. Why, then, does he not merely continue cutting where he had stopped—of care for featherless bipeds (men), there is care for the ill or the well, of care for the well there is feeding and exercise, and so on. This would enable him to differentiate physicians, trainers, and other nurturers and artisans from each other. One difficulty is that we could not then, in fact, reach the statesman because he has no specific knowledge of bodies. A perplexity familiar in other dialogues, say, Socrates' discussion with Polemarchus in the *Republic,* is evident here too; the statesman is apparently superfluous once other experts are available.[29] A second difficulty is that the Stranger's cuts have up until now been either/or: How, then, could the statesman command, say, both the physician and general, and adjust medical efforts to the needs of war, if the physician's or general's caring is completely separate from the statesman?

So, instead of dividing herd carers, the Stranger suggests that there was a second deficiency in their first effort, namely, that they ignored the distinction between being ruled voluntarily and by force. The statesman and the tyrant are in fact not identical (although apparently the god and tyrant are). But the

Stranger does not explore how consent would lead us to adjust our view of the statesman. Later in the dialogue, indeed, he again treats subjects' being ruled voluntarily as strictly irrelevant from the knowing ruler's standpoint. By introducing rival nurturers, the myth, and the consent of the ruled, the Stranger complicates his first picture (that statesmen rule tame bodily herds) by recognizing the sometimes limitless demands and recalcitrance (the privacy) of the body, and the thousands of artisans who serve it. But, in considering statesmanship, he has not yet recognized the complicated and independent human soul that he perforce has in view while educating young Socrates.

III

They therefore need a new way to understand statesmanship. This turns out to be exploring a paradigm or example of it, namely, weaving. They preface their procedure by discussing paradigms, yet another instance of how the *Statesman* parallels a discussion of politics and education. We need paradigms to indicate big things, because our "pathos" concerning knowledge is to "know" as if we are dreaming, not wide awake. The Stranger uses letters to illustrate his point— that is, he uses an example to show how examples help us to know. Our goal in learning letters is to see their identity in large and small words alike. We teach letters by beginning with small syllables. We then bring them side by side with large syllables in which letters are at first obscure, so that we can know the large syllables, or words. By acting as if knowing syllables is knowing letters, however, the Stranger abstracts from letters' order, the ways we can combine them, and their different capacities for being combined. (By contrast, he distinguished consonants from vowels in the *Sophist*.)[30] He treats letters as if they are herded into words; the difference between words is only that some are longer than others.

Learning letters exemplifies how to know (that is, how to discover the same root elements in all things, large and small, for letters stand for these elements) and how paradigms work (namely, by letting us see "the same similarity and nature" in what we compare.)[31] The likeness or sameness of weaving to statesmanship, however, will prove subtler than the identity of letters in different syllables. This accounts for the comparison's limits. Weaving is a first step toward understanding the statesman as combiner or synthesizer. So, the elements of weaving and statesmanship that the Stranger will compare are similar "coefficients," that is, causes and contributory causes. Spindle makers function in weaving coats, say, as tool makers do in cities. But, while each syllable is equally a syllable, and while the same letters in them function identically when separated, statesmanship and weaving do not rule or use their causes or contributory causes equally. Weaving does not match the scope and complexity of statesmanship: statesmen rule weavers. Wool's nature, moreover, is like the nature of the hard and soft characters that the statesman will weave in the city but not identical to it. So, weaving both will and will not exemplify the scope and complexity of politics.[32]

III A

The first similarity between weaving and statesmanship is that both use causes and contributory causes. These coefficients are ways the Stranger discusses associations among arts: "coefficients" state the connections among weaving, carding, fulling, spindle making, and so on, in caring for and producing woolen cloaks. The second similarity proves to be the hardness and softness we see in both warp and woof and courageous and moderate citizens. After reflection, we notice that weaving and statesmanship also share types of combining, namely, the intertwining of warp and woof in coats and of human characters in the city, and the enveloping that belongs to using both a woven cloak and a statesman's law.[33]

The Stranger's analogy between statesmanship and weaving indicates how the statesman can deal with rival artisans or nurturers.[34] He institutes in the city a relation of subordination among arts that is similar to the relation between the weaver and his carders, fullers, and spindle makers.[35] This analogy, however, makes evident that politics' end here is still unclear.[36] We can see this by looking at weaving itself. What, for a weaver, is a well-finished coat can once more be set in motion politically. The weaver is subordinate to the general, who tells him whether he needs heavy, light, long, or short coats for war and distributes materials and personnel accordingly. The general's battles, in turn, are subordinate to the city's common good. This good, however, is still obscure.

We can also observe this unclarity in the way the Stranger reaches his definition of weaving. He divides repellents and defenses, in order finally to reach woven coats that keep us warm. In these divisions, however, the Stranger treats as independent, arts, such as carpentry, that in his first division were not independent but subordinate to house building.[37] And, he separates arts of repelling as if all are equal, repeating for defenders his procedure with nurturers. Moreover, in some divisions he imposes overall descriptions on actions that we use in different crafts, where the actions are less practically comprehensive and less useful than the crafts themselves.[38] That is, he again treats arts and artisans as if we could classify them in many ways other than the ones he happens to choose or that we choose practically. This muddies considerably the question of their interrelation, subordination, independence, and purpose.

The question of the independence and dependence of arts also exemplifies the general question of whole and part. The Stranger and young Socrates continue to discuss more than what political scientists must know or, if one likes, political science goes beyond knowing political things narrowly. The central questions are how things that are separate can join together coherently (as they manifestly do) yet retain their independence and fullest nature and how we can grasp them independently when we see them only together with each other. The Stranger discusses, mentions, employs, and teaches young Socrates a number of such possibilities. These include his explicit statements about things that are both classes and parts, things (such as words) that differ yet have identical elements, arts (such as carpentry) that can stand on their own but primarily contribute to larger products, and arts that are called instances of two things at once, as weaving and fulling are instances both of caring for wool and of putting together and taking apart (syncritics and diacritics).[39]

The Stranger also suggests the variety in wholeness itself. He deals in his first divisions with genera whose classes or members are not ranked as better or worse but are cut in half. Shortly, however, he will talk about what "fits," that is, about wholes whose parts can be unequal. When he divides defenses in order to discover weaving's product (woolen cloaks), moreover, he mentions "envelopments," such as seamless wholes, and "composites." These general terms (which the Stranger uses to describe animal skins and sewing) call attention to several more ways that something can "cover," or be a whole.[40] Especially relevant, again, are differences between what covers its members equally (laws and cloaks) and what may not (wholes, such as cities that fit together unequal members such as rulers and ruled, or realized aspirations, which are not equal to what belongs with them through imitation or longing.)[41]

IV

The dialogue's next section concerns measuring.[42] It ostensibly answers a complaint that their discussion of weaving is too long. One part of the art of measurement measures "lengths, depths, widths, and speeds relative to their contraries"; it measures large and small relative to each other alone. The other art measures "relative to the mean, the fitting, the opportune and the needful." Arts such as politics and weaving attend to the mean and produce "everything good and beautiful" by preserving it. (If the arts are, it is, and if it is, they are, the Stranger claims.) Although they would need to "show forth" the precise itself, the Stranger says that for now their discussion is beautiful and sufficient.

The political importance of the mean is obvious. The Stranger introduces the beautiful (noble) and good, having previously suggested their significance only implicitly. He does not say what the mean is politically, however, or (at this point) what is being measured relative to it. He also does not display the mean in weaving: presumably he has in mind warps and woofs suitably hard and soft to produce cloaks that protect against (this or that degree of) cold.[43] So, although the Stranger introduces a new standard for political science, he says little about how it works and to what it applies.[44]

We learn more about measuring through the Stranger's explicit turn once again to education. We converse both for the sake of a single problem and to be more skilled in a subject generally. Their discussions here are "for the sake of our becoming more skilled in dialectics about everything."[45] We measure too much and too little talk by this end. Unlike things for which "perceptible similarities" are "naturally there," however, with bodiless things (which are the "biggest," "most honorable," and "greatest" things) we have no images to use to fit to our senses.[46] We can show them clearly only in speech, which is why we must practice in smaller examples such as weaving. In general, when one first perceives what many share one should divide into species, and when one first perceives dissimilarities one should comprehend with one genus what is kin.

IV A

After the Stranger introduces the mean, he turns to statesmanship, as weaving exemplifies it.[47] He cuts the city's possessions into parts, as he had cut acquisitions and productions to reach weaving's product, protective woolen cloaks. But he does not describe the city's product or purpose. Indeed, the city he outlines is essentially a city for the two-legged pigs reached before the myth, with the god of the myth removed and men left to their own devices, including our arts, and our mastery of plants and other animals. The city remains for the moment primarily bodily or, as we might say, economic.[48]

The Stranger splits the city's possessions into tools, vessels (for safekeeping), seats, defenses, playthings or imitations for pleasure, bodies (bodily materials), and nurture (bodies for the body). We should note several features and peculiarities of these divisions. One is the Stranger's claim that the sixth cut, the "first born" species of minerals, skins, and such, could have been first. Why, then, not place it first? A second is his pointing out the idea of coins and stamps, which he says he could distribute between playthings and tools.[49] A third is his statement that from a certain viewpoint everything is a tool.

One implication of these peculiarities (and the substance of the divisions) is that this city has no significant natural order among its possessions. All could be contributing causes, which is how tools are described. A second implication is that this city is bodily or economic; its purposes beyond nurture are mere pleasure and defense. Anything higher is lowered to this level. A third implication is that the classifying here is not very restrictive. Bodies are placed in two classes and could be placed in almost all; animals are placed in several ways in various classes. The variety, however, is not infinite. We can explain it by the Stranger's beginning with the city at its most basic or bodily level.[50]

The obvious result of these divisions is to allow the Stranger to clarify political science by using the distinctions among causes, and between causes and contributory causes, that he uncovers while discussing weaving. He quickly passes this by for now, however, because the parts of this economic city do not bring out the statesman's rivals for rule.[51] When we leave the city's purpose unclear (and in practice treat it only as bodily agglomeration), each class is equal and its membership is largely interchangeable. How, then, can we measure the classes by a mean, and to what could we fit them? The kind of causal rivalry for which the Stranger is looking (on the analogy of weavers and fullers, and still, ostensibly, to solve the problem of the statesman's rival nurturers) is still missing.

Even when the Stranger later discusses virtue, he tries to confine it to this city's limited purpose. Virtue, however, breaks from these confines.[52] Indeed, part of Plato's intention is to show the natural movement (although not the automatic path) from man as animal, to man as artfully using reason to serve his animality, to man as reasoning (and feeling) virtuously beyond his animality. The useful is a healthy ground from which to consider the beautiful and just.[53] Even when we are politically self-ruling, we begin as economic animals whose other traits are devoted to need. Men as reasoning, erotic, and spirited, however, must finally be opened to ends suitable to these powers and not only to their secondary uses. But these powers must then be reintegrated into the common good, something that happens only imperfectly. This movement also is characteristic when philosophy, not political rule, is the end.[54]

V

The Stranger turns next to the statesman's rivals. He begins with those who might be rival rulers but are not—the slaves, free artisans, and priests. The discussion of priests then opens to discussing the statesman's true competitors, whom the Stranger calls the greatest sophists.[55] These imposters first come to light as prideful priests who become kings or enjoin sacrifices upon kings. The imposters are then visible as lions, centaurs, satyrs, "and the weak and wily beasts," who exchange their looks and powers.[56] More concretely, these great sophists, the rivals to knowledgeable statesmen, are the rulers in cities' ordinary regimes—in monarchies, tyrannies, aristocracies, oligarchies, and democracies. Because they have no fixed looks (because, say, the genus of priests can force its way into the genus of kings), these regimes cannot be the wholes from which political actions take their measure. Rather, only what the statesman forms and rules knowledgeably can be a true standard for action. Our better actual regimes imitate this one right regime.

The Stranger's discussion of how actual regimes imitate and fall short of the statesman's regime centers on the problem of law. Humans (and our actions) are dissimilar and "almost none of the human things is ever at rest," so no art could command something "simple about all and over the entire time" that would comprehend "the best and the most just" "for all simultaneously." The regime based on knowledge, therefore, should not be hedged in by strict laws but needs flexibility to deal with variation. The difficulty with ordinary regimes, however, is that when they employ such flexibility their rulers use it for unjust gain. A statesman, by contrast, should no more be restricted in improving the city (in aiding its justice and nobility) than should a physician in curing the sick. Codes should not limit what their scientific judgment tells them to do. True statesmen do use inflexible codes when they need to be away, however, but revise and ignore them if necessary upon their return.[57]

V A

We usually distrust complete flexibility. Physicians not controlled by criminal and commercial laws are free to kill with impunity. Their wish to gain might lead them to use this liberty. How, then, could we allow to a city's rulers the complete freedom we rightly fear in physicians? Even more, how could we, who are not knowers, differentiate the putative political scientist from the would-be tyrant? Our problem is exacerbated because the soul's health (say, justice) is more disputable than the body's health. We can recognize, even if too late, failed treatment from physicians. Our knowledge of what we wish for and fear from our souls however, goes only so far.[58] The ruled cannot know clearly who is a true statesman. In any event, moreover, most of us believe we should not be ruled: we think we or our group (of, say, rich or poor) understands sufficiently the community's justice and health.

On the other hand, were ordinary regimes to imitate the complete legal inflexibility that the Stranger argues is the statesman's substitute for not always being able to be present, their permanent rigidity would become increasingly useless and foolish, that is, increasingly unscientific.[59] These difficulties make the practical political problem insoluble because rigidity is always in some cases stupid, and full flexibility is in all ordinary cases dangerous. Only luck would work, and perhaps even the luck of having a statesman among us is not enough. For, when the political scientist is away or lost in thought, the laws he leaves behind inevitably will produce some unjust results.

Although the political problem is insoluble, however, we could minimize mistakes were there enough statesmen who cared to be available or were we enough alike that the right set of inflexible laws would usually produce just results. The first possibility cannot work, unfortunately, because the number of statesmen is always small. The second alternative is less unlikely. This is why the Stranger depicts what is worthwhile in ordinary regimes more as an imitation of the statesman's legal inflexibility than of his flexibility, and why the Stranger continues to picture men as a herd whose economic well-being and safety are the statesman's goals.[60] He leaves largely undefined a more complex sense of what a statesman tries to achieve: the justice, benefit, and beauty in terms of which his regime ought to be measured.

As the Stranger now presents the statesman, he is the human equivalent of the god of the first division, caring either with the precision of an eye that is (almost) always on the sparrow, or freezing matters through quasi-divine laws. To consider either alternative just is to suggest that self-government by ordinary men is problematic.

V B

The political implications of the Stranger's teachings on law and flexibility become still clearer when we consider his classification of the usual regimes. He introduces dimensions for classifying them that are similar but not identical to Socrates' in the *Republic* or to Aristotle's in the *Politics*. The dimensions are one/few/many, rich/poor, law/lawfulness, and forced/voluntary. He does not say that regimes are governed by their ruling character or their understanding of what is good—say, honor or wealth—as in the *Republic*. Nor does he parallel the regime to the soul (as in the *Republic*) or treat it as the soul of the city. His regimes, furthermore, are not formed by an understanding of justice of the sort we see in Aristotle's *Politics*. What is decisive in ranking regimes, rather, is how much or how rigidly they adhere to (basic) law. The regimes imitate the law that a statesman implements (as his second best alternative to being there on the spot) by being more or less rigid, that is, by extent or degree, rather than by being closer to and further from the right regime by subtle similarity and difference in a variety of aspects, or by the subtle reflection of "erotic" yearning and attempt. The relation of the one right regime to the other six is a relation of greater stiffness and relaxation.[61]

The Stranger's emphasis on law is coupled with a de-emphasis on institutions, self-rule, and, to this point, character. He does not attempt an amelioration of the dilemma of flexibility and inflexibility of the sort we see in America's separation of powers. (The closest he comes is his view that democracy is the least harmful bad regime because rule is distributed among so many.) The reason for his omission is that he does not see statesmanship's goal as trying to unleash individual freedom in large numbers of men. His regime's goal is not individualism and economic growth (as opposed to sufficiency); our kind of choice, to say the least, is not fully permitted.[62]

The Stranger does not portray the peak of good politics as citizens' sound exercise of (necessarily imperfect) judgment, moreover, as he would were his purpose to generate prudent self-rule, or greatness of soul, for some. Rather, his right regime tries to completely control willfulness by reason, either legally or on the spot. Were the statesman's end to perfect political self-rule, however, he would not consider everything but his unchallenged immediate or legal presence to be unsatisfactory. Allowing room for imperfection would belong to the perfection he is trying to achieve. Government that properly mixes the flexible and inflexible is apparently more favorable to individual freedom and understanding than is either extreme.

The Stranger reserves for his educating of young Socrates the possibility of imperfection and one's own (individual) freedom. He portrays the need for agreement among discussants; that is, he permits young Socrates' volition. A stupid law that bans questioning is the antithesis of learning. Were everything truly and not merely conventionally rigid and unchangeable, we could not even begin to inquire. On the other hand, were nothing rigid nothing could be learned or said, and our search would be empty or mute.[63]

VI

The Stranger has been strangely silent about what the statesman knows and toward what end he acts. He mentions ends (justice, improvement, and happiness) but does not (yet) discuss their substance. It is only now, after discussing imposters, that the Stranger tells us just what it is that statesmen do.

The Stranger turns first to the statesman's closest congeners or kin, namely, rhetoricians, generals, and judges.[64] Although he does not say why they are kin, we can see that, like statesmen, rhetoricians, generals, and judges try to produce or secure a good for the whole city, not merely a part. The statesman is like other nurturers (such as shepherds) because he deals with a species comprehensively (man as opposed to sheep), and like weavers because he uses subordinate knowers and plaits a web. He also differs from these likenesses. Plato's typical political analogies function in different ways.

The discussion of law sets the stage for the statesman's kin because it makes the city's scope evident. The need to discuss kin, in turn, further enables us to see why law cannot altogether capture statesmanship. The statesman's knowledge precedes law and makes possible artful legislation; the political scientist is not as such a legislator. Indeed, law cannot tell generals, rhetoricians, and judges everything that they must do, because persuading, fighting, and judging require artistic or practical judgment. Especially with judges, the Stranger acknowledges the need for virtue; force and persuasion are insufficient. Virtue thus becomes the theme of the dialogue's last section, although it remains close to herd and economic matters. The justice the Stranger mentions, for example, concerns contracts but not distributing offices. This is left to the educators, guided by the statesman.

Although the Stranger says little about the statesman's goals, he does elaborate his difference from those he commands. The statesman tells citizens whether or not an art is to be learned, chooses that about which rhetoricians should be persuading the many, decides whether force should be used or friendship sought externally, and establishes the laws that judges are to guard and preserve. The other artisans are experts whose full purpose is provided outside their art.[65] The statesman's connections to the rhetorician and his kin are thus like the weaver's to the carder's and his. Unlike the weaver, however, the statesman apparently takes orders from no one, and rules "those who have the capacity to act, in [his] cognizance of the beginning and initial impulse of the greatest things in cities in regard to opportunity and lack of opportunity."[66]

This statement about opportunity leads us to think again about the precise in itself and about the Stranger's lessons concerning learning, species and part, dialectic, elements, using examples, and the greatest things. The exact range of the statesman's knowledge is unclear: Does he know the opportune itself, that is, apart from cities, or does he know the opportune only in relation to the beginning of the greatest things in cities? Does he know the true beginnings themselves, that is, apart from cities, or only the beginning of the greatest things in cities?[67] Can he as such also find the opportune way to bring forth the greatest things in individual or private souls? The statesman would apparently need to be guided by what he knows or hears about the beginning of the greatest things and the opportune simply, in order opportunely (or legally, as necessary) to command his rhetoricians, generals, and judges. In this sense, the statesman's knowledge is subservient to that of the philosopher, or the statesman is also a philosopher. More generally, the statesman is subservient to things as they are, such as the precise in itself. Moreover, although the Stranger says that learning, music, instruction, and myth are subservient to the statesman's commands, the statesman must in another sense follow them, for he is ruled by his own education and the broader whole it opens.[68]

It is unclear if we can make the necessary mutual subordination (and, therefore, independence) of politics and education fully coherent. The Stranger's educating of young Socrates counters or improves his city's combining of the virtues, and of the flexible and rigid. Can such education be made fully compatible with the city? The Stranger's discussion of sciences in the legal regimes indicates that it could not, although he does give the rhetoricians, generals, and judges some freedom here, in technique if not in purpose.[69] Perhaps thoughtful guidance from the start would allow cities properly to control and not improperly to fear learning, by providing sensible limits. Nothing, however, could guarantee that such guidance would be implemented perfectly. Socrates will always seem to some Athenians to be a sophist. The Stranger will always be a stranger in the city.

Because the Stranger identifies the scientific ruler and advisor, moreover, he need not even mention the problem of the coincidence of statesmanship (or philosophy) and actual rule. In fact, he leaves unexplored how the statesman persuades or commands the rhetoricians, generals, and judges to begin with. However he does this, he must do it imperfectly, using means—say, divine or priestly means—that will limit learning and statesmanship. On the other hand, although young Socrates is educated in the limits of law, he is also affirmed in law's necessity, and the Stranger sketches a nonutopian picture of acceptable regimes. The imperfect fit between philosophic education and political life need not be destructive.[70]

VII

The Stranger turns next to the statesman's own activity; the statesman weaves a web between two virtues, courage and moderation, or between manly and orderly human beings. We often praise quickness, speed, intensity, and keenness in bodies, souls, sounds, images, and thoughts. We call them manly or courageous; this is the name common to all these natures. But, he and young Socrates continue, we also praise quiet, slow, and soft doings in thought and actions, and smooth and grave sounds, calling them moderate and orderly.[71] If the quick and soft are inopportune, however, we reproach them as insolent and manic, or as craven and stupid.[72] The moderate and courageous natures, moreover, are hostile ideas that do not mingle. Those "who have them in their souls are at odds."[73]

The political difficulty this causes is that an excessively moderate city is passive and weak, too soft and slow, liable to being enslaved by enemies. An overly courageous city, however, is too actively aggressive, too hard and quick, liable to being destroyed through excessive risk.[74] One so fears war that it is easy to defeat; the other so welcomes it that the city is always in jeopardy. Each nature's excess inevitably becomes harmful when it is in complete control. The statesman's task, thus—the one "that is truly by nature"—is to weave the good and suitable examples of the two natures (that is, the ones capable of being limited by the other) and to give appropriate parts of rule to the two tendencies.[75] Like "any of the compounding sciences," the statesman's science puts together "things, which are both similar and dissimilar, by bringing them all together into one" and crafts "some single power and look."[76] The statesman does not directly educate these souls, however, but directs or supervises the educators who nurture them so that only the good become part of the web.

Proper material, however, does not guarantee that the web will be well woven. What weaves together these opposites, refined so that their extreme tendencies to manic insolence, godlessness, injustice, craven foolishness, and excessive humility have been controlled? Good marriages produce bonds between the orderly and manly and help to ensure that they do not become simple, bestial, and unmixably extreme by marrying only their own kind. More significant still than these animal bonds (and a condition for them) are the steadfast bonds of shared opinion about the beautiful, just, and good, and the honors that reinforce them. Political offices are entrusted to the two types in common, with a part of each mixed. In some cases, moreover, the two virtues come together in one soul. When "a need arises for one ruler . . . the royal weaver entrusts the one with both virtues."[77] So, the political scientist's care for human beings turns out to be directing the producing and educating of properly courageous and moderate people, plaited and bound by marriage and opinion so that the city is neither too aggressive nor too passive, and remains beautiful and free. The courageous become willing to "share in the just things," and the orderly "become(s) in its being moderate and intelligent within the limits of a regime."[78]

It is more difficult to connect the courageous than the moderate to the web because the courageous must be tamed in order to be useful to the herd, while the moderate are already tame and tend to be too tame.[79] Connecting the independent ones to the city is the crucial problem, more than stiffening the soft and yielding. As we also saw in the *Republic,* once we step away from considering men only as pigs, tying the courageous to the city so that it can be free becomes the urgent problem.[80] Indeed, young Socrates is himself often called manly, is quick to make divisions, and is filled with the human pride that leads him too quickly to dismiss our likeness to other animals. The Stranger's laborious discussions are intended, among other effects, to slow him so that he will better understand matters as they are or connect himself to a differentiated whole of things and not dissolve them in mathematical identity.[81]

VII A

One wonders whom this woven cloak of the moderate and courageous covers, and against what it defends. It covers all in the city, slave and free, and apparently defends them against conquest or keeps free those among them who are free already. The political scientist (the royal ruler), protects all in the city, primarily or exclusively by weaving the moderate and manly.[82] In fact, the Stranger now says that the moderate and manly are the rulers.[83] This is surprising because we might believe the statesman to be the only ruler here. The Stranger is reminding us, however, that the statesman is one remove from the rhetoricians, judges, and generals, telling them what to do either on the spot or through constitutional laws but not himself acting, and one remove from the educators, supervising those who prepare and bind the two types of virtue.

None of these citizens learns to be a statesman or to found a regime. The closest are those who mix both virtues and rule where the city needs individuals. But the Stranger does not mention how they might themselves learn the nature of courage and moderation, and no one in this regime is taught the truths behind the opinions that are their divine bonds. So, although the Stranger introduces the virtues, they do not open to the soul's taking flight nor belong to a discussion of the soul's powers. Instead, they are a refined instance of a soul that serves a whole city, still guided by something animal, namely, nurture and defense. Indeed, even the bonds of opinion about the beautiful, just, and good are not secured simply or primarily by the element of reason in them. The binding is "a drug by art."[84]

The Stranger thus elevates our animality to our rationality through law, virtue, opinion, and art, but he does not show us citizens in a fuller rationality.[85] Dialectic, and any discussion of how to bring it about, is missing from this city. The statesman presumably directs those who produce the opinions that protect the regime, because he knows more than those governed solely by opinion. But he does not provide an obvious place for his knowledge to be sought by his own citizens. So, the Stranger's regime is not Plato's *Republic,* although it is close to the *Republic* before the introduction there of communism and philosophy. Only in his inferior regimes might philosophy be permitted or useful. Anything unbridled in human action, including thought unbridled by political limits, is in practice allied with something corrupt.

VII B

We should compare the discussion of virtue in the *Statesman* to our earlier analyses. As Charmides does at first, the Stranger connects moderation to the quiet and orderly. As in the *Protagoras* and the example that Socrates gives Laches, the Stranger connects courage to quickness and boldness. The first general point, therefore, is that the Stranger treats human virtues as measured or appropriate directions of the soul's nonrational movements.[86] The place, or absence, of prudence here strengthens this view. Where is courage as the *Laches'* prudent endurance, or moderation as the *Charmides'* self-knowledge? Knowledge's place is taken here by the opinions that bind the quick and the orderly (and that govern their marriage), and the laws that nurture them.[87] The Stranger does not even credit with prudence the single ruler who has both virtues; as we said, this city does not train the statesman who founds it. The connection between prudence and what is good is abstracted from individually for these citizens and considered only politically. The common good—defending the city and its opinions about justice and nobility, vague though these are here—is that to which virtuous character is oriented, and the knowledge such virtue needs is basically found in the statesman or his law, not in the courageous and moderate rulers. The judges, rhetoricians, and generals are not bereft of knowledge, for they have arts, and the rulers hold offices. Nonetheless, cleaving to the city's enduring opinions, rather than exercising practical judgment, is the order of the day.[88]

The two virtues, courage and moderation, largely cover or include piety, justice, and wisdom here, for impiety and injustice are treated as defects of courage, and simple foolishness as a defect of moderation. These citizens' deeper justice and wisdom is primarily found outside them, in their opinions and bonds. We also note that cowardice is a defect here of moderation, an effect of excessive softness, and insolence is a defect of courage, an effect of excessive hardness and intensity. Plato does not separate the virtues transparently; in other places, as we have seen, licentiousness is a vice of moderation or an excess of untamed desire or eros, and cowardice is a vice of courage or an excess of fear.

Another feature of the Stranger's discussion is to connect virtue to a range of qualities or media. Courage is opportune quickness of sounds, bodies, and images, as well as of souls and thought.[89] It is connected to quick or not quick enough as measured by the product (this is what makes it opportune), and also to quickness as measured against other numbers or a familiar steady state (this is what makes it quick). Many sixteenth notes in a row are quick but may be too quick or slow for a composition. Human beings are quick or slow naturally, or appear quick or slow naturally when we consider using them in war, in fighting slavery, and in preserving freedom and peace.

If we consider quickness, intensity, and slowness in men (or generally) to be natural (as the Stranger says), then virtue improves nature. It produces proper quickness. It is unclear how rare the nature is that one could train to virtue. Some, but perhaps not many, are so extreme that (the Stranger says) they need to be exiled or enslaved. The unity of virtue in a few souls is a more unusual political excellence; the nature necessary for this is presumably also unusual. Perhaps a unity that is truly rare, however, occurs only philosophically. Virtue improves nature but in a noble and good direction that nature sets.[90]

VII C

The tendencies of hard and soft become courage and moderation in the good city. Both become virtues. This raises the question of what virtue is as a whole and how it has parts. In fact, the Stranger began the section on virtue with this reflection: virtue, which is or seems to be one beautiful thing—namely, virtue—has two parts that conflict, namely, courage and moderation.[91]

The Stranger does not claim that either courage or moderation is an imposter. Nor does he say that the seeming two are in fact one. Rather, he suggests that each needs the other to be a virtue or that each is a virtue only as part of the kind of mixture (bound by reason or reasoned opinion) that his web exemplifies.

Does the importance of mixing the two virtues mean that we cannot conceive separately a courage that is not insolent or a moderation that is not dull? Is each a vice when separate? Rather, we should say that each when alone tends so readily to be insolent or dull that we in fact grasp neither as a virtue wholly apart from the other. We can, nonetheless, differentiate courage as opportune quickness and hardness from moderation as opportune slowness and softness. Only when they are together in a whole, however (here, the city), can the hard and soft be proper or opportune and, therefore, visible as separate virtues. The virtues are virtues only as a mixture or, if one prefers, as a pair that belongs to a whole. Neither is a dispensable part (as is, say, one more piece of iron in a pile). The virtues are active only together, not when isolated from a city, soul, or other common unit.[92]

Does this also suggest that each virtue is in the last analysis unintelligible as a separate idea and that ideas, too, are wholes only as parts of something common? The way the Stranger trains young Socrates to tame himself indicates that the virtues we exercise in seeking to know are also virtues only as a pair within a task directed to what is common: the Stranger and young Socrates search together. In fact, we can discover courage and moderation in their nature only when we see both together in and for the whole of things, for otherwise we will see one or the other excessively. Each is itself only as an excellence in a whole.

We might wonder, nonetheless, just what the difference is between the two characters once they are combined properly. They become visible as virtue, but can we still discern their difference, as we can when the quick and the slow are excessive? Members of a herd, after all, lose almost all distinctiveness in their likeness. A motion or action is just right (neither too quick nor too slow) when measured by the mean implicated in a whole one produces, understands, or acts within. Will not all things that are just right look the same? Something may start as too quick or too slow and courageously or moderately perfect itself, but what becomes neither too quick nor too slow would seem to be both moderate and courageous, or virtuous simply.

This again suggests that the differences in the virtues are more visible in the imperfections from which they begin than in the perfection we strive to attain. What is visible from that final point of view is how things look when everything fits. As fitting, the courageous and moderate look the same: they fit. Yet, at the same time, they do differ, even if this difference seems harder to discern in excellence than in imperfection. They differ in the motions and openness that tend to make them independent or that enable them to fit differently in different products. They may also differ in the mutually relative measure, as do hard and soft threads as measured neutrally, or different notes, rhythms, and timbres that all fit a composition yet still differ. The possible utility of different materials becomes visible from the standpoint of the completed product to which they belong.

How courage and moderation are alike and differ in the very propriety that makes them virtues (and not only in their being properly quick or slow in a soul, city, body, sound, or imitation) is perhaps another question. In any event, it is in their being properly opportune—here, in their being correctly known and measured by the statesman for the city—that they are both virtues; virtue is the propriety, or prudent combination, of confidence, endurance, enjoyment, and self-control. The natural or artificial independence of things, their extremism, helps bring about a good only when it belongs to a whole that limits them; from the point of view of this whole, differences tend to dissolve in fitting harmony. The city, therefore, may begin inadvertently to eliminate the very material it needs, as intermarriage of the quick and the slow may ultimately bring about what is merely ordinary. Only with philosophy is this dilemma more perfectly, although not perfectly, resolved for men. When we understand things as they are, we are the same as others yet remain at the peak of our own powers.

VII D

It will be useful to remind ourselves of what we have learned about courage and moderation in the dialogues as a whole. To speak comprehensively, our courage is prudent endurance and confidence, or proper quickness that pushes away what threatens; does not break; closes off; defends the particular, precise, and independent; separates; protects; and in this unitary way defeats, overcomes, or incorporates. Moderation is prudent or self-controlled quiet, or proper slowness that refuses improperly to join with or fall into what attracts but that, knowing what it lacks, opens, reaches out, embraces, and in this way combines. These two virtues are types of motion, and of separating and combining—the courageous pride that secures independence and the moderate eros that brings together. Neither is possible without reason or understanding, which itself works primarily by separating and combining. The difference between what Plato brings out in the Stranger's discussions and in Socrates' are most visible in the phenomenon of eros and, thus, of moderation, as proper reaching up or transforming, and not only as reaching out or peaceful yielding. For, this reaching up or transforming helps to constitute the experience of the incompleteness in our actions within any apparently sufficient whole, such as our political community, that opens to another, higher, more beautiful, perfect, or complete whole. The possibility of the erotic movement of the soul that we see in the *Phaedrus* or *Symposium,* which exemplifies this incompleteness, is hardly visible in the *Statesman.* Consequently, the virtues and the city can seem more complete in the *Statesman,* the connections between dialectic and political virtue both less problematic politically and harder to discern intellectually, and the place of wonder and laughter less visible.[93]

Socrates and the Stranger

We should also discuss more conclusively than we have the several ways of dividing and grouping that we have been considering, for their variety could leave one excessively confused about Plato's thought. Which does he believe to be correct? To some degree, these differences are differences between the Stranger and Socrates, and I will explore matters in these terms. But, as I have suggested, the differences between the two become less clear as one develops the discussion. The argument points, in the end, to certain dualities in the articulation of things and in the attempt to know them philosophically that are invitations to continued reflection. What is important always is to recognize the priority of the question of 'what is,' in Plato's understanding, and to retain sight of his basic articulations of the virtues, regimes, beauty, what is good, and the like, as we have discussed them previously.

At first sight the difference between Socrates' and the Stranger's articulations is that the Stranger's are flat and Socrates' hierarchical. The Stranger's species seem to equalize their members. Each horned animal is as such identical to every other horned animal. Each art that issues another's commands is as such equal to the others; the coxswain and herald are from this point of view identical. The Stranger's species flatten. Socrates, by contrast, sometimes seems to treat members of a class as if they belong to it unequally. A visible example is the presence of beauty in the *Symposium*'s account of our movement from a beautiful body to beauty itself. The ideas are uplifting, not leveling. True beauty attracts more completely than do its images or is what is attractive in its images. One is pulled toward the immortal and, therefore, the most immortal.

To make this same point differently, the Stranger's cuts allow us to see the average or identical qualities that allow each member to belong to its class and do not reduce lesser members to imperfect versions of more complete ones. The best member of a class does not have priority. Socrates' dialectic, by contrast, does suggest this direction, especially when he is pointing to the philosophic life and, often, when he is considering what is good or beautiful. One question, then, is whether Socrates' and the Stranger's ways of dividing can recapture what is prominent in the other.

This leads us to examine more carefully how deep the difference between the two actually is or the unity of Plato's analysis. To turn first to Socrates, we may wonder whether, say, the beauty in body is a pale reflection of the beauty in soul and both a pale reflection of beauty itself or, rather, whether different circumstances allow the same beauty to shine through with greater purity, clarity, and truth. In the *Laches,* indeed, Socrates suggests courage's range and its connection to prudence without specifying a way that courageous acts are gradated in their courage. And in the *Euthyphro,* he suggests that piety belongs to justice and awe to fear, leading us to think that had he chosen to he might have begun a Stranger-like division in which members are not ranked but equalized. Moreover, throughout the dialogues, that the ideas are described as pure, eternal, and unmixed suggests as much that ideas in things fall short by being occluded, distorted, and mixed, as it does that the idea in the thing merely reflects, yearns for, or imitates the idea itself. To use quickness as an example of what an idea is, is to say that an idea has, in its instances, full, if not completely clear, presence. The same is true of mud.

Socrates' picture of the excess in what beckons us (which is correlated to our madness, openness, or dissatisfaction), however, is perhaps not altogether cap-

tured by this view. The way in which the full power of the just, good, or beautiful cannot be contained in any particular body, act, or thought seems to go
beyond its merely being occluded.[94] To wish to be noble is, ultimately, to wish
to be altogether noble; virtue deranges even as it orients. One might then suggest, in reply, that the full power of an idea is indeed present, but not fully
visible, in particular souls, actions, and bodies not only because the idea is occluded by the fleeting but, more generally, because the full conditions it needs
to flower are not present. Consider, for example, how the power of political
justice in the *Republic* requires the community of wives, children, and property. The full idea needs the proper conditions, including the proper partners
with which to mix, if it is to flourish completely. Its complete nature is otherwise present, as it were, only in its possibility. Despite occlusion, moreover,
ordinary clarity does allow us to see the average visibility or power of what
exists completely only potentially.

This way of grasping the imperfection in the connection of a member to its
species begins to amalgamate the Socratic to the Stranger's view. Socrates' understanding of the several ideas or classes within an idea in the *Philebus,* and
his emphasis there on the connection between goodness and purity, are also
steps toward this amalgamation.[95]

We can also close the gap between Socrates and the Stranger, starting from
the Stranger. His divides equal classes, yet in the *Sophist* some cuts are said to
purify. Perhaps, indeed, some classes are more complete than others that are
said to be like them, as the god is grander, and commands and is obeyed more
fully, than the statesman.[96] The earlier cuts in a sense include those below
them. One may reply, however, that there is a further difference between the
Stranger's cuts and Socrates', namely, that it is easier to see in Socrates' how
the ideas can be causes and not merely groups because they (or, at least, some)
cause by attracting. What attracts us in something beautiful is the true beauty
it imitates or that is occluded in it. Yet, here too we see that in the Stranger's
discussion of weaving, some of his cuts are of causes and others only of co-
causes, as weavers differ from helpers. The other causal arts, moreover, recognize that the weavers have the largest part of treating cloaks but not the only
part of it.[97] So, although the averageness of identity in which, say, the Stranger's cuts group statesman and builders may not as such allow better and worse
among a species' members, the Stranger's working with the different scope,
completion, causal power, and purity of what he cuts goes a long way toward
meeting Socrates' criteria of what is good, say, in the *Philebus.*

I am not suggesting that these points fully overcome the absence of imitative yearning in the members of the Stranger's classes. This absence is perhaps most obvious in seeking to understand why one should try to know or be just. Even here, however, the Stranger makes evident young Socrates' courage; that is, he indicates that there must be some link between virtue in his city, virtue simply, and virtue in education.[98]

We should also make clear in this discussion that the mode of connection between an idea and its members, and among ideas themselves, need not be identical. Indeed, although we may think of an idea's members as gradated, we are less likely to think of one idea as being uplifted by the next idea, as if some are shadows. It is more obvious to think of ideas as equal or as belonging to or nested within a more comprehensive original cut (such as cognitive commanding, or what has a soul). The Stranger cuts species that exemplify this equality, even though he is discussing arts and other changeable things. When he discusses being, rest, motion, sameness, and difference, moreover, what can and cannot be combined does so in the flat way of consonants and vowels, or nouns and verbs.[99]

This leads us to recall, however, that there is something arbitrary about the unity from which the Stranger begins in the *Statesman*—he puts together cities and houses—as there is something arbitrary about the wholes that contain the species (and, thus, their relation), as he understands them.[100] What is missing is openness to what is attractive. He works with the artistically knowable city, not the most just city. His way of seeing how the city knits together its parts does not fully explore the power of their independence. It is as if all excess or excessive desire could be eliminated. His city's goal is restricted to defense and nurture. For the Stranger, it is the species within a separated and then fixed composite that dominates, not a whole, and, therefore, parts, that attract beyond the composite. What is greatest are the five separate and connected but not organized genera. The knowledge in his city remains outside it, and our wish to know is not fully grasped.

These complexities would need to be more fully addressed in order for the Stranger's view to be altogether adequate. Perhaps, indeed, the Socratic view better allows us to understand the reasons for the shortcomings or likely arbitrariness of any city or whole. It surely seems to allow us to grasp more clearly the ambiguous place of thought itself in any community, disputes about the noble and good, and the eruption of the ridiculous. The central issue, one might say, is the connection of wholes or mock wholes to each other, not merely the connection of ideas to each other and of things to ideas.[101] From this standpoint, ideas or their instances can have something of a hierarchical relation to each other. Yet, one might ask of Socrates whether he shows us as fully as the Stranger does the characteristics and possibilities of things when we group and manipulate them as equally divisible, or whether he clarifies what the Stranger clarifies in his discussions of the five genera and the precise itself. Plato shows us through the Stranger how much we still can know even if we have not fully uncovered the whole.

The Political Dialogues

The *Laws,* the *Statesman,* and the *Republic* differ in several ways, but each is closer to the other than it is to the modern notions of politics. In each, happiness is judged in terms of the whole rather than the separate parts or individuals, virtue is fundamental, organizing for war is vital, acquisition of wealth and property is restricted or downplayed, and some form of knowledge is basic. Each also contains ways in which to consider imperfect regimes, moreover, with this imperfection being a central topic in the *Statesman* and the *Republic.* Each teaches about founding, from its own thematic standpoint, furthermore, and has something to show us about the connections and tensions among knowledge, the soul, and the gods. The regime of the *Republic* is directed to philosophy, as the regimes of the *Statesman* and *Laws* are not. Yet, the *Laws'* regime opens some of its citizens to reflections that might lead to philosophy, and the Stranger in the *Statesman,* although not the Stranger's city, educates young Socrates. The *Laws* displays the scope of political life as such, the *Republic* displays the restrictions that politics places on justice and on seeking to know, and the *Statesman* displays the possibilities of politics' being guided strictly by knowledge.

Conclusion

We examine Plato in order to immerse ourselves in the first, basic articulation of the core elements of human thought and action. This articulation points to the importance of the life devoted to the continuing attempt to understand. Our several explorations in the preceding chapters, therefore, are truer to Plato, and to the phenomena he studies, than any inevitably arbitrary summary is able to be. An elaborate conclusion about an ongoing activity would be misleading. Nevertheless, it is useful to recall the major directions that we have taken.

The configuration that Plato uncovers orients human understanding, not because he imposes it arbitrarily but because it is how everyday matters present themselves once we begin to explore the problems that lie on their surface. These problems are normally veiled, sometimes thinly, sometimes powerfully. The questions of the best way of life and best form of government, to take the central ones, become visible once we can no longer take for granted usual or traditional practices.

From this standpoint, we began by addressing the immediate impetus for Socrates' conversations, the reasons that occasion his discussions, and the usual arguments, evidence, and knowledge on which he relies. Our purpose was to clarify the elements of the mostly co-philosophical world as they point to, but also as they restrict, political philosophy, the unbridled exploration of human affairs. Socrates' conversations arise from fathers' concerns about sons, young men's political ambitions, compulsion, hopes for love, and pleasure in conversation. They remind us of men's basic goals and motives, then and now. At the same time, Socrates' conversations also remind us of our uncertainty about these goals, and our wish for knowledge about them. Knowledge is not an abstract or academic phenomenon but belongs to the everyday world. We therefore discussed Socrates' use of the arts as his ordinary examples of knowledge, and we looked at the standards of clarity, sufficiency, precision, and noncontradiction that he and his interlocutors employ. We discussed as well the presence and authority of sophists, for once one's world is so freed from its traditional ways that the need for guidance and advice becomes pressing, the fraudulent teacher may seem more worthy than the genuine one.

We then turned to Socrates' principle explorations of virtue—of wisdom, piety, courage, moderation, justice, and their unity—because Socrates often makes clear that his interlocutors' goals depend on, or should be transformed into, virtues of character. "Virtue," understood as Plato (or Aristotle) sees it, and freed from much of its contemporary residue of weakness and naiveté, remains the most compelling guideline for happiness. Some of Socrates' discussions of the virtues in chapter 2 appeared inconclusive and some did not. In each case, however, Plato uncovered the phenomenon he addressed in its major dimensions and its major uncertainties. We continued to develop throughout the book our view of Plato's judgments about the virtues' specific qualities and possible unity, ending with the discussion that concluded chapter 9.

One goal of Plato's prescriptions for politics involves protecting and advancing ethical virtue. This goal is elaborated most fully in the *Laws*. There, he develops the institutions and practices of a regime devoted to virtue, while being practically mindful of the restrictions that the need for popular consent places on political excellence and good legislation. He also explores the standpoint of piety and ritual on which happiness at first, and to some degree always, rests. This standpoint, indeed, is the ground of the powerful securing of the veil that may cover but never eliminate the natural problems that are rooted in ordinary actions and things. The *Laws'* explicit orientation to virtue, indeed, makes visible those natural features whose shape law and piety must at once follow (and in that sense clarify) and modestly cover up (and in that sense occlude). Study of the *Laws* in chapter 3 also offered an opportunity to observe the contrast and continuities between ancient and modern politics and freedom.

It is not possible to understand Plato's presentation of the central elements of human thought and action, and their possible combinations and differences, without considering the phenomena from which philosophy begins directly and which provide its continuing impulse. Plato mentions and discusses these phenomena throughout his works, of course, and he clarifies several of the most important among them without devoting dialogues to them. We therefore turned in chapter 4 to wonder, perplexity, laughter, and nature. These phenomena help to make visible the nature of the questioning and attraction with which philosophy begins, the object of its search, and the links among philosophy's objects and ordinary—yet extraordinary—experience. Plato's grasp of our capacity for seeing the connection between true and false, for recognizing things in combinations and divisions, and for noticing the differences and likenesses among images and their sources are revealed in his understanding of these subjects.

We then turned in chapters 5 and 6 to phenomena that are linked to or unite the virtues but are not themselves virtues, and which clarify further elements of Plato's philosophical understanding. We considered, first, nobility or beauty, crucial for virtue because the virtues are thought to be noble, and we then explored the good. Indeed, our discussion of the *Republic* centered on attempting to clarify how Plato understands goodness, or the good, and its connection to justice and politics. It considered as well Plato's portrait of philosophy and how it both intensifies and articulates virtue. Plato, as we saw, understands the philosophical and political lives to be united in their wish to grasp what is good, but he also sees them as being in tension because of the difference between philosophy's intellectual radicalism and the opinion and ritual on which political life must rest. We also developed in the *Republic* a discussion that we continued in the *Statesman* of Plato's understanding of the variety of forms of government, or regimes, an understanding that is the first detailed articulation of this central political phenomenon and one that is unsurpassed in its cogency.

We then, in chapter 7, considered in greater detail important phenomena that we began to explore in the *Republic:* the nature of the connection between soul and body, the soul's parts and powers, and the human good's orientation to pleasure and intelligence. Plato's discussion of the elements of pleasure, a phenomenon that becomes especially important as the salience of piety and the other virtues wanes, shows both its significance and its subordination to the mind. The importance of mind, in turn, compels a more complete analysis of the elements and possibility of opinion, image, and knowledge, vital in Plato's discussion in the *Republic,* and the subjects of Socrates' and the Stranger's discussions in the *Theatetus,* the *Sophist,* and the *Statesman.* The *Statesman* also continues Plato's political analysis by showing how a political end can function as a measure or standard, and by examining a variety of ways in which classes, such as the virtues, are able to combine with each other while remaining what they are. Plato's pioneering articulation of the core elements of human thought and action proves, eventually, to extend to the fullest ways in which what is intelligible is open to and attracts the mind.

II

Despite what I have just said about the importance, for Plato, of the continuing attempt to understand, our discussion in chapters 7–9 might leave the impression that Plato reaches a comprehensive conclusion. The *Sophist*'s analysis of rest, motion, being, sameness, and difference, however, stops well short of elaborating their full nature or the connections among them. It also leaves open the relation between these discussions and those that concern ideas such as moderation, justice, and courage, and beauty, measure, precision, and the good. The *Philebus'* exploration of pleasure and thought leaves insufficiently examined the madness, or excess, in philosophy. The *Statesman* leads us to ask about the connection between the regime it elaborates and the philosophic life, and between its methods and discoveries and those of the *Republic.* These three dialogues are, in the end, no more conclusive than is a "typical" Socratic conversation.

The inconclusiveness that arises from the continuing attempt to understand, however, does not obviate the acuity of Plato's basic articulation itself. Nor does it nullify our summary remarks in earlier chapters about Plato's understanding of the phenomena he explores. What is clear in Plato is the centrality of political virtue and philosophy, and the links and tensions between them. Intellectual action is rooted in the false perfection of everyday life, perfect because directed by and toward excellence within communities that attempt to be comprehensive, false because everyday life and community is in fact inadequate and incomplete. The political virtues of soul and city that Plato clarifies remain the heart of practical excellence. They are the soul's natural orders as we deal with and enjoy the pleasures, honors, beauties, and fears of life, together with other men. Nonetheless, they are imperfect, because reason cannot satisfy itself in political life alone. None of the usual goods allows reason to be fully itself or fully excellent. The goods for which we usually wish, however, and the powers we use more or less virtuously to secure them are, despite this, versions of what the intellectual life seeks, and its action in seeking it. The philosophic life extends and enlarges but does not exclude these excellences.

The kinds of connections and differences that exist among these powers and goods are one of Plato's central subjects. So, too, is the nature of the beautiful completion of things we produce and how what guides us can be a standard or measure. No other thinker has uncovered and then probed with such precision and intensity the question of whole and part, or one and many. Such examination also clarifies the motions of the soul and mind that are open to these unities. Plato discovers reason's power to discriminate and combine, and its connection to the true extent and meaning of erotic and spirited passions. He elaborates in their full range what grounds or causes human action, the goals, forms, motions, and conditions that direct and limit our affairs. He uncovers the world beyond the world.

Philosophic life is not only a transformative extension of everyday satisfaction and excellence. It is also rooted in ordinary understanding, the amazing powers of intellectual sight, or noetic comprehension, that we take for granted. Perplexity and wonder stand ready to be experienced in their striking presence. Laughter makes visible our immediate grasp of the difference and connection between what is and what merely pretends to be. Political thinking and choice can become aware of the scope and complexity of human affairs and our orientation to what is not merely human. We rarely examine the questions, problems, truths, and comprehensiveness that these experiences reveal. But we are able to follow these phenomena unflinchingly to where they lead. Plato shows the mutual connection of everyday and philosophic life, not just in what we seek but also in what and how we see.

Practical and philosophic excellence is each impossible without justice. Plato's rational articulation of things thus initiates the reasonable understanding of political affairs. The *Laws,* the *Republic,* and the *Statesman* attempt to secure virtue and, in different modes, to address the relation between philosophy and politics. Plato clarifies the strength and limit of law, the connection between law and piety, the importance of founding, and the status and limits of political knowledge. On the whole, his work inspires rational defense of freedom, love of its excellent use, and the effort to establish, prudently, political orders devoted to these ends.

Notes

INTRODUCTION

1. See *Lovers* 133E–135A, *Theatetus*, passim.

2. See Martin Heidegger, "Phenomenology and Theology," in *Pathmarks*, ed. William McNeil (Cambridge University Press, 1998; originally *Wegmarken*, Vittorio Klostermann, 1967).

3. Consider Hegel, *Lectures on the Philosophy of Religion*, introduction.

4. Among the exceptions are George Klosko, *Plato's Political Thought*, 2nd ed. (Oxford University Press, 2006), and Malcolm Schofield, *Plato: Political Philosophy* (Oxford University Press, 2006). These books are more historical or developmental in their approach than mine.

5. Consider *Republic* 337A, *Lovers* 133D.

6. Nicias is the other character in the *Laches* who offers an opinion about courage.

7. Plato also arranges the dialogues so that their result gives the title character or practice what it strives for, knowingly or not, but what it distorts when it remains as itself. The *Sophist* shows how sophists could attain the dominance of speech, and the being of negation, that they seek. The conditions under which sophistry could have what it seeks transform it, however, so that sophists would no longer look as they once did. The *Republic* shows that to have the justice that cities seek requires a new regime that would radically transform actual cities and, indeed, would go beyond anything political.

8. The importance of the fact that Plato writes dialogues, not treatises, is now widely acknowledged. The return to this view was spearheaded in recent years by Jacob Klein and Leo Strauss and their students. See, e.g., Jacob Klein, *A Commentary on Plato's* Meno (University of North Carolina Press, 1965), and Leo Strauss, *The City and Man* (Rand McNally, 1963). The question of the order of composition of the dialogues, however, remains unclear. The chronological question once seemed to scholars to be central, but it now seems philosophically less important. After all, in the absence of other evidence, one could hardly grasp the dialogues' order of composition, or decide that a dialogue transmitted to us as genuine is not, unless one understood it on its own. This task of understanding is difficult and rewarding enough by itself. Moreover, Plato often links dialogues by putting them in a clear sequence, as he does the *Euthyphro, Theatetus, Sophist, Statesman, Apology, Crito,* and *Phaedo;* by using similar or connected characters and references, as he does in the *Symposium* and *Protagoras,* or the *Lysis, Euthydemus,* and *Menexenus;* or by using similar dialogic devices such as having some dialogues narrated

and others performed. These and still other observable mechanisms more directly reflect Plato's intention than could a presumed order of composition. Nonetheless, Plato, who lived from c. 427 to 347 BC, did not write each dialogue all at once, so it is plausible to think that he might have changed his mind on important matters. (This is why chronology might matter intellectually.) I believe, however, that one cannot point to any place where one can say confidently that this has happened. One does see, of course, that Plato considers subjects from different, and perhaps broader, thematic points of view, or with different procedures.

One challenge to this claim of an essential unity in Plato's understanding, whatever the order of the dialogues' composition, is the presence of the *Sophist* and *Statesman*. These "late" dialogues, use the Eleatic Stranger, not Socrates, as the chief interlocutor, and sometimes employ a procedure of division (diaresis) that we do not see in that exact form in other dialogues. I discuss some of the substantive questions of the connection between Socrates' understanding and the Stranger's when I discuss these dialogues. For now, however, we should recognize that Plato embeds these dialogues in the order I mentioned earlier, which includes a "typical" Socratic conversation (the *Euthyphro*) and an emphatically Socratic one, his own trial or apology. In the *Philebus*, Plato puts in Socrates' mouth "methodological" statements and substantive concerns that are reminiscent of the *Statesman*. In my judgment, moreover, the political differences among the political dialogues, the *Laws, Republic,* and *Statesman* stem from different purposes and themes, not different understandings.

One might also claim that, whatever the importance of the unknown order of composition or the status of the *Sophist* and *Statesman,* it is significant that in five dialogues (*Parmenides, Timaeus, Critias, Sophist, Statesman*) Socrates is not the chief interlocutor, although he is present. In another (the *Cleitophon*) he speaks only briefly at the beginning, and in two others (the *Laws* and *Epinomis*) he is not present at all. One must plausibly explain these and other similarly baffling matters, such as why Plato visibly groups certain dialogues, has Socrates narrate some and directly perform in others, and so on. One possibility is that the dialogues where Socrates is not the chief speaker reveal Plato's break with, or criticism of, him. It is plausible that Plato would question Socrates' views, for he surely appears to question those of Heraclitus, Parmenides, and other thinkers. The difficulty, however, is that we do not know what the views of "Socrates" are, because we see him only as a character in Aristophanes, Xenophon, and Plato, and Plato presents him as claiming to know only his own ignorance, i.e., as not having any doctrines to criticize. Moreover, little that is critical of Socrates in dialogues where his role is small or in which, say, he is a young man, is not also said to or by Socrates (or easily enough inferred) in dialogues where he is more prominent. As I said earlier, the major subjects and procedures of the *Sophist* and *Statesman* appear elsewhere, sometimes not so systematically, but sometimes in detail. My conclusion, therefore, is that differences in Plato's arguments stem from the different themes of his presentations and the complexity of his subjects themselves. They do not stem from a fundamentally changed understanding that he depicts by reducing Socrates' visible importance. The safest path is to seek and expect consistency in Plato's overall political philosophy. If we cannot find it, we should blame ourselves or recognize the difficulty of what we are trying to understand.

These issues are usefully discussed by Catherine Zuckert in *Plato's Philosophers* (University of Chicago Press, 2009) and by Thomas Pangle in his introduction to *The Roots of Political Philosophy* (Cornell University Press, 1987). Zuckert organizes her study by helpfully and painstakingly arranging the dialogues in terms of the dates, from 450 to 399, during which Plato indicates each one took place. She does not claim that this is the only way to arrange the dialogues, however, and she should not, because several dialogues offer no indication of performance dates, others have dates about which one can at most speculate, and still others refer to events that did not coincide and people who could not all have been assembled at the same time. There are other plausible ways in which to group the dialogues, moreover, as I suggested, such as grouping those narrated versus those performed, or those with similar characters. And, of course, one may also group dialogues with similar or connected subjects. Indeed, that the dialogues can be connected to each other in several combinations is itself instructive.

9. I indicate during the course of the book why I discuss each dialogue when I do. In some cases my discussions of dialogues are too condensed to make visible many of the dialogical points I discussed above. In other cases, however, as in much of chapters 2 and 5, I summarize and comment on dialogues in enough detail that I am able to make explicit at least some elements of how Socrates orients his argument to the characters, wishes, and limitations of his interlocutors. In all cases, moreover, my view of Plato's understanding has been attentive to such matters.

10. My notes are meant to refer to dialogues where Plato addresses a subject that I am discussing. I also give references for points I am making about, and quotations from, dialogues that I am interpreting directly. I also occasionally use notes to expand my arguments. I note the editions and translations that serve as the basis of my discussions in chapter 1, note 3. I also mention other useful editions or books, especially for the *Laws, Republic,* and *Statesman,* in the appropriate chapters. Otherwise, I refer sparingly to secondary works, usually to indicate a good or important discussion of a subject that I have not developed or to point to an argument that I am aware is an immediate source of my own. To fully address and confront the literature on Plato would require a volume of its own.

CHAPTER 1: The World of the Dialogues

1. A rhapsode publicly performed the *Iliad, Odyssey,* and other poems. Plato examines the rhapsode Ion in his *Ion.*

2. These are anomalies not just for us but for many of Plato's characters.

3. For the Greek text of the dialogues, I have used *Platonis Opera, Volumes 1–5* (Oxford University Press). Volumes 2–5 are edited by John Burnet (1901–1907). Volume 1 is edited by E. A Duke, W. F. Hickken, W. S. M. Nicoll, D. B. Robinson, and J. C. G. Strachan (1995). (When the translations that I list below choose readings from the Greek that differ from this edition, I have followed the translators.) For the basic translation of the *Theages, Laches,* and *Greater Hippias,* I have used Thomas Pangle, ed., *The Roots of Political Philosophy* (Cornell University Press, 1987). I have also benefited from the translations of, and commentaries on, other dialogues in the Pangle volume: *Hipparchus,* trans. Steven Forde (Allan Bloom commentary); *Minos,* trans. Thomas Pangle (Leo Strauss commentary); *Lovers,* trans. James Leake (Christopher Bruell commentary); *Cleitophon,* trans. and commentary, Clifford Orwin; *Theages,* trans. and commentary, Thomas Pangle; *Alcibiades I,* trans. Carnes Lord, (Steven Forde commentary); *Laches,* trans. and commentary, James H. Nichols, Jr.; *Lesser Hippias,* trans. and commentary, James Leake; *Greater*

Hippias, trans. and commentary David R. Sweet; *Ion,* trans. and commentary, Allan Bloom. For the basic translation of the *Euthyphro* and *Apology,* I have used *Four Texts on Socrates,* trans. with notes by Thomas G. West and Grace Starry West, intro. by Thomas G. West, rev. ed. (Cornell University Press, 1998). This volume includes Plato's *Euthyphro, Apology of Socrates,* and *Crito,* and Aristophanes' *Clouds.* For other basic translations I have used the following volumes, which also contain useful introductions and commentary: Thomas G. West and Grace Starry West, trans., *Charmides* (Hackett Publishing Company, 1986); James H. Nichols Jr., trans., *Gorgias and Phaedrus* (Cornell University Press, 1998); Robert C. Bartlett, trans., *Protagoras and Meno* (Cornell University Press, 2004); Thomas Pangle, trans., *Plato's Laws* (Basic Books, 1980); Allan Bloom, trans., *The Republic of Plato* (Basic Books, 1968); Seth Benardete, *The Tragedy and Comedy of Life: Plato's* Philebus (University of Chicago Press, 1993); Seth Benardete, trans., *Plato's* Theatetus (University of Chicago Press, 1986); Seth Benardete, trans., *Plato's* Sophist (University of Chicago Press, 1986); Seth Benardete, trans., *Plato's* Statesman (University of Chicago Press, 1986); Eva Brann, Peter Kalkavage, and Eric Salem, trans., *Plato's* Phaedo (Focus, 1998); Albert Keith Whitaker, trans., *Plato's* Parmenides (Focus, 1996). For the basic translation of the *Euthydemus,* I have used W. R. M. Lamb, trans., *Laches, Protagoras, Meno, Euthydemus* (Loeb Classical Library, Harvard University Press, 1953). I modify these translations as necessary. Debra Nails's *The People of Plato* (Hackett, 2002) is a comprehensive discussion of what is known about the characters in the dialogues.

4. *Laches, Theages, Euthydemus.*

5. See *Alcibiades I, Theages.*

6. Consider the *Greater Hippias'* discussion of Sparta, 284B–286A.

7. Consider the beginning of the *Theatetus.*

8. See *Alcibiades I,* 106B–109C, and *Republic* 506A.

9. These are among Socrates' criteria for being an expert. Socrates also likes to say that something is teachable if we can point to teachers and learners. See, e.g., *Meno* 89E–90E, and *Laches* 185B.

10. See *Theages* 126D–128C, *Protagoras* 316B–318A, *Gorgias* 487A–D.

11. In fact, it is not obvious that what Lysimachus and Melesias want is identical, because distinction for one son may reduce it for the other.

12. Perhaps these difficulties are overcome when one seeks Socrates' advice. After all, he seems above payment, content with his relative poverty, modest in his claims to know, and unconcerned with victory in argument, although those he defeats do not always see it this way. Indeed, these practices—his poverty, professed ignorance, and gentleness—belong to the aura of purity or, at least, otherworldliness that seems to us and to interlocutors such as Alcibiades and Euthyphro to emanate from him. (Consider, however, the difference between the perplexity of ignorance and the assuredness of saintliness.) Socrates' claimed ignorance about courage, wisdom, and the other concerns of fathers and sons, however, appears to be overstated. So, too, is his trustworthiness less clear-cut than in our idyllic picture of him. Socrates does not cheat, but he does not do all he can, even for his friends. Rather than educating Critobulus or Nicias' son himself, for example, he recommends the music teacher and sophist Damon. Perhaps he does no more or less for these young sons than they are capable of doing for themselves. Does he help them as much as he could, however, or give the fathers what they thought they might be receiving?

13. Lysimachus' father was Aristeides "the just," a statesman who helped lead the Greeks against the Persians.

14. See *Alcibiades I* 118B–119A. Pericles was Athens' chief statesman during much of Socrates' early life.

15. See *Lysis* 208A ff.

16. See *Republic* 487A–D.

17. Socrates, who lived from 470 to 399, was convicted and executed in 399. *The Apology of Socrates* presents Plato's version of the trial.

18. See, e.g., *Alcibiades I, Theages,* and *Protagoras.*

19. See, among other examples, *Alcibiades I* 106B–116E, and *Gorgias* 494C–495A.

20. See *Meno* 70A–73C, and Polus' and Callicles' discussion with Socrates in the *Gorgias.*

21. See *Symposium* 177D, *Theages* 128B, *Theatetus* 148E–151D, and *Charmides* 154BC. For a recent discussion of the *Symposium, Phaedrus,* and *Lysis,* consider Mary P. Nichols, *Socrates on Friendship and Community* (Cambridge University Press, 2009).

22. We see subtle references to his Daedelus-like ability to set statues, or fixed opinions, in motion. Consider, e.g., *Euthyphro* 11BC and *Meno* 97D. On Socrates' demon, see, e.g., *Theatetus* 151A, *Theages* 128D, and *Apology* 40AB.

23. See *Meno* 80AB, *Greater Hippias* 301B.

24. See *Greater Hippias* 286CD, *Protagoras* 335B–336B.

25. See *Meno* 76AB, 80B, 94E–95A, *Symposium* 213B–215B.

26. See *Symposium* 174A, 215A–222D.

27. See *Alcibiades I* 103A–106A, the conclusion of the *Republic,* and the *Meno.*

28. See *Greater Hippias* 297E, *Lysis* 223A.

29. See the beginnings of the *Parmenides, Protagoras, Charmides.*

30. See *Lysis* 204B–205A, *Symposium* 183A–D.

31. This link is most visible in the *Laws.*

32. Consider *Republic,* Books II and III, and *Laws,* Book I.

33. See *Protagoras* 335A–C, 342A–347A; *Phaedrus* 237A–241D; and the conclusions of the *Gorgias* and *Republic.*

34. *Symposium* 174E–175B, *Protagoras* 335D.

35. *Apology* 38A.

36. I will not distinguish here between sophists and rhetoricians.

37. See *Euthydemus* 304C–306D.

38. Consider *Protagoras* 337CD.

39. Consider Leo Strauss, *Studies in Platonic Political Philosophy* (University of Chicago Press, 1983), chap. 3.

40. See Callicles' discussion of pleasure with Socrates in the *Gorgias* and Protagoras' discussion of pleasure with Socrates in the *Protagoras.*

41. *Greater Hippias* 282DE.

42. Consider *Gorgias* 449D–451E.

43. *Greater Hippias* 281A–D, 304A–E; *Meno* 89E–95A.

44. *Protagoras* 337CD, *Euthydemus* 277E, *Laches* 197D.

45. See, e.g., the *Alcibiades I* and the *Statesman.* I am not here distinguishing between art (*techne*) and science (*episteme*).

46. See *Gorgias* 465A, *Laws* 857CD.

47. Consider *Timaeus*, passim, and the discussion of the arts that precedes and follows the myth that the Eleatic Stranger tells in the *Statesman*.

48. See *Symposium* 221E–222A.

49. *Laches* 184E.

50. See *Statesman* 283B–284D.

51. And in the *Republic* 595C–597D, Socrates discusses the "ideas" of beds and couches to which the carpenter looks when he is making something other than houses.

52. See *Meno* 73B, *Statesman* 259B.

53. Consider the opening of the *Theatetus* and *Gorgias* 464B–466A.

54. See *Laches* 198E–199A, *Statesman* 290DE, 301CD.

55. See *Lysis* 209E.

56. *Philebus* 44C.

57. See *Alcibiades I* 106C–109B, *Euthydemus* 279A–282D.

58. Several dialogues, the *Theatetus* most obviously, discuss knowledge at length. I will examine the *Theatetus* in the eighth chapter. Even the *Theatetus*, however, is not epistemological in the modern sense. It does not seek an absolute foundation or an always effective method but, rather, subjects various opinions about knowledge to Socratic examination. As with other topics, Plato's philosophical understanding of the elements of knowledge and their correlatives extends, but does not overthrow, ordinary comprehension. I also discuss perplexity at greater length in the fourth chapter and return in the seventh and ninth chapters to measure, sufficiency, and precision. I should also note that the criteria of knowledge and of what makes something good are curiously connected. The *Philebus* explores this connection in the light of pleasure.

59. See, e.g., *Euthyphro* 4E, 14B, *Protagoras* 329C, *Meno* 85D. See, too, the Eleatic Stranger at *Sophist* 223A.

60. See, e.g., *Symposium* 201A, 204B, 206C, *Euthyphro* 5C; and see the Eleatic Stranger at *Sophist* 238DE, 242B, 223A, 254B, 226C, 242C, 243D, 245B, 261E, 262C, and *Statesman* 262C.

61. See, e.g., *Symposium* 177E; *Euthyphro* 12E, 14C; *Theatetus* 148E, 169D, 201B; and the Eleatic Stranger at *Sophist* 221B, 221C.

62. One can see this procedure throughout the course of the *Laches, Charmides, Euthyphro, Meno, Protagoras,* and *Gorgias*.

63. See *Charmides* 159A–161B.

64. See *Euthyphro* 11E–12E.

65. See, e.g., *Euthyphro* 6A; *Protagoras* 339B; *Meno* 82A, 96A; *Alcibiades I* 116D–117A; and *Republic* 436B–437A.

66. Consider, for moderation, *Charmides, Protagoras, Meno,* and *Laws,* in which insolence is still another opposite.

67. Consider the *Euthydemus*, passim.

68. Consider the *Republic*, Book VII, and the discussions throughout the *Parmenides*.

CHAPTER 2: Virtue

1. Justice, courage, moderation, and wisdom, but not piety, are the *Republic*'s four virtues of city and soul. So, piety's independent status is questionable. Plato also mentions other virtues, such as magnificence, in the *Meno*.

2. Although the dialogues' subtitles are suggestive, it is not clear that they stem from Plato himself.

3. When I am exploring particular dialogues, I proceed by discussing a portion of Plato's argument in a section headed by, say, Roman numeral II. I then, if necessary, comment further on some of the portion's less obvious elements and implications, in a new section with that same Roman numeral followed by a letter, say, II A. (I vary this procedure for the *Gorgias*, as I indicate when I begin to discuss it.) In this chapter I am examining the *Theages, Euthyphro, Laches, Charmides, Gorgias, Meno,* and *Protagoras*. Chapter 1, note 3, contains general information about the Greek edition and translations of these dialogues that I am following.

4. For the *Theages* generally, consider the discussion in Christopher Bruell, *On The Socratic Education* (Rowman and Littlefield, 1999).

5. *Theages* 122A.

6. It turns out that Theages and Demodocus want to engage Socrates himself; Socrates need not have remained poor.

7. Cf. the *Statesman*'s discussion of weaving.

8. Themistocles lived from c. 528 to 442 BC and was a contemporary of Aristeides. He is credited with devising the naval strategy that was instrumental in the Greeks' triumph over Persia.

9. *Theages* 126D.

10. Cf. *Lysis* 207D–210D.

11. See *Gorgias* 516DE.

12. Plato's *Sophist* examines nonbeing, or difference. Some sophists (and rhetoricians) work by exacerbating differences and jumbling similarities. See, e.g., the *Euthydemus*.

13. *Theages* 131A.

14. One practical intention of Socrates' discussions of virtue is to moderate his interlocutors' ambitions, or to make them less dangerous to themselves, the city, or the philosophic way of life, even if the discussions sometimes reach no explicit conclusion.

15. *Theages* 129D.

16. Cf. *Laches*, where Aristeides is present.

17. *Theages* 130E.

18. *Theages* 131A.

19. The privacy required for conspiracy is what tyrants must oppose. Cf. Aristotle, *Politics*, Book V.

20. And, in another example, claiming to have warned Timarchus not to try to kill Nicias. For the Sicilian expedition, see Thucydides, *History of the Peloponnesian War*.

21. His father hints that Socrates, not his demon, does the opposing, and Plato quietly indicates the difference between praying and deliberating. Theages' apparently excessive credulity may be why Socrates presents his demon not just as warning him (as

he does elsewhere) but also as warning his friends (through him), and as linked to un-canny foresight.

22. "Primarily" means, however, that immediate questions about the public place and degree of religion can be politically controversial, as is evident in Supreme Court cases.

23. Only a government that believes itself to embody philosophical truth precisely and sufficiently, so that citizens need not seek understanding for themselves, is an equal or greater threat.

24. It is fortunate that in Athens and similar cities, which are among the few places where philosophy and political philosophy were at all likely to have been discovered, they were indeed discovered. I explore Plato's view of the inevitable tension between politics and philosophy in subsequent sections and chapters.

25. In the terms outlined in the first chapter, the *Euthyphro* combines a father's con-cerns indirectly expressed—Euthyphro's father is not present—and a son's ambitions (although we might at first hesitate to connect Euthyphro's piety to a desire for honor.)

26. Cf. the opening of the *Theages*. For Socrates' trial, see the *Apology of Socrates*.

27. *Euthyphro* 4D.

28. *Euthyphro* 4E.

29. In the course of these conversations Euthyphro mentions discovery, contempla-tion, precise knowledge, wonder, and astonishment. Socrates' search for piety elevates these passions or judgments. He does not, however, name philosophy. (See 5A–6D.)

30. Does he hope he can moderate him?

31. This multiplicity, indeed, is exemplified by the two terms that Socrates now uses for pious, *eusebes* and his usual *hosion*, and by Euthyphro's adding *hieron*. *Eusebes* and its variants often connote being observant and what is observed, and *hieron* and its variants what is sacred or revered. For the connection between gods and ideas, see the *Republic*, and Leo Strauss, *The City and Man* (Rand McNally, 1964).

32. See *Alcibiades I* 117AB.

33. See Homer's *Odyssey*.

34. Monotheism does not overcome this difficulty as long as there are competing monotheists or polytheists. Even were there only one god believed in by all, his indica-tions of what he loves would need to be stable and clear.

35. Is a "what" a problem that permits or encourages further questioning?

36. I am using *pious* and *holy* interchangeably here.

37. Consider Nietzsche, *Beyond Good and Evil*, on the connection between saintliness and cleanliness.

38. He still does not clearly treat piety as a virtue; he never mentions the soul.

39. See the *Apology*, and Socrates' discussion in the *Meno* with one of those who in-dicts him, Anytus.

40. See Socrates' discussion with Thrasymachus in the *Republic*, Book I, and the first set of divisions and the myth of the *Statesman*.

41. *Euthyphro* 14C.

42. *Euthyphro* 14E.

43. See *Sophist* 216CD, *Phaedrus* 244A–257B.

44. See *Charmides* 160E.

45. I use *courage* and *manliness* interchangeably. Consider Harvey C. Mansfield, *Man-liness* (Yale University Press, 2006), and, for courage in Plato generally, Linda Rabieh,

Plato on the Virtue of Courage (Johns Hopkins University Press, 2007). For the *Laches*, also consider Bruell's *On the Socratic Education*.

46. See *Lovers* 134A–C.

47. *Laches* 184C.

48. *Laches* 190D.

49. We are halfway through the dialogue, at 190D, when this happens.

50. If courage is enduring pains and fears, what could its relation be to pleasures and desires? Perhaps we display it when we push pleasures away. In this way, courage deals with the attractive as well as the repulsive and prevents us from being overwhelmed by either. Moderation would then be yielding appropriately to pleasures (and fears, e.g., fear of ill repute).

51. See *Laws*, Book I.

52. Cf. *Protagoras* 349E–351B.

53. Laches had earlier attested to Socrates' courage at the battle of Delium. Socrates' words are worth listening to, he claimed, because of his courageous deeds.

54. See *Republic* 536B.

55. See *Statesman* 306A–308A.

56. Cf. *Statesman* 284E.

57. He is concerned that forethought and success might eliminate risk and, hence, courage. But might not forethought and success, through small victories, enable grander risks that the army may take for larger victories? Could forethought or art not reduce risk to a point where overcoming it can be ventured courageously, rather than foolishly? One might think of the example of careful planning in advance of a mission that remains dangerous when undertaken.

58. Sight was said to be the eyes' perfection, but it is only part of health. In the *Charmides*, by contrast, a headache can be cured only by considering both the whole body and soul, and, finally, by moderation. The *Laches* confuses whole and part in virtue by making a part (courage) the whole, and the *Charmides* confuses it by making the whole (knowledge) a part (moderation).

59. This suggests that separating or distinguishing can itself be noble: if there is courage in search, this courage could be noble separating, or separation of what is noble.

60. Cf. *Philebus* 39C.

61. This need not be so if the whole is merely the addition of "parts" that are only artificially discriminated amounts of the same virtue; Nicias' mistakenly dividing courage as a third of knowledge treats virtue as a whole of this type. Therefore, we must assume that the parts of virtue are not of this type. But we cannot say from the *Laches* whether they are like parts of the face, parts of the city, parts of the class "animal," or like the participants within each virtue itself. Moreover, good and evil are underdeveloped here. Cf. *Protagoras* 329D, *Philebus* 16C–17A, *Greater Hippias* 301E–302D.

62. Boldness or courage, nonetheless, always remains a principle of one's own separate life.

63. The *Theages* indicates the degree to which Socrates helped the boys.

64. See *Republic* 430E–432A.

65. In the *Protagoras* (as we will see) he describes some of his strategies in argument—his superiority as an ordinary sophist, so to speak. See *Protagoras* 330E–331A, 335BC, 339E–340A, 362A. In the *Gorgias* he claims he is especially just and the only true political ruler.

66. Whatever pious rituals or reunion with his family occur happen off stage. The battle occurred early in the Peloponessian War and ended in 431.

67. *Charmides* 154A.

68. *Charmides* 154C.

69. Cf. *Protagoras* 328D.

70. See *Charmides* 155D.

71. Consider Laches' fear of ridicule.

72. *Protagoras* 314E–316A, 317CD.

73. See *Meno* 80AB.

74. Cf. *Republic* 518C.

75. *Charmides* 159A.

76. Socrates sets up moderation as the possible topic, but it is Critias who actually chooses it (157A–D). Critias later became one of the Thirty Tyrants who ruled briefly after the Peloponessian War. They were overthrown in 403. Charmides collaborated with Critias. Both were killed in battles with the democratic opposition.

77. Strong or beautiful bodies sometimes require special attention. See *Lovers*, where Socrates gives the healthy body more independence.

78. Laches also generalizes, from citing the courageous action of not fleeing in battle to seeing courage as endurance of the soul.

79. We should note the appearance of fear in all three virtues we have discussed. A full understanding of the virtues needs to account for their mutual connection in fear and what we fear, and in pleasure and what we desire.

80. *Charmides* 162BC.

81. We are reminded of the *Republic*'s view of justice, and Polemarchus' taking over of his father's argument in *Republic*, Book I. Socrates' statement about Critias' anger and endurance also suggests the connection between one's own and courage. We should, further, note the link with the previous discussion: awe that causes shame keeps one in one's own, i.e., not too big for or beyond oneself. But, as Socrates indicates, one's own may be more open and needy than awe suggests. We learn in the *Lesser Hippias* that Hippias the sophist makes for himself much of what is done better by artisans in a city; he seems ridiculous, or extreme. One's own is open to what is useful or good for oneself but not obviously equivalent or reducible to oneself.

82. Cf. *Protagoras* 332AB.

83. *Charmides* 167A. Cf. *Lovers* 137A–138A.

84. See *Apology* 20C–23B. Critias adds knowledge of what one does not know only after Socrates' prodding.

85. It is need or lack that links moderation to both ignorance and desire. Hence, moderation has two groups of opposites, silly foolishness/hubris, and ascetism/licentiousness.

86. *Charmides* 167B.

87. Cf. *Theatetus* for a different view, which involves common sensing and immaterial perception.

88. See *Meno* 75B.

89. *Charmides* 167D. Can one—can Charmides—be moderate unless he believes he knows what moderation is? Does not moderation require choosing to be moderate?

90. *Charmides* 168A.

91. *Charmides* 169A.

92. Cf. *Republic,* Book I.

93. See *Alcibiades I* 106C–109A and *Republic,* Book I. See, too, *Statesman* 304A–305E.

94. Socrates has done this despite the fact that Critias has not quite said that knowing knowledge must include nothing whatsoever of what knowledge knows. Would he disagree that one must know what shoes are, and how we use them, in order to know that one is not a shoemaker?

95. At *Charmides* 171E.

96. But cf. *Lovers.*

97. See the *Laws, Statesman,* and *Alcibiades I.* We will discuss the *Republic* in chapter 6.

98. In addition to James Nichols's discussions accompanying his translation, one should consider Seth Benardete, *The Rhetoric of Morality and Philosophy* (University of Chicago Press, 1991), and Devin Stauffer, *The Unity of Plato's* Gorgias (Cambridge University Press, 2006).

99. When a dialogue is named after one character but more than one speaks, Plato is considering two or more elements of its subject and how they modify each other, and examining how the title, the thematic element, modifies the other element in Socrates' own philosophic enterprise.

100. *Logos* means speech, reason, and account.

101. *Gorgias* 452D.

102. Cf. *Protagoras* 323B, 348C.

103. *Gorgias* 463AB.

104. *Gorgias* 465A.

105. As cooking is to medicine, further, cosmetics is to gymnastics. Cf. *Statesman* 282A, 289A.

106. He had earlier told Gorgias that he refutes and is refuted with pleasure, for there is no evil greater than false opinion about the things their argument concerns, and it is a greater good to be released from evil than to release others.

107. See *Theages* 124D.

108. See *Greater Hippias* 295B–297E.

109. *Gorgias* 480E.

110. Cf. *Republic,* Books I, II.

111. *Gorgias* 485DE. Cf. *Euthydemus,* beginning and end.

112. See *Republic* 578C.

113. *Gorgias* 491B.

114. Just before asking this he had agreed with Callicles' rebuke that Socrates always says the same things and added that he says them about the same things.

115. *Gorgias* 491E.

116. Callicles says that Socrates should be ashamed of his argument.

117. Socrates makes philosophy the true having more, as well as the true intelligence, courage, self-rule, and dominance of the soul. He transforms Callicles' more ordinary view of these matters and of pleasure, although, as we soon see, these views are not fully Callicles' own. Socrates also acts here as if one could ignore the body and its strength.

118. Compare this with Socrates' manipulation of the conversation in the *Protagoras,* discussed shortly.

119. *Gorgias* 499E–500A. See *Laws,* Book I.

120. *Gorgias* 503C. Cf. Socrates' funeral oration in the *Menexenus, Meno* 93A, and

Euthydemus 306B. Militiades commanded the Athenians at Marathon in their victory over Persia in 490 and was Themistocles' contemporary. Cimon, also a significant statesman, was Themistocles's son.

121. *Gorgias* 505B.

122. *Gorgias* 506E. See *Republic* 443C–444D.

123. *Gorgias* 507A.

124. *Gorgias* 508C.

125. *Gorgias* 510A.

126. Cf. *Lysis* 214BC.

127. Cf. Theodorus in the *Theatetus* and Hippias in the *Greater* and *Lesser Hippias* for other versions of extremism in speech not, however, matched in practice.

128. See *Gorgias* 458A, 509B–D.

129. In general, the precise place of knowledge in virtue is unclear here.

130. See *Republic, Sophist,* and *Statesman.*

131. Is the human good proper satisfaction?

132. Cf. the discussion of pleasure in the *Philebus,* which we examine in chapter 7.

133. *Gorgias* 525C.

134. Cf. his own reference to guessing about Gorgias, and the fact that the *Republic,* whose theme is justice, also features an afterlife story.

135. Consider Hippias' treatment of Sparta in the *Greater Hippias* 283D–286C.

136. This issue is the heart of the *Laws.*

137. The *Meno* reminds one of the *Gorgias* because Meno agrees that his view comes from Gorgias. It reminds one of the *Apology* because its third character is Anytus, one of Socrates' accusers. It reminds one of the *Phaedo* because both dialogues present Socrates' suggestion that we are able to know the most important things today because our immortal soul is recollecting what it has seen before. It reminds one of the *Theatetus* because knowledge is an explicit topic, and a mathematical discussion is important in its argument. It reminds one of the *Protagoras* because it opens with Meno's abruptly asking Socrates if virtue is teachable.

138. Cf. similar suggestions about justice in the *Republic,* Book I.

139. Cf. *Phaedrus* 248D, and the *Statesman,* where city and household management are equated.

140. *Meno* 72A.

141. *Meno* 75B.

142. Meno's is the tyrannical command of a beautiful youth in bloom. Cf. Charmides' conduct in the *Charmides.*

143. Meno prefers, as his answer, a universal how (emanation) to different whats. This answer is universal because it works with sound "as well as smell and many other such things" (*Meno* 76DE).

144. *Meno* 77A. He hints at but does not give Meno examples of different types of wholes, as he will with Protagoras. The emanation explanation points toward the different virtues being like pieces of gold, more and less of the same.

145. *Meno* 78C.

146. Cf. Socrates' treatment of Alcibiades in *Alcibiades I.* Socrates is ambiguous about whether longing to know arises from perplexity itself: Would one in all cases of perplexity need or desire to discover how things are? For the slave discussion generally, see Jacob Klein, *A Commentary on Plato's* Meno (University of North Carolina Press, 1965).

147. *Meno* 86B.

148. *Meno* 86BC.

149. See *Protagoras* 323C.

150. He cannot, in fact, discuss virtue's teachability without assuming something about the soul.

151. Cf. the discussion of fathers and sons in the *Laches,* and the discussion of lineage in *Alcibiades I* 120E–124C. Contrast what Socrates says or indicates about the merits of such figures here with what he says in the *Gorgias.*

152. *Meno* 94E.

153. See *Republic,* Book X.

154. Socrates does not point out the sometimes useful directness or narrowness of mere opinion and experience.

155. Cf. Socrates' rebuke of Nicias in the *Laches.* To be divinely inspired is not to know.

156. *Meno* 100B.

157. The sophists Hippias and Prodicus, Charmides, Eryximachus, Phaedrus, Pausanias, Agathon, and (shortly) Alcibiades and Critias, are also at the house. We should compare this group to the characters in the *Symposium.*

158. *Protagoras* 319A.

159. For this myth, consider Seth Benardete, *The Argument of the Action* (University of Chicago Press, 2000), and Robert Bartlett's discussion accompanying his translation.

160. *Protagoras* 322E.

161. *Protagoras* 323D.

162. *Protagoras* 326C.

163. *Protagoras* 327B.

164. *Protagoras* 329E.

165. On the close connection between justice and moderation, compare what we have just seen in the *Gorgias* and *Republic,* Book IV. On their difference, consider the *Statesman.*

166. Socrates claims soon that he lacks the memory for long speeches. As we know, by contrast, he is in fact able to follow and make them. (Consider what he hears and says in the *Symposium, Protagoras* 336D ff., *Phaedrus* 244A–257B, the conclusions of the *Gorgias* and *Republic,* and his speeches in the *Apology*). Socrates is so unashamed to admit ignorance or inability that he claims it falsely. He and Protagoras lie about their skills, for different reasons.

167. Cf. *Theatetus* 167E–168A.

168. How much does philosophic search require conversation with others and permit a community of equals—justice, in a sense, but not rule? Together, we do "have greater resources with regard to every speech and deed." If one "observes alone," he seeks another "to whom he may point this out and with whom he may make certain of it" (*Protagoras* 348D). See, too, 351E.

169. On interpretation, see *Hippias Minor,* and *Ion.*

170. How, then, is each or all "virtue"? That is, how do they participate in or compose a whole such as a face?

171. Cf. *Protagoras* 349D.

172. See *Hipparchus* 310D.

173. *Protagoras* 350D–351C. Cf. the discussion in the *Euthyphro* of the relation between justice and piety, and fear and awe.

174. Cf. *Protagoras* 323CD. The nature and nurture of which Protagoras is thinking are unclear. He presumably means habituation and training of natural gifts. The habituation may be aided by art, as moderation is aided by proper rhythms, but courage itself is not knowledge, although it could be aided by calculation. The nature he has in mind may simply be one that is not incurably vicious, rather than one with abundant spiritedness. Courage may thus mean trained confidence or boldness that, say, overcomes convention and rules in the service of one's pleasure.

175. Socrates ironically gives Protagoras what he wants (the teachability of virtue), as he does with other title characters.

176. Cf. 351B–E. We can smooth the apparently abrupt change in topic by remembering Socrates' suggestion to Polus in the *Gorgias* that one has power only if it is good for one.

177. Cf. *Sophist* 235D–236C. In this way Socrates also captures the connection between courage and endurance featured by Laches—here, enduring a present pain to achieve greater future pleasure—but not mentioned by Protagoras. But, he ignores the discrepancy between courage and pleasure to which Laches, and risking one's life, point.

178. *Protagoras* 352A.

179. *Protagoras* 353A.

180. Socrates also chooses pleasure because it appears to be a more immediate natural good for men than is, say, justice, and because calculating reason (and, thus, the other virtues such as courage that Socrates is equating here with wisdom) seems more completely teachable than do law or opinion. Socrates thus suggests the conditions for the full teachability of virtue—that it be, seek, or grasp a fully natural good that is completely open to reason. Pleasure and calculating it, however, are not this end.

181. *Protagoras* 351C.

182. See Socrates' discussion with Callicles in the *Gorgias,* and *Philebus* 21A–D.

183. Cf. *Theatetus* 151D–183D and *Protagoras* 329B–D.

184. How much does free or bold action change matters, so that advance calculation can never be fully accurate?

185. These points will be more fully grounded once we have discussed the soul in subsequent chapters.

CHAPTER 3: Virtue and Politics

1. See *Symposium; Greater Hippias;* Fustel de Coulanges, *The Ancient City* (Johns Hopkins University Press, 1980; originally, *La Cite Antique,* 1864); and Thucydides, *History of the Peloponnesian War.* Chapter 1, note 3, contains general information about the Greek edition and translations of the dialogues that I am following.

2. See, e.g., the openings of the *Charmides* and *Lysis.*

3. Here, the divine bonds and binding drug are identified as much as possible with the statesman's artful weaving. See *Statesman* 304C, 310A–311C.

4. Consider the *Sophist,* which we discuss in chapter 8.

5. See Mark Blitz, *Duty Bound: Responsibility and American Public Life* (Rowman and Littlefield, 2005).

6. Plato generally understands freedom in conjunction with the nobility and self-

mastery of virtuous citizens. Ultimately, indeed, freedom requires, or is, philosophy, or intellectual excellence.

7. Slavery is not discussed as an institution in the *Republic*'s just regime, and, there, the arts that slaves might practice belong to citizens. It is, however, alluded to. See 433B and 469BC.

8. *Laws* 832C.

9. *Laws,* Book I.

10. In the *Phaedrus'* ordering of the souls that have seen most of the truest things, philosophers are ranked first and statesmen third, together with household managers and "businessmen." The lawful, warlike, or commanding king ranks second; he is like the *Statesman*'s royal ruler, or a step below him. In the *Statesman,* however, the king and statesman are equated (248D).

11. In addition to Burnet's *Platonis Opera* and the translation I follow [Thomas Pangle, trans., *Plato's* Laws, (Basic Books, 1980)], editions of and books on the *Laws* that one can usefully consult include E. B. England, *The* Laws *of Plato* (Manchester, 1921), Seth Benardete, *Plato's* Laws: *The Discovery of Being* (University of Chicago Press, 2001); Leo Strauss, *The Argument and the Action of Plato's* Laws (University of Chicago Press, 1973); and Glenn R. Morrow, *Plato's Cretan City* (Princeton University Press, 1993).

12. *Laws* 627D.

13. I concentrate on the substance of the *Laws'* argument, and I proceed by discussing a portion of the *Laws* in sections headed by Roman numerals. One should not conclude from the fact that the Athenian Stranger (whom Aristotle in his *Politics* identifies with Socrates) often speaks at length, however, that the conversational byplay with the Spartan Megillos and Cretan Critias is window dressing. Their sometimes reluctant and sometimes eager responses teach us something about the bases of opinion in belief, training, experience, rivalry, and nature, and the way these shape the Athenian's presentation. Consider, e.g., the different responses of Cleinias and Megillos to the Athenian's proposed laws about sex (842A) and the times when the Athenian engages with Cleinias in what approaches dialectic.

14. Cf. *Republic* 544C, 545A, 549A.

15. *Laws* 624A. See *Meno* 99D.

16. *Laws* 630C. Cf. *Statesman.*

17. See this suggestion in the *Laches.*

18. In defending symposia (drinking parties, or banquets), the Athenian challenges Sparta's proscription of them, as well as Megillos' defense of Sparta. Seeing different laws helps us grasp "the vice and virtues of the lawgivers themselves" (637D). It is also an aid in discovering what is natural.

19. *Laws* 647AB. See 671D.

20. Consider Strauss, *Argument,* Books 1 and 2; and *Symposium* 176A–178A, 212D–215A.

21. *Laws* 650B.

22. Megillos and Cleinias are friendly to Athens. Their reasons for their friendliness show the importance of love of one's own and its connection more to benefits given than to those received. When Megillos was young, his family represented Athens in Sparta; Cleinias' ancestor helped Athens against Persia.

23. Plato's attention to children's moral education clarifies the public importance of what is for us primarily private.

24. One should consider the difference between virtue seen as correct habit and passion and virtue seen as prudence in securing what is good.

25. Choral performances are coordinated with holidays in which rest from labors helps set right the education in pleasure and pain that becomes corrupted during the course of life (*Laws* 653CD).

26. *Laws* 656D–657B.

27. *Laws* 660A.

28. *Laws* 669A.

29. *Laws* 670E–671A. See *Charmides* 155E–158C.

30. Cf. the "true" city discussed in Book II of the *Republic*. Consider, also, Catherine H. Zuckert, *Plato's Philosophers* (University of Chicago Press, 2009), chapter 1. The discussion that begins Book III replaces a discussion of the gymnastic training that would instill bodily virtue.

31. *Laws* 687C.

32. See Strauss, *Argument*, Book 3; and *Gorgias*.

33. *Laws* 701E. This is also why, from different points of view, moderation, justice, and prudence has each seemed central in the Athenian's discussion. The issue is preserving a due measure.

34. *Laws* 708D. Cf. Machiavelli, *The Prince*.

35. The Athenian now basically equates the rule of law with the rule of god and hides the discrepancy he suggested earlier between reason (prudence) and law. He reaches his point about just vs. unjust regimes by reporting on a story about rule during the age of the god Kronos. See *Laws* 713C–714A.

36. *Laws* 723B ff.

37. *Laws* 720D. Cf. *Gorgias* 456B–459B.

38. *Laws* 723DE. The interruption may indicate that the insistence of the body, and of necessity, can never be ruled fully by virtue and persuasion.

39. *Laws* 726A.

40. *Laws* 730D.

41. *Laws* 732A. Compare this statement to Socrates' arguments in the *Gorgias*. We should note that in discussing what the citizens will hear about the ranking of the divine, honorable, and praiseworthy, the interlocutors do not differentiate between philosophic and political virtue.

42. Cf. *Protagoras*. In the account in the *Laws'* prelude, pleasures differ according to their source and cannot all be added together in a single calculus.

43. Cf. 734E–735A with *Statesman* 305E ff. To begin a city usually requires purifying its prospective populace, as one might a herd, and settling preexisting debts. We can assume a purified populace and no preexisting strife about property in this city in speech. Similarly, a legislator would not change preexisting sacred rituals.

44. This regime is at least one remove from the *Republic*, in which citizens hold as much as possible in common. Here, such commonality is said to require a city of gods or children of gods. Although this regime is "second best," in point of unity, it too is a city in speech. Were it to exist in deed, the size of its population would be adjusted in light of its territory and neighbors. Whether it could exist in deed without being significantly modified is unlikely, however, because some facts on which it relies—say, the purified populace, a beginning free from all economic controversy, a free hand with regard to ritual, and favorable territory—would, as the Athenian indicates, be difficult

to achieve in deed. When he treats the city in speech as if it actually is to become Megillos' colony, he permits preexisting imperfections to continue, such as original differences in wealth. The second best city is a city in speech that he treats as if it could become a city in deed. Therefore, not every aspect of the model need be followed. (See 745E–746D.)

45. *Laws* 747D. See *Greater Hippias* 285BC.

46. *Laws* 756E.

47. Consider the mention of Zeus in *Laws* 761AB.

48. *Laws* 760A–763C.

49. *Laws* 765E. See our discussions of the *Theages* and *Euthyphro*.

50. See *Statesman* 310A–E.

51. Slaves may also be freed (*Laws* 915B).

52. Cf. *Republic*, Book II, and the discussion of the utility of Stesilaus' art in the *Laches*.

53. *Laws* 799E–800A, 794A, 816D.

54. *Laws* 794A. Book XII considers ways in which the citizens might improve their laws.

55. *Laws* 794D. See Strauss, *Argument*, Book 7, and *Laws* 909E.

56. *Laws* 801C.

57. *Laws* 807E.

58. *Laws* 816D, 817BC.

59. *Laws* 818C. Teaching these subjects redresses Cretans and Spartans "habitual unfamiliarity with such things" (*Laws* 818E).

60. See Strauss, *Argument*, Book 8, p. 119.

61. Cleinias (though not Megillos) does not fully accept the Athenian's law.

62. *Laws* 846D. See *Republic*, Books II–IV.

63. See *Protagoras* 322D.

64. This is the first mention of philosophy in the *Laws*, and, appropriately, the ensuing discussion is a conversation between the Athenian and Cleinias. The Athenian goes on to say that they are inquiring about the whole regime and therefore have no necessity to legislate but are trying at leisure to "discern in what way the best and also the most necessary would each come into being" (858A). The regime of the *Laws* deals with what is best, but with the best as it must be modified by necessity.

65. *Laws* 861D.

66. Cf. *Protagoras*. See also Lorraine Smith Pangle, "Moral and Criminal Responsibility in Plato's *Laws*," delivered at the American Political Science Association annual meeting, Chicago, Illinois, 2004.

67. The discussion thus comes around to possible replies to the apparent split between the noble and just. We might say that undergoing just punishment is not disgraceful if it improves the miscreant. Or, we might deny the identification of the just and the noble: in practice, obeying defective laws (and being punished for breaking them) may be just, but not noble. Even in the best regime, the intellect is subservient to and serves other, lower, virtues. See 875A–D.

68. See *Euthyphro*.

69. *Laws* 869E.

70. *Laws* 881B.

71. Cf. Socrates' discussions in the *Gorgias* with Polus and Callicles.

72. *Laws* 875A–D. See also the *Statesman's* explanation for law, which we discuss in chapter 9. The discussion of voluntary crime shows how we could reduce crime that deals with ordinary goods and passions by making the law's demands visible, and by making punishment for breaking the law regular or, indeed, inevitable. Voluntary crime, strictly, would then cover only those things above the laws, such as dedication to knowledge simply.

73. *Laws* 884A.

74. The Athenian's proof is limited to serving its task. Even if true, it does not prove the truth of each thing that the laws say about the gods.

75. For versions of these views, see *Gorgias* and *Protagoras*, and the discussion of Protagoras in the *Theatetus*. Consider also Socrates' discussion of the gods with Adeimantus in the *Republic* 362D–367E.

76. *Laws* 897B. See the outlining of the prelude to the laws in *Laws* Book V, and *Phaedrus* 244A–257B.

77. Cf. *Gorgias* 504D–507A.

78. *Laws* 896A.

79. See *Laws* 896D–897C, 889D; and Strauss, *Argument*, Book 10.

80. *Laws* 896A.

81. Consider, e.g., the gods depicted in Homer's *Odyssey.*

82. See Strauss, *Argument*, Book 10, p. 150.

83. *Laws* 889D, 892A–C, 893E–894A, 896BC.

84. Cf. *Republic*, Books II–IV.

85. Cf. *Euthyphro.*

86. See *Laws* 909B.

87. Cf. the conclusion of the *Sophist.*

88. One sees again the difference between a liberal regime such as ours that liberates acquisition and a free regime such as this, directed toward virtuously using what one owns. But one also sees the similarity, because in neither case is the "material" feared. Virtue is not asceticism or renunciation.

89. See Strauss, *Argument*, Book 11, and *Laws*, Books IV, V, and X.

90. *Laws* 926E–927A. Cf. *Republic* 554C.

91. See *Laws* 927B–928D.

92. Consider *Euthyphro.*

93. *Laws* 931B–E.

94. Is he subtly reminding us of the limits of the sacred or divine, because of the problem of priestly imposters, ridicule, and natural justice and questioning?

95. See 948B–949C, and Strauss, *Argument*, Book 12.

96. "As much as is possible everyone should in every respect live always in a group, together and in common—for there is not nor will there ever be anything stronger, better, and more artful than this for producing security and victory in war" (*Laws* 942C). See Books I and II.

97. Consider the beginning of the *Greater Hippias.*

98. *Laws* 951B.

99. *Laws* 952A.

100. Is the link among these topics truth or honesty?

101. The philosopher considers more than a city; he considers what is fully common, present inexhaustibly for each to understand. And, he strives to attend to it for the

perfection of his own soul. Unlike the good citizen, the philosopher is most his own when he imitates, through seeking to understand, what is least his own. See Strauss, *Argument,* Book 12.

102. *Laws* 965D. See Strauss, *Argument,* Book 12, pp. 181–82.

103. *Laws* 966B.

104. See *Laws* 968E.

CHAPTER 4: The Roots of Philosophy

1. See, e.g., *Republic* 375A, 433A, 485A–486D, 507D–508A. Chapter 1, note 3, contains general information about the Greek edition and translations of the dialogues that I am following.

2. See Leo Strauss, *Natural Right and History* (University of Chicago Press, 1953).

3. This is also true of environmentalism, although to a lesser degree, for environmentalists argue more about what the dangers are to the environment, and what trades are appropriate among environmental and other "values," than about what nature is.

4. What is naturally just is, equivalently, naturally "right" because we can translate the German *recht* as either justice or right.

5. Plato also occasionally speaks of something's being naturally correct (*orthos*)—a name, say, or a law—which we also may translate as naturally right. "Corrections" or punishments, however, are not what we mean by natural rights.

6. I distinguish this concern from Plato's examination of the possible immortality of the soul in the *Phaedo* and elsewhere.

7. And, while he understands sex and love as profoundly as any man who ever wrote, we have seen in the *Laws* that when it comes to legislation he is guided by the natural link between sex and procreation.

8. In the *Gorgias,* as we saw, it is Callicles, not Socrates, who utters Plato's only use.

9. *Protagoras* 337D.

10. *Alcibiades I* 119B.

11. *Charmides* 154 DE. See, too, *Menexenus* 239A, 245D.

12. *Phaedrus* 252D.

13. *Parmenides* 132D.

14. *Critias* 116B.

15. *Parmenides* 153E.

16. *Phaedrus* 245E.

17. *Phaedrus* 266B. Cf. *Statesman* 265E.

18. *Protagoras* 325B.

19. *Protagoras* 330D.

20. *Protagoras* 358D.

21. *Sophist* 255AB. We can capture all these meanings and see something of their differences and complex interrelationship by considering *Phaedrus* 269E–272B.

22. We should not assign strictly different senses to these prepositions.

23. *Laches* 192C.

24. *Protagoras* 320DE.

25. *Phaedrus* 270C.

26. See *Greater Hippias* 295D, *Alcibiades II* 120E, *Lysis* 220A, and the discussion of education in the *Laws* and the *Republic.*

27. Consider Diotima's discussion with Socrates in the *Symposium, Hipparchus* 226D, *Phaedrus* 276A, 276E–277A.

28. *Charmides* 154E.

29. See *Philebus* 58AD.

30. See *Euthydemus* 303C, *Symposium* 210E–211A.

31. A thing that needs certain circumstances to be its own in the full sense may, therefore, have what we could call its ownmost or proper circumstances.

32. Consider the course of Plato's discussions in the *Gorgias* and the *Republic*. See *Republic* 586DE.

33. Furthermore, if a thing's nature is its defining characteristic, then things whose origin is artificial are also natural in this sense—chairs, say, that are all made with a certain use or shape in mind, or laws that are all intended to establish a single opinion about justice.

34. *Meno* 81CD. See also *Philebus* 58A, 58D.

35. We can further understand the natural as the complete once we consider Plato's view of the beautiful and good.

36. See, e.g., *Sophist* 245B–249D, *Laches* 192B.

37. See the understanding of artisans as producers in the *Republic,* the *Sophist,* the *Statesman,* and other dialogues.

38. See, e.g., *Republic* 369BC, 507B–509B, *Sophist* 266E.

39. We uncovered some of the substance of this natural understanding when we discussed virtue and regimes.

40. A version of these possibilities is gathered in Diotima's statement to Socrates in the *Symposium,* 211B ff.

41. *Theatetus* 155CD. Cf. Aristotle, *Metaphysics,* Book I, and Martin Heidegger, *Basic Questions of Philosophy,* trans. Richard Rojcewicz and Andre Schuwer (Indiana University Press, 1994; *Grundfragen der Philosophie,* Vittorio Klostermann, 1992), chap. 5.

42. Amazing, terrific, and great are substitutes for this meaning but do not always share the wonderful's emphasis on the desirable. Outstanding comes closest here as a synonym.

43. The wonderful as defying explanation is especially pressing if explanation is attempted in terms of external causes and does not mean deeper and wider description of the wonderful thing itself.

44. One may at leisure wonder or gaze at what was unusually or impressively frightening. Unlike wonder, terror at the terrifying points to avoidance and discombobulation, or to awe as frozen obedience. Such fearful awe differs from reverence in the sense of uplifting admiration. Wonder at the baby's wonderful development contains such reverence for this singular one in his inviolable power and wholeness.

45. In the full sense, this is wonder at excellence. One begins to account for the surprising by seeing the full range of its power or nature.

46. This admiration is not always easily separable from enjoying these powers, as one enjoys and wonders at the excellent pianist.

47. *Charmides* 159A.

48. *Theages* 128B.

49. *Symposium* 216C.

50. *Symposium* 221CD.

51. *Greater Hippias* 282D.

52. *Gorgias* 456A. See, too, *Euthydemus* 283B.

53. *Parmenides* 134E.

54. *Protagoras* 361B.

55. *Philebus* 14C. What happens when someone is released from eye disease?, Socrates asks Callicles in the *Gorgias.* "Is he then released from health of the eyes too and does he end up having been released from both at the same time?" "Not in the least," Callicles replies. "For I think," continues Socrates, "that becomes something wonderful and irrational, doesn't it?" Rather, one "gets and loses each in turn," as with strength and weakness, speed and slowness, "and as regards good things and happiness and their opposites" (496B).

56. *Phaedo* 97AB. For further analysis of the *Phaedo,* see Ronna Burger, *The* Phaedo: *A Platonic Labyrinth* (Yale University Press, 1984), and Peter Ahrensdorf, *The Death of Socrates and the Life of Philosophy: An Interpretation of Plato's* Phaedo (SUNY Press, 1995).

57. *Phaedo* 60BC.

58. *Phaedo* 58A.

59. *Protagoras* 329B–D.

60. *Theatetus* 161C.

61. Questioning wonder at the unclear seems closest to Socrates' own wonder and what he points out to Theatetus. Indeed, he wonders at apparently petty matters. But are they in fact petty, or are they not themselves extraordinary, and impressive? Does philosophy transform the unusual and impressive into the questionable by seeing in it cause and contradiction, then being further struck by our human ability to be impressed and to question, and then further questioning this? Such dialectic is the heart of the soul's free openness. Socrates can use wonder at something very odd to start someone on the way to deeper questioning. "Son of Cleinias," Socrates begins the *Alcibiades I,* "I suppose you wonder why it is that I, who was the first to become a lover of yours, alone persist in it now that others have left off and yet have not as much as spoken to you during the many years that others came clamoring to converse with you" (103A).

62. I am tall in relation to others, but my finger is short, and so on.

63. *Philebus* 14D–15C. Popular wonders may include extraordinary creations such as chimeras, or the content of the Stranger's myth in the *Statesman,* or Euthydemus' actions.

64. *Symposium* 210E–211D.

65. *Theatetus* 144A, *Lesser Hippias* 372. Cf. *Charmides* 158E, 164D.

66. Socrates' shamelessness shows the difference for him between wonder and fearful awe. Awe lacks wonder's questioning of the false, irrational, and apparently inexplicable. It tends to unquestioning obedience.

67. *Quandary* is also an apt translation.

68. *Meno* 80CD.

69. We see these procedures in, e.g., *Theatetus, Meno, Charmides, Republic, Sophist, Statesman,* and *Euthydemus.*

70. *Sophist* 243BC.

71. See also *Sophist* 217A, 231C, 236A, 243BC, 249B; *Theatetus* 145DE, 158A, 169A, 187D; *Statesman* 263D.

72. *Greater Hippias* 286CD.

73. *Laches* 194BC.

74. *Greater Hippias* 297D. See *Lysis* 207A, *Euthydemus* 275D, *Theatetus* 87D, 90B, *Statesman* 284B, *Sophist* 231C, 238A, 239DE, 247D, *Euthydemus* 292E.

75. *Greater Hippias* 304C.

76. *Lysis* 216C, *Theatetus* 187D.

77. *Hipparchus* 231C.

78. *Sophist* 236E.

79. *Lysis* 207A.

80. *Greater Hippias* 297DE.

81. *Euthydemus* 300E–301A. See, too, *Timaeus* 49B, *Sophist* 217A, 231C, 245E, 249D, *Theatetus* 175D.

82. *Euthydemus* 306D. See, too, *Charmides* 167BC.

83. *Charmides* 169C. Socrates occasionally distinguishes true from merely popular or ill-informed perplexities, as he distinguished true from popular wonders. See *Sophist* 251BC. Cf. *Parmenides* 135E.

84. See, too, *Theatetus* 174B–175D.

85. *Lysis* 206AB.

86. *Euthydemus* 275D, *Lysis* 213D.

87. *Laches* 194A.

88. *Laches* 194B. Cf. *Lovers* 135A.

89. See *Laches, Meno; Republic, Gorgias and Laws; Protagoras, Greater Hippias, Lesser Hippias, Lovers; Laches, Theages, Euthydemus; Theatetus, Republic and Lysis.*

90. See *Greater Hippias,* and the Stranger's procedure in the *Sophist.*

91. *Parmenides* 136DE.

92. *Lysis* 222E–223C.

93. The "friend" of seeking to know is neither completed knowledge that one sets aside nor ignorance that believes it knows. Rather, its friend is ignorance that recognizes itself and what can be known, the knowable as it is present for our longing. (See, too, *Sophist* 245A.)

94. Perplexity and wonder differ because perplexity is struck by difficulty and wonder by beauty or magnificence. The difference is not strict, however, because wonder can also be about the unusually contradictory or unaccountable, and in both wonder and perplexity we are stopped in our tracks. In philosophic inquiry, moreover, some of what perplexes attracts and is seen in its height, and the wonderful becomes a perplexity for whose resolution one searches. Perplexity's searching-resourcefulness comes to belong together with wonder's observant-examining. This spiral of wonder and perplexity characterizes reason's dialectic. Wonder, and responding to it properly, furthermore, belongs primarily to the yielding, lingering, and completion we associate with love, while perplexity, and responding to it properly, belongs primarily to the pride, overcoming, or conquest we associate with spiritedness. Both work together, however, and are elevated in the reasonable dialectic that seeks to grasp fully what naturally is.

95. *Laches* 183D ff.

96. *Laches* 184BC.

97. *Greater Hippias* 286D; *Euthydemus* 300D, 299B; *Phaedrus* 262C.

98. *Phaedo* 64AB, 77E.

99. *Philebus* 48B ff. Consider, too, Ctessipus' ridicule of Hippothales in the *Lysis* 204BD.

100. See *Protagoras* 319C, *Lovers* 134B.

101. *Parmenides* 128C, *Republic* 531A, *Phaedrus* 260B, *Crito* 53D.

102. *Charmides* 156A, *Sophist* 227A.

103. *Republic* 527A.

104. *Republic* 527D, 531C; *Meno* 71A, 95A; *Gorgias* 462E. Cf. *Republic* 517A.

105. *Phaedrus* 268D.

106. *Gorgias* 485B ff., *Laws* 643BC, *Phaedo* 77E, *Parmenides* 130C.

107. *Lysis* 207C.

108. *Phaedo* 115C, *Protagoras* 358B.

109. *Theatetus* 174AB, *Phaedo* 115C.

110. *Phaedo* 59A, 84D, 86D.

111. *Philebus* 48C ff., *Lesser Hippias* 364CD, *Republic* 337A–D, *Republic* 518AB.

112. *Euthydemus* 272C. Cf. *Symposium* 199B.

113. *Republic* 517D ff.; *Theatetus* 172C ff.; *Gorgias* 484E ff.; *Philebus* 62B.

114. *Republic* 451A ff., *Republic* 509C, *Gorgias* 473E, *Euthydemus* 305A.

115. See *Meno* 80A; *Cratylus* 413B; *Republic* 385D ff.; *Symposium* 189B, 212A, 222C; *Philebus* 65C–66A.

116. *Republic* 457A, *Lysis* 205BC.

117. See Leo Strauss, *Socrates and Aristophanes* (Basic Books, 1966).

118. As more natural or spontaneous they can also be closer to the possibly rare or "ideal," the purity or "perfection" of their conventions, as opposed to their practical existence. Adolescents can be more natural than adults, not only as more erotic and closer to the ridiculous but also as possibly more righteous. This direction toward purity, however, together with inexperience and imprudence, can also lead adolescents to be mastered by convention's tyrannical wish to be truly supreme, as with religion, or by conventional fashion and goals. Their degree of true justice depends on the substance of their conventions and their openness to what is truly natural or cosmopolitan. See *Lysis* 205B.

119. See *Philebus* 65C–66A; *Symposium,* passim.

120. See *Republic* 331D, *Lovers* 134B.

121. *Phaedo* 115C.

122. *Euthydemus* 305A, *Menexenus* 236C, *Theatetus* 194C–E ff.

123. *Theatetus* 174B ff.

124. *Euthydemus,* passim; *Apology* 30D; *Laches* 184BC, 194A.

125. *Lysis* 208E, *Theages* 128BC.

126. Laughter is a confident (although misplaced if too low) recognizing of the natural as it irrupts into the conventional and a confident recognizing of the unconventional (as a different convention or practice, even if more natural, as is Socrates' studying) in its gap from one's own convention.

127. *Theages* 122B; *Republic* 493D, 613BC; *Euthydemus* 273D; *Lysis* 221A. When Socrates claims to Theages that he cannot educate him because he knows about nothing but erotic things, Theages accuses him of joking, of not being serious.

128. *Theages* 122C, 128BC, *Gorgias* 481C, *Apology* 24C.

129. *Greater Hippias* 300D, *Euthydemus* 276BD, *Symposium* 222C.

130. *Euthydemus* 277D–278C.

131. These pratfalls reveal the ridiculous ignobility, indignity, and dependence that lurk in even the most formal occasions; they reveal the human pretense that we can be perfect or complete.

132. *Euthydemus* 283C, 287A.

133. The links among wonder, perplexity, and laughter are suggested near the beginning of the *Parmenides*. "If then someone shall try to show that for things such as stones and wood and the like, the same things are many and one, then we will say that he's demonstrated that some thing is many and one, not that the One is many or the many's one. He's not even said anything wonderful but only what in fact all of us should readily agree upon. But if someone, as I just said, shall first distinguish the forms as separate in themselves, such as Likeness and Unlikeness and Multitude and the One and Rest and Motion and all the like, and then will show that in themselves these things can be mixed together and separated, I'd admire that with wonder, Zeno," he said. "Now I do believe that you've worked over these things quite courageously; but, as I've said, I would admire this much more; if someone could demonstrate that even in the forms themselves—in the things grasped by reasoning—there is everywhere tangled up that same perplexity which you proved is present in the things we see." "While Socrates was speaking, Pythodorus said, he himself thought that at each word both Parmenides and Zeno were going to get angry. But they kept their mind on Socrates and, with frequent glances to one another, they smiled as if admiring him which is, in fact, what Parmenides told him, once he was done" (129D–130A).

CHAPTER 5: Beauty and Nobility

1. See *Republic* 402B–D, *Charmides* 159C. Chapter 1, note 3, contains general information about the Greek edition and translations of the dialogues that I am following. For the *Greater Hippias* I follow *Greater Hippias*, trans. David R. Sweet, in Thomas Pangle, ed., *The Roots of Political Philosophy* (Cornell University Press, 1987). I proceed in my exploration of the *Greater Hippias* by discussing a portion of Plato's argument in a section headed by, say, Roman numeral II. I then, if necessary, comment further on some of the portion's less obvious elements and implications, in a new section with that same Roman numeral followed by a letter, say, II A.

2. The Greek term *kalon* is translated either as nobility or beauty, and occasionally as fine. We have already encountered the sophist Hippias in the *Protagoras*.

3. Consider Aristotle's discussion of progress or innovation in *Politics*, Book II, 1268B23–1269A27.

4. On envy, consider Laches' view of Stesilaus, and the discussion of laughter in the *Philebus*.

5. *Greater Hippias* 283B.

6. Socrates must perplex Hippias because wonder is so trivial for him.

7. See *Hipparchus*, *Gorgias* 467D–468E, and the discussion of oligarchy and democracy in the *Republic*, Book VIII.

8. *Greater Hippias* 284B. The regime that is outlined in the *Laws* helps us to understand this standpoint.

9. *Greater Hippias* 285B.

10. *Greater Hippias* 286A. See *Lesser Hippias*.

11. We see in the *Laws* how the Athenian attempts to close this gulf, while remaining visibly on the side of law and tradition.

12. Cf. Socrates' discussion with Thrasymachus in the *Republic*, Book I.

13. *Greater Hippias* 288C.

14. This someone later proves to be the son of Sophroniscus, i.e., Socrates himself, his objecting alter ego. By questioning Hippias through a third party and sometimes answering for him, Socrates maintains the fiction that Hippias is wise.

15. *Greater Hippias* 288E.

16. *Greater Hippias* 289B.

17. See Protagoras' statement about some of the variety in good things, *Protagoras* 334A–C.

18. Cf. *Lysis* 216CD.

19. *Greater Hippias* 287D.

20. Cf. the discussion of the pious in the *Euthyphro,* and the kinds of distinctions the Eleatic Stranger will make in the *Sophist* and *Statesman.*

21. This duplicity is one source of the ambiguity in beauty, justice, and the like.

22. *Greater Hippias* 288A.

23. Consider *The Odyssey* and Odysseus' relation to Athena. It is noteworthy that Socrates chooses to bring out the ambiguity or ugliness of human beauty by comparing us to gods above and monkeys below rather than, say, by reminding us of the beautiful girl's ugly old age. We should note, too, how Socrates has suggested varieties in the ways beauty is, and is known—sufficiency, precision, causality, disputability, excellence, utility, and wholeness or form.

24. *Greater Hippias* 290E–291A. Socrates presents this example as one pressed by his unyielding objector: he agrees that Hippias would not converse with him, for "it wouldn't be fitting" for Hippias, with his beautiful clothes and reputation for wisdom, to be so filled with words.

25. *Greater Hippias* 289D.

26. We remember that in the *Gorgias* Socrates distinguishes the false flattery of cosmetics—adorning makeup—from gymnastics' production of beauty and strength. This pair is in turn analogized to sophistry and legislation. The truer beauty of the Spartan virtue brought out by its laws is compared in the *Greater Hippias* to the false beauty of Hippias' wealth and adornment, procured through his pretty speeches, and the false wisdom of his speech is compared to the truer wisdom of Socratic dialectic—speech that, here, seeks the beautiful.

27. *Greater Hippias* 291DE.

28. See their conduct in the *Euthydemus.*

29. Cf. *Greater Hippias* 283E–285B with 292AB.

30. See *Greater Hippias* 292C–293B.

31. See *Charmides* 169CD, *Meno* 86D–87C, and *Lysis* 223A for other instances of how Socrates escapes or tries to escape from apparent roadblocks.

32. *Greater Hippias* 293E.

33. See Laches on appearing to be courageous, *Laches* 184BC.

34. Perhaps Socrates uses this example because some beautiful things are "excessive," outstanding, magnificent, and remarkable at the same time they are fitting.

35. Cf. *Lysis* 217DE.

36. Even the "excess" is not obviously excessive or the most excessive.

37. See *Greater Hippias* 291D, 292E. Cf. *Phaedo* 100C, *Symposium* 211E–212A.

38. *Greater Hippias* 289D.

39. *Greater Hippias* 294BC.

40. Consider Socrates' discussion of gymnastics, cosmetics, legislation, and soph-

istry in the *Gorgias* 464A–466B, and the Stranger's discussion of two types of image in the *Sophist*.

41. Hence, the various statements in the dialogue about what seems or appears to be true.

42. See Glaucon's speeches about justice in Books I and II of the *Republic*.

43. This complexity is how the discussion of appearance in this first general opinion is allied to Hippias' first concrete statement (that beauty is a beautiful girl); we must remember that each opinion is linked to the others. Socrates hints that beautiful things can be ranked—something implied by appearing closer to and farther from beauty or other beings—when he mentions imitation. Anyone can see that noble practical pursuits are more beautiful than a pair of pretty shoes or that gods are more perfect than men. Yet, the question of such a progressive or hierarchical appearance of beautiful things is, after being alluded to in Hippias' first opinion, not discussed. (Contrast the *Symposium* and *Phaedrus*.) The formal search for the beautiful is for something that covers all beautiful things equally.

44. Consider the *Laws*, where laws concerning many commercial matters are just but not noble.

45. Consider the connection between size and beauty in Aristotle, *Nichomachean Ethics*, Book IV, chapter 3. See, also, *Charmides* 158A.

46. See *Greater Hippias* 295A–296E.

47. If the excess is not tamed, it can be garish or mad. The beautiful as the splendid and fitting fits together into a magnificent whole a straining excess of separate beauties, i.e., of things that seek independence, something we especially see in the soul and among men in the city.

48. Cf. *Menexenus* 234C–235C. These characteristics help capture the noble as an end in itself, or as chosen for its own sake, although in fact it may fit further ends. It is not suitable to destroy the noble, as one might a merely fitting flea. One cannot with propriety merely redistribute the parts of something noble.

49. My italics.

50. *Greater Hippias* 295B.

51. *Greater Hippias* 296A.

52. Consider the connection between Hippias' view of politics and power and Callicles' view in the *Gorgias,* and the connection between Socrates' view in the *Gorgias* of the soul's order and his view of use here.

53. *Greater Hippias* 298A.

54. *Greater Hippias* 300B. Cf. *Theatetus* 184D–185D.

55. *Greater Hippias* 302AB.

56. Cf. Callicles' opinion in the *Gorgias*.

57. *Greater Hippias* 304B.

58. See 289D, 302B, and the discussions of pleasure in the *Gorgias, Republic,* and *Philebus*.

59. *Greater Hippias* 304A.

60. Cf. *Theatetus* 184D–185D.

61. Socrates argues in the *Gorgias* that persuasion is mere flattery, i.e., that it involves what pleases the audience. Hearing the pleasurable things that Hippias says is not necessarily hearing noble and good things.

62. See *Lesser Hippias* 368BC.

63. See also *Republic* 537E–538D.

64. See *Euthyphro* 11BC.

65. Perhaps this duality is why Socrates splits himself in this dialogue, rather than merely inventing an anonymous spokesman to make certain arguments, as he does in other dialogues.

66. See *Greater Hippias* 292E ff.

67. See *Republic* 509A.

68. The gentleman (*kaloskagathos*) is why it seems wrong to common opinion to separate the noble and good. See for the beautiful, e.g., *Euthyphro* 13E; *Laches* 182B; *Phaedo* 116D; *Theatetus* 142B, 151E, 184A; *Statesman* 266C, 289A, 309B; *Sophist* 216C, 251A, 265C.

69. *Phaedo* 86A, 110A; *Theatetus* 142C, 185E, 195E; *Sophist* 228A–C, 236A; *Statesman* 273C, 275A, 277A, 282A, 311B.

70. *Euthyphro* 9E; *Phaedo* 73A, 77A, 94A; *Statesman* 258D, 267A, 271D.

71. *Laches* 191C; *Sophist* 228A ff., 247E, 251A–E, 261C; *Statesman* 278A.

72. *Phaedo* 70A, 89B, 99A, 110C; *Theatetus* 143E, 157D; *Statesman* 269C, 283D; *Charmides,* opening scene.

73. *Philebus* 17E.

74. *Phaedo* 58E, 65CD, 70B, 79D, 98A; *Sophist* 222C, 227C, 258B; *Statesman* 262B, 284B–D, 311B.

75. *Phaedo* 114C; *Laches* 179C, 192C; *Sophist* 236BC; *Statesman* 297C, 301A; *Meno* 80C.

76. As we suggested, what is independent and fitting could still be petty.

CHAPTER 6: Philosophy and Politics

1. We will again consider the beauty or nobility of virtue in chapter 9.

2. In addition to Burnet's *Platonis Opera,* and the translation I follow (Allan Bloom, translation and commentary, *The Republic,* 2nd ed. [Basic Books, 1991]), there are other editions, commentaries, and collections that someone who wishes to study the *Republic* further will find enlightening. Useful editions and translations include James Adam, *The Republic of Plato* (Cambridge University Press, 1902); and Paul Shorey, *Plato's* Republic (Loeb Classical Library, Harvard University Press, 1953). Bloom's translation remains the best. Useful discussions include Bloom's, which accompanies his translation; Seth Benardete, *Socrates' Second Sailing* (University of Chicago Press, 1989); Eva Brann, *The Music of the* Republic (Paul Dry Books, 2004); Leon Craig, *The War Lover: A Study of Plato's* Republic (University of Toronto Press, 1994); various essays on the *Republic* in David Lachterman, ed., *St. John's Review* 39, nos. 1 and 2 (1989–1990); Stanley Rosen, *Plato's* Republic (Yale University Press, 2005); Devin Stauffer, *Plato's Introduction to the Question of Justice* (State University of New York Press, 2000); and Leo Strauss, *The City and Man* (Rand McNally, 1964). The chapters on the *Republic* in John Sallis, *Being and Logos,* 3rd ed. (Indiana University Press, 1996) can also be consulted profitably. Collections of essays primarily from the analytic point of view include Richard Kraut, ed., *Plato's* Republic: *Critical Essays* (Rowman and Littlefield, 1997), and Gregory Vlastos, *Plato I, Plato II* (Anchor Books, 1971). Chapter 1, note 3, contains general information about the Greek edition and translations of the dialogues that I am following. This chapter is based on Mark Blitz, *Plato's* Republic, printed at Claremont McKenna College, 1999.

3. It therefore does not present a regime that is possible in the flesh.

4. Cf. *Alcibiades I*, 106D–109B; *Charmides* 173A–D. I proceed in my exploration of the *Republic* by discussing a portion of it in sections headed by Roman numerals.

5. See *Laches* 194C–196A.

6. This order is also basic in clarifying how, if justice is a form of knowledge it, unlike other sciences, will not be used improperly. Cf. the discussion in the *Gorgias* of the soul's order, 503D–504D.

7. Socrates' discussion in Books II–V, to which we now turn, ostensibly originates in the wish of his two chief interlocutors, Glaucon and Adeimantus, that he prove that the just man is happier than the unjust one. Glaucon in particular has questioned this, in ways familiar to us from the *Gorgias*. Books II–V and, indeed, II–X, are a model for how we might expand the discussions of the *Laches, Charmides,* and *Euthyphro*.

8. Consider the centrality of war and ruling in the *Laws*.

9. These practices are discussed in Books II–IV.

10. *Republic* 433C–E.

11. These practices are discussed in Book V.

12. Full communism is impossible in the flesh.

13. *Republic* 413E–414A.

14. See Hobbes' *Leviathan,* chapters 13 and 14.

15. Socrates often goes shoeless but not always. Consider *Symposium* 174A.

16. Cf. *Statesman* 267D–276B.

17. *Republic* 414B ff.

18. As we said, Socrates' discussion in Books II–X originates in the wish of his two chief interlocutors, Glaucon and Adeimantus, that he prove that the just man is happier than the unjust one.

19. See Book IV.

20. Consider Books II and III.

21. See *Greater Hippias* 286D, 291E–292B, 295AB, 296AB, 298BC, 304C–E; *Laches* 194A; *Theatetus* 151DE.

22. They therefore help to enlarge and make precise the assembling, disassembling, analyzing, and synthesizing that are philosophy's own activities. Cf. our discussion of the virtues in chapters 2 and 9.

23. See the Stranger's divisions in the *Sophist* and the *Statesman* and his encouragement to his interlocutors, and Socrates' discussions of love in the *Symposium* and *Phaedrus*.

24. Cf. the peculiarity of Socrates' claim in the *Gorgias* (521D) to be the one who "alone of the men of today" "practice[s] politics." His discussion of justice in the *Republic* does not contradict his discussion of justice in the *Gorgias,* but it does deepen it. In the *Republic,* he more fully analyzes the soul's parts (and, therefore, its just order), the link between opinion about and knowledge of what is good, philosophical activity itself, and philosophy's connection to and split from politics. See *Gorgias* 486A ff.

25. Consider the status in the *Laws* of the Athenian Stranger.

26. *Republic* 505D.

27. See *Republic* 586DE.

28. See *Republic* 504D–518B, the conclusion of Book VI, and the beginning of Book VII.

29. We will consider this relationship in chapter 8.

30. Consider our discussions of the *Euthyphro, Laches,* and *Greater Hippias.*

31. Cf. *Greater Hippias.*

32. Consider *Sophist* 253D–260B.

33. Socrates does not elaborate in Books VIII and IX a regime that is better than what we have now but less unlikely than the just city of the *Republic.* This is a task of the *Laws.*

34. See our discussions in chapter 1.

35. See *Laws,* passim, and *Statesman* 294A–C.

36. See *Republic* 551A.

37. This discussion of pleasure supplements our discussions in the *Gorgias, Protagoras,* and *Greater Hippias* and, in the next chapter, the *Philebus.* By showing philosophy's superiority to tyranny as pleasure, and by indicating too its superior use of reason and spiritedness, Socrates has shown that the just man (the philosopher) is happier than the most unjust one (the tyrant.)

38. *Republic* 479A–480A. See the *Euthyphro* 10A–11B.

39. See Strauss, *The City and Man,* pp. 135–37, and the Athenian's discussion in the *Laws* of the poets' subordination to law.

40. This is why Plato is so concerned to direct poets in the cities of the *Laws* and *Republic.*

41. *Republic* 506E, 435D.

CHAPTER 7: Pleasure and the Soul

1. I draw on all the dialogues for my analysis. Soul is especially significant in the *Phaedo, Timaeus, Phaedrus, Laws,* and *Republic.* Chapter 1, note 3, contains general information about the Greek edition and translations of the dialogues that I am following.

2. See *Gorgias* 464BC.

3. See *Phaedo* 105B ff. One may doubt whether Plato truly believes that souls are immortal. Neither the discussion in the *Laws* or the *Republic* demonstrates that they are.

4. *Theatetus* 185A–E.

5. *Phaedo* 64B–67D, 82D–84B, 114D–115E.

6. *Statesman* 261B3–C12.

7. See our discussion of the *Laws,* and the discussion of soul in the *Timaeus* and *Phaedo.*

8. *Alcibiades I* 128A–131D.

9. See *Gorgias* 464B–465D, and the discussion of gymnastics in the *Republic,* Book III.

10. Consider the *Protagoras'* discussion of calculating pleasure and the discussion of the order and justice of the soul in the *Republic.*

11. For error, perception, and common sensing, consider especially the *Theatetus,* for thought and pleasure the *Philebus,* for love and beauty the *Phaedrus* and *Symposium,* for image the *Sophist,* for measuring the *Philebus* and *Statesman,* and for causality, the *Republic.*

12. In the *Phaedrus* the spirited aspects of the obedient part are less clear.

13. Plato's discussion of spiritedness (*thumos*)—whose virtue is courage, and which is the source of anger, indignation, ambition, pride, and the like—is an important cor-

rective to modern thought, which tends to reduce the nonrational soul to desire and to reduce desires' objects to what money can buy.

14. On love and friendship generally, consider Mary P. Nichols, *Socrates on Friendship and Community* (Cambridge University Press, 2009).

15. Consider the concluding section of the *Protagoras.*

16. It does appear in the *Laws* and *Euthyphro.*

17. See, e.g., the *Alcibiades I, Protagoras, Euthydemus,* and *Greater Hippias.*

18. See, too, the suggestion we discussed that courage is steadfastness against pleasure as well as against pain.

19. See the discussion of spiritedness in Books II and IV of the *Republic,* and *Euthyphro* 3C.

20. See our discussion in chapter 2.

21. See *Theatetus, Meno, Protagoras, Sophist, Statesman, Philebus,* and *Republic.* We explore knowledge more fully in the next chapters.

22. *Republic,* Book VI.

23. *Philebus* 11D.

24. In this way I will also be examining these phenomena themselves. See *Republic* 505B–D.

25. Cf. *Republic* 505AB.

26. *Philebus* 12C. The *Philebus* is like other dialogues in which interlocutors take over each others' arguments; see, e.g., Lysis and his friend Menexenus in the *Lysis,* and the brothers Euthydemus and Dionysodorus in the *Euthydemus.* The *Philebus* is also evidently connected to the *Gorgias* (because Gorgias is mentioned later in the dialogue), and to the *Sophist* and *Statesman* because of its indication of the presence of "middle" things between one and unlimited that allow dialectic rather than mere eristic talk.

27. *Philebus* 12D. I follow Seth Benardete, trans., *The Tragedy and Comedy of Life: Plato's* Philebus (University of Chicago Press, 1993). I proceed in my exploration of the *Philebus* by discussing a portion of Plato's argument in a section headed by, say, Roman numeral III. I then, if necessary, comment further on some of the portion's less obvious elements and implications, in a new section with that same Roman numeral followed by a letter, say, III A.

28. See *Meno* 75B–76D.

29. *Philebus* 15BC.

30. *Philebus* 16E–17A.

31. *Philebus* 17B.

32. *Philebus* 21DE. Consider also the Athenian Stranger's distinction in Book II of the *Laws* between charm and benefit or correctness: pleasure is the charm in food and learning, but healthiness and truth are their benefit.

33. *Philebus* 22B.

34. Consider the myth in the *Statesman.*

35. *Philebus* 23C ff.

36. See *Statesman,* Aristotle's *Ethics,* and Seth Benardete's commentary in *The Tragedy and Comedy of Life.* On the *Philebus* generally, see also Robert C. Bartlett, "Plato's Critique of Hedonism," *American Political Science Review* 102, no. 1 (February 2008): 141–51.

37. *Philebus* 28A.

38. *Philebus* 30C.

39. *Philebus* 31C.

40. *Philebus* 31C. See *Phaedo* 60BC.

41. *Philebus* 33AC. Cf. *Lysis* 216C.

42. Consider the discussion of memory and sensation in the *Theatetus.*

43. See *Philebus* 52B ff.

44. Cf. *Theatetus.* One can complicate matters even more, for there can be true or false writings about true or false memories.

45. *Philebus* 40C. See also *Republic* 585A–586A.

46. *Philebus* 40D.

47. The elements of this grounding of pleasure might also allow us to understand coherently the pleasure of action as well as that of restoration, and to distinguish the pain of dissolution from mild longing and melancholy, as well as from equanimity. Awareness of bodily pleasure can be awareness of burgeoning health, of complete or sufficient action, of readiness for activity—ways we recognize pleasures that are not a filling of emptiness but that are connected to sufficiency and perfection. (The sweetness of some sensations, e.g., foods that pleasantly fit our senses whether or not we are hungry, is connected to this recognition.) Indeed, does not philosophy take pleasure in its (image of) full awareness? There is pleasure in the mind's awareness of the soul's powers being fully and fittingly active and in its wonder at the beautiful. The pleasure of knowing also involves ignorance, however, not as a pain of loss, dissolution, or failure, but within the activity itself, because of ever-present or, indeed, expanding perplexity. Knowledge involves knowing what is not, cannot, or will not be known. Hence, its pleasure, however pure, is not free from poignancy and regret.

48. If we still wish to think of (much) pleasure as experienced in a filling, we would say that what is filled has many nooks and crannies that allow for excess and deficiency, that the filled section cannot easily be separated from the rest of the surface or container that encloses it, and that there is a certain seamless connection among our various containers. Falseness, impurity, reverberation and depth abound. Even the pleasure of bird-watching is sooner rather than later greater for trained bird-watchers than for the rest of us.

49. Cf. narcotics.

50. We should remark that a false pleasure could also simply be one that we could have replaced with a greater one at the time, had we calculated better. One might consider the *Protagoras* in this regard. Are not all pleasures connected and never truly isolated even when they seem so, which further allows the possibility of falseness in settling on one? Consider the discussion we are about to begin.

51. *Philebus* 44A.

52. Consider Socrates' discussion of pleasure with Callicles in the *Gorgias,* 493D–494C; cf. *Philebus* 58AB.

53. *Philebus* 45E.

54. *Philebus* 46C–47C. See *Republic* 402E–403C.

55. Consider the *Sophist* for further discussion of this question.

56. Consider the pain and reward of childbirth.

57. *Philebus* 47E.

58. The strong can take revenge and are frightening, so we do not laugh at their seeming.

59. *Philebus* 50B.

60. Consider chapter 4 and our discussion of the passage we have just summarized, and of Plato's view of laughter generally. One might connect the pleasure of laughter with recognition of the natural and restoration to it, but it is also connected to pleasure in the natural activity itself. One should also consider the subtle relations between nature and convention.

61. Cf. *Republic* 586BC.

62. Consider and contrast our own comics' attacks on the politically powerful.

63. *Philebus* 51D. Cf. *Greater Hippias* 288DE. If in no way, how are both pleasure?

64. Cf., however, *Republic* 584B and 585B ff.

65. His third way at first lacked all pleasure. He now adjusts it to include pure pleasure.

66. Consider *Republic* 504E, and see *Timaeus* 91D. One reason hearing pure sounds falls short, we might argue, is that they are not complex enough, and, therefore, do not address or satisfy our full powers and can thus easily become boring.

67. Purity also suggests piety. Protarchus seems to treat the pleasure of what is noble and just as coming from rewards in an afterlife. Cf. *Phaedo*, 65E–67D.

68. We should notice that Socrates does not now go on to discuss mixtures of different pure pleasures, or of pure and impure pleasures.

69. *Philebus* 55A. See *Philebus* 33B.

70. *Philebus* 55AB.

71. See *Philebus* 54E–55A.

72. Cf. *Theatetus* 194C–195A.

73. For carpentry, cf. *Theages, Statesman, Lovers,* and *Alcibiades I.* For guesswork and practicing, cf. *Gorgias, Protagoras,* and *Meno.*

74. Cf. *Statesman* 284D for a discussion of precision.

75. *Philebus* 57B.

76. *Philebus* 58A.

77. *Philebus* 58AB.

78. *Philebus* 58D.

79. *Philebus* 59C.

80. *Statesman* 258D–259D. There, however, the Eleatic Stranger distinguishes the carpenter from the master builder who commands him but does not act. Statesmen belong to the master builder's class.

81. *Statesman* 284B–D, 304A–305A. Consider Socrates' earlier remarks in the *Philebus* about hubris, limit, and law.

82. What remains here of the highest and greatest—say, the most causal and attractive things—is only its unmixed permanence. The nature of true things is their purity, and purity is mathematical. The science in carpentry and the merchant's craft, here, is only in numbers.

83. See *Republic* 505DE.

84. *Philebus* 62B.

85. *Philebus* 63C.

86. *Philebus* 63E–64A.

87. *Philebus* 64C.

88. *Philebus* 65D.

89. See *Laws* 819E–820A.

90. See *Meno.*

91. Consider Laches' separating courage from victory. Socrates mentions in the *Philebus* virtues such as justice and moderation, and refers to law and order, and to right opinion. But he does not explore virtue explicitly at length or connect his discussions to political science.

92. *Lysis* 217D–218B.

93. Consider *Republic* 486A. When "a nature is philosophic," its "understanding [is] endowed with magnificence and the contemplation of all time and being," and its "soul . . . is always going to reach out for the whole and for everything divine and human." See, also, *Republic* 485D. "Therefore the man who is really a lover of learning must from youth on strive very directly for all truth." His "desires incline exceedingly" to learning, and he will "be concerned with the pleasure of the soul itself with respect to itself." Consider, too, *Republic* 582A.

94. See *Statesman* 284C ff. Socrates exemplifies such extreme inquiry in the *Philebus* more than he grounds it. One should consider the manic aspect of philosophic eros.

95. *Philebus* 65E.

96. See *Gorgias* and *Meno*.

CHAPTER 8: Knowledge and Illusion

1. Cf. *Philebus*. Chapter 1, note 3, contains general information about the Greek edition and translations of the dialogues that I am following.

2. See *Theatetus* 184A. For the translation of the *Theatetus* and the *Sophist,* I follow Seth Benardete, trans., Plato's Theatetus (University of Chicago Press, 1986), and Plato's Sophist (University of Chicago Press, 1986). I proceed in my explorations of the *Theatetus* and *Sophist* by discussing a portion of Plato's argument in a section headed by, say, Roman numeral V. I then, if necessary, comment further on some of the portion's less obvious elements and implications, in a new section with that same Roman numeral followed by a letter, say, V A.

3. Plato's brief references in the opening to poor memory, negligence, or duplicity, and Theatetus' resemblance to Socrates further bring out these points. The ensuing discussion of the limits of memory and speech subtly reinforces them.

4. *Theatetus* 145A. The opening scenes suggest still other elements, conditions, or instances of knowledge: wonder and perplexity, evidence, bearing witness, one's own examining, artistic vs. unskilled speaking, adequacy, and not making mistakes (145A–C).

5. Socrates ignores here the place of rank and resemblance in knowledge. He makes knowing a thing identical to knowing it fully and equally. The merely material might satisfy this requirement: hence, Socrates' example, mud.

6. Socrates also suggests that something's name is misunderstood unless we know what it is. We can see, however, that identity in name is one way we first notice what is common.

7. *Theatetus* 152D.

8. *Theatetus* 153A. Cf. *Philebus* and *Sophist.* The question is the permanence and purity of the standard for measuring.

9. Cf. *Philebus.*

10. *Theatetus* 155D. See chapter 4.

11. See *Sophist.*

12. *Theatetus* 159E. This argument is based on Socrates' supposition here that the healthy and sick are wholly other and dissimilar.

13. *Theatetus* 164B.

14. *Theatetus* 164C.

15. See *Charmides*.

16. *Theatetus* 165B–D.

17. Cf. *Philebus*.

18. *Theatetus* 167C. This statement does not prevent (Socrates as) Protagoras from calling conversation that sets opponents upright rather that competitively tripping them up more "just."

19. *Theatetus* 172B.

20. One might consider in this regard the openings of the *Euthyphro* and *Charmides*.

21. Cf. *Statesman* 286CD.

22. *Theatetus* 174A.

23. *Theatetus* 174B.

24. Cf. Thrasymachus' remarks in Book I of the *Republic* and the discussion of expected or anticipated pleasure in the *Philebus*.

25. *Theatetus* 180AB. The view that knowledge is perception was said earlier to coincide with Homer's and Heraclitus' views.

26. Cf. whiteness and purity in the *Philebus* 53AB and *Charmides* 154B.

27. *Theatetus* 184D. Consider Martin Heidegger's examination of this discussion in his 1931–32 lecture course "*Vom Wesen der Wahrheit*," Part Two, chapters 1 and 2, in Ted Sandler, trans., *The Essence of Truth* (Continuum, 2002).

28. Cf. *Greater Hippias* 302B–D.

29. They bracket in between matters such as learning or forgetting.

30. For Socrates himself, doubt or its possibility is always embedded in his opinions. Does perplexity uncover the possibilities in the actualities that pride, politics, and piety defend, as wonder uncovers the actualities in the possibilities that eros longs for and seeks?

31. We mistakenly think that the ugly is beautiful, not that it is in fact ugly but is merely being asserted to be beautiful. Socrates disregards here the difference between what is beautiful and partial beauty, and so on. Earlier, good was said to require some evil (*Theatetus* 176A).

32. *Theatetus* 191A.

33. *Theatetus* 194E.

34. What is the status as knowledge of their own examination here?

35. These respects could include different aspects, forms, motions, materials, and media. Consider the discussion of opinion in the *Republic* 476D–480A, where the power of opinion is "neither ignorance nor knowledge" but looks "darker than knowledge . . . and brighter than ignorance," and the opinable participates in both "to be and not to be."

36. *Theatetus* 200D–201A.

37. *Theatetus* 200E.

38. Cf. Leo Strauss, *Natural Right and History* (Free Press, 1953), chap. 3.

39. *Theatetus* 201D. In thinking about this view, we should consider the possibility that an explanation in speech can be faulty, that how we connect elements in an expla-

nation is crucial, that each element must be recognized as an "element," and that it seems odd to separate perception from knowledge altogether. (See *Sophist* 264AB.)

40. *Theatetus* 202AB. Cf. Samuel Scolnicov, trans., *Plato's* Parmenides, with commentary (University of California Press, 2003), for similar arguments in the *Parmenides*.

41. *Theatetus* 202B. Consider the discussion of this issue in the *Sophist*, and compare the use of letters in the *Theatetus, Sophist, Statesman*, and *Philebus* with that in the *Republic*.

42. *Theatetus* 202C.

43. *Theatetus* 206B.

44. *Theatetus* 208C. Perhaps, then, knowledge as recognition is neither perception nor discursive speech alone but is noetic, and then discursive, and then noetic, and so on. The usual noetic seeing or understanding often proves to be about what is somewhat false and fleeting.

45. *Theatetus* 208D.

46. The whole, and even the elements, might still be in question.

47. See *Theatetus* 197CD, and *Sophist* 226C, 228C.

48. Cf. *Statesman*.

49. See Locke's *Essay Concerning Human Understanding* and Nietzsche's *Beyond Good and Evil*. Cf. Mark Blitz, *Duty Bound* (Rowman and Littlefield, 2005), chap. 9.

50. Political knowledge is most obviously knowledge of combining or making common.

51. The *Sophist* brings forward the question of images and what is not, but not directly from the standpoint of need or erotic yearning as we see it in, say, the *Symposium*.

52. Consider, for this link, the status of the opinions about justice in the *Republic*, Book I; the discussion of opinion in *Republic*, Book V; and the fact that the parts of the divided line belong together on a single, connected, line.

53. It is not obvious why Plato uses the Eleatic Stranger rather than Socrates as his chief interlocutor here and in the *Statesman*, just as it is not obvious why Plato uses the Athenian Stranger in the *Laws*, and Timaeus in the *Timaeus*. The issue thus occasions much scholarly debate; one can find good discussions in Catherine Zuckert's *Plato's Philosophers*. I wonder whether, if we knew in advance the subject matter and approach of these dialogues but not the chief interlocutor, we would have predicted Plato's substitutions, or whether we are primarily involved in after-the-fact explanation. Neither the Athenian's code of laws nor Timaeus' detailed cosmodicy seem to people to be Socratic. But, is not this impression governed by knowing in advance that he is not the chief interlocutor? Are the legal code and cosmodicy so different from the *Republic* and the stories that conclude the *Republic* and the *Gorgias* that Plato could not have made Socrates deliver them at an appropriate time? What in the *Laws*, for example, opposes Socrates' "usual" views to a greater degree than in different dialogues Socrates sometimes seems to oppose himself—say, on the scope of the virtues or the worth of pleasure? It is occasionally suggested that the Eleatic Stranger replaces Socrates in the *Sophist* and *Statesman* so that Socrates, who is present for these conversations, can hear accusations of his sophistry and democratic unorthodoxy prior to his trial. But nothing one might take as the Eleatic's indications about this are things Socrates has not heard in other dialogues, such as the *Meno*, or things a reasonably intelligent man would not already know. Moreover, the *Sophist* and *Statesman* are embedded in a group of seven (or eight) dialogues, the other five (or six) of which are Socratic, a fact that one might claim

as clearly shows their unity with Socratic dialogues as their difference from them. Even the kinds of divisions practiced at the start of the *Sophist* and *Statesman* are, as I said earlier, suggested, if not worked out, in the *Philebus* (and the *Phaedrus*).

Nonetheless, it is a fact that Plato uses different chief interlocutors. If we are in need of a formula to capture the apparent differences among them and to explain why Plato does not always use Socrates, we might suggest the following. While Socrates is both citizen and philosopher, both citizen and "Stranger," the Athenian in the *Laws* is the citizen (acting) as Stranger, the Eleatic is the Stranger (acting) as Stranger, and Timaeus, who constructs a politically or ethically useful cosmology, is the Stranger (acting) as citizen. Plato chooses to bring out the elements of Socrates' combination on their own, as it were, while also indicating their separate shortcomings. Our recombining of these elements, keeping in mind their shortcomings and the limits of this recombining, is once again Socratic or Platonic, which is why one can speak in a unified way of Socrates or, obviously, Plato. The *Sophist* and *Statesman* pursue a path that tries to retain the Parmenidean or Eleatic notion that being is intelligible, while still allowing more than one being (e.g., different ideas). The path thus works through and around the perplexities with which Socrates typically deals, but it does so in a different way. While he tends to discuss phenomena by keeping in mind their appearance in the highest things (one cannot understand, say, justice without looking at its presence in philosophy), the Eleatic Stranger tends to discuss phenomena without considering rank. His arguments are less erotic. Yet, we should not overstate this difference, because Socrates too attends to what is equivalent but unranked (consider his examples of quickness and mud), and the Eleatic Stranger discusses, at length, the problem of imitation. And, while Socrates more visibly than the Eleatic Stranger tries to educate his interlocutors ethically or politically as well as intellectually, the Stranger also educates, although more obviously intellectually. Both, moreover, must consider wholes, parts, and the separate wholeness of parts. As I suggested, the two look most visibly alike in Plato's presentation of Socrates in the *Philebus,* with his emphasis on measure. I conclude that we may treat the Eleatic Stranger and Socrates as fundamentally the same, as well as different from each other, in the ways I have indicated. Plato or, if one likes, Socrates, is not at root contradictory. I discuss these issues again at the conclusion of chapter 9.

54. The importance of splits in two, and what counts as such a split, seems connected to what Socrates says about numbers and precision in his discussion with Philebus.

55. In our discussion of the *Statesman,* we will point out still another central feature of the Stranger's way of dividing.

56. *Sophist* 221B.

57. Do they themselves hide while seeking sophistry? Does the Stranger secretly master Theatetus? Is what they seek in some sense compliant and not only resistant? See Benardete's commentary to his translation of the *Sophist.*

58. Consider Socrates' claim to have the erotic art. One might differentiate him from sophists at this point in the following manner: he hunts by giving, as does an expert in erotics, rather than by merchandising, as does a seeker of wealth. He produces the conviction of one's own ignorance, rather than of (sham) virtue. He gives—and the sophist sells—speeches, but how their form and content differ would as yet be unclear. Consider, also, *Sophist* 227D–229A.

59. Cf. Socrates' understanding of sophistry in the *Gorgias* as a phantom of legislating and as analogous to cosmetics, the phantom of gymnastics.

60. Cf. *Protagoras* 339E.

61. Cf. *Statesman* 282BC.

62. The many agree that the soul's illness, but not its ignorance, is vice.

63. Cf. *Gorgias*. Consider there and in the *Laws* the connection between education and legislation, and between ignorance and crime.

64. Cf. *Philebus* 55D ff.

65. Cf. Socrates' alter ego in the *Greater Hippias* and the argument of the *Philebus*. One must consider the possible connections among knowing what is pure, purifying the soul, and pure pleasure.

66. *Sophist* 230E. Cf. *Philebus* 51D–53C, 58C–E.

67. *Sophist* 231B. For dogs, consider also *Statesman* 266A, and *Republic* 375C–376C. The dog is individual but tame, or tamable, and loyal to what he knows. This canine likeness to the philosopher in the city may be one reason "by the dog" is, for Socrates, a characteristic oath.

68. Cf. *Gorgias* and the reference to physicians at *Sophist* 230C, with *Sophist* 247B. We also should note that the split between the soul's illness and ugliness is not hard and fast.

69. *Statesman* 291C.

70. *Sophist* 226E.

71. One should consider the conditions of battle with which a general must deal.

72. *Sophist* 232B. The Stranger's summary divides the sophists' exchanging in three —merchandising, retailing, and self-selling—more visibly than he had previously.

73. Cf. sophists' claims and practices in the *Greater Hippias, Protagoras,* and *Euthydemus.* Consider Martin Heidegger, *Platon: Sophistes* (Vittorio Klostermann, 1992), and Martin Heidegger, "Das Ding," in *Vorträge und Aufsätze* (Neske, 1954).

74. Cf. *Gorgias* 456A–457C. One way in which Socrates apparently educates—purifies through refuting—is by contradicting. The contradictory involves what is improperly combined, although this may be rooted in a prior improper grasp of the separate things that are being combined.

75. As is true of Socrates, the Stranger too does not suggest that men can be completely wise.

76. Cf. *Theatetus* 206CD, 208C, on speech as spoken image.

77. *Sophist* 239C.

78. *Sophist* 236E. Cf. the discussion in the *Greater Hippias* of being beautiful and appearing to be beautiful.

79. *Sophist* 239B–240A. Consider how in asking about the one "image" the sophist would be imitating Socrates' procedure. Mirrors show images only if we know, or first see, what images are and what they image.

80. How can "image" be possible, at the level, say, of the *Philebus'* pure objects? The ensuing discussion means to clarify this. One should also consider the use of images in thinking, as the divided line in the *Republic* is an image of connection and difference among things we can know. See Jacob Klein, *Greek Logistic and the Development of Algebra* (MIT Press, 1963); Jacob Klein, *A Commentary on Plato's* Meno (University of North Carolina Press, 1965); Jacob Klein, *Plato's Trilogy* (University of Chicago Press, 1977); Stanley Rosen, *Plato's* Sophist (Yale University Press, 1983); and Stanley Rosen, *Plato's* Statesman (Yale University Press, 1996).

81. Consider plaiting and weaving in *Theatetus* 202B and *Statesman* 279B ff.

82. In doing this they will try to refute Parmenides' speech that being is one, as in

the *Theatetus* Socrates and Theatetus refuted Heraclitus. (See, too, the *Parmenides*.) Both Parmenides and the Stranger come from Elea. Philosophers learn from but do not remain chained to their origins, just as sons learn from but do not remain chained to their fathers' admonitions or to what they learn from sophists. As the Stranger suggests at 234D, when they in time come near to things and experience them in their vividness, the apparitions in these speeches are "totally inverted" by the works in their actions. Yet, perhaps this nearness also distorts—perhaps there is something true in sophists' apparitions. True education does not rest in its radicalism but always remains dissatisfied with presumed self-knowledge. Consider Socrates' reference to madness at 216D and the Stranger's reference to it here, at 242B.

83. *Sophist* 243E.

84. *Sophist* 245E.

85. *Sophist* 247BC.

86. See *Theatetus* 156A.

87. *Sophist* 248A. Cf. *Philebus* 58A and *Republic,* passim.

88. See *Euthyphro* 11A and *Greater Hippias* 301B.

89. *Sophist* 249A. See *Republic* 524E.

90. *Sophist* 249B.

91. *Sophist* 249D.

92. *Sophist* 252D.

93. *Sophist* 253C.

94. Dialectic or conversation is, therefore, apparently not identical with the divisions or diaresis the Stranger used to find the sophist. Those divisions divided, more or less in half, arts that are concerned primarily with what becomes.

95. *Sophist* 253D.

96. For *Sophist* 253D ff., see Klein, *Plato's Trilogy,* chap. 1.

97. *Sophist* 254A.

98. *Sophist* 255E.

99. *Sophist* 256E.

100. *Sophist* 258C.

101. *Sophist* 258E.

102. Yet, each has a nature, although this is hard to state alone.

103. See *Sophist* 260A.

104. Heidegger makes the Stranger's discussion of the power to mix with or be common among all the genera the center of his discussion.

105. Consider, too, the discussion of the mixture of pleasure and mind, and its relation to purity, in the *Philebus.*

106. In this sense, a power can become a cause, such as an art that makes or produces something. See, e.g., *Sophist* 265B.

107. *Sophist* 254C.

108. For power see, among others, *Gorgias* 466B–468E, *Republic* 359C, 473CD, 477B–478B, Greater *Hippias* 295D–296E, *Philebus* 29B.

109. The Stranger continues to point out to Theatetus the importance of confidence in advancing intellectually, as one does when seizing a city.

110. Cf. the meanings of speech in the *Theatetus.*

111. *Sophist* 263A.

112. Cf. *Charmides* 158E–159A, the link between pleasure and expectation in the *Philebus,* and the *Theatetus'* account of perception.

113. Theatetus mentions, but neither he nor the Stranger develops here, the status of similarity in imitation. Given the course of the argument, their presumption is that otherness is the key to making phantastic images.

114. See *Republic* 392A–396E.

115. Here, the sophist ironically pretends to know what he does not. Socrates, by contrast, ironically pretends not to know what he does or ironically pretends to be speaking only to the ordinary opinion or audience.

116. See *Theatetus* 210C.

117. *Sophist* 265DE.

CHAPTER 9: Knowledge and Politics

1. Among Plato's dialogues, the *Statesman* presents an especially strong link between its subject, political knowledge, and its theme, political knowledge from the standpoint of the possible rule of a single political knower. As with the *Sophist,* its chief interlocutor is the Eleatic Stranger. Socrates, Theatetus, and Theodorus are also present, but the discussion is conducted chiefly with "young" Socrates. Both dialogues are occasioned by Socrates' asking Theodorus if Eleatics consider sophists, statesmen, and philosophers to be one or three. A possible examination of philosophers' likeness to the mad (for they are also said to seem sometimes to be mad) is silently omitted, although the manic appears near the *Statesman's* end, as a defect of the quality whose virtue is courage. Perhaps this omission is connected to the downplaying of eros in these dialogues.

2. The *Sophist* is about the likeness of sophists to teachers and philosophers. It seems to founder by reaching a point where the fakery or falseness of sophists is fully split from the truth of what they are like. The dialogue then uncovers the possibility of this likeness, or togetherness, while preserving the difference. The *Statesman* is about the difference between statesmen and others (other knowers) and seems to founder by reaching a point where their difference is submerged, or exists only as the difference between gods and men. The dialogue then uncovers the possibility of this difference, while preserving the likeness, or togetherness.

3. In addition to Burnet's *Platonis Opera* and the translation I have primarily followed (Seth Benardete, *Plato's Statesman* [University of Chicago Press, 1986]), other useful editions and discussions include Joseph Cropsey, *Plato's World* (University of Chicago Press, 1995); Jacob Klein, *Plato's Trilogy* (University of Chicago Press, 1977); M. S. Lane, *Method and Politics in Plato's* Statesman (Cambridge University Press, 1998); Stanley Rosen, *Plato's* Statesman (Yale University Press, 1995); *Statesman,* trans. C. J. Rowe (Hackett, 1999); "Reading the 'Statesman,'" Proceedings of the Third Symposium Platonicum, Bristol, ed. Christopher J. Rowe., *International Plato Studies Bd.* 4 (1995); Kenneth M. Sayre, *Metaphysics and Method in Plato's* Statesman (Cambridge University Press, 2006); and Leo Strauss, "Plato," in Leo Strauss and Joseph Cropsey, eds., *History of Political Philosophy* (Rand McNally, 1968). Chapter 1, note 3, contains general information about the Greek edition and translations of the dialogues that I follow.

4. As we suggested, measure (and production according to measure) links the *Statesman* and *Philebus.* One might say that the *Statesman* clarifies the knowledge that the guiding legislator in the *Laws* must possess.

5. I proceed in my exploration of the *Statesman* by discussing a portion of Plato's argument in a section headed by, say, Roman numeral I. I then, if necessary, comment further on some of the portion's less obvious elements and implications, in a new section with that same Roman numeral followed by a letter, say, I A.

6. The Stranger does not proceed as he had in the *Sophist* by first dividing arts into making and acquiring.

7. Cf. the discussion of carpentry and arithmetic in the *Philebus* 55D–57A.

8. That is, the advisor is identical to the man we would like to call the "actual" ruler, the one whose orders are obeyed by citizens. Cf. *Gorgias* 455D–457C.

9. See *Phaedrus* 248D, Socrates' first discussion with Lysis in the *Lysis*, and *Lovers* 138C.

10. *Statesman* 259B. Cf. *Meno*. This, too, looks odd, for it seems true only if the aim of the knowing ruler and the household manager are the same. But can the house nurture or sustain virtue or the arts, as the city can? (See Aristotle, *Politics*, Book I.)

11. *Statesman* 260A. Statesmen are cognitive commanders because the proper standard or measure that they know is used to produce or compose what is fitting. Mathematicians simply count or measure, or know how to count or measure. Whether statesmen can know their measure apart from commanding fitting productions or, rather, can know it only for producing what is good politically, is unclear.

12. We cannot help wondering, of course, how the purely cognitive "ruler of workmen" ensures that his commands are obeyed. But it is possible to imagine an artisan who must use others to produce his works and knows what they should do, even if he cannot successfully convince anyone to do anything.

13. See *Greater Hippias* 289B. Perhaps the rule of knowers whose injunctions are obeyed without using force or persuasion can arise if the ruled are thunderstruck or in awe, immediately instructable, or are in no way recalcitrant or independent. Later in the dialogue, law takes the place that interpreters and diviners occupy here.

14. See Benardete's commentary in *Plato's* Statesman.

15. That men are featherless or bare becomes explicit only when the Stranger shows young Socrates that they might take two paths once they see that we are pedestrial: we are hornless, non-interbreeders, and two footed; or we are two footed and featherless. Consider also Aristophanes' speech in the *Symposium*.

16. *Statesman* 261BC.

17. Cf. Protagoras' myth in the *Protagoras*. The multiplicity of man's connections to animals indicates why, to understand us properly, we must distinguish ourselves from animals through a variety of ideas, as the Stranger tells young Socrates, and not all at once. We recall Socrates' discussion with Protarchus about ideas early in the *Philebus* 16C–17A.

18. Consider Aristotle, *Politics*, Book I.

19. Consider chapter 4.

20. *Statesman* 306E. Cf. the example of quickness in the *Laches*.

21. This is one cause of organizational peculiarities such as programmatic overspending. Cf. Stesilaus in the *Laches*.

22. Still another way we can grasp Plato's intention here is to reflect on the Stranger's reprimand of young Socrates for at first splitting men from all beasts. This split, he suggests, results from human's believing ourselves to be august. The Stranger himself, however, had said that the statesman supervises the souled, not the soulless, because

the souled are better born (or nobler) (261C). But, the Stranger then proceeded to ignore everything in humans that is in fact nobler. Splits that do not allow us to distinguish noble and base are splits where both members participate in their unity equally; where, when more or less of their unified quality exists, it is additive rather than measured; and where the members are not hierarchically arranged. (One might consider different pieces of gold and different days of the week in contrast to ruler and ruled, or a man and his painted image.) Splits that allow the distinction of noble and base members are splits where the members participate unequally, some demonstrating or aspiring to a greater proportion of the defining quality. When the Stranger ignores cuts in terms of the more or less noble, therefore, he ignores several reasonable and not merely proud or passionate ways of dividing. There are kinds of unities, wholes, or species that are not comprehended in the Stranger's discussion up to this point that become significant later: the way the Stranger chooses here is coherent with his seeing humans as equal herd animals but not as reasonable or divine. (The relation between these two kinds of splits and splitting on the basis of purity, as the Stranger discusses this in the *Sophist*, is still another matter.)

23. Plato draws our attention to this through the Stranger's educating young Socrates, for such education has little place among the men who are here the explicit object of statesmanship. Moreover, the Stranger mentions to young Socrates that he displays eagerness and manliness, addresses him as "dear," and mentions the goodwill he has for his "nature"; that is, he indicates that he does not simply have a herd soul.

24. Part of the Stranger's education of young Socrates occurs in discussion of what counts as a cut of species rather than a cut merely of parts. Male and female is a more "beautiful" (i.e., a more complete) cut of human beings than is Greek and barbarian. The central point seems to be that a beautiful cut is one in which the half that one continues to cut must not borrow characteristics from what one has left behind—usually, without one's knowing this. Violating this procedure is what causes the mistakes to which the Stranger points as they proceed along their way—not explicitly distinguishing domesticated from savage animals, for example, as he remarks at 264A. But he leaves it to us to discover the grounds of his procedure, and to consider its connection to the fact that their hasty dividing has led them to "accomplish it more slowly," which suggests the upcoming discussion of the two types of measure.

25. *Statesman* 267D–E. One may wonder what the relation is between nurturing or caring in the *Statesman* and the division of arts between production and acquisition in the *Sophist*. As we said in our discussion there, several arts could be placed in either half. Nurture helps something to reach or return to its natural end.

26. Cf. Protagoras' myth in the *Protagoras* 320C–328D.

27. For obvious reasons, it is unlikely we would or could do so. Further analysis of the myth's substance, structure, and implications can be found in Rosen, *Plato's Statesman* and Benardete, *Plato's* Statesman.

28. See *Statesman* 271E. Cf. Hippias and Socrates' discussion of Hippias first attempt to say what beauty is in the *Greater Hippias*.

29. See *Alcibiades I* 106C–109B.

30. One should consider the *Republic*'s argument, seemingly opposite to this one, that we can grasp the small, there, justice in the soul, by first looking at the large, there, the city.

31. The difference between similarity and nature here is unclear. It might refer to the

features of a thing being compared or exemplified, with different generalities, so that, say, all elements are ("similar" as) parts but only some parts share a nature as elements; all letters are (similar as) elements, but only some elements share a nature as letters; and all vowels are (similar as) letters, but only some letters share a nature as vowels. Vowels could then share a nature and a similarity with some letters, while differing in nature from most of them. Or, the difference between similarity and nature may point to sameness in order vs. identity in substance as, e.g., legislation and gymnastics each orders or perfects (the soul or body) but differ in substance.

32. These two examples of paradigm point to an additional complexity. Weaving and learning letters share some things—here, being used as examples and being involved with combining and separating (syllables are themselves "weavings")—but not most. Letters cannot keep one warm, nor can one read a warp or a woof. As is true of the first divisions, the question arises: From what point of view do we notice resemblances? Are all points of view equally appropriate, dependent simply on immediate utility? How can we learn what statesmanship is if we can compare it to so many things and place it in so many classes? Are there natural limits here, and do they guide us? For a discussion of the question of paradigms and examples generally, consider Eva Brann, *The Music of the* Republic (Paul Dry Books, 2004), and Rosen, *Plato's* Statesman.

33. This intertwining of characters, however, is supplemented by a "divine" bond. On weaving also see *Phaedo* 84A, 87B–E.

34. That is his ostensible reason for studying it.

35. See the earlier discussion of the master builder.

36. Nurture and defense of the body are the two purposes discussed so far. They are too broad to capture political science (because it is not the only nurturing and defending art) and too narrow (because these purposes still lack human soul.)

37. In the *Theages,* as we saw, carpenters themselves use subordinates, and in the *Philebus* they are distinguished by their precision, and, therefore, can be grouped with the other precise arts.

38. He places roofing within the wider but less useful (say, when one needs a new roof) "bolting." See *Statesman* 280B–E.

39. See *Statesman* 282A–D.

40. Cf. the day or daylight, as discussed in the *Parmenides.*

41. A mediocre tennis player both does and does not exemplify a good one.

42. See *Statesman* 283B ff.

43. Is the function to protect lastingly, or for a short time? Is it (also) to allow motion (i.e., to fit the wearer's shape and size)?

44. The full relation between the mean and a fitting production that it serves is unclear. A beautiful whole is useful because it is fittingly measured, but it is not identical to either the good end it serves or the precise as such. Moreover, looking at matters such as the precise or true may itself be the end toward which our souls can be fittingly ordered. In the *Philebus,* after all, the arts are well below the pure in rank, and the carpenter's and mathematician's precisions differ. On the mean generally, consider Benardete, *Plato's* Statesman, Klein, *Plato's Trilogy,* and Rosen, *Plato's* Statesman.

45. *Statesman* 285D.

46. Perhaps, then, the pure pleasures of the *Philebus* (which are connected to seeing these greatest things) can indeed have their own magnitude or extent.

47. *Statesman* 287A ff.

48. We should note again the earlier equation of the large house and small city, an equation not withdrawn even after tyranny is replaced by the voluntary.

49. Cf. the earlier mention of stamping *eide* at *Statesman* 258C.

50. Cf. the earlier placing of everything soulless into one kind at *Statesman* 261C.

51. The artisans who are coordinated with these parts—carpenters, house builders, painters, leather cutters, farmers, and so on—do not as such compete with the statesman for rule. This is not to say, however, that they might not compete with him as citizens in democracies.

52. The fact that it does so indicates a narrowness in the Stranger's procedure.

53. See *Republic* 369B–372E.

54. Cf. *Republic*, passim.

55. See *Republic* 492AB.

56. On the relation between animals and men in the *Statesman*, see Mark Blitz, *A Study of Plato's* Statesman (PhD diss., Harvard University, 1971).

57. Presumably, questioning and examining, one manner in which the statesman might be away from affairs, also might issue in improvement. Cf. Socrates' delay in going to Agathon's banquet in the *Symposium* 174D–175D. See, also, *Theatetus* 174C–E.

58. See *Protagoras* 312BC.

59. Cf. *Greater Hippias*, on Sparta, 283C–286C.

60. See *Statesman* 294DE.

61. See *Statesman* 297D–300D. If a scientific ruler needed to give laws to aristocratic, oligarchic, democratic, monarchical, or tyrannical rulers who imitated him, one could defend not deviating from these laws more confidently than one could recommend never deviating from the laws of ordinary democracies, aristocracies, and so on, although these too ultimately imitate the one right regime. The Stranger counsels against practices, including innovations in arts, that violate basic, original laws. But it is not clear that all improvements or discoveries lead one to violate original laws, even if the laws originate from nonknowers. Socrates, after all, refused to engage in corrupt practices but did not violate any of the democracy's laws. And, the Athenian in the *Laws* recognizes the occasional need to touch things up.

62. Moreover, he does not attempt an amelioration of the dilemma of flexibility and inflexibility such as the Athenian's preludes and his complex discussion in the *Laws* of political offices, because the statesman here need hardly deal at all with the independence of individuals.

63. Consider *Sophist* 248A–249D.

64. The place of rhetoric here should be compared to rhetoric, false and useful, in the *Gorgias*.

65. *Statesman* 303E–305E.

66. *Statesman* 305D.

67. Does the statesman even know the greatest things in cities as opposed to the opportune in regard to beginning them? These are not identical; the weaver might weave good coats but not as such know the full worth of all their uses.

68. See *Statesman* 304A–C.

69. See *Statesman* 299B–300A.

70. See *Statesman* 293E.

71. Cf. *Laches* and *Charmides*.

72. See *Laws* 934D.

73. *Statesman* 307C.

74. *Statesman* 307E, 308A.

75. See *Phaedo* 71A.

76. *Statesman* 308C.

77. *Statesman* 311A.

78. *Statesman* 309E.

79. See *Statesman* 308E–309A.

80. Consider Benardete's discussion of this in *Plato's* Statesman.

81. There is an easy to overlook link between mathematics and the spiritedness that may issue in courage. The link is in the swiftness, the agglomeration, the seeing of all outside (and, for the mathematician, all inside as well) as a unity, not a whole with parts. Hence, too, there is a characteristic separating in both, where all ones are equal, and differences are different agglomerations of units. This does not mean that a mathematician is spirited in all things, for we should contrast Theatetus with young Socrates. (But we should also remember the start of the *Theatetus,* where Theatetus is reported to be injured in battle.) The spirited defense of oneself or one's city protects and pushes away and, therefore, secures and illuminates an independence that one does not believe to be identical to rival unities. As such, however, mathematical thinking is swift and "aggressive," not erotic or languid. See, also, *Republic* 522C–E, 525A–526E.

82. *Statesman* 305E, 311C.

83. *Statesman* 311A.

84. *Statesman* 310A. Cf. *Statesman* 304CD.

85. We also should again point out an important difference between the binding of warp and woof and of courageous and moderate. The first occurs through intertwining that needs no third thread, but the second needs divine bonds of opinion. The passions require speech even when it is speech as an enchanting drug, that is, even when speech appeals to passions rather than elevates them directly. The passions, nonetheless, are indeed ultimately elevated here because they become part of the common good. This common good, however, is in one sense independent—as is a finished woven coat—but in another sense is not. As a coat is finished to the purchaser's perhaps imperfect specifications, so the divine bonds of opinion necessary in this regime reflect, but are not simply and fully, what we can grasp of the beautiful, good, and true. The statesman imitates even in his own regime. What is good in the city is found in and made possible by the greatest things. It is dialectic, however, not command, that comes closest to those things.

86. These two virtues also remind us of the moderation and courage that are connected to desire and spiritedness in the *Republic.*

87. Consider here the conclusion of the *Meno*—the unity of virtue in practice comes from law, that is, a genus that tries to serve the same end as, but falls short of, the philosophic genus.

88. The Stranger does not mention training in prudence or practical judgment and only barely mentions thinking that is connected to employing the virtues. (See *Statesman* 306E, 307B, 309DE.)

89. Cf. *Laches* 191CD.

90. *Statesman* 308D, 310A.

91. *Statesman* 306A. The *Laws* also features this issue in Book XII. Plato's discussion

here adds to what he indicates in the *Laches, Protagoras,* and *Charmides,* and to what he shows about the complexity of whole and part elsewhere in the *Statesman.*

92. The virtue of lovers and the way they are good for each other is never apart from a whole—a yearning, a child, an education—that takes each one and both together beyond itself to something that neither can be apart or merely together.

93. One might also consider similar issues from the viewpoint of courageous intensity.

94. See *Phaedo* 74E–75B. This differs from suggesting that, say, the power of justice is not altogether in any act or body because it must also be in other acts and bodies.

95. Consider, also, the discussion of the ideas in the *Phaedrus* 270 CD.

96. Or, would this only mean that the Stranger has overlooked a relevant characteristic by which one should differentiate cognitive commanders?

97. *Statesman* 281B.

98. And he does not fail to refer to wonder, although more as what is puzzling than as what is stunning.

99. Indeed, it is not clear of what the five genera are genera—the whole of things, the precise itself, intelligibility? We should consider also the variety of modes of combining we see in the dialogues, including weaving, binding, imaging, resembling, kinship, friendship, unity, and community.

100. Consider our earlier discussion of the horned and hornless.

101. One also sees the significance of this standpoint by considering the relation of the subject of a dialogue to the implicit whole in which it takes place, something that Plato shows us in the dialogue's action.

Index

moderation, 61, 62, 76, 79–81, 93, 97, 169, 176–177, 257–263; in *Charmides,* 53–62

motion, 60, 218, 220, 234–236; and nature, 118–119, 122, 251; in soul, 80–81, 107–109, 195, 259, 263; and virtue, 262–263

Mozart, 152

music, 75, 84, 94–95, 102

nature, 21, 29, 76, 97, 100, 108, 116–122, 201, 235–236, 240, 244–245; and beauty, 64; and cause, 122; and convention, 23–24, 64–65, 70–71, 116–117, 183; and ends, 119, 122; and essence, 119, 122; and form, 122; human, 106; and justice, 173; and laughter, 138–140; and law, 64, 68, 117; in *Laws,* 91–93; and limits, 117, 122, 167; and measure, 122; and motion, 118–119, 122, 251; and origin, 118, 120–121; and perplexity, 213–214; and pleasure, 204–205; and power, 122, 238; and reason, 120, 121; and rights, 116–117; and speech, 183; and statesmanship, 91; and virtue, 257, 260; and whole, 122, 261

Nietzsche, 116, 226

nobility, 56–57, 60, 81, 85, 91, 95, 153, 265; and courage, 78; and *Greater Hippias,* 143–165; and justice, 105; and lie, 172; and virtue, 77, 260. *See also* beauty

Odysseus, 148n23

Odyssey, 16, 108n81, 148n23

Old Testament, 9

oligarchy, 182–184

Olympian, 109, 112

opinion, 4, 12, 56, 74, 96, 105, 167–168, 196, 202–203, 210, 219–220, 259, 260; and action, 57; false, 239–240; and knowledge, 221–225; and politics, 219

order, 108–109, 168; and city, 81; and good, 65–67; and knowledge, 180–181; and power, 238; and soul, 65–67, 81, 195

Pangle, Thomas, 5n8

paradigm, 247

Parmenides, 119, 127, 142n33, 217

passion, 33, 35, 80, 94, 192–194, 194–195

Pericles, 14, 63, 66, 73, 91

perplexity, 12, 21, 54, 130–135, 165, 233–234; and advice, 11; and contradiction, 132–133; and ends, 133; and experience, 131; and goals, 17; in *Greater Hippias,* 155, 157, 158, 159; and ignorance, 131; and inquiry, 135; and nature, 213–214; and philosophy, 213–214; and politics, 134; and reverence, 134; and shame, 134; and Socrates, 72, 217; and soul, 208. *See also* problem

Persia, 49, 94n22, 96

persuasion, 1, 4, 12, 25, 63, 160

Phaedo, 19, 20, 21, 22, 127, 128, 129, 162

Phaedrus, 17, 18, 19, 120, 122, 143, 193–194, 205

Phaenerete, 18

Philebus, 22, 25, 27, 30, 127, 128, 129, 137, 196–214, 217, 230–231, 265, 272

philosophy, 62, 64–65, 69–70, 98, 105, 111–112, 234–235, 246, 262, 272–273; and aspiration, 40; and beauty, 176, 193–194; and courage, 62; and ends, 251; and eros, 55; and experience, 116, 167; and freedom, 105, 219, 234, 236–237; and good, 167, 180; and law, 21; and moderation, 61, 62; and perplexity, 213–214; and piety, 2, 41; political 1, 9, 219, 269; and politics, 64–65, 67, 68, 166–187; 219–220, 270–271; and purity, 209–214; in *Republic,* 166–187; roots of, 115–142; and sophists, 23; and soul, 175–178; and spiritedness, 176–177; and the statesman, 256; and virtue, 36, 67, 79, 115–116

piety, 2, 35, 81, 83–84, 92, 109, 151, 193, 260, 264; and being, 219; in *Euthyphro,* 41–47; and law, 20–21, 41, 103; and politics, 23

Pittacus, 144

Platea, 49

play, 94, 140–141, 250

pleasure, 21–22, 24–25, 94–95, 98, 184–185, 250–251; and beauty, 157–160; and calculation, 77–79; in *Gorgias,* 62–71; and laughter, 137; and nature, 204–205; in *Philebus,* 196–214; and philosophy, 213–214; and punishment, 205; and purity, 207–208; and reason, 24–25; and wonder, 124

poetry, 58, 77, 92, 94, 227; and education, 102–103; and knowledge, 185–186; and politics, 84–85, 169

political art, 75